ENCHANTED GROUND

This painting of Abigail and Jonathan Koons, believed to have been created in 1860 after their move from Ohio to Illinois, has been preserved by their descendants for over 160 years. The artist's identity is unknown. Photo courtesy of the estate of Judy Stahlberg Berg.

ENCHANTED GROUND

The Spirit Room of
Jonathan Koons

Sharon Hatfield

SWALLOW PRESS / ATHENS, OHIO

Swallow Press
An imprint of Ohio University Press, Athens, Ohio 45701
ohioswallow.com

First paperback edition 2022

To obtain permission to quote, reprint, or otherwise reproduce or distribute material from
Swallow Press / Ohio University Press publications, please contact our rights and permissions
department at (740) 593-1154 or (740) 593-4536 (fax).

Printed in the United States of America
Swallow Press / Ohio University Press books are printed on acid-free paper ⊗ ™

28 27 26 25 24 23 22 21 20 19 18   5 4 3 2 1

Hardcover ISBN 978-0-8040-1208-9
Electronic ISBN 978-0-8040-4096-9
Paperback ISBN 978-0-8040-1239-3

Library of Congress Cataloging-in-Publication Data

Names: Hatfield, Sharon, 1956- author.
Title: Enchanted ground : the spirit room of Jonathan Koons / Sharon Hatfield.
Description: Athens, Ohio : Swallow Press, [2018] | Includes bibliographical
  references and index.
Identifiers: LCCN 2018032213 | ISBN 9780804012089 (hc : alk. paper) | ISBN
  9780804040969 (pdf)
Subjects: LCSH: Koons, Jonathan, 1811–1893. | Spiritualists--Ohio--Biography.
  | LCGFT: Biographies.
Classification: LCC BF1283.K66 H38 2018 | DDC 133.9092 [B] --dc23
LC record available at https://lccn.loc.gov/2018032213

A NOTE ON SOURCES

Spelling and punctuation varied widely during the mid-nineteenth century,
especially the spelling of proper names. The quotations from original sources used
in this book transcribe the original spelling, punctuation, and grammar. In some
passages the author has inserted clarifying information in brackets.

For Jack

The Messiah taught the doctrine of peace, love, goodwill and forgiveness to all mankind in general; which of itself was sufficient for Christians without the brimstone.

—Jonathan Koons,
Truth Seekers' Feast

We remained there till Sunday morning, and then, on foot, we took up the line of march towards the enchanted ground. We ascended the hills, which are piled one upon another, to a fearful and dizzy height. It seemed to me that we were travelling quite away from the earth sphere. About 11 o'clock, on Sunday, the 26th, we arrived at Mr. Koons', a farm house, situate upon a small farm, among these everlasting hills.

—A pilgrim, circa 1855,
in T. L. Nichols, *Religions of the World*

Koons took no fees. Indeed, he generously housed and fed the visitors from a distance. The reader may construct his own psychology of the matter.

—Joseph McCabe,
Spiritualism; A Popular History from 1847

Amiable and beloved Father farewell not on this perishing stone, but in the book of life and in the hearts of thy afflicted family is thy worth recorded.

—Inscription on gravestone of Cyrus S. Hughes,
nephew of Jonathan Koons

Contents

Illustrations

GALLERY THREE
Following page 222

Preface

When I moved to Athens, Ohio, in 1985, I had no idea that one day I would explore what a nineteenth-century commentator has called "the weird celebrity" of the place. As a new arrival from my native Virginia, I thought it was a just a picturesque, progressive city where I would eventually earn a master's degree in journalism from Ohio University. Only in 2010, as an author and longtime Athens County resident, did I turn to explore the deeper history of my adopted home. That was when I settled on researching the medium Jonathan Koons, a life that continues to intrigue me even after several years.

I had first learned of Koons through the local newspapers while in graduate school. Around Halloween time he would dutifully take his place in a recap of Athens County's spooky stories—haunted cemeteries linked by a pentagram, the abandoned insane asylum overlooking the city of Athens, and of course his own dark séances where ghostly musicians played and instruments floated about the room. But in those pre-internet days I could scarcely imagine that Athens would eventually gain notice online as one of the "most haunted" places in the United States. Not until I began my recent study did I learn of Koons's contribution to the mystique—some would say superstition—that has attached itself to the area. For he drew hundreds, perhaps thousands, of people to Athens County in the 1850s with the promise of reconnecting them with dead loved ones, thus putting the locale on the map of the spiritualist press. It was from the rocks and forests—the very landscape itself—that psychic forces were able to gather strength, or so the theory went. This idea has persisted for at least 165 years—and perhaps much longer, if one considers legends about Native Americans in this place.

Yet Jonathan Koons has little mention in the history books of Athens County, Ohio; he lives on mostly through oral tradition. Not surprisingly, that tradition has reshuffled facts even as it has enlarged certain themes and diminished others, memorializing yet obscuring the person who lived here. What's more, the story of Koons's wife, Abigail Bishop Koons, is a wisp of smoke compared to that of her husband, not due to any lack on her part but the sheer fact that the nineteenth century was indeed a man's world in which women's lives were seldom detailed—or their names even mentioned—in published sources. From the scraps of information available, it is clear that Abigail and Jonathan were full partners as together they explored the counterculture of their time.

When I began looking into the Koons story, I thought I would be writing a book about psychic abilities—traits that the Koons family was said to possess. I thought I would use my journalistic skills and the latest research to find out exactly what was genuine and what was false about the Koons phenomena. But I soon realized that the story was as much, or more, about the power of ritual and belief than about an actual physical reality. Some visitors to the Koons séances reported transformative encounters, whether their perceptions were "real" or not. For that reason I do not presume to judge the validity of the religious experiences reported in this book. To avoid a ponderous writing style, I decided not to overuse qualifiers such as *purportedly* and *supposedly* in every account of what visitors to the Koons séances saw or heard. I invite readers to enter the sphere of the nineteenth-century spiritualists and look at the world the way they saw it—playful, mysterious, and ultimately kind.

IN his fine book *Wonder Shows,* Fred Nadis makes the provocative statement that "every historical study is a veiled autobiography." Although that maxim may not be uniformly applicable, it resonates for me. I have always been attracted to mysteries large and small. As a child and enthusiastic member of the Nancy Drew book club, I was transported to a world where fictional mysteries unfolded like clockwork in old hotels, larkspur lanes, and hidden staircases. In the real world I wondered who had made the arrowheads that farmers routinely plowed up from the fields around our home. As I began to study science, more curiosities presented themselves: the dark side of the moon, the stars, the dinosaurs, Mendel's peas, and Schrodinger's cat—and I wondered what future discoveries might reveal about the cosmos. I even dreamed of becoming a scientist myself.

But mysteries of the supernatural resided in a category all their own. I waited in rapt anticipation for my grandma to open the book of Grimm's fairy tales and begin to read. I shivered as other relatives told of a headless horseman patrolling a lonesome hollow in our neighborhood. Such flights of imagination led me to speculate on what magical creatures might dwell in the misty folds of Cumberland Mountain, whose high rocky rim dominated the landscape of my youth. And in church we learned of magical feats such as walking on water or through fire, how Gideon's fleece changed from dry to wet, and why the hand wrote on Belshazzar's wall. The difference was that these stories, unlike "Hansel and Gretel," were believed to be literally true.

Over fifty years later I am still as interested in mysteries as I was back then—both of a scientific and metaphysical kind. I have gained much comfort, and perhaps some insight, from reading the works of poets, philosophers, scientists, and assorted radical thinkers. As a young child I had feelings of déjà vu that I could not really articulate, but years later I instantly recognized them in Wordsworth's verse from 160 years before:

> Our birth is but a sleep and a forgetting;
> The Soul that rises with us, our life's Star,
>> Hath had elsewhere its setting
>> And cometh from afar;
>> Not in entire forgetfulness,
>> And not in utter nakedness,
> But trailing clouds of glory do we come
>> From God, who is our home:
> Heaven lies about us in our infancy!

That sense of glory predictably faded over time, but from reading the works of Carl Jung and his disciple Joseph Campbell as an adult, I have experienced a feeling of connectedness with water, rocks, trees, and animals—both human and not. Jung demonstrated how many cultures throughout the world share the same archetypes, although they have different expressions—perhaps an indication of a great mind or consciousness that unites not only humans but other forms of life. Jonathan Koons and his fellow believers were attempting to tap into this vast reservoir—although other religions could claim other, equally valid, pathways. Koons was the product of a time and place, just as I am. And though this book was not intended as a "veiled autobiography," I will be the first to acknowledge that by learning his story I have been able to trace some philosophical dilemmas of my own. I hope the reader will find illumination as well, and, if not, will simply be entertained by Jonathan Koons's tale.

FEW visible structures remain from the world that Jonathan Koons and his extended family created when they settled on a high ridge in Dover Township in the 1830s. Both Koons's 1852 Spirit Room and another built about 20 years later have succumbed to the ravages of time. One artifact that survives is a small hilltop cemetery where his daughter and brother lie buried. As the Koons family stood around the fresh graves of their kin in the mid-nineteenth century, they grappled with the perennial questions that the death of a loved one brings. What can we know in this life about the next, if there is one? It is a search, as one Victorian letter writer put it, for evidence of "the continued life." But the path they took to seek that truth, that is what makes this story.

1

The Frenchman's Visit

IT WAS an age that loved its wonders—the bizarre, the spectacular, and the arcane. In the 1850s sightseers could tour Barnum's American Museum in New York City to gawk at wax figures of Siamese twins and of a giant and giantess in Quaker dress. The visitors could pause to admire the miniature costume of mulberry-colored velvet worn by General Tom Thumb to his audience with Queen Victoria—or on a lucky day meet the diminutive Tom himself. But in the backwoods of Ohio, hundreds of miles from that center of commerce, the curious were flocking to a remote country cabin whose marvels would rival any of P. T. Barnum's attractions. The farmer-turned-medium Jonathan Koons had built a special house where it was said that the dead spoke to the living, where the ancient spirits of the place deigned not only to reveal the wisdom of the ages to visitors but to serenade them with celestial music.

Like hundreds before him, Joseph Barthet had heard of the mysterious goings-on at Koons's hillside farm, only 7 miles distant but far removed from the county seat and university town of Athens. So renowned was the rustic cabin called the Spirit Room that Dr. Barthet, a mesmerist and devotee of spiritualism, had traveled more than 1,000 miles from New Orleans to see it for himself. He joined a restive crowd, some dressed in homespun and others in city attire, that had already gathered outside, awaiting admittance to the evening's demonstrations.

Barthet was ushered into a log structure that he estimated to be 15 feet long, 10 feet wide, and 7 feet high. He found himself in a one-room building with a most peculiar contraption at one end: a wooden table the size of a coffin affixed with a bewildering profusion of wires, metal bars, tin plates, pieces of glass, and small bells. Some wires ran to two drums, about 5 feet apart, that were fixed to a frame hoisted above the table. Barthet had heard that the device had been constructed under the guidance of the spirits to energize the room and help focus their essence. On the table itself sat a tin trumpet about 18 inches long with a small mouthpiece. A hand bell, tambourine, accordion, and harmonica also adorned this unlikely altar. Writing paper, a pencil, a book, and two sheets of sandpaper coated with phosphorus completed the eerie tableau.

No stranger to a séance, Barthet scanned his surroundings with a discerning eye. A decade or so earlier the French émigré had organized mesmerists in New Orleans as the Magnetic Society, men who thought that a fluid with electrical properties permeated the universe and, with the aid of hypnosis, could be harnessed for its healing powers. From there it was just a short step to believe that entranced individuals also could be in touch with the healing spirits of the dead. As the spiritualist craze spread to New Orleans from the North in the 1850s, Barthet had become a leading voice of the new religion of spiritualism, initiating some of the first circles in the city. Although he had come to this gathering in Ohio as part true believer, Barthet would not disavow the habits of mind that had made him a dispassionate observer. He watched curiously as the 20 or so guests filed into the spirit room and his host prepared for the evening's performance.

Jonathan Koons's hair was the color of hickory nuts, and he wore it long and parted in the middle. With his full beard and heavy brows over deep-set dark eyes, Koons wore a mantle of grave intellect about his person. But even in middle age he carried the livelier traits of the performing artist as well, for it was said that he could hear a tune whistled just once and effortlessly reproduce it on his fiddle. Tonight, with violin in hand, Koons took his place at a second, smaller table that had been pushed up in front of the rectangular one that supported the two drums and the other musical instruments. His son Nahum, a tall, fair-haired teenager known as Nim, took a seat on the opposite side of the smaller table, which was reserved for the mediums and special guests. Although most visitors sat in two pews facing the tables, Barthet was given a place of honor at Jonathan Koons's right. On Barthet's right was his traveling companion, M. L. Their host's custom was to give special accommodations to visitors from far away, especially those learned men who could best appreciate the phenomena. Sizing up the arrangements, Barthet noticed how crowded the room had become and how difficult it would be for anyone to get up and move around. To make matters worse, a little stove straddled the space between the smaller mediums' table and the first bench.

Koons put out the candle, plunging the room into total darkness. Something immediately struck the mediums' table with two violent licks. Barthet guessed that it had been the mallet for the large drum. The fiddle began to play a jig at a rising tempo as the two drums kicked in behind it, sometimes drumming together and sometimes separately. Some little bells rang too, perhaps from the vibrations of the whole assemblage. Barthet found the noise unpleasantly loud, but he thought the timing of the drums and violin impeccable. He imagined some invisible conductor leading the band through a medley of tunes. When it was time to switch to another melody, the conductor would change the rhythm, delivering a few offbeat licks. The fiddle would then commence another hornpipe or quickstep, and the drum would resume keeping time. Barthet assumed that Jonathan Koons was playing the fiddle with both hands. He wondered how anyone else could have moved to the drums so quickly without detection—or even whether one person could have managed to play both drums at once.

The drums fell silent, and a tambourine flew across the room, keeping time with the violin. Barthet got the impression that two hands were working the tambourine, one shaking it and the other hitting it. He could also hear a handbell that seemed to be aloft. The New Orleans mesmerist strained to pick up any evidence of human motion but could not. With no light at all, he was depending on his ears alone to make sense of what was unfolding.

Now it was time to test the capabilities of the acrobatic tambourine. On its first pass around the room, the instrument had lightly tapped Barthet's knee before continuing on to touch others in the audience. Now he silently placed his hands on either side of his body at knee level, one hand next to his knee and the other 8 inches from his body. Barthet wanted the tambourine to touch his hands without groping around or brushing against his knees—a feat that he thought would be difficult for a person to do in pitch darkness. As if by magic, the tambourine returned and immediately did as he had willed.

The Frenchman placed his hand on the table palm up, and soon the tambourine fluttered down onto his hand. He could feel the side and the drumhead of the instrument. Barthet dared to push his hand forward. An alien palm came in contact with his. The temperature of the hand was unremarkable, but the outsize fingers caught his attention. Barthet wanted to palpate the strange extremity, but all too soon it flew away. He assumed that the person still playing the violin was Jonathan Koons. Common sense told Barthet that the only person who could reach him in the cramped space was young Nahum Koons, who sat opposite his father. Barthet had his doubts, though. Nahum would have had to get up from his chair and lie nearly flat on the table to touch Barthet's hand. The mesmerist did not think Nahum could have done this without making some telltale sound; besides, the young man's fingers were much smaller than the ones Barthet had just felt. The mesmerist had made a careful observation of Nahum's fingers before the séance began. The only way he could imagine the teenager's fingers being that thick was if they were swathed in heavy gloves.

The tambourine returned to the table and the violin performance stopped. Barthet's reveries were interrupted by a high-pitched voice flowing out of the trumpet, which he surmised was now floating above them. The voice was speaking with Jonathan Koons, but at first Barthet could not make out what it was saying.

"King, play the accordion," Koons commanded.

The instrument immediately began to sound, but to Barthet it was just noise. Whoever or whatever was behind it—the entity called King—obviously did not know how to play.

"Koons, this accordion is like a lot of people," the voice in the horn complained. "It seems well on the outside, but it doesn't have anything good on the inside."

"King is jovial," Koons said, perhaps addressing the spectators as much as the voice. "But he is right in this case because nothing good has come from this instrument that is, for that matter, very mediocre."

The voice tried a different tack. "Koons, tell me to get the violin."

"Very well, pick it up."

Barthet heard the violin being plucked, rather than played with the bow. Soon the accordion joined in, but the result was no better than before. Barthet found the sound discordant. The invisible being was certainly no musician.

No sooner had the violin fallen silent than a high-pitched voice emanated from the harmonica. Barthet deduced that the harmonica was functioning as a megaphone, just as the trumpet had earlier. Although the voice sounded natural to him, he still could not make out the words. The music started up again shortly, this time a racket of accordion and harmonica that hurt Barthet's ears. He felt something lightly tap his skull several times just above his right ear, almost like a caress. Whereas the tambourine had tapped his knee and hands, this time he thought the accordion was dancing around his head.

Now the voice in the trumpet requested a fiddle tune and began to sing, but Barthet remained unimpressed. He found the lyrics childish and the falsetto voice that delivered them unpleasant, nothing like the celestial music he had read so much about in glowing accounts of the Koons phenomena. Mercifully the singing lasted only about a minute. But the tapping soon began on the other side of Barthet's head; he believed it was the trumpet. Annoyed as he was with the musical performances, the hypnotist marveled at the demonstrations on his person. He was convinced that only an entity that could see in the dark, or was reading his mind, could land these taps at precise locations—and, so far as he was concerned, clairvoyance did not exist.

A flash of light shot through the darkness near the back table and was quickly extinguished. Barthet heard the rustling of paper. Something that looked like a small lantern appeared 2 feet in front of him. He leaned closer. The lantern came within 8 inches of his face, and by its light he could see a hand holding a pencil as if poised to write. The hand itself was giving off a modicum of light, as if it had a glowworm in its grasp. It began scribbling on paper, first a couple of lines and then a long paragraph that filled the page. The paper flipped over, and a hand again appeared above it. Barthet did not know if it was the same hand. The writing continued on the reverse side of the paper until the light was gone. He heard what sounded like paper sliding across the table toward him and grabbed it.

"Koons, I have something to tell you," came the voice through the trumpet.

"Well?"

"*Bon soir,*" said King, taking his leave with the thump of the tin horn on the table.

Jonathan Koons lit the candle, and the men pored over the document. Barthet found a message signed "King" that had been written out in a precise, backward-slanting hand on a piece of stationery:

> To the friends and visitors of this assembly we glad to meet you here in this our humble retreat. Let the light illuminate your spiritual vision and perception we have afforded you on this occasion, and freely as we bestow so freely confer on those who seek.

On the back of the stationery, more words had been written in a different hand, with more space between the letters and fainter characters. The calligraphy even showed signs of corrections to some of the strokes. Barthet read:

> Friends, disregard the <u>medisance</u> of those who dispute statements, for their <u>manqué d'experience</u> leads them to lamantable states dereglements.—A FRIEND

Running a critical eye over the page, Barthet could see four French words that were written correctly except that some accent marks had been left off. Curiously, three of those words were underlined but the fourth, *dereglements*, was not. Barthet also thought that the last word should have been placed in parentheses, as it was restating the two words just before it. He also noticed that the English word "lamentable" had been misspelled. Even with the errors and lack of specificity, Barthet found meaning in these few words from his native tongue. The message said: "Friends, disregard the malicious gossip of those who dispute statements, for their lack of experience leads them to lamentable states craziness." He thought it referred to skeptical comments he had heard during his trip to Ohio. Beyond that, he was convinced that no one in the Koons household—or any of their visitors, save himself and his traveling companion—knew a word of French.

✳ ✳ ✳

BARTHET had to cut short his stay at the Koonses' because the food served there made both him and his companion sick, a complaint voiced more than once by city folks. But he would not be the first or last learned person to investigate the strange phenomena that had made Jonathan Koons a celebrity attraction in the spiritualist world. Upstanding citizens from all walks of life—"persons of undoubted respectability . . . whose testimony would not be refused in any court of justice in the world"—were flocking to an estimated 2,000 mediums throughout the United States. Among the converts were several writers of prominence and achievement, including Harriet Beecher Stowe, William Cullen Bryant, and James Fenimore Cooper. A few nationally known judges and politicians also espoused the new religion, including Judge John Worth Edmonds of New York and Nathaniel P. Tallmadge, formerly a US senator from New York and governor of the Wisconsin Territory. And just a decade later First Lady Mary Todd Lincoln would be hosting séances in the White House. But spiritualism was not a movement for the elite alone; thanks to its optimistic emphasis on human improvement and the equality of all souls, one to two million Americans in a national population of 23 million were said to have joined its ranks by 1850.

In the years leading up to the Civil War, spiritualism must have seemed to its devotees like a moral compass that could guide a rapidly changing society. Railroads and steamships had revolutionized transportation, and key inventions like the cotton gin and interchangeable parts had the United States careening from a nation of farmers to an industrial powerhouse with centers located mainly in the North. Along with German and Irish immigrants, millions of rural Americans moved to the cities to work in factories, creating the beginnings of the middle class—and liberating a pent-up desire for progress. Optimism was the order of the day; citizens in the East believed in a divinely sanctioned manifest destiny that entitled them to virtually all the land between the Atlantic and the Pacific.

But those years also had a dark side: overcrowding in the booming ports and cities resulted in poor living and working conditions and outbreaks of disease; infant mortality was high and industrial accidents horrific. The federal government had removed Native Americans from the South by treaty, or at the point of a bayonet, from their homelands east of the Mississippi, clearing millions of acres for slaveholding white settlers. Wars had been fought out West to gain more land, and with each new acquisition of western territory fresh controversies would erupt about whether that territory should enter the Union as a free or slave state. From the shining new cities of the North to the colonnaded verandas of the South, the threat of violence hissed and simmered.

Religion, too, was in ferment; in the late eighteenth and early nineteenth centuries a wave of religious fervor called the Second Great Awakening had swept across the United States and on to the frontier. Along with a renewed emphasis on a personal relationship with the Savior, some Christian believers looked forward to a new millennial age, all the while working to purify society so that Christ could return to Earth.

Nowhere was this revivalism more prevalent than in western New York, where spiritualism was born in 1848. This region eventually became known as the Burned-Over District because so many religious fires had swept the population that few people were left to convert. The Second Great Awakening not only fueled Protestant denominations such as the Methodists and Baptists but spurred the rise of churches that believed in direct communication with spirits. The Shaking Quakers, or Shakers, for one, had long been known for their ecstatic rites—whirling and stamping dances and speaking in tongues, as well as their propensity to fall under the influence of spirits as they worshipped. Mediums, also called instruments, heard from entities as diverse as Napoleon, Native Americans, and even neighbors who appeared at their own funerals to console the living. And in 1823 an angel had appeared to Joseph Smith, revealing to him the location of inscribed golden tablets buried near Palmyra, New York, and providing the foundational text for the Mormon religion. Other residents of the Burned-Over District had once discarded their worldly possessions, believing the preacher William Miller's prediction that Jesus Christ would return to Earth no later than March 21, 1844.

The desire to cleanse a wicked world in advance of the Second Coming also spilled over into the social arena. Reformers in central and western New York, some inspired by their Christian faith, sought to improve society across a broad swath of issues affecting the here-and-now, not just the hereafter. The first women's rights convention ever held in the United States took place in 1848 in Seneca Falls, where Elizabeth Cady Stanton shocked listeners with her demand for the vote. Intertwined with the women's movement were campaigns for temperance, prison reform, and the abolition of slavery. Utopian societies also flourished there for a time, experimenting with new ways to live. When the sisters Kate and Maggie Fox introduced spiritualism into the cauldron, it must have seemed just as plausible as other "isms" that residents had entertained over the years.

Spiritualism began in a rented farmhouse in Hydesville, New York, where Kate, Maggie, and their parents heard mysterious noises in the night. Soon Kate, 11, and Maggie, 15, reported that they could communicate with the spirit of a murdered peddler through raps—two for yes and silence for no. Within weeks, hundreds of curiosity seekers had visited the farmhouse, upsetting the Foxes' daily routines but ensuring notoriety for the two girls. Shepherded by their older sister, Leah, the pair first moved to Rochester and eventually wound up in New York City, where all three siblings became internationally famous mediums known as the Rochester Rappers.

Now, just a few years after the Fox sisters had made their debut, Jonathan Koons was attracting an ardent following. Most visitors, like a Cincinnati businessman delving into the séances, came away convinced that the ghostly hands and unearthly music were "the work of an invisible intelligent power." "Hundreds, and I believe thousands, (judging from a register kept there) have been there from almost all parts of the United States," the businessman wrote, "and I have yet to hear of the first one who has gone away skeptical as to the genuineness of the performance."

Even so, the French mesmerist Barthet was left to wonder about what he had heard and seen. The velvety blackness of the séance room seemed to produce sheer magic, but returning to the light sent questions seesawing through his mind. Barthet tumbled the evidence over and over as he left Athens County, never to return. Was Jonathan Koons a martyr for the spiritualist cause, an unlikely scientist harnessing yet unknown powers of the universe, or—as his critics charged—merely a charlatan of the highest order? Answering these questions would not be easy. But from 1852 on, the spiritualist movement would claim Jonathan Koons as one of its most charismatic figures—a backwoods seer whose legacy would rival even that of the famous Fox sisters for a place in its history.

2

"The Place of My Nativity"

IN THE fall of 1833, 22-year-old Jonathan Koons set out to see a new world. He was bound for the Ohio Country, where the corn was said to grow 14 feet high in the river bottoms and the juice of wild strawberries could reach a horse's knees. Venturing out from his home near Bedford, Pennsylvania, he traveled first to Pittsburgh and then to Mercer, Pennsylvania, on the Ohio border, where his two uncles lived. Over the next several months he would traipse through 14 Ohio counties, eventually finding the one in which he would cast his fortune as an adult.

Koons was not alone in his desire to see the western lands. For over 30 years his fellow Pennsylvania Germans had been crossing the mountains in search of new opportunities. The pace had accelerated in 1811—the year Koons was born—with the start of construction of the National Road at Cumberland, Maryland. Even then the presence of Pennsylvania Germans was considerable in places like Lancaster, Ohio, in the southeast, where signs were printed in both English and German, and settlers could peruse a German-language newspaper. "I enjoyed this trip very much—scarcely a day passed by, but what I met with some friend or acquaintance from the place of my nativity," Koons wrote.

His trip was something of a rite of passage. He had just completed an apprenticeship as a carpenter and joiner—surely a handy trade in a new land where buildings were multiplying and Ohio's population was nearing one million. Two and a half years earlier, when he had left home for the first time at age 19, Koons had apprenticed himself to a master carpenter, Elias Gump of Reinsburg, Pennsylvania. The small town (now spelled Rainsburg) was located in a valley called Friends Cove, about 11 miles south of Bedford toward the Maryland state line. Along the town square Gump had built a house and a carpenter shop where his employees turned out cabinets. In addition to acquiring the fine woodworking skills of a joiner, Koons had learned how to play the fiddle while in Reinsburg. As he would later write, a "vast plain of social relations" soon opened up to him: "The love of music was also a prominent feature of my character which led me into a practical performance of the same. It was not long until I acquired an admirable degree in the skill of its performance—which became an agreeable source of recreation, and it also opened a channel through which I gained admission in social society and assemblies that would have denied me admittance under any other qualification, except wealth and pomposity." With his connections in the carpentry business and his newfound talent for music, Koons soon found himself feasting at a cultural banquet. "These humble professions gained me admittance to . . . public orations, delivered by patriotic and able minds at military picnics, festivals and balls," he wrote. "They also opened my way into social family circles, private halls, [singing] parties, discussions, religious assemblies, weddings, huskings, raisings, theatrical performances, etc., etc., which were constant contributors to my little store of practical, experimental[,] exemplary, and theoretic knowledge. Scarcely an act or idea ever escaped my consideration."

Whether he brought his fiddle along on the journey is not known, but he certainly carried his curiosity with him as he made his way south through Ohio in 1833. In Canton he could not resist joining the multitudes who flocked to see a murderer hanged in the public square. That November, while boarding at New Harrisburg, in Carroll County, he stumbled half-dressed into the street to witness a spectacular nighttime meteor shower but was equally fascinated by the reaction of the townspeople—"some were praying, some laughing, some weeping, and others mocking; while at the same time the surrounding elements seemed all on fire." Years later he was able to joke: "Thinks I, surely, Hughes and Miller [millennialists] are true prophets; and they only made a slight mistake in computing the time of the destruction of the world by fire."

＊ ＊ ＊

IN a letter Koons described his father's side of the family as being "of German extraction throughout." In the Old World the family name may have been spelled Countz. Upon reaching the colonies the family used the German spelling of Koontz, but later generations took up the more Americanized spelling of Koons. Jonathan's father, Peter, who fought against the British in a German unit in the Revolutionary War, had settled with his wife, Margaret Snyder, on Clear Ridge in Bedford County, Pennsylvania.

Growing up on his parents' farm with four brothers and five sisters, Jonathan was a sickly child, given to physical ailments and prone to anxiety and depression. "I became afflicted with rheumatic affections at an early age, by exposure and hard labor, which caused my aching limbs at times to disobey the volition of mind in the discharge of their physical office," he recalled in his 1856 autobiography. "This in effect afflicted the mind also, and I would have ofttimes cheerfully dispensed with my frail physical bark, and launched my mental existence upon the mysterious ocean of a future state." The only thing that kept him from suicide was the thought of the "horrible scenes and penalities" that religion prescribed.

Peter Koons was from the "old school Presbyterian church," and accordingly the infant Jonathan was baptized there, among the Friends Cove congregation. But his Lutheran mother, Margaret, provided most of his religious instruction at home. "The first education I received on the subject of man's immortality, or soul, was impressed on my mind by my kind and affectionate mother," he wrote. Margaret taught her son Bible stories about the Creation, the flood that wiped wickedness from the earth, Jonah and the whale, Joseph with his coat of many colors, and the downfall of Sampson. From the New Testament she related Christ's miracles and his mission of redeeming humanity from original sin. "In that age I did not doubt the correctness of all she taught out of her rule of faith—being at that time led by her fascinating charms into implicit confidence of all she declared unto me," Koons explained.

Despite the trust he had in his mother's wisdom, young Jonathan was nonetheless possessed of a questioning mind. As he grew older, he wrote, "I was considered a tedious pupil, in consequence of being prone to inquire into all the whys and wherefores of my mental attractions, while under the instruction of my preceptors." This contrariness caused problems for the boy, as his mother had taught him that God would hold him accountable for "every idle thought" as well as for words and deeds. To covet someone's property was just as bad as actually stealing it, and "the conception of a false conclusion was the same in effect with God, as if we had proclaimed it." Jonathan persisted nonetheless; "every pebble in the pathway of my life was turned up under the expectation of finding an index to true knowledge," he would later write. He asked his mother why God had created hell and the devil. Her answer was that God was an "unfathomable mystery"—and to doubt his word was to sin against the Holy Ghost, "which sin cannot be ratified under the atonement of Christ, neither in this world, or in the future state of man."

Over the course of these lessons Jonathan became convinced he was going to hell, a certainty that propelled him to a mental health crisis. He told of a short period in his youth (no age given) when he became anxious at bedtime—"a haunted and fearful condition." He could not sleep, he said, for fear that "Satan would snatch me from the arms of kind Morpheus." Jonathan would ask his mother to pray with him. She would oblige and tell him a Bible story, which would usually put him to sleep. But the boy's dreams were filled with "horned and cloven footed devils" that dragged his playmates into hell with evident delight. Jonathan dreamed they were chasing him, too, and he would wake up in the act of jumping out of bed. The nighttime terrors soon became so strong that sunlight could no longer dispel them, and he sank into a deep melancholy from which his loved ones could not arouse him. "This sad predicament of my mind caused me to sob and sigh aloud," he recalled. "All the kind entreaties of the family for an explanation of the cause, were made in vain."

Finally, Jonathan fell into a trancelike state in which he imagined that a stranger—"a pure and noble personage"—was leading him through "successive plains [planes]" of heaven, where he recognized "the old prophets and patriarchs." They eventually reached the zone of ultimate perfection, but Jonathan was allowed only to behold it without actually entering. He begged his guide to let him stay, but he had to go back to Earth to perform important duties before he could return.

When he woke up, Jonathan was troubled to find himself still in mortal form. "The thoughts of prolonging my days upon the earth after [this] experience, afflicted my mind very grievously," he wrote. "This vision gave me a sort of foretaste of what I began to hope for; and the idea of spending my earthly career in such doubts and fears as those I had already experienced, was painful in the extreme." Once again the boy turned to his mother for help. She listened intently as he told the story of his visit to the realm of light. "She informed me of her faith in the guardianship of angels, whom she believed hovered around us, and exercised their kind protecting influence in our favor, against temptations of Satan," he recalled. At last Jonathan had found the comfort his soul required. Perhaps the kind stranger who had led him through heaven was an angel himself.

The healing vision replaced the dark thoughts that had clouded Jonathan's young mind: "From that time forward . . . I became newly inspired with dawning hopes and prospects, that God could not reasonably act so cruel in his judgments as he is represented by the clerical Bible canonaders of the day and age. I hoped most anxiously that God would be kind enough to overlook my unavoidable fruits of imperfection." Jonathan Koons not only found a more positive worldview but became intrigued with the altered state of consciousness that was the instrument of his deliverance. From then on, he would meditate—and in doing so, find the space to turn his theological world upside down.

THE stories Koons heard from his father were entirely different from those of his saintly mother. Sitting around the fire at night back in Bedford, Peter and other relatives would tell tales of magic and wonder—of haunted groves in the woods, a mysterious light seen steadily traversing the ridgetops, and witches shape-shifting into animals. As a grown man, Koons remembered those tales and took the time to write them down. "These were listened to attentively, with a sort of reverential awe, and were generally believed," he wrote. "Many of these occurrences, as was claimed, took place within my father's family and circle of friends. This inspired me with a sort of fear and desire to see a 'ghost' or 'spook' as the Germans denominated a spirit, although I can not positively say that my desires were granted until recently."

One such story involved his father and a neighbor woman named Mrs. ——, whom the family referred to derisively as "that old rib." On a Sunday morning Peter went out to round up his cows and took along a rifle in case he chanced upon some game. As the family prepared breakfast, they heard several shots fired in quick succession. They guessed that he had come upon a flock of turkeys. Breakfast was postponed, and the family's expectations grew high as they waited for Peter's return. Soon he appeared with the cows—but minus the birds or any type of wild game.

Disappointment spread among the children, but as the head of the household Peter was not questioned. The family silently took their places around the breakfast table. Young Jonathan could tell that something was bothering his father. In fact, Peter had no appetite and Margaret had to beseech him to even sip a cup of coffee. Finally, Solomon, the second-oldest son, who had already taken a wife, summoned up the nerve to ask his father what had happened.

"When I came upon the cows I saw a small deer in the midst of the herd," Peter related. "I fired upon it. This only caused it to give one or two bounds, and stopped without manifesting any fear or alarm. I repeated my firing; this caused it to act with a sort of contemptuous defiance, with-out expressing the least degree of alarm. Thus I continued to fire at my object which at times was within five or six paces, until all my balls were exhausted." When the smoke cleared, the little deer had vanished.

Without another word Peter rose from the table, grabbed his hat, and set off, all the while mumbling something to himself. The family knew ex-actly where he was headed: to see a witch. Jonathan listened in fascination as his brothers and sisters, sister-in-law, and mother speculated about what would happen next.

"I wonder if that old rib will be able to relate the morning transaction without personal information as she is in the habit of doing," said Margaret.

"I have no doubt of it," her daughter Rachael replied, "for she appears to know everything that transpires in the neighborhood, and of course she will know the present occurrence."

"I wonder how she comes by her intelligence," said Lewis, one of the Koons brothers.

"Why! The Devil brings her the intelligence, and it was none else but Satan who transformed himself, to deceive father," Rachel explained.

"Moderation, children," Margaret broke in. "You must not be so pro-fane. Let us look to God for protection, and we need not fear the power of Satan."

"I will not judge, but I can not avoid an opinion," said Solomon. "If half the reports are true, she evidently is a witch."

The group fell into a discussion of the evidence against the "old rib." Solomon's wife Nancy said that one night she had been alone in her bedchamber awaiting her husband's arrival when someone entered the room. She assumed it was Solomon and lifted her head from the pillow; by the light of a few coals from the fire, she saw Mrs. —— standing by the bed in a nightdress. Nancy found herself pinned to the bed, rendered powerless to move, and felt a weight upon her breast. Solomon quickly dismissed his wife's experience as a classic nightmare, but his sister Elizabeth insisted that the same thing had happened to her.

"Hark," Margaret said, silencing the back and forth. "Father is coming home. Let us wait and see what discoveries he has made."

As Peter entered the room, Solomon's wife could not resist teasing her father-in-law. "Been taking abroad, eh?" she asked.

"Yes," Peter replied with a smile playing on his face.

"Suppose we shall have a wedding soon, seeing [as] you visit Mrs. —— so frequently?" Nancy continued. She turned to Margaret. "What do you say, Mrs. K, do you not entertain fears of your husband's becoming espoused to Mrs. ——?"

"Judging from previous visits, we might presume so," Margaret said.

"All but the wedding," Peter shot back. "I have peculiar objects in view, besides her personal beauty and deportment, which incite my frequent visits."

When his audience could bear the suspense no longer, Peter explained that he had hurried to the woman's house so that he would be the first to see her after his encounter with the deer. He had long entertained suspicions about "that crooked rib" and her ability to tell of events she had not personally witnessed or heard about. He wanted to outrun any news that might have traveled about the peculiar animal in the forest. Mrs. —— was waiting for him at the door, as if she knew he was coming.

"Well Mr. Koons," she said, "you have been shooting at a deer this morning, and you did not get it either."

"Yes," Peter said, "and a tormenting deer it was too! I shall take a little further trouble in ascertaining the character of such mysterious forms."

"Oh, you need not take that trouble," his neighbor assured him. "The next deer you fire upon you will get."

Peter left her home feeling a bit sheepish about the prediction. If it proved to be true, he would have game for the family—but would have been "out generaled" by the witch, his reality shifted.

About a fortnight later Peter set out again with his rifle. At a spot about 4 miles from the home of Mrs. ——, he took down a deer from an unusually long distance. He was surprised to have hit it, but he wasted no time in hanging the carcass up in the woods and made a beeline for his house, where he dropped off the rifle without a word to his family. Soon he was back at the doorstep of Mrs. ——.

"Well! Mr. Koons, you got your deer this time, eh? Did I not tell you so?"

WITH such recollections to amuse him as the days grew shorter, 22-year-old Jonathan continued south on his journey through Ohio and eventually reached Athens County. By the time of his visit Europeans had been living in the area for more than three decades. Athens County had been established in 1805 and the town of Athens—the county seat and home to Ohio University (founded 1804)—was incorporated in 1811. The first generation of settlers, erstwhile wearers of coonskin caps and tanned deer hide, now garbed themselves in linsey-woolsey or calico. These elders and grandparents had stories to tell any newcomers willing to learn from the prior generation's hard-won experience.

As the old-timers would recall, the end of the Revolutionary War had left many American veterans, in the words of the historian Charles M. Walker, "with an abundance of liberty but no property, and their occupation gone." In the Northeast many set their sights on the frontier west of the Alleghenies. Two veterans, Rufus Putnam and Benjamin Tupper, advertised their new firm, the Ohio Company of Associates, in the hope of raising the capital necessary to purchase western lands from the United States government. After several investors bought subscriptions and the firm completed negotiations with Congress in 1787, the Ohio Company bought 1.5 million acres in the Appalachian foothills of the future state of Ohio. The acreage lay just north of the Ohio River, with Virginia on the other side. The entrepreneurs planted their initial settlement at Marietta at the confluence of the Muskingum and Ohio Rivers in 1788, giving that city the distinction of being the first permanent settlement in the North-west Territory.

To reach the frontier from the Northeast, the so-called Wilderness Yankees had to move their belongings by wagon to the headwaters of the Ohio near Pittsburgh, where flatboats or large canoes could be sent down-river. The 48 pioneers in the first group—all men—floated down the river to the mouth of the Muskingum, where they erected a fort called Campus Martius. Tall tales—both inviting and ominous—soon spread back East by word of mouth. These legends told how brandy flowed from underground springs, how cloth grew on trees, and how poisonous hoop snakes could chase the unsuspecting to their deaths. Mostly, though, the fertility of the land was an enticement that overcame the threat of animal or Indian attack—the saying went that the rich Ohio farmland "needed only to be tickled with the hoe to laugh with the harvest."

The settlers had kept coming, not only from New England, New York, and Pennsylvania but from Virginia and Kentucky as well. By 1790 Marietta boasted 100 cabins, and a second outpost had been established farther west at Cincinnati. The Delaware, Shawnee, and other Indian tribes were not about to go quietly, however, when confronted with the loss of their hunt-ing grounds. In response to stepped-up attacks from the native people, the federal government sent troops to drive out the estimated 15,000 Indians living in the future state of Ohio. Two US armies were roundly defeated, but a third, led by General Anthony Wayne, crushed a confederation of Indian tribes at the Battle of Fallen Timbers in western Ohio in 1794. The Indians were forced to cede all but the northwest corner of Ohio to the government in the Treaty of Greenville. Soon the unbroken forest would ring with axes as the trees were felled to make way for farmland.

In this postwar period settlers spread out from Marietta into the in-terior of the vast Ohio Company purchase. Meandering across southeast Ohio on a northwest to southeast diagonal was the placid river the Dela-ware Indians had called Hockhocking, or bottle river. The Hockhocking and its tributaries, fringed by white-barked sycamores, soon became rolling highways. In 1797 several families from Marietta ascended the Hockhock-ing and established the first permanent settlement in what would become Athens County. They paddled as far as the present-day town of Athens, said to be "40 miles by water from the Ohio." Others attempting an overland route had to navigate through virgin forest where oaks, maples, and hickories towered above and raccoons and red foxes scampered below among thickets of sassafras, dogwood, witch hazel, pawpaw, and hornbeam. They quickly subdued the land. The last buffalo was captured and put in a traveling show in 1799, and bears and wolves were hunted down and scalped for bounty money. By the time Koons arrived in 1834, other towns and settlements dotted the county map. The Indians had been forced out decades before, giving way to European excavators who would uncover treasures of stone, copper, and shell that the ancestors of the exiled Native Americans had secreted in burial mounds. A nascent saltworks—soon to become the dominant industry of the county—had supplanted one of the Indians' former haunts where Sunday Creek joined the Hockhocking.

Why Jonathan Koons chose this place above all others he visited in Ohio is not clear. Perhaps he felt at home in the hilly landscape, which may have reminded him of mountainous Bedford County and the Juniata River that flows through it. He set his sights on acreage 7 miles outside Athens, a tract that was too steep to be considered prime farmland but could be had for as little as 25 cents an acre. In his autobiography he merely said: "Enroute for home, I purchased the property upon which I now reside, without a dollar to advance on the contract—save a rifle worth about seven dollars, which I had procured in exchange for an old silver watch, during my sojourn in Athens County. This exchange [for the rifle] was made for the purpose of enabling me to sport amongst the Athen's hills that abounded with game at that time."

The records of Athens County, however, do not mention any of the colorful details that Koons has supplied. They say simply that in February 1834 Koons bought 262 acres in Dover Township. He paid $65 to James and Lucinda Fuller for the tract. Whether by impulse or careful design, Koons had started the trip as a tourist; now, at only 22, he had become a landowner.

Koons returned to Bedford in the spring of 1834 and worked as a joiner to raise cash for the farm in the Ohio Country; he supplemented his income by teaching school the following winter. By the spring of 1835 he was ready to cross the mountains a second time, to Athens County where his own land awaited him.

3

Putting Down Roots

JONATHAN KOONS had been in Athens County for a little more than a year, plying his carpentry trade, when he met 24-year-old Abigail Tuck Bishop in the summer of 1836. Though most of his brothers and sisters had chosen spouses from Bedford, Pennsylvania, he fell for a woman from Coos County, New Hampshire, way up on the Canadian border. His musical or woodworking skills, or perhaps a visit to church, may have gained him entrée to the Bishop family, but in any case Koons soon felt he had found a kindred spirit in Abigail. "The young lady was a member of the Episcopal Methodist church,—but liberal in her views, having been favored with facilities [faculties] leading to higher views than those entertained by many of her order," Koons recounted in his autobiography. "Her profession was that of a school teacher, which during her avocation, brought her in contact with many free thinkers, who inspired her with a desire to be also mentally free." Abigail's free thinking may have led to her membership in the Methodist church, a somewhat unusual arrangement, given that her own father, Samuel Gaylord Bishop, was a Calvinistic Baptist minister.

In considering Jonathan as a prospective bridegroom, Abigail must have realized that here was a man who had mostly given up on organized religion. Back in Pennsylvania during his apprentice days, he had decided to undergo formal instruction in the Presbyterian church, partly as a way to honor his father. But Koons quickly found church doctrine unappealing—a worldview that "threatened the wandering and disconsolate pilgrim with eternal woe and despair, every step he advanced." Once his studies were finished, he quietly left the church into which he had been baptized as a baby and never looked back. "[I] set my course for a more fair and happy land, under the compass and sail of individual sovereignty and self preservation," he would later write.

Though Abigail may have been more conventionally religious and better educated than Jonathan, they shared the world of ideas. As a farm boy rich in oral tradition but bereft of formal schooling, Koons had struggled to become a learned man. In his autobiography he reveals that except for "a few quarters" in school when he was young, he was largely self-taught. At the time he began his apprenticeship, around 1830, he was "without a literary education—except that of an indifferent reader." In his early twenties Koons sought to remedy that lack of refinement by fashioning his own library, which included "a carpenter's architecture, practical geometry, common arithmetic, mensuration of solids, Comstock's natural philosophy, Guys' pocket encyclopedia, Gall and Spurzheim's phrenology, Walker's dictionary[,] Buck's theological Dictionary, Josephus' History of the Jews, and a few others of less importance." These texts supplemented what was probably the first book he had ever owned—"an old Bible," which he obtained "in exchange for little articles of traffic, when a little sportive lad at home." Though lacking in academic credentials, Koons had prepared himself to converse with the schoolmistress on the topics of the day.

If the minister's daughter were to accept Koons's suit that summer of 1836, she would not be getting a pious husband but, as an admirer later wrote, an intelligent one whose restless mind "was full of ideas that ring like true metal." By that fall it was a bargain she was ready to make.

✳ ✳ ✳

ON October 27, 1836, Jonathan and Abigail's summer romance turned into a lifetime commitment when the two were married in Athens County by a justice of the peace. It remains a mystery why her father did not preside over the ceremony and what the Bishops thought about the fiddle-playing Pennsylvania Dutchman who had captured their daughter's heart.

What is clear is that Koons had married into a family of some means. In 1814—when Abigail was about three years old—her father had bought land in Athens County, presumably sight unseen. For the sum of $3,200 Bishop acquired 1,600 acres in northern Ames Township. Though he perhaps did not realize it, he may have been sitting on a fortune. His $2-an-acre domain lay in the Sunday Creek watershed, which would eventually become known for the vast coal deposits that had lain under the dense tree cover for millions of years. In the early decades of the nineteenth century, however, it was simply a remote area where the burr oaks grew thick, showering the forest floor with their showy fringed acorns.

In addition to being landowners, the Bishops prided themselves on being part of the learned class. Samuel Bishop was born in 1769 in Connecticut and married Abigail Tuck, the daughter of a Harvard-educated minister, in 1800. At their wedding at the Pittsfield Meeting House in Rockingham County, New Hampshire, the presiding cleric gave a sermon on "the importance of right views in matrimony." The theme held good auguries for the couple, who were to become lifelong partners. Less than a month before, Bishop had taken the podium to eulogize the recently deceased George Washington. The minister soon had his speech published so "that the reader may know what a good and virtuous example is, and be excited to copy it."

In 1833, when Bishop had owned the Athens County acreage for nearly twenty years, he brought his family to Ohio. Why he decided to relocate to the wilderness at age 64 is not known, but apparently only his wife, Abigail, and three of their seven children—Almira, James, and Abigail—made the move. Soon after their arrival, Samuel laid out 20 town lots for a settlement he called Bishopville and eventually built a home there.

The next year Bishop divided his Athens County property among his heirs, reserving a small swath along Sunday Creek for himself and his wife. Their daughters, Abigail Tuck Bishop and her older sister, Almira Bishop Fuller, received a portion of their father's considerable holdings in what was now known as Homer Township, as did three of his sons and Almira's husband. In all the deeds Samuel Bishop mentioned his love and affection for his children. The amount of land allotted to each heir varied, but what is striking about these arrangements is that the women reaped more than a token inheritance. In a time when sons often acquired all the land and daughters were lucky to get a cow or feather bed, Abigail and Almira received a hefty slice of their father's estate.

On the land that Bishop gave to the then-unmarried 22-year-old Abigail, the elderly minister hoped to carry out an ambitious plan. He had decided to start a secondary school in Bishopville amid the acreage he was deeding to her. From Abigail's holdings he reserved "a plat of house lots containing in their midst a common of about three acres on which it is calculated to erect a school house for the instruction of youth by the name of Bishop's Fraternal Calvanistic [Calvinistic] Baptist Seminary." He also set aside three lots to construct housing and work space for the instructors and students.

Bishop soon deeded a 100-acre tract adjoining the school grounds to five local Calvinistic Baptist men who agreed to serve as trustees. He was donating the land, he said, because of "the love and goodwill that I bear to the present rising and future generations and the earnest desire that I have to be instrumental of promoting learning morality and piety in them all." Bishop envisioned an academy whose male and female students could work to pay all or part of their tuition and living expenses. He promised to compensate students "at a reasonable price" for cultivating the donated land around the school. He had a soft spot for impoverished scholars, who could "pay in whole by their labor if they should wish[,] for it is given for that express purpose and for no other." Bishop also authorized the trust-ees to "erect shops" on the school grounds and to "furnish materials for mechanics, for the same purpose: also, furnish places and stock for female labor, sewing, braiding, and all such other kinds of labor as may be deemed expedient."

Bishop did not explain why he had decided to locate the seminary within Abigail's land. Could he have expected that she, as the unmarried school-teacher daughter, would play a role in the new school? Or was it simply the best location on which to build? Whatever her father's intention, Abigail soon leased the 40-acre plot surrounding the proposed school grounds back to her parents for their lifetime use, "in consideration of the love good will and affection" she had for her "honored Father and Mother." The rent was to consist of "one ear of corn to be paid to me my heirs or assigns from year to year on the first day of January" and only "when demanded." After her marriage Abigail would sell this land back to her parents, retain-ing a separate tract of over 100 acres as her inheritance.

❊ ❊ ❊

SHORTLY after Koons's move to Ohio, his mother, Margaret, fell gravely ill back in Pennsylvania. Though he was far away, Koons felt a close tie to her, writing that she was "as honest, amiable, kind and affectionate a mother as ever graced the earth." As she lay dying, Margaret told the family she could not go peacefully without one final visit with Jonathan, to whom, in his words, she had always extended "one of the most tender threads of her affection." There was not enough time to send a letter bidding her son to come home, so it appeared her final wish could not be granted. As friends and relatives gathered around the unconscious woman to witness her final breath, Jonathan Koons was having a synchronistic vision. As he later wrote: "Her spirit left its senseless tenement a sufficient length of time to pay me a visit in Ohio, three hundred miles distant, and then returned back, and reanimated her frail remains, that had been partially adjusted with the funeral habiliments, and delivered the unexpected tidings of her visit, in the relation of which she announced that she had now seen me, and was prepared to depart in peace. She even related what I was engaged at, and the condition of my person, which proved to be strictly true."

Jonathan's brother Lewis wrote to him soon after their mother's death. He was curious to confirm Margaret's account—seemingly gained by clairvoyance. Jonathan swore to Lewis that his mother's information was correct in all respects.

UPON their marriage in October 1836, Jonathan and Abigail, both 25, set up housekeeping in Amestown, a farming settlement some 10 miles distant from the patch of virgin forest in Dover Township that they would eventually call home. Koons continued to work as a carpenter for paying customers while slowly carving out a working farm on their own land, which by now had swelled to 522 acres, the result of a second real estate purchase he had made that summer.

Except for floods along Federal Creek, Amestown and the surrounding Ames Township had much to recommend to the young couple. Pioneers arriving there in 1798 in dugout canoes had brought with them progressive values that included an emphasis on education. One of the earliest schools had Harvard graduates on the faculty and students reciting the words of

Cassius and Brutus at a school assembly. According to the 1833 *Ohio Gazette*, the township "contains two stores, a number of mills, a handsome brick Presbyterian meeting house, two brick school houses, [and] an incorporated circulating library." Before the end of the decade the village of Amesville would be officially established, but even that designation did not relieve women of the necessity of crossing the main street on horseback when the thoroughfare was muddy, thus keeping their skirts and pantalets dry.

The idea of a circulating library might have been especially appealing to Abigail, the former schoolteacher, and to her husband, given his love of books. As early as 1803 or 1804, settlers in Ames Township (the western part of which would become Dover) had created the Western Library Association to have a circulating book collection in their community. Residents bought shares or memberships in the WLA in exchange for the opportunity to borrow books. The money was used to purchase the library's volumes. Cash was hard to come by on the frontier, so some of the founding members had paid with raccoon or bear pelts instead, earning the enterprise the colorful moniker Coonskin Library.

Along with a desire for literacy, a strain of antislavery sentiment ran through Amestown, one probably shared by Abigail, whose father was noted to be a "strong Abolitionist." One Ames resident recalled that when he was a small boy, his father instructed him to take food to a certain rock deep in the woods and leave quickly. When the coast was deemed clear, escaped slaves would emerge from their hiding place in a cave to claim the provisions. The boy's father would eventually escort them to the next station on the Underground Railroad.

The extent of Jonathan and Abigail's involvement in the activities of the Amestown community is not clear, but while living there in October 1837, they welcomed their first child, a little boy they called Nahum Ward Koons. The baby was given the name of Nahum Ward of Marietta, the man from whom Koons had bought his second tract of land. Ward was a philanthropist as well as Marietta's former mayor and a successful land speculator; his name is scattered through the deed books of several counties. Not only did Jonathan and Abigail's baby bear the name of one of the area's luminaries, he had a Bible name: Nahum was a visionary prophet of the Old Testament. Perhaps this combination of worldly success and heavenly guidance resonated with the young couple.

In June 1838 they moved to their Dover Township property with little Nahum. Over time the family would clear about 60 acres, plant 500 fruit trees, and build a sturdy log house, barn, and other outbuildings. But for now this high ridgetop on the lower end of Sunday Creek—crowned with a knoll that would later be called Mount Nebo—was still a place given over to wildness; only one neighbor could be found within 2 miles. In these solitary environs survival would depend on their resourcefulness—and, upon occasion, a touch of divine intervention.

ONE cold morning that December, a young man named E. Johnson ran to Koons's house calling for help. Johnson and his coworker, M. Linscott, both of whom were boarding with the Koons family, had been out making rails. Linscott had struck himself in the foot with an ax and lay badly injured. Could Koons bring a horse and some bandages? While gathering up the supplies, Koons remembered a form of old folk magic practiced by his father back in Bedford. "Having a theoretic knowledge of the modus operandi in the 'witch' system of treatment, I thought this was a good opportunity for experimenting," Koons wrote. "I accordingly applied the remedy, as previously directed, simply by invoking the impelling agents that actuated Christ, for their special care and protection in behalf of the afflicted."

Johnson led Koons into the woods, where he found the helpless Linscott lying on a steep bluff, his blood staining the frosty ground. The young boarder was so weak that he could not stand. Strangely, though, his wound had stopped bleeding. They took him to the Koons house and placed him on a mattress on the floor. When his shoe and stocking were removed, Koons was horrified to see that Linscott had chopped his foot nearly in half. Nonetheless the foot was bandaged without stitching together the severed blood vessels, and in the process only a single spurt of blood hit the wall of the cabin. Linscott spent just a week recovering, with no further blood loss or complications, and experienced a pain-free convalescence at the Koons home. "I do not claim, however, that I was instrumental in producing these happy effects," Jonathan Koons wrote. "I simply give the facts."

When Koons reflexively used the chants of white magic to staunch the flow of blood from Linscott's foot, he was following a tradition long established among the Pennsylvania Dutch. Jonathan's father, Peter, as well as a cousin on the Koons side, had been called powwow doctors back in Bedford. This term had nothing to do with Native Americans but was a system of European folk magic dating back hundreds of years. The overwhelming majority of its practitioners considered themselves Christians, believing that divine aid could flow through them to help stop bleeding, heal burns, or cure other ailments.

Of his father Jonathan Koons wrote: "He was possessed of powerful magnetic forces, and many wonderful cures were performed through and by him, with what was called the laying on of hands." Jonathan recalled a time when Peter cured his son Solomon of a raging fever when the boy had been given up for dead. Peter would also blow his breath on severe burns to prevent them from blistering. His care extended to animals, such as horses with colic and other illnesses. "He believed that his healing powers were transmitted, or conferred by certain spirits, whom he universally invoked on his healing occasions," Jonathan Koons explained. "The spirits he generally invoked on these occasions, were 'Jesus of Nazareth,' 'John the Baptist,' and some of the apostles of Christ." Several other men and women in Jonathan Koons's childhood also had been considered healers, though the source of their power led to much speculation. "For fear of evil, many were afraid to enter their company," he later wrote.

Jonathan Koons had carried over from Pennsylvania a respect for his father's traditions. Although he had rejected Peter's stout Presbyterianism, Jonathan was still attracted to his father's mystical side; here in the Ohio Country he would find his own way to tap into the lode heretofore mined by their ancestors. In so doing he would become, for a season, one of the most highly admired mediums in antebellum America.

BACK in Bedford, most of Jonathan's siblings soon joined an exodus to Athens County, leaving Lewis behind with their elderly father. By 1840 the area around Mount Nebo was fast becoming an enclave of the Pennsylvania Koonses and related families. Jonathan and Abigail had been living on their farm for two years and had welcomed baby Filenia, born in 1839, as a little sister to 3-year-old Nahum. Jonathan's sister Elizabeth lived on the next farm over with her husband, Joseph Hughes, and their children. Their sister Mary, who went by her nickname, Polly, had married Nicholas Border back in Bedford, and they, too, settled nearby. In 1838 Jonathan and Abigail had sold 200 acres of their farm to the youngest Koons brother, George, for $200. With a homestead to offer, George wed Chloe Weimer, whose dowry consisted of a trunk, looking glass, and sidesaddle. The oldest Koons brother, Michael, had come west with his wife, Sarah Border. Another sister, Rachel, had migrated with her Bedford husband, Aaron Evans. Brother Solomon, too, had bought a farm a few miles away. All told, the Koons brothers and sisters had several hundred acres at their command as the 1840s began.

With more families settling around Mount Nebo, the demand for public education grew. Schooling had to be worked around more immediate matters, such as planting and harvesting crops, hunting, and chopping wood for winter, yet the Dover Township area was known as a place whose residents were often literate and valued an education for their children. In 1847 the family of Elizabeth and Joseph Hughes leased land rent-free to Dover School District No. 2 for the construction of a school. As school district directors, Jonathan, his brother George, and their neighbor Joseph Tippie did "agree to build or cause to be built a comfortable school house in a reasonable time." Census records show that Jonathan and Abigail's children were attending school in 1850, likely in the new building.

ABIGAIL Bishop Koons, surrounded by in-laws, had no dearth of relatives around Mount Nebo, but she must have relied mostly on letters to stay in touch with her own blood kin. If she traveled 15 miles north to the Bishop enclave in Homer Township during this period, perhaps she did so to console her elderly father on his legal entanglements. Toward the end of the 1840s Samuel Gaylord Bishop's dream of operating a high school lay in tatters. By then legal wrangling about the proposed Bishop's Fraternal Calvanistic [Calvinistic] Baptist Seminary had been ongoing for about 10 years. At some point a handsome two-story building of locally crafted bricks had been erected, but no classes were ever held there.

Prospects for the school had seemed bright at first. After it was incorporated by the state legislature in 1835, Bishop went on a lengthy out-of-state fundraising trip, returning in September 1836 with donated money and other valuables. But he and the trustees had a falling out, and Bishop apparently decided to go it alone. His erstwhile collaborators demanded an account of the donations he had collected for the seminary, but he refused. With the bonds of Christian fellowship now torn asunder, the trustees sued the elderly minister for damages in 1839. Years of litigation dogged Samuel after that, as first the Athens County Common Pleas Court and later the Ohio Supreme Court ruled against him. (By 1845 Homer Township had been portioned off from Athens County and made a part of Morgan County, but the case remained in Athens County.) The high court ruled that "there was in the hands of the said Samuel G. Bishop after deducting a competent amount to him for his services in collecting the same, for the use of the complainants the sum of $1,369.60." As no payment to the victors was forthcoming, an 80-acre chunk of Bishop's property was sold at public auction in 1849. But the litigation was destined to drag on, a nettle in what might otherwise have been a comfortable old age for 80-year-old Samuel and his wife, Abigail, five years his junior.

JONATHAN Koons's ancestors had been blessed with the gift of longevity, with one forebear surpassing the century mark and several others living well into their eighties and nineties. Back in Pennsylvania, his father Peter died in 1847 at the age of 87 or 88. Peter's second wife agreed to allow his son Lewis to administer the estate. Lewis had his father's 385 acres in Monroe Township auctioned off to pay his creditors, putting the estate in the black. Lewis wrote to Jonathan that the exact amount of Peter's legacy, $263.39, would be divided equally among the 10 heirs. Whether Peter ever saw any of his grown children after they crossed into Ohio is not known. However, a few years later Jonathan would come to believe that his father had sent him an affectionate poem—mysteriously rendered in Jonathan's journal by the spirits—as a token of Peter's survival in the afterlife.

AS Ohio had continued to fill up with settlers, time had shown that the land in southwestern Ohio was superior for farming; the hilly acres of the Ohio

Company purchase in the southeast, prone to erosion and packed with clay, had proven a poor match for the loamy plains of the state's bread-basket farther west. Nonetheless in 1849 the *Ohio Cultivator,* an agricultural journal, was predicting a prosperous future for Athens County farmers. "The time will come when the hills of old Athens will not be numbered among the least of those tributaries to your laudable agricultural exertions in Ohio," it said. "The vast mineral resources of the county, consisting of Salt, Coal, Iron and Lime, (not yet wrought) will bring and are bringing in a large number of miners and manufacturers. The population has to be fed, insuring to the farmer here a home market, and good prices for all the products of a farm."

Such prognostications must have been welcome news to Jonathan and Abigail, who by 1850 had a family of seven children to support. Their two daughters were 11-year-old Filenia and 8-year-old Quintilla. Nahum, 12, was the oldest son, followed by Samuel, 9; Sanders, 6; Daniel, 5; and John A., 4. In just a few years, some newspapers would call Jonathan Koons a "well-to-do" farmer, while others would describe him as poor. In truth he seemed to be a typical farmer in Dover Township with real estate valued at $2,000. In addition to the farm, Koons had $90 worth of "farming implements and machinery" and livestock valued at $200. But Abigail stood out among the women of her neighborhood in that she owned land valued at $1,000—the Sunday Creek acreage near Bishopville that her father had given her.

By now Jonathan and Abigail had sold off more of their sprawling farm, paring it down to a more manageable 160 acres—100 acres they had improved and 60 that were unimproved. Like farmers' lives everywhere, the Koonses' revolved around the cycles of planting and reaping, as well as the birthing and slaughtering of animals. From their ridgetop fields they produced 130 bushels of wheat, 100 bushels of Indian corn, and 10 bushels of Irish potatoes while harvesting 6 tons of hay for the livestock. Some of the children were old enough to help tend to the two horses, four "milch cows," 30 sheep, and 9 pigs that the family owned. From the sheep they collected 100 pounds of wool; from the cows' milk they made prodigious quantities of butter and cheese. They also kept honey bees. It was a life-style that made trips to town largely unnecessary.

Koons and other ridgetop farmers in the area found the higher ground well suited to growing fruit trees, with the higher altitude maintaining higher temperatures during cold spells. He was especially proud of the orchards that he called the Koons Fruit Farm. In addition to selling fruit and other produce as a cash crop, the Koonses sought more ways to bring in money. In 1850 they created $31 worth of unspecified "homemade manufactures," and Koons performed marriages and other services as a justice of the peace. It is also possible that his wife's property in Morgan County was producing income in some way, perhaps supplying timber for a nearby sawmill.

Jonathan and Abigail were comfortably settled on Mount Nebo among the Koons clan, but their lives were soon to be upended. They would become entangled in religious quarrels that would sweep their community— and even divide their own extended family.

AT dusk on April 20, 1850, Jonathan Koons walked steadily up the path, scarcely noticing the white object bobbing 10 to 15 paces ahead of him. His thoughts were heavy as he considered his youngest brother, George, to whom he had ministered day and night on his sickbed. After several days of such duty—perhaps spelling George's wife, Chloe, as she tended to the couple's four little boys—Jonathan needed to return home to see about his own family. With his dwelling just a half-mile away, he cut through a strip of woodland and reached the top of Sand Ridge, where several roads intersected at a clearing. Coming out of his reverie, he noticed that the object—more of a form, really—was still in front of him. Now he really began to pay attention. He walked faster, making a beeline for a clump of bushes that the form had darted behind. When Koons finally reached the spot, the shadowy image was gone.

He shrugged off the incident as an optical illusion and hurried home, eager to see if the farm was being kept up in his absence. Once he had satisfied himself that all was well outside, he went in and joined his children by the fire. They were anxious to know how their uncle George was doing. As Jonathan began to describe his brother's condition, a deafening crash ripped through the upper story of the log house right over their heads.

"George is dead," Jonathan blurted out, surprising even himself. The youngsters wanted to know how he knew.

"Did you not hear the token?" their father exclaimed.

Koons instantly wished he could recall the words. He would later write: "Of this I immediately repented, for two causes. First: I feared it would cause the children to be timid in case they believed in tokens and omens. Second: It was not in accordance with my general faith. Had I been asked ten minutes previous to the occurrence, if I believed in omens, I would have candidly told them I did not."

As the children continued to bombard their father with questions, he recovered and began to assure them that a board must have fallen on the second story. They all trooped up the stairs to inspect, but nothing out of the ordinary revealed itself. "Not feeling prepared to reply to further inquiries on the present subject, I, instead thereof, entered a list of orders to the children, relating to their ordinary duties, and retraced my steps to my brother's residence," Jonathan recalled. "About two-thirds of the distance, I met a messenger on his way to inform me of my brother's decease. I immediately inquired for the precise time of his departure, which corresponded very nearly, if not quite, to the minute the crash at my house was produced."

George was dead at age 36. His family buried him in a high meadow near his home. Once Jonathan's grief had subsided, he began to reflect on the meaning of George's untimely passing. He even wondered if the otherworldly signs given to him had been real after all. Jonathan soon became "profound[ly] skeptical," discounting the validity of "specters, witches and spiritual admonitions and tokens." But his mind was not quite settled. "Notwithstanding this conclusion," he wrote, "I cannot say but what frequent silent whisperings admonished me otherwise, which I could not at all times pass unheeded."

Beyond the ordinary obsequies that had been observed for George, Jonathan would soon find another way to come to terms with his loss.

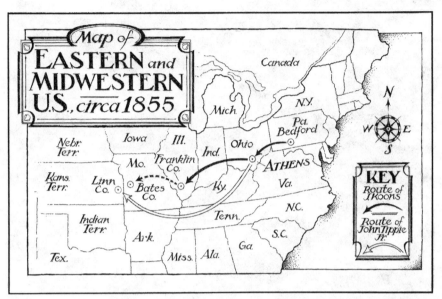

1.1.   Jonathan Koons and John Tippie Jr. joined a tide of westward migration during the nineteenth century. The solid line shows Koons's movement from Pennsylvania to Ohio to Illinois; the broken line depicts his intended destination in Missouri. The white line shows Tippie's disastrous relocation to Bleeding Kansas. The actual routes the families took between 1835 and 1858 are not known. Map by Sandy Plunkett.

1.2 Jonathan and Abigail Koons, ca. 1852–55. Photograph courtesy of Brandon Hodge, MysteriousPlanchette.com.

1.3 Nahum Koons, shown here with his father ca. 1852–55, when Nahum, born in 1837, would have been in his mid- to late teens. Photograph courtesy of Brandon Hodge, MysteriousPlanchette.com.

Koons Cemetery, 1939

4.1a. Tombstones in Koons Cemetery as they appeared in 1939, looking northeast. William E. Peters Papers, Mahn Center for Archives and Special Collections, Ohio University Libraries.

4.1b. Vista of Koons cemetery as it appeared in 1939, looking north. William E. Peters Papers, Mahn Center for Archives and Special Collections, Ohio University Libraries.

4.1c. This 1939 photograph shows the headstone of George S. Koons, Jonathan's younger brother, who was 36 when he died in 1850. As the administrator of George's estate, Jonathan helped the widow, Chloe Weimer Koons, settle the family's financial affairs. William E. Peters Papers, Mahn Center for Archives and Special Collections, Ohio University Libraries.

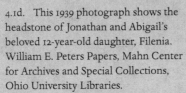

4.1d. This 1939 photograph shows the headstone of Jonathan and Abigail's beloved 12-year-old daughter, Filenia. William E. Peters Papers, Mahn Center for Archives and Special Collections, Ohio University Libraries.

1.5   Alfred Ryors, Ohio University president (1848–52) and a Presbyterian minister, who declined to preach the funeral of Koons's young daughter Filenia in 1851. Ryors's wife, Louisa Walker Ryors, was among 106 people in Athens County who signed an 1854 petition asking the US government to scientifically study spiritualist phenomena. University Archives, Mahn Center for Archives and Special Collections, Ohio University Libraries.

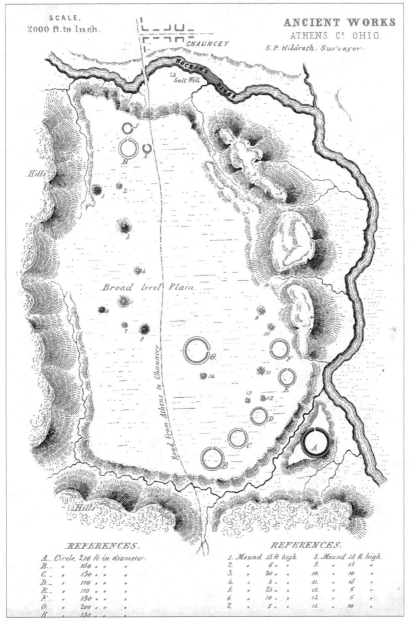

SCALE.
2000 ft. to Inch.

ANCIENT WORKS
ATHENS C^o OHIO.
S. P. Hildreth. Surveyor.

CHAUNCEY

Salt Well.

Hills.

Broad level Plain.

Road from Athens to Chauncey.

Hills.

REFERENCES.

A. Circle, 210 ft. in diameter.
B. „ 150 „ „ „
C. „ 130 „ „ „
D. „ 110 „ „ „
E. „ 110 „ „ „
F. „ 130 „ „ „
G. „ 200 „ „ „
H. „ 130 „ „ „

REFERENCES.

1. Mound 15 ft. high.
2. „ 6 „ „
3. „ 30 „ „
4. „ 8 „ „
5. „ 24 „ „
6. „ 10 „ „
7. „ 5 „ „

8. Mound 15 ft. high.
9. „ 15 „ „
10. „ 10 „ „
11. „ 15 „ „
12. „ 6 „ „
13. „ 6 „ „
14. „ 70 „ „

1.6 In Jonathan Koons's day Indian mounds and enclosures abounded in Athens County, as shown in this early surveyor's map of the Wolf's Plains complex just a few miles from the Koons home. Koons believed that he received messages from spirits of Native Americans and participated in excavating their burial sites on two occasions. Map by S. P. Hildreth reproduced from Ephraim George Squier and Edwin Hamilton Davis, *Ancient Monuments of the Mississippi Valley*, 1848.

4

"A Striking Specimen of Beauty"

IN THE very first years of settlement, the wild reaches of southeastern Ohio must have seemed like an American Eden, a place where believers could distill Christianity to its purest essence. Far from the religion of the Old World, with its prescribed rituals, they were free to improvise when it came to worship. One Athens County pioneer recalled,

> There were no churches or meeting-houses in the county. Religious services, when any were had, were held in some private dwelling, or barn, or perhaps rude school house with oiled-paper windows to admit the light, and fitted up with rough benches. Such shelter was sought in cold weather. In the summer, the congregation generally assembled in the open air under the spreading branches of the trees, where, seated on benches hastily prepared for the occasion, they listened to the welcome message of the traveling preacher, who was either an independent missionary or sent on a missionary tour by the body to which he belonged.

One such voice crying in the wilderness was that of John Chapman, the woodsman and tree planter better known as Johnny Appleseed. Born in Massachusetts in 1774, he became a living legend on the American frontier, walking thousands of miles across Pennsylvania, Ohio, and Indiana not only to plant apple trees but to spread the spiritual teachings of Emmanuel

Swedenborg. Chapman was a follower of the eminent Swedish scientist and mystic whose philosophy inspired generations after his death in 1772. He had converted to the Swedenborgian church, called the Church of the New Jerusalem (or just New Church), while living in Pennsylvania. Although he was a businessman who sold seedlings and saplings to the pioneers, Chapman also was a pacifist, vegetarian, and deeply religious man who distributed Swedenborg's texts all across the frontier. Upon arriving at a settlement, Chapman would shout, "News! Fresh from heaven!" as he handed out chapters of the books and collected pages that had already been read. When he was invited into a local home to spend the night, he would sit around the fire extolling the virtues of his faith.

Chapman probably told his hosts about Swedenborg's great renown as a clairvoyant back in his native land, how in 1759 the seer had remotely viewed Stockholm in flames from 250 miles away—long before couriers could deliver news of the fire. Swedenborg believed that, in addition to this psychic gift, he had been specially chosen as a channel for communication with spirits of dead human beings that inhabited various rungs of heaven and hell. In his view, dead souls abiding in heaven had an existence much the same as they had on Earth except they now were not burdened by sin. This spiritual world was reflected in the physical world; everyday things harbored a deeper hidden meaning. The Bible, too, contained symbolic meanings and could be interpreted in a radically different way by considering the correspondences woven into its language. Above all, the "good news" Chapman was spreading was Swedenborg's promise that salvation was open to all, that people had some measure of control over their final destiny. In fact, it would be the recently dead individual, rather than God, who would review earthly deeds and judge him or herself accordingly. This was a message that spiritualists would embrace in due time.

Chapman had begun his wanderings in Ohio as early as 1801. He refined his business practices into what became a familiar ritual: he would collect seeds from commercial cider presses, identify places in the wilderness that he thought would be settled in a year or two, and plant orchards in those areas. Though he often lived in the forest with little shelter, Chapman sometimes built cabins or bought property to use as a base for his operations or simply as an investment. For three decades he owned land in eight Ohio counties and planted apple orchards in nearly twice that number. Even more important, in his eyes, was his influence in establishing Swedenborgian societies; although this faith would never become widespread in the state or the nation, Ohio by 1843 had several hundred members of the Swedenborgian church.

In Meigs County the fruits of Chapman's spiritual labor were seen in the Grant family, converts who entertained the holy man at their home and established a Swedenborgian congregation inspired by his teachings. Apparently no such society existed in neighboring Athens County, but Chapman did travel through the area, often stopping to spend the night at the Dover Township farm of Abraham Pugsley, a Baptist minister. Local tradition has it that Chapman planted his last orchard in southeastern Ohio on Elder Pugsley's land before moving his operations farther west. If his path had ever crossed that of Jonathan Koons, they could have passed many lively hours parsing theology in addition to mulling the finer points of growing apples. Chapman's twin legacies would linger in southeastern Ohio for decades after his 1845 death in Indiana.

While Chapman was bringing a mystical strain of Christianity to the area, he might have encountered the Reverend James Quinn, a Methodist missionary based in Marietta who traversed the wilds on his horse, Wilks. In December 1799 Quinn had made his first pass through the Hockhocking Valley, preaching at any settlements he could find. Although he enjoyed comfortable lodgings in Athens, he endured many lonely hours on the trail, once carving his name on a beech tree after taking a solitary meal of "pone and meat." After several years as a circuit rider, Quinn helped organize what was likely the first camp meeting in Athens County—a four-day affair that drew excited participants with its evangelical style of preaching and singing. Methodist societies eventually formed in Athens and Alexander Townships, cementing that denomination's influence in the area.

Just a year or two after the town of Athens was incorporated in 1811, the Methodists built a brick church in the village. The Presbyterians followed with their own building in 1828, having previously worshipped at the courthouse. Although they were several years behind the Methodists in actual church construction, the Presbyterians were highly influential. At least three presidents of Ohio University were ordained ministers of that faith, as were many faculty members.

The elders of the Presbyterian church took their duties seriously, disciplining members of the congregation who drank to excess, neglected prayers, questioned religious doctrines, or committed fornication or adultery. In 1828 the elders set their sights on Samuel Baldwin Pruden and his wife, Mary Cranston Pruden. Baldwin at age 30 was an enterprising merchant and miller who was developing the Bingham mill in Athens as a wool-carding operation. Within a few years he would make his fortune by establishing his own flax oil, grist, and saw mill, and a saltworks just south of Athens. Mary was the daughter of a well-to-do family in New York State and a descendant of two colonial governors of Rhode Island. As a youth she had survived a harrowing voyage down the rain-swollen Ohio River, during which she was nearly swept away by a flash flood, before reaching Athens on foot.

In the spring of 1828 Baldwin Pruden was brought before the Session, the governing body of the local Presbyterians, for failing to attend services for more than a year. When questioned by the church elders, he said "he disbelieved the authenticity of the Holy Scriptures and that he did not believe in the future punishment of the wicked." He was excommunicated on May 10, 1828, "until he manifest repentance."

Mary Pruden may have continued to attend services after the ouster of her husband, but her adherence to church doctrine was also suspect. The contrary ideas entertained by the couple were thought to stem from their reading of the *New Harmony (Indiana) Gazette*. New Harmony, founded in 1814, was a utopian community in southwestern Indiana that sought an egalitarian lifestyle for all its residents. The Scottish industrialist Robert Owen, who was widely regarded as an infidel, had purchased the town in 1825. The newspaper, edited by his son Robert Dale Owen, provided a platform for free thinking—questioning the norms of society that most people took for granted. The paper weighed in on slavery, women's right to divorce, child labor, free education, and other reform issues. Above all, the paper challenged the very pillars of religious orthodoxy.

"Our ancestors drowned old women for a knowledge of witchcraft and burnt heretics, because they were guilty of heterodox sentiments," an 1827 editorial noted, "and we, their successors, if we have lessened the punishment, have not become more rational in our accusations. In the nineteenth century, we accuse our fellow-men of candor, and impeach them of sincerity. An atheist is a blameless character so long as he dissembles; but let him be guilty of honesty, and his character is lost."

A stubborn dalliance with this newspaper continued to cause problems for the Prudens. Just a month after her husband's removal from the church, Mary Pruden was called to answer similar charges. "We charge you with questioning the truth of some parts of the Holy Scriptures—Expressing doubts about some of the leading doctrines of the Gospel—and industriously propagating infidel principles from a certain weekly paper called the *New Harmony Gazette,*" the indictment declared. Mary Pruden pleaded not guilty.

A formal trial commenced on July 19 with the Reverend Robert G. Wilson presiding. Wilson was pastor of the church as well as president of Ohio University. The jury of six elders was made up of male church members of high standing in Athens—four merchants, a lawyer, and a justice of the peace. At Mary Pruden's request, the lawyer, Joseph Dana, was allowed to assist in her defense. She also asked questions of the witnesses herself.

A handful of witnesses testified about their sometimes startling conversations with Mary Pruden. One said she "heard Mrs. Pruden say she did not believe there was any witches or Devils" and that she "doubted their being either a Heaven or Hell." Another quoted her as saying that "God was an object of imagination." Multiple witnesses reported that she had read to them out of the *Gazette* or talked to them about books she found interesting.

One of the elders, Alvan Bingham, testified about a conversation in which Mary Pruden seemed to discount the literal truth of biblical miracles. "She said, it was said that Bonaparte marched his army across the Red Sea at the same place where Moses with the Israelites crossed: Moses being well acquainted with that Country knew the exact time at which he could cross on dry ground. . . . She said that she believed the Bible as much as any minister of learning."

"What were your impressions from what Mrs. P. said?" asked Dana.

"It made me feel disagreeable from her saying that she believed the Bible as fully as any minister of learning," Bingham responded. "The impression was that Educated Ministers do not believe it, and she did not."

"Did you express your fears to Mrs. P. about the consequences of reading the papers?" Dana queried.

Before Bingham could answer, Mary Pruden interjected, "He did repeatedly and scolded me."

She said nothing further in her own defense. The panel unanimously found her guilty on all counts but stopped short of pronouncing her punishment. Instead they delayed sentencing and asked the Reverend Wilson and Dana to speak with her privately.

On August 9 the Session met again. Wilson reported that he had visited Mary Pruden, but "she was not willing to make any further concessions than what she had made before and would not agree to abandon the practice of reading infidel publications." With the recalcitrant Mary Pruden remaining a challenge to church authority, she was excommunicated that day.

It is not clear whether Baldwin and Mary Pruden suffered any social ostracism as a result of being kicked out of the church for heresy. But nine years later Baldwin Pruden was barred from testifying in a civil suit in Athens County Common Pleas Court after an attorney objected to his religious beliefs (or lack thereof). Baldwin Pruden's businesses continued to prosper, and in time he became a trustee of Ohio University, a state legislator, and—ironically—an associate judge of the Court of Common Pleas. In 1840 he and Mary built a red brick mansion they called Harmony, perhaps in honor of the publication that had brought them so much trouble—and so much delight.

BY 1850 the number of churches in Athens County had grown to 24, with the two oldest groups, the Methodists and Presbyterians, leading the count with 12 churches and 8, respectively. The Second Great Awakening had set the stage for the growth of these two religious powerhouses, but other denominations had a foothold as well: the county had two Baptist churches, one Roman Catholic, and one Universalist.

From this smorgasbord of religious sentiment, Jonathan Koons had tasted nothing that would satisfy his soul. Behind the trappings of an ordinary farmer, he harbored beliefs that were far from common in Athens County. Koons had long been alienated from traditional Christian teachings, even though he was married to the daughter of a Baptist minister. As he would later write, he was, in fact, an infidel:

> I had become an advocate in defence of atheistical sentiments, through the perversion of Christian orthodoxy, under the

instructions of which I had been placed at an early age, and which
for a time had taken hold on my mind. But soon finding myself
sadly disappointed in my vain expectations of receiving those
spiritual gifts and blessings which I anticipated at the mercy of
God, through my devoted teachers, I soon became subjected to
the title of backslider by those from whom I had departed in faith,
and simultaneously heaped their scorn and derision upon me with
such heated fury, until I was racked with fears, and was frequently
constrained to cry, Oh Lord, save or I perish. But not withstanding
all my repeated efforts to reconcile myself to their wedded faith;
my researches after truth were only instrumental in disclosing
new fields of ideas, which would not admit of any corresponding
connection with the attributes of an allwise, benevolent and
merciful God.

In particular Koons had trouble reconciling his childhood religious
teachings with the notion of a merciful God. The steady diet of Calvinist
theology emphasized humans' sinfulness, the depravity from which no
amount of good works could cleanse a person over the course of a lifetime. Adam and Eve's error would always be visited on him, his children,
and their children until the end of time. Worse still, humans had no free
will with which to seek salvation; God had already predestined who would
be saved and who would be lost; the former, called the elect, would never
have to face the fires of hell.

After his conversion to spiritualism, Jonathan would put those fears to
rest, confidently stating,

Let us strictly avoid the propagation of the preposterous notion,
that any distinguished sect, party or person, above all others, is a
"special elect" favorite of a universal Deity, or some man-made
Bible-God; a doctrine that has cursed and retarded the progress of
the human family in all ages of the world, from the date of Adam
hence to modern Calvinism; which, last, and worst of all, teaches
"that all those, and those alone, who were from eternity elected to
salvation, are given Christ by the Father," or God. . . . In place of
the doctrine of election, let all reformed teachers to the contrary
consider themselves . . . the common and legitimate heirs . . . of
one and the same universal paternity.

Spiritualists offered a kinder, gentler religion espousing many heavens, no hell, and room for every soul. They believed in a universal brotherhood in which all had a chance, and indeed a responsibility, to improve themselves, not only in this life but after death. Spiritual evolution was a process. Individual spirits progressed through a series of concentric circles stretching out from Earth. The longer a person was dead, the more likely he or she was to lose contact with those on the planet. Some souls, however, chose to stay near, to assist loved ones on Earth as well as prove the existence of life after death. Thus spiritualism had a strong attraction for the recently bereaved. If its promise were true, mediums could provide the connecting link between survivors and those gone on, conveying the proof of survival so desperately sought.

IN late 1851 Koons's uneasy relationship with the church became public knowledge in a most unseemly fashion. Twelve-year-old Filenia, Abigail and Jonathan's second child, died of an enlarged heart on September 1. How long she had suffered from this condition is not known, but she had been well enough the previous summer to present the editors of the *Athens Messenger* newspaper with a basket of fruit on some unspecified occasion.

"Her disease . . . bid defiance to all the medical aid that could be procured on her behalf," her obituary stated. "She was a striking specimen of beauty, intelligence and piety. She was the pride of her doting parents, but, like the untimely flower, she faded and vanished from their sight, leaving many friends to mourn her departure." The notice concluded with 12 lines of poetry stating the conventional sentiment that Filenia, having escaped sorrow and suffering, was now in a better place. What is striking about the poem, however, is that the word *Communicated* appeared at the end of it, rather than an author's name. This suggests that whoever submitted the obituary to the newspaper believed that the spirits were already communicating with the family.

That chasm of time in September must had been exquisitely bittersweet for the Koons family, as Abigail gave birth to a boy on September 2, before her daughter's body had even been buried. Jonathan's lack of faith made the little girl's death even more devastating. "What rendered the occurrence [of Filenia's death] more trying than otherwise was my skepticism relative to the immortality of the soul, which, with myself, had been a subject of doubt for some years," her father would later write. "Fearing that this would be our final separation, and the blotting out of all her mental functions and sensitive powers, I viewed death as the final destroyer and extinguisher of all our physical charms, sorrow and pleasures. In this state of mind, I was prevailed upon to consent to the formal ceremony of a funeral discourse. I accordingly dispatched a friend for a clergyman, with instruction to employ the first one he met, without regard to his disciplinary profession."

After that the story diverged in its retelling—not so much in the facts themselves but in their interpretation. Along with Filenia's obituary in the *Athens Messenger* appeared a scathing letter signed "A Friend" and authenticated in a preamble by Jonathan Koons himself. The anonymous person wrote:

> Messrs. Editors—On the occasion of the death of Miss Koons, in accordance with the wish of mourning parents, a friend was dispatched in pursuit of some (soul-loving) Divine to deliver a funeral address, with instructions to pay no regard to sect or name of religion—thinking that the most suitable time to make lasting impressions upon the young minds of the surviving brothers and sisters. But alas! the mourners were sadly disappointed to learn from their friend that he met with a positive denial both from the Rev. Mr. —— of the Methodist Church and the Rev. Mr. —— of the Presbyterian order (residents of Athens) after an earnest solicitation on his part: and after being induced by the latter to state the character, religious denomination and family circumstances of the deceased—and for no other reason than that the sun shone too hot for them to ride out at that time. However, the funeral procession was made up with a respectable assembly of friends and well-wishers of the deceased who contributed due respect to the occasion by an honorable interment and a full manifestation of their sympathy for the surviving relatives: and it is hoped that the friends will yet find someone to favor them with a funeral sermon: someone with equal mental abilities and a physical constitution which will enable him to endure the electric rays of a scorching

sun or the inclemency of a mild and gentle breeze after a regaling shower, which proved to be the case on that occasion.—A FRIEND

Addressing the questions supposedly posed by the Presbyterian minister, Koons might have revealed that he was both an infidel and a Whig. Instead he distilled his beliefs into two short sentences: "I will only add to avoid future enquiries as to my religious and political creed, that the former is 'Do unto others as you wish others to do unto you'—the latter is 'Vote for righteous measures and men who are just and true.'—Yours with respect, JONATHAN KOONS."

Thus began a war of words in the local newspaper, with the two ministers trying to defend their reputations. Both men maintained that their inaction had nothing to do with Jonathan Koons's beliefs but stemmed from far more pedestrian circumstances. The Reverend Alfred Ryors, who was not only the local Presbyterian minister but president of Ohio University, tossed back a biblical salvo, accusing Koons of violating the Ninth Commandment (Thou shalt not bear false witness) by vouching for the acrimonious letter. Ryors identified the man who asked him to preach Filenia's funeral as "Mr. Hughes" (probably Jonathan's brother-in-law or nephew, through Jonathan's sister Elizabeth Hughes) and assumed that Hughes had written the letter. But the minister cast the events in a much different light as he explained them from his perspective.

Ryors wasn't feeling well on a hot, late-summer day when Hughes approached him around 11:00 a.m. with a request to officiate at the funeral at 1:00 p.m. Ryors was unprepared to travel the 7 miles from Athens to the Koons farm, but more important was that he did not know the family. While denying that he had asked about the Koonses' politics, he acknowledged that he had asked several reasonable questions: Were the parents religious and, if so, of what denomination? What had caused the girl's death, and did she die peacefully? Ultimately, however, his concern for his own health had led him to refuse Hughes's request.

The next letter to the *Messenger* came from the Reverend W. F. Stewart and gave his version of events: Koons's emissary ("a stranger") came to the parsonage specifically seeking a Methodist clergyman to preach the funeral. The unnamed man "urged me to go, saying that Mr. K., tho' not a member, frequently attended the Methodist Church, and would like to have a minister of that denomination." But Stewart demurred, explaining that he was leaving town the next day and "was much pushed for time." In his published letter Stewart delivered a stinging rebuke to Koons and "A Friend" for their "strange and indelicate" public mention of "matters thus connected with the dead." "I am willing to make sacrifices for the consolation of the bereaved," Stewart fumed, "but I do think it unkind that those who seek shelter in no branch of the Christian Church should not only expect the minister of the gospel to run at their call, but hold him up in the public prints when prevented by previous engagements from doing them service."

Koons sent a somewhat conciliatory letter to the *Messenger* the following week in which he backtracked, suggesting that his original letter may have been misunderstood. But after brief apologies, he could not resist one final barb: "Since the law of retaliation is neither congenial to common sense or moral virtue, I heartily recommend a truce with my competitors, ere the sheep's clothing be rent from the wolf."

Was Jonathan Koons simply unlucky, taking a last-minute chance on finding a speaker for his daughter's funeral when he had no pastor of his own? Or was the religious edifice of Athens stacked against him? It is clear that neither Ryors nor Stewart knew the Koons family, and therefore they did not refuse to come to their aid out of disapproval or spite. More likely, neither pastor felt a necessity to go out of his way to assist someone who was not a member of his church. Not having a "church home" left the Koonses with no one to officiate at weddings and funerals, although the absence of Abigail's father, the Reverend Samuel Gaylord Bishop, is hard to fathom.

Koons's withering exchange with the ministers shows his combativeness and nimble tongue but also reveals his sense of exclusion from Christianity, even from established society. He had even gone so far—on the heels of his apology—as to characterize members of the clergy as "wolves in sheep's clothing." Why he cared so much is a mystery, given his unorthodox views. Yet Robert L. Daniel, in his book *Athens, Ohio: The Village Years*, notes that "the churches of the village remained the most important groups in which Athenians participated. . . . Membership tended to confer an aura of respectability, given the penchant for disciplining the wayward. . . . At the same time, keen denominational rivalries precluded cooperation between the churches."

Reflecting on the incident five years later, Koons was still bitter toward the ministers, now claiming that *three* clergymen had refused him. Perhaps unwilling to appreciate the social advantages of church membership, he wrote, "[When] three 'preachers' were solicited, of different denominations—all strangers to myself—each in turn drew the religious and temporal history of my family from my friend; and finding we were not members of their respective orders, they all denied their service, under some feigned excuse, none of which, however, justified their denials in our judgment. Had the examination of my family history been omitted by them, their excuses would have been received. But as the case stood, I could not consider them faithful stewards in the discharge of their professed duties."

Koons had taken the ministers' rejection deeply and personally. As he stood in the rain-cooled breeze at his daughter's graveside, he resolved to challenge the orthodoxy of the Christian sects at every opportunity—and they in turn would brand him as worse than an infidel.

5

At the Spirits' Command

WORD OF mysterious rappings heard in Rochester, New York, in late 1849 reached Jonathan Koons by way of the *New York Tribune,* in which he read a report attributing the noises to the work of spirits. Koons developed a keen interest in traveling to Rochester to see for himself but soon realized he could not afford it. He would have to bide his time until spiritualism reached him.

By early 1852, according to Koons, "there arose quite an excitement" in Athens County "on the subject of Spirit-manifestations." The zeitgeist sweeping from the Northeast all the way to the backwoods of Ohio was "causing so much fear and alarm through my own neighborhood," he recalled. Koons claimed that initially he was as skeptical of the new religion as he had been of the old. "Some were bold enough to declare that it must be the devil, some that it was electricity, some said that it was biology in a new form, and others that it was a deception." Like his father traipsing to the witch's doorstep, Jonathan Koons set out to investigate. He assumed it was all a fraud but was "hoping at the same time that it might prove to be what it purported to be, the acts of the Spirits of men."

DESPITE the strange occurrences surrounding the deaths of his mother and brother George, Koons had never actually seen a ghost. As a young apprentice back in Bedford County, he had once spent the night at a home where a man had recently committed suicide. Koons and a companion, the schoolteacher William Alexander, were abed in an upstairs chamber when footsteps sounded in the hall. The bedroom door opened and closed. They could hear more footfalls in their room. Alexander buried his head beneath the covers, but Koons strained his eyes in the dark to see what was there. "I gave myself little or no alarm," he later wrote, "as I could not conceive the possibility of a 'Ghost' producing tangible footsteps." Seeing nothing, he quickly fell asleep.

Koons's inconclusive brush with a ghost could not compare with the stories told by his oldest brother when Jonathan was a youngster. Michael had lived at the old Fletcher place, about 6 miles south of the Koons family home near Bedford. As Jonathan later described it, "The dwelling was constructed in old-fashioned style, with a chimney in the centre, and a fire place on both sides." The house was essentially a duplex with one party living on one side and another—often a boarder—occupying what was called an "apartment" on the other side. Over the years several folks had lived there but not for very long, thanks to what seemed to be apparitions and strange influences about the place. Despite this reputation Michael's family moved in and apparently occupied the entire farmhouse. In good weather they noticed how the cattle, lying near the house while chewing their cud in the evening, would suddenly get spooked and run into the woods. Horses returning from a hard day in the fields would all at once take fright and become unmanageable.

In wintertime the family sealed off the far side of the house and did not use it. One snowy night they heard the outside door to the apartment open and close. "They accordingly repaired to the room to see who had entered," Jonathan Koons wrote. "On entering the apartment a spotted dog was discovered lying upon the bed, which, by the rays of dim light, was mistook for their own, and no one thought any different." The dog was bidden to leave the room and did so immediately. When the family returned to their quarters, they began to ponder over the experience. How could the west-facing door have gotten open when an enormous snowdrift was piled up against it? Looking outside, they found the door closed and the snow without blemish. "Their own dog was lying quietly in his kennel without a single trace in the fallen snow, of his departure or return," Jonathan Koons recounted.

Though Koons was well acquainted with his brother's troubles at the old Fletcher place, Jonathan as a boy found nothing in the tales to prove a hereafter. The same could be said for the times he saw a jack-o'-lantern or will-o'-the-wisp, sometimes called *ignis fatuus,* or swamp gas. "One of these luminous forms was frequently seen to travel a path accurately, leading from my father's residence across a ridge to an adjoining neighbor, which was frequently mistook for the actual approach of some person with a lantern." Travelers on the turnpike between Bedford and Bloody Run also complained of "ignescent forms" that stalked them with a bright white light or blocked their passage on the road.

Sifting through these stories as a youth in Bedford, Jonathan was not sure what to make of them. Years later in Ohio, as he reflected on his childhood and adolescence, he wrote, "My own personal experience in matters relating to tangible spirit manifestations were very limited, so much so at least that it left my mind in constant doubts and fears that all the remarkable appearances of forms, were nothing but hallucinations which give rise to many serious doubts on the subject of man's future or spiritual existence."

But the spirits he would encounter as a middle-aged man were not something to be feared but earnestly to be desired, for they alone could finally put his doubts to rest.

THE spiritualist fervor had entered Athens County through an improbable route—from the west rather than the epicenter in the Northeast. Joseph Herald, an Athens County resident, encountered a rapping medium while on a trip to Indiana.

"Is there a medium in my county?" Herald inquired of the spirits.

They responded, presumably through raps, that one Mary Jane Paston was a rapping medium. Upon his return home Herald called upon the Paston family, none of whom knew anything about spiritualism. Undeterred, Herald asked them to sit around a table with him to form a traditional circle that included 16-year-old Mary Jane. To their complete amazement they soon heard raps.

The Pastons were a bit perplexed by this development, as the father was an atheist and the mother a Methodist. Mr. Paston especially was skeptical about any spiritual origins of the messages, holding firm in his rejection of the afterlife. Nonetheless the family continued to hold séances and began attracting crowds. The father, however, soon tired of visitors' frequenting his home and taking up the Pastons' time with this newfound obsession. He was also concerned about his daughter's participation in what many regarded as a shady enterprise. Determined to put a stop to the craziness, he forbade Mary Jane to continue rapping or sitting for circles. Henceforth anyone who stopped to inquire about the medium within was turned away at the door.

Even as weeks or months of relative peace and quiet ensued, Paston nursed a worried mind. Perhaps he had acted rashly in shutting down his daughter's activities; perhaps there really was something to be explored. He contacted someone he knew to be of his own religious persuasion— the infidel Jonathan Koons. Around February 1852, Paston invited Koons to visit and join him in investigating the mystery, apparently relenting on his edict to Mary Jane. As Koons's interest was already piqued by newspaper stories about spiritualism, he needed little urging to accept the invitation. "But as far as this matter concerned my own faith, I supposed it to be a fraud imposed upon the credulous part of [the] community, by a set of designing aspirants for power and gain," he wrote. "I accordingly set out with a firm and assiduous zeal to detect their fraud and make a full exposure of their designs."

Once Mary Jane had seated herself at a table and placed her hands on top, her father began the dialogue.

"Is there a spirit present?" Paston asked.

A rap was heard in the vicinity of the table. As Paston continued to query the spirit, it would rap once to indicate yes but would pause or remain silent to signal no.

"This however, was not very satisfactory to me," Koons recounted, "as I chose to present my own questions, many of which were asked mentally, which were all correctly answered. And amongst the various questions given by me I enquired for mediums in my own family, naming them over in order, and behold the lot fell upon myself." Koons must have been amazed and gratified to learn that he possessed these undeveloped talents. He further learned that at an appointed day and hour, the spirits would reveal themselves to him and begin his initiation as a medium.

Koons's encounter with Mary Jane Paston went a long way toward erasing his skepticism. He went home and immediately began to meditate, hoping to make contact. Nothing happened for several days, until the hour the spirits had decreed finally arrived. According to the *Spiritual Telegraph* newspaper, Koons's hand was "seized by some strange influence" and he began writing at terrific speed, filling three or four sheets of paper in a few minutes. The scribbles appeared to be in some kind of language, but he could not read it. The automatic writing continued to produce this alien script for two weeks, until Koons grew weary and concluded that the source was not spirits but "some unconscious mental action of his own." Abigail, however, was not persuaded. "His wife had observed its influence on him, and did not believe the intelligence and force originated in him or in any other person present," the *Telegraph* said, "and while they were discussing the matter, his hand was moved to write a communication to them in English, the character of which entirely disproved his theory."

Once the breakthrough of using English had been made, it became the lingua franca of spiritual communication in the Koons household. Koons began experimenting with various types of mediumship over the next six months. He was encouraged to learn that his wife and children, even the 7-month-old baby, George Eaton, also had extrasensory abilities. (Koons reported that he by then had nine children, including son Cinderellus, born in 1849, as well as an adopted daughter, 5-year-old Eliza, whose origins are not clear.)

"Soon finding several medium developments in my own family, I was no longer at a loss for proper means to detect the supposed fraud, and from that time the manifestations have progressed in my family," Koons wrote. Soon not only he but others in the Koons household were writing out messages. In what must surely have been one of the strangest home schools in the country, Jonathan taught the children to develop their own psychic specialties, which he called "these strange spiritual gifts": "One for rapping, another for [table] tipping, another for writing, another for speaking, another for seeing, and so on."

In a letter to a friend Koons explained how his group of mediums got better with practice:

> During the latter part of the summer 1852, our circle had assumed
> a considerable degree of order and precision. Alternate groups

of different classes of spirits, would preside, as it were,—over the deliberations of our circle—to wit,—the spirits of late deceased friends, Christian martyrs, Jewish rulers, American Indian chiefs, and antediluvian, and pre Adamite spirits. Also, a class of spirits, who called themselves *primitive Americans*. At this time, we were confined to the tedious method of holding correspondence with the departed, by the tiping of tables, and stands, to the successive letters of the alphabet, that were required to form the syllables, words, and sentences, of which the communication thus received, was composed. If a spirit desired to indict a communication, it would enter a notice of the same, and would appoint a time, for the special purpose.

Koons grew increasingly perplexed as he tried to decipher the meaning behind the messages. Just as ordinary mortals hold contradictory views, so did the invisibles. Did their silly babbling contain any spiritual lessons at all? As his impatience grew, Koons felt that the cacophony of advice—though given in English—was almost as useless as the original spirit writing that he could not read. "After communicating with Spirits of every grade, and those of every sect and party of men that ever inhabited the earth, each claiming to hold, with sometimes slight variations, the same views that they entertained while living in the body, he got provoked that he could find no oracle upon whom he could rely," the *Spiritual Telegraph* recounted.

On August 15, 1852—after six months of recording the bizarre messages—Koons began to feed his manuscripts into the flames of a stove or open hearth in his house. The dwelling began to shake and the furniture was thrown about. Strange noises resembling logs rolling across the roof or trees falling on the cabin scared him, and as the shaking continued, he feared the house would fall down around him. Koons stopped his headstrong act to ask the spirits what they wanted. He was told to hold on a little longer and all would be well. Koons demanded to know whom these reassurances were coming from. Through calling out the alphabet and listening for raps at the appropriate letter, the Koons mediums were able to spell out the identity of the forceful intruder as "King and Master of Paints, Servant and Scholar of God." His fear perhaps consumed by curiosity, Koons demanded to know King's history. The spirit agreed to give it two days hence, at 3:00 p.m. on August 17. He asked Koons not to burn any more manuscripts in the meantime and not to abandon his quest. Should Koons decide to accept the offer, he, King, would corral the entities at future circles. King would banish the base spirits that muddled Koons's mind. All the Koons family had to do was accept King as their spiritual guide.

ON August 16, 1852—the day after the spirit King made himself known to the family—Nahum Koons took up a pencil and began to draw. Supposedly acting at the direction of King, Benjamin Franklin, and other entities, the 14-year-old sketched a diagram of what the spirits called "an electrical table" that would enable them not only to speak but to create vocal and instrumental music. Jonathan Koons set to work. He hired a man to help him build the table although he could ill afford the expense. Even with the diagram, Koons apparently had to do some experimenting to get it right, and the task soon proved frustrating. "Sometimes Mr. Koons fancied they [the spirits] altered their original drawing, or else he had not fully understood it," the *Spiritual Telegraph* reported.

Just as he had done when learning automatic writing, Koons eventually became discouraged enough to consider jettisoning his quixotic scheme. After a week or two of fruitless effort, he sought in vain for a sign that the spirits would fulfill their promises. "Being in a state of gloom and great despondency, with his relatives and friends chiding him for the foolish expenditure, and reporting that he was crazy, etc., it was more than he could bear," the *Telegraph* explained, "and he resolved again to abandon the whole thing and burn up the several parts of the table which he had made."

Magically, as Koons was about to consign the electrical table to the flames, the now-familiar aural sensation of trees or logs rolling on the cabin roof and falling to the ground started up again. As before, Abigail begged him not to do anything rash and to keep working. The furniture lurched around the cabin as husband and wife debated the issue. Nahum walked into the room in the midst of the turmoil. Koons told his son to "go to the table and find out what those devils want." With Nahum acting as the medium, the spirits tipped out a stern rebuke: Jonathan must stop his impulsive behavior and finish the project. But Jonathan, by now in a combative mood, refused to work any further unless the spirits renewed their commitment. Finally the invisibles gave specific instructions on how to assemble the table, telling Jonathan they would soon communicate in the manner they had promised.

He dropped his plans to scuttle the machine, and by the next evening the pieces of the apparatus had been put in place according to the spirits' directions. Jonathan refused to join the circle that surrounded the prototype that night and threatened to burn it up if nothing happened. Presumably Nahum, his mother, and other family members conducted the strange vigil. "A few moments after the circle was formed, the wires of the machine began to pulsate as it were, and increased in strength until the whole machine shook like an aspen leaf, and even the whole house trembled," the *Spiritual Telegraph* recounted. After half an hour of disturbance, something rapped out FAREWELL FRIENDS, thus encouraging Jonathan to complete the table.

The final product was a contraption made of metal and wood whose purpose was "collecting and focalizing the magnetic aura used in the manifestations." Sometimes described as a "novel battery," "retainer of electricity," or "spirit machine," it was really an apparatus that was placed on top of a six-legged wooden table about 6 feet long and 30 inches wide.

A wooden post 4 feet high rose up perpendicular to the tabletop. Fastened to each side of the post was a carved piece of wood. The upright post had two or three iron bars passing through it parallel to the table. Hanging from the iron bars were what one observer called "a wire woven into a kind of net work with copper and tin plates, and small bells." Others thought that the metal plates were made of copper and zinc; almost everyone agreed that they were fashioned in the shape of doves. Jonathan had stocked the drawers underneath the tabletop with paint, brushes, and paper that the spirits might need. Down near the floor, a horizontal wooden bar with eight sides was suspended by copper wires.

During the next few days the spirits began to assert themselves through the machine. According to the *Spiritual Telegraph*, "The spirits wrote on the table with chalk, time was beat to music, Spirit-bands were organized, etc." From this cacophony a clear demand emerged: the spirits gave Jonathan a list of instruments required for their music making. He had no idea where to find items such as a drum, accordion, harmonica, banjo, cornet, tambourine, and bells, but he was told to travel to McConnelsville or Malta, two towns that faced each other across the Muskingum River some 30 miles from his home.

Jonathan and Nahum quickly embarked on the quest. Arriving in Malta on horseback, the two could find no store that sold the instruments. "He [Koons] felt that he had been humbugged," the *Spiritual Telegraph* reported, "but, after putting up the horse, they went out with a piece of paper and pencil, and seeing a buggy wagon standing under a shed put the paper and pencil in it, and stepped [to] one side a rod or two; after remaining some minutes they went to the wagon and found written upon the paper, 'Cross over the river to McConnelsville and inquire of the first man you meet if he knows who has musical instruments.'"

Once in McConnelsville Nahum and Jonathan encountered a stranger who directed them to the private residence of a man who owned a drum. They struck a deal and left the man's home with not only the drum but directions to the owners of other instruments. The pair went house to house and almost miraculously were able to procure all the items on the spirits' wish list.

Upon returning home the Koonses arranged the musical instruments as the spirits wanted. The electrical table was fitted with two drums, a bass and a tenor. They were placed opposite each other, attached to two curved pieces of wood sticking up at the back of the table. The Koonses laid the other instruments on the tabletop. With the angel band configured, the Koonses had done all they could. Now they could only wait until dark— the time the spirits liked best—for the invisibles to bring the instruments to life. Before long, it would not be Jonathan Koons playing his fiddle solo at the Koons farm; a whole heavenly host would join him in song.

AS their fascination with spiritualism continued to ramp up, word of the Koonses' nighttime activities had begun to spread. Curious neighbors, as well as folks from outside the area, started to gather at the Koons farm. The house consisted of two cabins, each 18 by 22 feet, connected dogtrot style by "a rough shed" that served as an entryway. Wooden shakes held down by heavy poles covered the exterior. Their friend David Fulton from Amesville was a frequent visitor to the circles along with other members of his family. Fulton was by necessity an overnight guest, as he lived too far away to return home safely after the séances. He described the scene:

> One end of the dwelling, or one of the cabins, was occupied (one or two years) for the "Spirit Manifestations." This caused the other to be very much thronged, especially in cold weather, it being the kitchen, parlor, sitting-room and bed-room altogether. Here I have seen, again and again, one or two tables filled with persons not of their own family. Then comes bed-time; the floor has to be cleaned, and beds have to be divided and divested of part of their covering and arranged upon the floor to make accommodations for those who remain. Morning comes: some, not too distant, leave for home; others remain till after breakfast, and if any would summon up resolution to inquire what he charged his universal reply was, "Not anything, that he made no charge;" and thus, taking advantage of his generosity, would leave.

Despite the constant uproar in their home, Jonathan and Abigail impressed Fulton with their hospitality: "I must truly say that I never in the first instance have seen a frown on his countenance, or that of his amiable lady, who is certainly one of the finest women in the world."

EVEN with the construction of the electrical table and the gathering of the musical instruments and art supplies, the spirits' demands were not yet sated. They instructed Koons to erect a separate building exclusively for their use, a structure that soon was called the spirit room. As Koons's friend David Fulton recalled it, half of the Koons residence—one of the two connected log cabins—was used for séances for "one or two years," presumably before the spirit room was built. But Koons told it differently, and in his accounts the spirit room was up and running by December 1852, about 10 months after his conversion. Later some of Koons's more imaginative followers would liken it to the psychomanteums of ancient Greece, where pilgrims seeking initiation into the mystery religions went down into underground caverns and, with the aid of priests and psychoactive drugs, were believed to communicate with spirits of the dead.

Just 6 feet from his own house, Koons built a one-room, mud-chinked log cabin with a peaked roof. Visitors variously estimated its size as 18 feet long by 15 feet wide by 9 feet high or 16 feet by 12 feet by 7 feet. The door and shuttered windows fit so tightly that the light was blocked out when they were closed.

Inside, the rectangular table supporting the spirit machine was placed at one end of the room with enough space for someone to pass behind it. The wall behind the electrical table had rustic shelves. At the other end of the cabin Koons placed benches in a tiered arrangement that resembled theater seating. In the middle, between the electrical table and the audience, as many as eight mediums and guests would sit around a second table that abutted the long one. This second table has variously been described as a "common cherry breakfast table" and "a common fall-leaf table, about 3 ½ feet square." The mediums sat in a semicircle that connected with both ends of the electrical table. Between the mediums' backs and the front row of audience seating was a coal-burning stove; the clearance on either side was only a foot, which made it difficult to walk around. The stovepipe passed through a planked ceiling and low garret before piercing the peaked roof. Over time the garret would be filled with "old shoes and other old trumpery." Koons's list of props for the spirit room had now expanded to include two accordions, bass and tenor drums, tambourine, guitar, banjo, harps and bells, toys to give to the audience, and several pistols.

ONCE the Koonses had accepted his guidance, the spirit calling himself King dominated the séances. He provided his history to the family as promised on August 17, 1852, when he claimed to be the head of a band of 165 spirits. King daringly declared himself, as well as the earth, to be "of more ancient date than Adam." He claimed to have lived 14,000 years earlier and that "he belonged to a people whose organization would in these days be called giants, and in consequence of this superior physical endowment, they were called a nation of kings. Hence his cognomen is King," a Buffalo newspaper explained. A great congress of entities from the various "spirit-spheres" had recently adopted a plan to communicate with humans through raps, and King—because of his evolved spiritual nature—was among those deputized to proceed. The cosmic outreach was proving wildly successful.

Though King sometimes did communicate by rapping, the entity also was said to provide written messages, which he signed "King, Servant and Scholar of God." Sometimes the names of multiple male authors would appear at the end of a document, such as "Moses, King, Adam, David" or even "King 1. King 2. Adam. Moses." Some believed that "King 1" and King 2" had been a father and son while on Earth. The revered Swedenborg also was counted among the heavenly messengers. At other times King would step aside and give voice to an angel named Oress or to culturally exotic spirits such as Native Americans or Chinese. On one occasion, a spirit revealed that "he had lived in Africa, before the human family had progressed to language"—which would certainly have made him more ancient than King, the 14,000-year-old. King's most playful moniker, "Master of Paints," referred to the watercolor paintings supposedly produced by his band—one such creation being a bejeweled chariot called a spirit car.

Visitors to the Koons Spirit Room were often invited to read the sermons that the spirits had composed, though Koons's critics would say that the writing style suspiciously resembled his own. One visitor recounted that he "spent the afternoon in examining papers, purporting to have been written by the spirits, some of them written while the room was under lock and key, some written in the presence of many persons, *without the aid of a medium* . . . and some written through mediums. These papers were almost entirely upon theological subjects, and contained some of the most able arguments."

Interpreting these messages from the beyond, Jonathan Koons saw the spirits' philosophy as a positive, inclusive one. "I will now give you some of the leading features of the doctrines taught by our spiritual correspondents," he wrote to a spiritualist newspaper. "Viz: They teach that God is purely love. Also, that God has placed man under a law of progression, that all can become participants of his glory and divine blessings, by the consent of their own wills."

The purpose behind the manifestations was to free humanity from the perennial fear of death, to assure everyone that human personalities would survive physical decay. Jonathan and Abigail must have been overjoyed to receive the following poem with the dedication "To My Mother":

Rejoice in fullness of love,
In the smiles of your angel dove.
Who was plucked from your kind embrace,
From the branch of tender days,
Whose soul to you returns,
Whose love now purely burns,
For friends who yet do dwell,
In their weak mortal cell,
To teach God's love and will,
For their joys to fill.

Though their little daughter's earthly raiment lay nearby in the family cemetery, Filenia Koons had cast off the old coat and put on the new. She was reaching out to comfort those still in the body.

6

A Buried Man's Instructions

CITY DWELLERS making the pilgrimage through hilly southeastern Ohio to the door of Jonathan Koons in 1852 encountered what seemed to them a strange and exotic landscape, one sometimes called the Huckleberry Knobs. Farmers and merchants had access to faraway markets through the Hocking Canal, built in the 1840s, but a railroad would not reach Athens County for another four years. "This country is about 50 years behind the age," wrote a clergyman visiting the Koons homestead from afar. "The inhabitants are a plain, simple-hearted people, dressed in their plain, home-spun clothes, males and females; living in log cabins, such as the early settlers occupied about a century ago. A kinder-hearted people I never saw."

The clergyman failed to note the stately brick buildings and elm-shaded grounds of Ohio University just 7 miles from Mount Nebo, but it didn't take a wild-eyed romantic to see how remote the countryside actually was. Whether visitors were stoked by religious zeal or plain curiosity, just getting there required stamina and determination. Approaching from the west, a pilgrim would take a train to Lancaster, Ohio—the nearest point by railroad—and travel more than 40 miles by stagecoach or canal packet to Chauncey, a village in Athens County's Dover Township. Travelers from Columbus would have to take the stagecoach through Lancaster and proceed to the southeast on a journey spanning more than 70 miles. "I staged over a country that enabled me to fully realize the inspiration of that elegant song, 'Jordan is a hard road to travel,'" wrote a visitor from New York City. "But I feel myself amply repaid for the wear and tear of my journey, and would again undertake the same, as cheerfully as did ever a pilgrim to the holy land."

Some pilgrims coming from the east fared better by a water route: a steamboat carried them from Zanesville or Marietta to McConnelsville on the Muskingum River, where they were obliged to hire a private carriage for the last leg of the journey. Others approaching from Cincinnati could travel upstream on the Ohio River, disembarking at Pomeroy for the inland trip. When traveling by coach or carriage, however, "the miles bear no correspondence to the hours, for on every route they think they do well if they accomplish two and a half miles an hour," an Illinois passenger wrote. Once in Chauncey, weary travelers had to walk 2 or 3 miles to the Koons home or find a local willing to take them there on horseback or by carriage. "Fare, hog and hominy," quipped one wit, "and he needs to *endure* that travels in that country!"

Though visitors were still only in the foothills of the Appalachians, they faced an arduous climb to reach the Koons farm, poised more than 1,000 feet above sea level. "The way to Mr. Koons' house leads through several miles of mountainous woods," a visitor named J. B. wrote. "It is one of the wildest countries I ever saw. Here and there bright little streams come jumping over the rocks and down the mountainsides; echoes ring through the thick forest—it seems, indeed, the fit abode for Spirits."

"When you finally get into Koons's vicinity," an Illinois man reported, "you find the essence of hills personified; there is no such thing as a level spot large enough to put a house on. Koons's house is located on the southeast angle of a sharp ridge, some few rods below the edge of the ledge, and where, when the native trees occupied the ground, the lightning was wont to make frolic among them; and where it still likes to sport." During his visit "the stove-pipe above the spirit room was burst off, and a number of times during the sitting of the mediums, electric sparks were seen to play over the wires of the spirit table."

More than one writer would comment on the unusual electrical properties that seemed to infuse this locale. The chemist, professor, and author Robert Hare—one of the most prominent converts to spiritualism in the United States—believed that "there is something in the locality that favours mediumship." A curious person once asked the presiding spirit during a séance why the manifestations were seen in the vicinity of the Koons farm rather than elsewhere. "[He] was told that it was owing to the peculiar geological formation; the material on which, and by which, spirits act, existing there, in singular abundance. He said he had never seen such a rich out-cropping of minerals, combined with richness of vegetation, and salubrity." Another visitor called it simply "the enchanted ground."

Although the atmosphere may have been electric, the appearance of the Koons homestead bespoke thrift and industry rather than magical largesse. Koons's friend David Fulton wrote, "He is a plain, unvarnished farmer, having a large family of small children, [and] owns a small piece of very rough land indeed, has it well fenced in small fields, and cultivates it in the neatest manner; and in addition to his regular set orchard, he has his fence-corners generally set with the choicest of fruit trees. On this small, rough bit of ground, Mr. K. so managed it as to make a comfortable living for his large little family." An out-of-state visitor found the Koons home place "a very romantic spot among the hills," adding that the groves of apple and peach trees "give something of the appearance of comfort to the surrounding scenery."

When the spiritualist publisher Charles Partridge made the trip from New York City, on a spring evening he saw "from thirty to fifty men sitting on stones, logs and fences around a dilapidated log-cabin" with their carriages parked and horses tied nearby. "The men looked respectable, and their deportment and conversation bore the impress of a religious meeting," Partridge reported. In the same yard, not far from the Koons residence, sat the spirit room that was attracting crowds almost nightly. "I inquired [of the men] what Spirits lived there, and was told that it was the room where people go in to talk with their Spirit friends who have gone out of their earthly tabernacle," he wrote.

Adding to the spookiness of the place were stories about the Koons family's knowing things about their guests they shouldn't have known, had no way of knowing. Several high-profile visitors took deliberate steps to conceal their identity as a means of testing the Koonses. The Reverend Thomas Benning of New York, riding over the hills to the Koons homestead, "was suddenly impressed to maintain a profound incognito while there." Once inside the spirit room, Benning remained tight-lipped about his identity and place of origin, only to be astonished by the spirit King's words to Jonathan: "Do you know who you have got here? We do. He has come a long ways. We sent him." This statement alone did not prove that King, or Koons for that matter, knew Benning's identity. Perhaps it would have been easy to deduce from the minister's city dress that he had come a far distance. But when Benning entered the room a second time that same day, he found a letter "addressed to his initials and in the proper handwriting of his deceased wife," the *Spiritual Age* reported.

Benning was not the only one to be so greeted. When Partridge arrived at the Koons establishment, he, too, found that Koons was expecting him, although the two had not corresponded about the visit, much less met face to face. Just as a real telegraph carried messages in a mysterious fashion, the "spiritual telegraph"—the name of Partridge's newspaper— seemed to be operating between New York City and the wilds of Ohio. And a Pennsylvania medium, traveling with a friend by steamer down the Ohio River, made his way to the Koons place and got a hearty welcome from the family. Jonathan Koons "was aware of our coming," the medium explained, "for he had been in communication with me two days previously, by spirit power."

A November day in 1852 found Jonathan Koons digging for treasure. He was spading up the ground under a hickory tree in the woods near his house, just as the spirits had told him to. The adventure had begun the day before when his sons Nahum and Samuel, aged 15 and 12, were herding some cattle home from a pasture about a mile away. While passing by a scattering of stones that circled the hickory, the boys felt something plucking at their arms, grabbing their wrists, and trying to pull them off the path and toward the rocks. Spooked, they returned home and wasted no time in telling Abigail what had happened.

Their mother guessed that the spirits were trying to communicate, so she, Jonathan, and probably Nahum repaired to the spirit room to find the source of the boys' scare. The shade of an Indian chief revealed that he and another entity had accosted Nahum and Samuel to call attention to what was actually a burial place. Within the rocky circle, Jonathan would find the ashes of the chief's body, together with his weapons. The invisible gave his name as Jewannah Gueannah Musco and explained that his tribe had waged war on another tribe that was siding with the whites—an alliance the chief deemed traitorous. His warriors, Musco explained, had "persued them unto death, as they would the wolf and the bear."

Despite the ferocity of Musco's attacking force, he was fatally struck by an arrow. To honor his dying request, Musco's warriors burned his body on a pile of wood and buried his ashes and personal effects under the hickory tree, placing the stones around it. As proof of his authenticity and as an example to unbelievers, the spirit asked Koons to take two neutral observers to the spot and dig up the relics.

The message made sense to Koons and may have come as no surprise. He had whittled a rude homestead out of the forests of Mount Nebo, one of the highest elevations in the county, in an area prone to lightning strikes and carved in legend as a sacred spot for the Shawnee Indians. Maps made much later would depict the Mount Nebo Trail threading along the ridgetop, perhaps referring to a timeworn path trod by Native Americans. By the time Abigail and Jonathan took up farming there, the Indians had been driven out, yet here in this western land some believed their spirits still lurked among the glades they had once inhabited. Some people even told that Koons had been able to purchase the land so cheaply because others were afraid to live there.

Just a few miles southwest of Mount Nebo fanned out the broad expanse of Wolf's Plains, where monuments to a much earlier Indian presence remained. Here along the Hocking River the ancient people had constructed a 3-square-mile complex of earthworks. Settlers had noticed not only conical burial mounds but circular enclosures that reminded them of an old fort. Later scholars, however, would interpret these open-air structures as ceremonial theaters where shamans, often under the influence of psychoactive drugs, sought entry to the spirit world. Here in these sacred circles, perhaps two millennia before Jonathan and Abigail Koons's day, Native Americans had donned wolf skins and lit fires, performing their sacred rites under the light of the moon. In his role as ambassador and guide, the shaman would contact spirits from the other side, sometimes those of animals—and sometimes those of the dead.

The magnetic pull of the buried man's instructions led Koons to the woods where the boys had been affrighted. Koons had convinced two local men to join him and Nahum on the quest. They had walked southward only about three-quarters of a mile when they encountered a large hickory "near a broken strata of sand rock, that projected from the bluff point of an adjacent hill." With the two witnesses looking on, Koons scraped aside the ocher husks of the last summer's leaves and began to dig. The black loam of the forest yielded to red clay, but at a depth of 24 inches, still not a trace of anything unusual had turned up. The neighbors might have wondered whether they had been called away from their chores on a fool's errand. Finally, 3 feet down, came the clank of the shovel hitting something solid. Just as the Indian had foretold, Koons pulled from the grave a stone battle-ax, arrows, and a stone breastplate. These artifacts, Koons believed, would make a fine display at his home—yet another proof of the wonders, as if any more proof were required.

＊ ＊ ＊

AS Koons's spirit guide, King, had told him, Ohio was once deluged by a primordial sea. King's observation did not contradict the conventional wisdom, for everybody who read the Bible knew that in the beginning the earth was "without form and void, and waters moved upon the face of the deep." But that was just the starting point for King's controversial views; he was not satisfied with the six-day story of Creation. The earth had roiled with change through endless eons: "Periods of duration have elapsed too great for human powers to estimate," King advised. "Vast and successive revolutions have taken place. . . . The space of time since ADAM is but a single link, of the almost endless chain which stretches forth from the moment that matter first began to be brought together, by the Almighty Power and wisdom of God."

Early nineteenth-century geologists studying southern Ohio likely would not have faulted King's conclusions. The landscape told a story that did not support the time line of Genesis, either. Eons before, even before there were humans to behold them, some of the area's waterways had flowed in the opposite direction from what Jonathan Koons would have observed in his time. Starting in the Blue Ridge Mountains of North Carolina, a river of Nile-like proportions had cut a gorge as much as 500 feet deep through Virginia and West Virginia before entering southern Ohio and carving its way into Indiana and Illinois. Tributaries of the northwest-ward-flowing Teays River had drained all of Athens County about five million years earlier.

Much later, repeated intrusions by glaciers had changed all that, damming up the waterway and forming a giant frozen lake. When the glaciers retreated, they dumped their mighty load of silt and gravel into the Teays's drainage system, burying it and creating the Ohio River. The new channel, which flowed south, eventually brought European settlers to the newly contoured land. But the old pattern was not obliterated; the trained eyes of early geologists still could discern extinct valleys and dry riverbeds. And every so often a goose flying aloft would spy the ancient trace of the Teays and land by mistake as if on water; and in some places wild magnolias flourished along the riverbanks, far from their southern origins.

Human beings also were of much more ancient origin than commonly believed. Even though bitter debate about human evolution was still several years away, King provocatively declared that the planet "has been successively inhabited by new races of beings," of which his pre-Adamite order was only one. And even around Dover Township in the 1850s, oddities of a much more recent character were yet to be explained. The native people whom the Europeans first encountered in Ohio had no origin stories to attach to the numerous mounds and earthworks in the area, leaving early surveyors to speculate about who might have built them. Ruminations on the role of the ancient Scythians of Asia, Toltecs, and even "Hindus" would persist for the remainder of the nineteenth century. Koons would come to believe that he himself had found the key to the Indians' past. "I am in possession of a history of the origin of the red Men, given by a very ancient spirit . . . who claimed to be one of the ancient fathers of that race," he wrote.

Thus part of the angels' mission was to bring scientific truth to those who would open their minds to their true place in the universe. "Should I succeed in surmounting your sinful ignorance in this respect, then you may be visited by a host of ancient spirits, with healing in their wings," King informed the circle. But such startling messages—so out of step with the times—were easier for a spirit to utter than for a mere mortal to profess.

＊　＊　＊

ONE night, just before Christmas 1852, Jonathan Koons watched as flames licked at the smoldering remains of his barn. Gone were his crops from the past growing season, along with a new wagon, plows, and other farming tools. By the time the blaze had been discovered, about nine o'clock, nothing could be saved but a visitor's horse.

Koons knew immediately that the fire had been no accident. Threats of mob action had been bandied about the neighborhood, forming a dark undercurrent to his shining new life as a medium. "The fat was in the fire as soon as the news was spread abroad, that the spirits of the departed friends, were corresponding with their survivors on earth at my residence," he wrote. According to the *Athens Messenger,* "a gang of drunken rowdies" had been harassing the Koons family and their guests "almost nightly" for several weeks. Whiskey had finally given license to someone to light the torch.

Koons chafed at the injustice. "While my property was consuming, I asked, what have I done—what authority insulted—what law violated that I should suffer this malice and vengeance?" he wrote. "It was done because I persisted in affording opportunities to investigators: this, and nothing more." Still, he knew that it could have been far worse. The elements were on his side that clear and cold night, withholding any wind that could have spread the flames to nearby structures. "But for the calm, house, spirit-room, family, all, would have shared the common fate," he mused.

The *Athens Messenger* weighed in with a call for redress. "We sympathize with our friend [Koons] in his misfortune and hope the guilty scoundrels may be arrested and brought to justice," the newspaper said. Koons had a good idea of who had carried out the nighttime attack but decided not to press charges—owing to an act of piety, as he later said, or perhaps to a lack of proof. The identity of the arsonists would remain an official question mark. Yet in Koons's view, they were only a stalking horse for the religious establishment. "The clergy denounced me from their pulpits as a child of Satan, and a perverter of the Christian Church, saying that I ought to be burned out of house and home, with my family of mediums in the midst of the flames," he later charged. "These Christian incendiaries thought thereby to compel me to discontinue my séances, for the want of provisions for the use of my family and truth-seeking guests."

Koons also realized that the barn burning might be a harbinger of greater calamities. "I was well informed, that on a previous night arrangements were made to assassinate myself and eldest son, but were thwarted by the presence of a crowd of visitors," he wrote. Such gruesome knowledge must have given the husband and father pause, for ambush might be just a rifle shot away as the family went about their chores on this lonely woodland farm. But in his anger and despair Koons had turned to the spirits in the early morning hours after the evening fire. "Overcome by the calamity I retired to the spirit-room to see if the angel world could or would afford me relief," he recounted. "Immediately the trumpet sounded and the voice spoke words of consolation. 'Fear not, life and future welfare will be sacred.'"

Koons had found this illumination he had searched for since childhood. Buoyed by the spirits' promise, he would resist all attempts by his enemies to extinguish that light.

7

The Trumpet Medium

FOUR DAYS into the new year of 1853, Koons's circle was keeping a date set exactly four months earlier. At the close of a séance on September 4, a spirit had tipped the table to reveal that it wanted to make contact: "The circle is hereby notified, that Hommo, an ancient Indian chief, desires to favor the circle with a communication, when the circle is not otherwise occupied and engaged." The appointed hour was upon them, and the results promised to be all the more spectacular now that King no longer depended on tips or raps and was speaking through a trumpet.

The new Indian shade was much older than Jewannah Gueannah Musco, the slain chieftain who supposedly had lived during the time of white settlement in Ohio. Hommo, on the other hand, claimed to have lived 800 years previous to 1853, when the bow and arrow were replacing the spear in the Ohio Valley. But his purpose was the same as Musco's—leaving to earthly believers the ghastly task of exhuming his remains. In this case Hommo did not give his cause of death. He did explain, however, that his body was embalmed "in a composition of ashes, clay and charcoal; and was placed upon a select spot, with his head towards the 'rising sun,' and his face downwards; over which, a monument of earth was erected, about 20 feet [in] diameter at the base." To build the mound the Native Americans had carried dirt in what Hommo called luggagers, a type of stretcher consisting of an animal skin stretched between two branches of a forked stick to form a basket. Working in teams of three, the Indians would move the earth to the mound site, where for several days each member of the tribe would ceremonially cover the body with it.

Hommo told the Koons family that his body was enshrined in a mound about one and a half miles northeast of their home. He asked that they go there and find his body to "test his veracity." Jonathan Koons, however, had little enthusiasm for the mission, thinking of the sheer amount of labor involved. He would have demurred from the spirit's request had it not been for "two visiting investigators,—J. Hoisington and M. Handsberry," who were keen to make the excavation. Upon digging into the mound, the trio found a skeleton enclosed in what Koons called cement, which seemed dry and waterproof. Their inspection of the mummy was short-lived, however, as most of its bones crumbled upon being exposed to air. Nonetheless Koons found the enterprise to be yet another validation of predictions gleaned from the dead. "All we were told by the spirit, relating to his position and mode of preservation, was found to be correct, to a demonstration," he wrote.

Although Koons's digging today would be regarded as grave desecration or destructive amateur archaeology, what he did was commonplace at the time. He took home the few bone fragments that did not disintegrate, believing them to be Hommo's. He added them to the personal effects of the Indian chief Musco that had been recovered in the woods the previous November. Koons, like many spiritualists, believed the Indians' messages to be worthy of investigation. Actions that now seem discourteous or disrespectful must have seemed to him an attempt to honor the wishes of the dead.

FROM time immemorial the idea of a talking object has held the human imagination. "The creation of objects that could *talk* had long been presumed to be inseparable from the creation of objects that could *answer questions,* and that might therefore be used to divine secret or future knowledge," a twenty-first-century folklorist observes. In the tenth century one Gerbert of Aquitaine had created a metal head "by a certain inspection of the stars when the planets were about to begin their courses." The mysterious object was reported to deliver correct answers to yes or no questions. And Cervantes, in his 1615 novel *Don Quixote*, has an "enchanted head" that can field questions from guests. In 1853, in rural Ohio, the Koons family was carrying out a tradition as timeless as "mirror, mirror, on the wall"—yet transforming it into something as daring as the latest technological innovation.

With Nahum now developed as a trumpet medium, the Koons circle was free from the tedious business of rapping or table-tipping their way through the alphabet or limiting themselves to yes-or-no questions. Now spirits could deliver whole sermons or the circle could hold conversations with King or other spirits. Historians believe that Jonathan Koons was the first person in the spiritualism movement to develop "direct voice" communication through the trumpet. The Koons instrument must have been more like a metal megaphone than a musical instrument with valves; perhaps the women of the house used it to summon the men from the fields for dinner. It was described as "a tin trumpet about two feet in length" that had the magical quality of levitation. Before long the Koonses would incorporate multiple horns, of both brass and tin, in their séances.

The horn was placed on the mediums' table before the séance began. "Before using it for speech, it would be raised into the air, then a sentence would be distinctly articulated through it, when it would fall to the table," one set of visitors to the Koons circle told the *Cleveland Plain Dealer*. "When we asked any questions, as we did repeatedly, the horn would rise, the answer be given, and the horn again fall to the table. At our request they extended the horn to us, and allowed us to take hold of the large end of it, while at the same time conversation was directed through it to us. We observed, that after the horn had been used for a few moments, the small end was sensibly warmer than the large end."

Jonathan and Nahum could scarcely have imagined that use of the horn would still be debated well into the next century. The magician Harry Houdini, writing 70 years after the Koons demonstrations, was openly contemptuous of the trumpet medium and spiritualist practices in general. "As one who for 35 years has been freeing himself from every sort of bond, encumbrance, and restraint that human ingenuity can devise . . . please permit me to testify that for a medium to free himself from a spiritual circle and so get hold of the trumpet is child's play!" he declared in 1925.

In the article "How I Unmask the Spirit Fakers," Houdini explained how tricksters posing as physical mediums can deceive the gullible. The trumpet medium usually sits at a table with the people to his left and right holding his hands, leaving him no opportunity to touch the trumpet lying on the table. But all too often the fraudulent medium is able to get a hand or foot on the trumpet and move it around the room, sometimes with the help of a confederate, sometimes by "his own cleverness." The "spirit voice" that seems to emanate from the trumpet is actually the medium's as he or she holds the horn and speaks through it in a disguised voice. At other times, such as in daylight, the faker may use ventriloquism to project his or her voice, even while conversing with others in the circle.

Houdini related how he, along with a reporter and a county prosecutor in Cleveland, once attended a séance at the home of a well-established trumpet medium:

> The particular medium of whom I write performed most of the usual tricks with the trumpets. He also caused a guitar, placed on the table before him along with the trumpets, to be play[ed] while he sat with his hands apparent[ly] covering those of the persons who sat at his right and left. . . . And so, when the opportunity presented itself, I slipped out of the circle in which I sat and smeared lamp-black on the trumpets. I waited until the medium had completed his trumpet work; then I rose, drew an electric flashlamp from my pocket, and directed its rays across the table.
>
> It was a startling, though somewhat comical picture that the sudden light disclosed. For there in the circle sat the medium holding the guitar above his head, and his hand and face were as black as a coal heaver's from the lampblack I had used!

The exposed faker had held the hand of the person next to him and then withdrew it, replacing it with a handkerchief-covered rock that had about the same weight as his hand. The medium thus freed his real hand to manipulate the trumpet and the guitar. He was charged with fraud. The arrest sparked a police crackdown on 20 other mediums throughout the city.

Throughout the article Houdini tried to strike an evenhanded pose of scientific openness despite the scorn he felt toward mediums. "In regard to spiritualism I am not a skeptic," he wrote. "Although I have found no genuine physical phenomena medium, by which I mean one who does not produce his effect by purely natural means that any trained magician can duplicate, I still have an open mind. I am willing to be convinced—even to believe, if a medium can demonstrate to me that he actually possesses true psychic power."

Houdini also rebutted the idea put forward by some spiritualists, among them Sir Arthur Conan Doyle, that Houdini himself was a medium, that the spirits aided him in making his miraculous escapes from "handcuffs, ropes, chains, straight-jackets, locks, bolts, prison cells, trunks, safes and packing cases." As Houdini once told Conan Doyle, "If you were to build a packing case large enough to contain me and all the American spiritualists and the scientists that uphold them, weight it with pig iron, tie us up in it and throw it into the sea, I'd be the only one that would come up. But it would be trickery that would release me."

Houdini's contemporary E. J. Dingwall, a magician and expert in psychic research in the 1920s, took a more nuanced view of the trumpet séance. He maintained that a person might choose to visit a trumpet medium for a couple of different reasons, although they are not mutually exclusive. One person might go out of scientific interest, to try to peer behind the smoke and mirrors and see how the phenomenon works. Others, perhaps the majority, go to receive messages from the dead. These believers, Dingwall wrote, "are usually indifferent to the methods of producing voices to which they are listening. In other words, it does not really concern such sitters if the medium is really producing the voices by whispering down the trumpet if the information given is such that it contains matter which could not have been acquired by the medium normally." If the information supplied through the trumpet proved credible, then the medium must have been using the instrument as "an added attraction" on which her message did not depend.

But Dingwall cautioned amateur investigators to be suspicious of any mediumship conducted in the dark: "The first thing the spiritualist does is to pull down the blinds. He does not tell you that D. D. Home, the most famous medium who ever lived, derided dark séances. . . . Neither will he tell you that the greatest of all trumpet mediums (Mrs. Blake) sat in broad daylight, near the window. . . . If therefore an enquiry into trumpet mediumship is proposed, the beginner had better concentrate upon the voices and the information they give. Do not be led astray by elaborate apparatus."

When it came to voices from the beyond, opinions would continue to clash for decades.

THE burning of his barn had made Koons dig in his heels, vow to continue his spiritual investigations. As the stream of out-of-town pilgrims grew ever larger, news of the strange nocturnal rites of the Koons family must have brought mixed reactions from other residents of Athens County. The thunderous drumming that opened each spirit concert was loud enough to annoy the Koonses' neighbors, but they would have been few in that remote locale. Merchants in the nearby village of Chauncey, which had a large hotel to accommodate businessmen dealing in salt and coal, no doubt saw an uptick in sales to stagecoach passengers bound for the Koons Spirit Room. Other township residents simply must have been excited about the newest form of entertainment to reach their locale.

Most accounts in the press, however, tended to focus on the community's religious outrage. An enthusiastic visitor to the Koons Spirit Room described it with a touch of sarcasm: "I left the house fully convinced of two facts:—First, that the manifestations were produced by an intelligent power. Second, that that power was not human. These two facts are admitted by the whole neighborhood, with this addition, viz: that the power is 'The Devil.' And so firmly are they convinced of this, that some have thought to do God service by burning up the crop and barns of Mr. J. Koons . . . and doing sundry other acts of loving kindness, by which, they expect to cast the devil out."

Although this attitude may have been prevalent, at least a significant minority of local people embraced the message of love, harmony, and immortality that at times must have been overshadowed by the dramatic nighttime antics of the spirits. These seekers most assuredly became converts to the new religion.

Lovead T. Dean was probably one of them. He belonged to a branch of the Dean family that had moved to Ames Township from Massachusetts around 1815. His late brother, Colonel Nathan Dean Jr., had been an entrepreneurial force in the Mudsock community (near Ames Town) before his untimely death at age 49 in 1837. In addition to leading the local militia, the colonel had owned large tracts in the area and was a landlord to many. He had just assumed the position of postmaster, carrying the mail between Marietta and Ames Town, when a malady or accident befell him. The nature of the ailment is shrouded in mystery, but Dean recognized its severity. He swiftly dictated the terms of his will but died before he had a chance to sign a formal document, prompting two witnesses to swear to its validity.

Although 16 years had passed since the colonel's death, perhaps he was one of the family members whom Lovead T. Dean wished to contact through the Koons séances that spring of 1853. If so, 50-year-old Lovead must have been gratified to receive a poem said to have been composed by Nathan Jr. and purportedly written by a spirit hand.

> New fields disclose,
> To all of those,
> Who are to reflection given;
> Bright minds disclose,
> To all of those,
> Who seek the ways of heaven;
> But minds decline,
> When mark'd with crime,
> And to insolence are driven,
> And weary not,
> Dark crimes to plot,
> Against the throng of heaven,
> And horrors burst,
> Those minds who thirst,
> For crimes of wretched deeds;
> But those who cease,
> Their lusts to please,
> Shall glorious bounties reap.
>
> Could friends the luster but behold,
> Of those who seek their peace,

And see us shine like burnished gold,
Imbued with smiles of peace;
No longer would they seek to try
To shun our presence more,
But with my brother, swift would fly,
To greet our anxious love.

Besides Lovead Dean, participants in the circles in 1853 included John Tippie Jr. and his wife, Anna Margaret, son Ezra, brother Joseph, and nephew Wesley Tippie—a family that soon would be linked with the Koonses' own brand of spiritual practice. Koons's friend David Fulton also received a snippet of verse, decorated with a vibrant flower and said to be from his departed sister Emily. Lending credibility to the séances was George Walker of Amesville, a retired associate judge of the Court of Common Pleas whose wife had died three years earlier. Walker signed an affidavit stating that he had "witnessed the performance of music on a variety of instruments, also uttering language through the trumpet by the spirits, also the writing of a lengthy communication by one of the spirits in presence of the audience." One of Walker's former colleagues on the court, Judge Robert A. Fulton, visited the Koons circle and was listed in a spiritualist newspaper along with Koons, Tippie, and others who "affirm to have seen and conversed with spirits."

Within Koons's own extended family was a difference of opinion regarding his new avocation. His conversion to spiritualism must have made for interesting conversation at family get-togethers, if it was discussed at all. In addition to Koons's niece Anna Margaret Tippie, his sister and brother-in-law, Lydia and Thomas Morris, attended some of the séances. But Koons described his brother-in-law Aaron Evans as "an inveterate opposer" of the new religion, while reserving harsher words for another opponent, Jonathan's older brother Solomon. Back in Bedford, Solomon used to tell about getting spooked on his way home from courting late at night. As he walked along a country road, his route took him through a haunted spot in the woods, where ghostly footsteps pacing behind him made his hair stand on end. Solomon joked that he "found it necessary to support his hat with his hands, to keep his hair from crowding it off its head." But his youthful levity was no laughing matter now, as Solomon evidently believed that Jonathan had fallen under a devilish influence. "Whether or not this intrusion [the footsteps] led him to fancy the same or similar manifestation to be of a satanic origin is more than I am able to establish at this time," Jonathan Koons wrote. "This however being his conclusion in relation to what has recently transpired at my residence, leads me to infer a cause, and the most reasonable conclusion I can draw is, a lack of self confidence in his own judgment, in consequence of which, he walks in the council of his pastor."

The skepticism of even a close sibling with his own experience of spirits evidently ensured that Koons descendants would have different opinions about Jonathan Koons's legacy. In generations to come, some would proudly embrace the family connection, convinced that he indeed had psychic powers. Others would avoid any association with his peculiar brand of religion, even going so far as to change the spelling of their last name.

8

Communication from Angels

ONE OF the pilgrims climbing the ridge to the Koons Spirit Room in the spring of 1853 was Dr. J. Everett, a Columbus physician who had spent time in the Hydesville, New York, area when the Fox sisters burst upon the scene in 1848. The good doctor visited the Fox family on several occasions, found the sisters to be credible, and became a spiritualist himself. After hearing of new mediums who might prove to be every bit as dynamic as the Foxes, he was eager to investigate the goings-on in his own backyard.

On the first evening, May 11, Everett joined about 20 other people in the spirit room, where they heard music played on a variety of instruments and language uttered through the trumpet and harp. He believed that the beings who produced these sounds were angels, for the music was "performed with a skill and excellence that far surpassed any specimen that can be performed by any musician on earth." On occasions when the closed, crowded room would become stuffy, he felt breezes produced by angel wings fanning his face. On one particularly memorable evening Everett shook hands twice with one of the invisibles, who presented each member of the audience with a toy.

"The exhibition which I have been permitted to witness repeatedly from time to time during the eighteen days I have remained here, is not only of the most astounding character, but presenting us with the most overwhelming evidence that our sphere, earth, is being visited with an innumerable host of beings, who were once residents of this globe, and who have a mission to fulfil for the good and spiritual advancement of our race," he wrote in an affidavit. "They say to us that 'God is love' and all he requires of us is love to him and to each other, a life of purity and righteousness, in obedience to him."

Everett returned to Columbus determined to publish the revelations he had received. The result was *A Book for Skeptics: Being Communications from Angels, Written with Their Own Hands; also Oral Communications, Spoken by Angels through a Trumpet, and Written Down As They Were Delivered, in the Presence of Many Witnesses. Also a Representation and Explanation of the Celestial Spheres, As Given by the Spirits, at J. Koons' Spirit Room, in Dover, Athens County, Ohio.* The little volume of about 100 pages was issued by Osgood and Blake Publishers in Columbus in 1853. Everett was listed as the author, but he seemed to have served as an editor, for the book is a collection of Jonathan Koons's letters, as well as sermons said to have been delivered by the spirits. The book even included a sample of handwriting from the angel Oress—a patch of dots and strokes and squiggles that would have fit on a large teacup—with a translation given in English to show that "angels do write, and perform this by motions and signs, all in rhyme."

As reflected in the book's title, Koons maintained that information from the spiritual plane came to him in multiple ways. One was the strange writings he claimed to find in the spirit room—poems and messages that mysteriously appeared on paper while the room was locked and empty. Second, with the audience present, notes were scribbled with a pencil by a human-like hand during the séances. Third, using Nahum as a conduit, King spoke directly through the trumpet, which meant that someone at the circle had to write down his utterances in near-darkness or remember them and write them down later.

According to Emma Hardinge Britten, an early historian of the movement, "Many of the communications thus written or spoken, were of a highly philosophical character. In the former method, the spirits themselves phrased the writings, but in the latter, [the Koons] family or their visitors were obliged to take down the words from memory, and thus it happens that *the phraseology is far more characteristic of the Ohio scribes than of their spiritual authors*" (emphasis added). Speaking of the messages given through the trumpet, Koons acknowledged to a friend that by early 1853,

"I [could] only give the substance of the latter correspondence, as it had become impossible by that time, to keep a written note of all that was spoken, and transacted by spirits."

A pundit with a more skeptical bent than Britten's, the publisher J. R. Buchanan of Cincinnati, analyzed a message written by a ghostly hand at a Koons séance and found nothing otherworldly. "There was nothing at all angelic or supernatural in its appearance; on the contrary, it was a commonplace specimen of writing, which, if I had heard nothing of it, I should have pronounced to be the production of a man in the prime of life, evidently an American, of moderate or respectable education, and of considerable mental activity," he wrote. "It was placed on the forehead of a lady of moderate impressibility, and it gave her a decided impression of a keen, active mind."

Skeptics might have noted that this was exactly the profile of Jonathan or Nahum Koons. But others held out the hope that such wonderful physical manifestations *did* occur in the West, where, some believed, "mental and spiritual conditions were more simple and primitive than in the east." This hope would send the denizens of New York, Philadelphia, and Boston flocking to the domain of Jonathan Koons.

✷ ✷ ✷

OVER the past six months 15-year-old Nahum had been shown a series of heavenly visions. Under King's direction the young man entered into a clairvoyant state and was able to see the realms of heaven in vivid detail. First came a precise, almost mechanical, drawing of the celestial spheres—seven in number—that radiated out from a center point, O, in a series of interlocking shells. King supposedly had drawn the outlines and guided Nahum in painting the various sections. Then, on May 28, 1853, speaking through the trumpet, King revealed what the diagram stood for.

Although several world religions shared the archetypal notion of seven heavens, the idea was expressed through Nahum in Christian terms, especially in language drawn from the book of Revelation. The communication explains that in the drawing O represents "what was anciently the pit, lake, hell, and second death, &tc, into which all those whose names were not found written in the book of life, (agreeable to the language of St. John the divine) are cast forever." Far from being an imaginary or mystical place, O has a diameter that equals the combined diameters of Earth and the moon. The pit is dark, because it is far from the divine light, and it is teeming with electricity "which is productive of a constant chain of thunder, lightning, and quaking, from which circumstantial phenomena, the equivalent of fire and brimstone, were drawn by the inspired penman, St. John, who was spiritually led in like manner to those of the present day, who are conducted by the spirits in the superior or clairvoyant state," as King described it. But the unfortunate denizens of O were not bound to stay there forever; the term of imprisonment was thought to be one year, but as it was commonly known that 1,000 years was the same as one day with God, even King could not say for sure. Periodically these detainees would have access to the next level, sphere number 1, and could proceed outward "into a state of progression, under divine love and truth."

Each of the seven levels—eight, counting the pit—was geared to the moral refinement of the departed soul. The soul's placement depended on the deeds committed while in the body. "The peculiar arrangements of those spheres, and their respective orders, constitute a proper and perfect series of school rooms, adapted for the progression and advancement of their respective occupants into which each class is placed, respectively from the first to the sixth degree," the communication explained. "The sixth being that of the highest order in which they become fully qualified, and rendered fit subjects to go before the throne of God."

No one except God and the angels lived in the seventh heaven, but the enlightened souls in the sixth could freely pass over. It was a realm of light and color, with shifting scenes providing the angels with "a constant repast." Sometimes the visitors formed "celestial assemblies" to commune with the divine entity; they paired off in couples and stood hand in hand "around the glorious throne of their Heavenly Parent, where they offer their united praises, to the honor and glory of God's adorable name, during which celebrations their Majesty supreme responds in smiling accents," King reported.

But Christ, who traditionally sits at the right hand of God, was not present in this seventh sphere, which placed Nahum's vision outside the mainstream of Christian thought. Instead, at upper left, the drawing contained "an imperfect representation" of Christ's throne with crosses and a scepter beside it. Christ had his own throne, which was "classed among the innumerable numbers of similar thrones, which are occupied from time to time by personages of equal exalted dignity to that of Christ, from all the hosts of Heaven's combined worlds." Just as Christ's emblems were present to explain his mission on Earth, so the others had their symbols, which existed but were not depicted.

On the opposite side of the scheme was another, smaller, ring of concentric circles that represented "the depository," a record of all souls occupying the first six heavenly spheres. "These breast-plates or books of life, contain the picture, or character of man's deeds, done in the body during the course of his life," the communication explained. When someone died, he was shown the pictures and became "his own judge" of which level he should occupy. The books were updated as the soul progressed to a state of perfection. They also served as a celestial census containing the names and titles of the souls while they lived on Earth.

"This depository is open at all times, to which advanced spirits have access, which serves them in the room of a general record, of all those spirits embraced in the different spheres," the communication continued. "And which also serves them as a guide, in tracing out any individual spirit, since the names and titles of individuals are not known in heaven, peculiar to this world, only as recorded on each one's breast-plate, or book of life." The only exception was those in the pit, or center point, O; their records were not yet in the depository. Nonetheless they still had a chance to progress to the highest level, where they would become "as grand archangels of God, leaving all their errors and corruptions behind them."

The vision of heaven created by Nahum and King was printed as the frontispiece in Everett's *A Book for Skeptics*, illuminating the glorious future awaiting humanity.

EVEN as the faithful at the Koons circle contemplated Nahum's heavenly visions, life on Earth was proving far less sublime. On June 3, 1853, shortly after Everett's departure, something must have gone wrong at the Koons circle. Jonathan Koons did not say explicitly what happened, but the following day he sent Everett a stern message from the spirits for inclusion in the upcoming book. The communiqué warned that the mediums should not be interrupted during the circle. The spirits drew their ability to act in the physical world from the "nervo-vital fluid" of the mediums. If an accidental collision or shock occurred, the event "would immediately cause said medium, with his own involuntary power, to attract said fluid to himself," resulting in the object's falling to the floor. The warning concluded by repeating that mediums should not be bothered by the audience while "objects of value" were levitating around the room.

Reading between the lines, it appears that mischief had entered the spirit room that evening. Jonathan Koons was known to admit both spiritualists and nonbelievers to his circle, allowing them to sit within arm's length of the mediums. Perhaps a rogue guest had tried to grab a medium as a means of exposing fraud. During the melee a musical instrument might have crashed or gone spinning into the crowd. A sharp critic of the Koons demonstrations told a newspaper that "a man was knocked down with a drum-stick one night for endeavoring to pry into these mysteries [of the séance], so people have learned to be cautious." It appears, however, that the Koons family would have to learn to be careful, too. The soft dark of the séance room cloaked spiritual ecstasy for some, but it also concealed random destruction: one tambourine would be broken and several instruments damaged during the Koonses' public adventures.

SOMETIME in 1853 a man named M. B. Ashley was advised by a medium in Rochester, New York, to travel to Athens County. When he arrived at the Koons home, he asked Jonathan Koons if he might look inside the spirit room. The stranger was ushered into the space, then not in use, and his gaze swept over the musical instruments and other paraphernalia.

"The spirits have been writing," Koons said unexpectedly. He picked up a sheet from the table. "To M. B. Ashley, a person I do not know, which is not infrequent."

"That is my name," the visitor said.

"Then it is undoubtedly for you," Koons said and handed it to him.

Ashley was stunned to see the words written there. The message included the same language that the young female medium in Rochester had used, setting him on the quest.

The traveler needed no further convincing. He ended up boarding a full three weeks at the Koons residence, where he fell under the enchantment and attended numerous séances. Finally the day came when he had to return home. Ashley asked for his bill.

"Your board is already paid for," Koons responded.

"Who has paid it, and how has it been paid?" asked the astonished man.

Koons showed Ashley $15. "By the spirits, and in bank bills," was the reply.

✳ ✳ ✳

BY November 1853 Koons had begun to rethink his open-door policy. Someone apparently had visited his circle and decided it was all a humbug. The *Spiritual Telegraph* in New York City had received a "letter from Ohio" that attacked Koons's credibility, but several trusted men had assured the editors that the phenomena were genuine. To protect Koons's reputation, they rejected the critical letter and instead published Koons's own statement of self-defense, prefacing it with a note that vouched for the star medium: "Certain reports . . . have been industriously circulated, designed to discredit the claims of the manifestations at his place, and tending to excite the suspicion that he is himself the author of the wonders exhibited and described by the persons who have visited his premises. Neither the nature of the case nor the spirit of Mr. Koons' letter appear[s] to us to warrant this suspicion, and it is but just to say that the fidelity of his statements is supported by many intelligent witnesses. Ed."

In his letter to the *Spiritual Telegraph,* Koons railed against the "base and untruthful charges" leveled against his family and friends. "I have thrown open my house, and all the fixtures ordered by the spirits, for the fullest inspection," he wrote. The spirits had allowed investigators to sit beside him and Nahum while the séances were in progress "so as to prove that we were not guilty of fraud." Koons said no more changes to the circle would be made. People who come to his home "to detect me in the practice of the most stupendous imposition ever attempted, if it be an imposition, are politely requested to stay away." He believed that people who come looking for a hoax will confirm their belief, no matter what the evidence is.

Koons argued that he had nothing to gain by fraud. He pointed out that he didn't charge admission to his circles, which were draining for his wife and children: "The mediums of my family have sat up night after night, when they were scarcely able to move, and had almost to be carried into the room to accommodate visitors." Further, he freely gave away the spirits' written communications. Sometimes the documents went to "responsible men for publication," but other people, he feared, simply attended the séances to "gratify idle curiosity." Koons said he never expected to be paid in this life, beyond "the untold satisfaction of demonstrating beyond cavil that man lives after death, of which I had many doubts myself until they were removed by these demonstrations."

He also addressed a common criticism of séances—that they were held in the dark to make fraud less detectable. "The spirits make the demonstrations at their own time and in their own way," he wrote. "If they prefer darkness, I can not help it. If they choose light, I do not object to it. All I wish known is, that I do not do these things[,] that they are not done by any human agency."

In closing out his letter, Koons said that his house had been searched repeatedly over the past two years, with no evidence of skullduggery uncovered. On one occasion he and "an inquisitor" were going through the upstairs when Koons found two baby birds that one of his young sons had hidden there. Whether in anger or with cold determination, Koons wrung their necks in front of the man. The skeptic "heard the demonstrations afterward the same as before, and then went away and charged it on the poor birds." To Koons the episode demonstrated only how rabidly illogical his critics could be. To the reader it may have revealed something else: how far someone would stoop to protect his reputation.

9

Allies and Kin

WHILE JONATHAN Koons was defending himself from calumny in the pages of the *Spiritual Telegraph,* his neighbors were planning to open a spirit room of their own. An enthralled visitor to the Koons circle noted in his own letter to the *Telegraph* that "arrangements are being made for another circle and band of Spirits two and a half miles hence, which will produce wonders. The band will be composed of seven hundred and twenty advanced Spirits. In the family where this circle is forming is a child who has been influenced by Spirits since six weeks old; another, who is clairvoyant, sees and describes Spirits, and is only three years old. There is also a man in this family who talks with Spirits daily. But why detail—the half can not be told." The believer concluded with a strong endorsement of the Athens County phenomena. "I hope you will not listen to those men who basely slander the demonstrations at this place," he told readers, "and if you doubt, come and see for yourself."

✱ ✱ ✱

John Tippie Jr., the host of the new spirit room, had been born in Athens County in 1811. He shared his birth year with his future neighbor, Jonathan Koons. Both families had ties to Pennsylvania, but Uriah Tippie had brought his family to Ohio 30 years before the Koonses arrived, when the oldest son, John Tippie Sr., was a teenager. Uriah, a veteran of the American Revolution, settled north of Athens and pieced together a living from farming, a war pension, and work as a cobbler. As an adult the senior John Tippie farmed and reared at least four children in Ames Township. In 1850 he and his wife, Betsy, then in their sixties, still lived in the district with the widowed stepmother of John Sr. residing in their home.

Two farms over from his father's place, the younger John Tippie presided over a large household that included six children by his first wife, Phebe Denman (sometimes spelled Denham), who had died around 1846. On May 21, 1847, he had married a much younger woman, Anna Margaret Hughes, and they had started a second family. Anna Margaret, who was about 21 at the time of her marriage, was Jonathan Koons's niece, the daughter of his sister Elizabeth Koons Hughes. By 1850 John Jr. and Anna Margaret had eight children living with them, including two from their union—2-year-old Robert and the infant Lydia.

The Tippies became serious acolytes of the Koons circles, often traveling the backwoods paths at night from their farm two and a half miles away. One visitor noted that "the Tippie family did not manage to obtain the demonstrations from the spirits at their house until after they had, over the course of a year or more, very assiduously attended the séances of Mr. Koons." As in the Koons tribe, mediumship soon became a family affair for the Tippies. "The children . . . were clairvoyant, so that they see and play with spirit-children day by day, and considered it a great privilege to go into a dark room for the purpose of shaking hands with the spirits before retiring at night," another visitor reported.

Some observers might have thought that the Tippies' spirit room would be an affront to the Koonses, a competing enterprise that would draw visitors away from the original. Yet far from being competitors, the Koonses and the Tippies were in a sense allies as well as kin. One commentator believed that the psychic activities of the Tippies and others in the neighborhood boosted the spirits' "signal" at the Koons home, making the Koons family demonstrations more striking and dynamic. The two families also were able to swap out their boarding guests, providing each other with a break from the demand for spectacular entertainment several nights in a row. John Tippie Jr. could also be counted on to greet visitors arriving at the stagecoach office in Chauncey. Tippie won the gratitude of one footsore visitor from St. Louis by letting the man ride his horse and walking beside it as they made the arduous climb from Chauncey to the Koons farm.

In 1853 the younger John Tippie, wife Anna Margaret, son Ezra, brother Joseph, and nephew Wesley signed an affidavit supporting Jonathan Koons's presentations as authentic. That same year Koons wrote of an unusual circle at his home that involved one of the Tippie sons, probably Ezra. The 18-year-old gave a "spiritual address" to the assembled group "while in a somnambulic or clairvoyant state." During the trance the spirits conducted him through the spheres of heaven where he appeared to experience bliss. After Ezra woke up, he started repeating the information as if he were unaware that he had already said it. Koons declared the session "very satisfying, and convincing" and said he was impressed that the layout of the spheres reported by the Tippie boy matched the drawing that his own son Nahum had already prepared, "since the statement made by the spirits, and those made by the different clairvoyants in this place, all agree in the same."

Not surprisingly, when the Tippies opened their spirit room to the public in 1854, many attendees noticed the similarities between the original circle and its offshoot. One prominent visitor, Charles Partridge, editor of the *Spiritual Telegraph,* noted that "rooms and manifestations [are] very much alike, but the electrical tables are somewhat different in construction. Both spirits claim to be King." Joseph Barthet, the mesmerist from New Orleans, attended a Tippie séance and found the seating arrangements nearly identical to those at Koons's; Barthet was seated at the mediums' table next to John Tippie and opposite Ezra Tippie.

Other observers, such as a group of prominent Cleveland citizens, reported some differences between the two spirit rooms. At the Koons circle Jonathan often would play the violin and then the spirits would accompany him; the Tippie family did not play instruments at the gatherings but relied entirely on the spirits to animate the instruments. The Clevelanders visiting the Tippie séances found the music "more varied and interesting than at Koons's." However, the spirits relied on the trumpet for communication and on these particular nights did not produce any writing or the famed spectral hands that so impressed audiences. They did, at least on one occasion, perform parlor tricks for the benefit of their guests. According to one visitor's account, the invisibles ordered the lights put out and during "a short interval of darkness" stacked the musical instruments one upon the other to make a precarious sculpture. When the candle was relit, "the small bell had been placed on the table, with the sharp point of the handle upwards; upon this stood a drumstick, on its end, a book placed on the top of this drum-stick, edgeways, and another drumstick ended up upon the edge of this book."

The group of five from Cleveland stayed two days and two nights at both homes and found what seemed to be incontrovertible proof that their hosts—showmanship notwithstanding—drew deep meaning from spiritual endeavors. One morning they were passing the Tippie Spirit Room when they heard John and his son (presumably Ezra) asking questions of the horn in a private moment. A female voice was coming through it— evidently that of Phebe Denman, John's deceased wife. "To us that private conference was truly significant and beautiful," the Clevelanders reported. "The husband and child had turned from the family and friends to ask advice of, and listen to the gentle tones of the first wife and mother." Once the conversation was over, the visitors entered the room and found only John Tippie and his son.

Over at the Koons place the menu of special effects seemed to keep growing. Although many had reported that the tambourine flew about the room tapping visitors on various body parts, the accordion and violin had now gone airborne as well. "The violin was not on the table during the whole time [of the séance], but was carried by invisible hands all around the room, now passing near to our heads, now near the ceiling, and now resting on our persons," the Clevelanders reported. "It was placed on the knees of one of our number, and turned over, so that the strings were on the underside, and while his hands were passing all around it so as to cut off all connection with it, a tune was played. The accordeon was played on, not only while it lay on the table, but while it was floating through the air through all parts of the room."

The visitors—two of whom were supposedly clairvoyant—returned to Cleveland entirely convinced of the wonders they had beheld: "We advise any and all who wish to witness demonstrations of Spirit Power and Intelligence, . . . to make a trip to Athens county, where they cannot fail to be convinced 'that Spirits who once inhabited mortal bodies, still live, and can and do hold intercourse with the inhabitants of earth.'"

The city folks held the Koonses and Tippies guileless, because, in their view, the families were country bumpkins—people who could barely speak proper English, much less Latin or French. The Clevelanders' assessment of their hosts was laced with backhanded compliments:

> Were it possible that such manifestations could be made by
> mortals, they never could be made by Mr. Koons, Mr. Tippie, or
> any members of their families. Apparently, none of them have the
> disposition to deceive, and certainly none of them have common
> sense or intelligence in such quantities as would allow them to
> successfully impose on others, by any tricks of jugglery or sleight
> of hand.—Their every word and action evinces their honesty, their
> simplicity, their rusticity, their ignorance of men and manners. Their
> business is farming, and their farms unmistakably show that they
> are not qualified for a sphere of action of even so high a grade. The
> two traits of character, particularly noticeable, are their artlessness
> and integrity. Occasionally they are the media through whom
> communications of some intelligence are given; but the contrast
> between such written and spoken communications, and their
> writing and speaking while in the normal state[,] is readily seen.

AMONG the delegation from Cleveland were two women who were already gaining notoriety for their radical views of women's rights and other reform issues. Both Caroline S. Lewis—said to be both beautiful and married to one of the richest men in that city—and the red-haired Hannah Frances Brown, a crusading writer and editor, were followers of the spiritualist John Murray Spear. Even among free thinkers, Spear stood out for his outlandish schemes and projects, many of which involved sexual relations among his coterie. Lewis and Brown had spent time at Kiantone, Spear's utopian camp on the Pennsylvania–New York border, and had been involved in his efforts to build a perpetual motion machine. The so-called New Motor, which its creators scandalously claimed had gained the spark of life from an actual woman, failed to work and was destroyed by a mob in New York State just weeks before the women visited the Koons farm.

Women like Brown and Lewis drew the ire of more mainstream spiritualists by endorsing the doctrine of free love, a highly controversial plank in the spiritualist platform. According to the historian Ann Braude, free love was "generally understood to mean opposition to marriage as an institution, [and] many who applied the label to themselves fell far short of this extreme position. Proponents used it to refer to their opposition to marriage laws that discriminated against women, while detractors used it as a synonym for promiscuity or infidelity." Supporters of free love argued that all sexual relations ought to be between so-called affinities—people who are mutually attracted, whether married or not. Thus women should be free to reject their husbands' sexual advances, and divorce laws should be liberalized so that men and women did not engage in sex with partners they no longer loved. The trance speaker Lizzie Doten declared that free love did not mean "free lust," but in the popular imagination that was exactly what the term implied.

John Murray Spear's followers, considered some of the most radical on this issue, did nothing to dispel that impression. Lewis had already scandalized Cleveland society by posing nude as an artist's model. A few years later she would shock other spiritualists at a Ravenna, Ohio, free love convention by declaring that "I am married to all men,—to the Divine God principle—and it is for me to say what expressions or manifestations of love I shall give to all men."

Like Lewis, Brown believed that women should have control of their own bodies when it came to sex and childbearing. A native of New Hampshire, she was a former mill worker who had moved to Cleveland with her businessman husband around 1848. She tried for years to get a divorce after her marriage had soured and finally obtained one around 1856. In the meantime she had left the Universalist Church and converted to spiritualism, which she admired for its egalitarian handling of gender relations. Brown devoted her considerable energies to securing women's rights through her writing and speeches. She would go on to edit the *Agitator,* a paper devoted to radical reform, and write a book called *The False and True Marriage: The Reason and Results.* Brown eventually became licensed to perform marriage ceremonies at spiritualist weddings; she emphasized "true soul unions" rather than codified relationships that held women in bondage.

In his voluminous writings Jonathan Koons did not expound on free love, and though his marriage to Abigail seemed rather conventional, they must have endured a certain amount of guilt by association with such figures as Lewis and Brown. Nor is it clear what the sleeping arrangements were for visitors at the cramped quarters of Koons and Tippie, who may not have had the wherewithal to enforce rigorous standards of Victorian morality. No doubt some pilgrims came not only for spiritual nourishment but to have an off-the-record vacation from the mores of the time. That is why a disgruntled visitor to the Koons Spirit Room, sure that he had been humbugged, published a letter in which he included one bit of salacious gossip: "The doctrines taught there are perfectly detestable. *Free love* is made a cardinal principle, at least so we were informed, and their theory is reduced to *practice.*"

2.1 Maggie and Kate Fox, credited with starting the spiritualism movement in New York State in 1848. The sisters, known as the "Rochester Rappers," later were joined by their older sister, Leah Fox Fish, and became internationally famous mediums. 1852 daguerreotype by Thomas Easterly. Courtesy of the Missouri Historical Society, St. Louis.

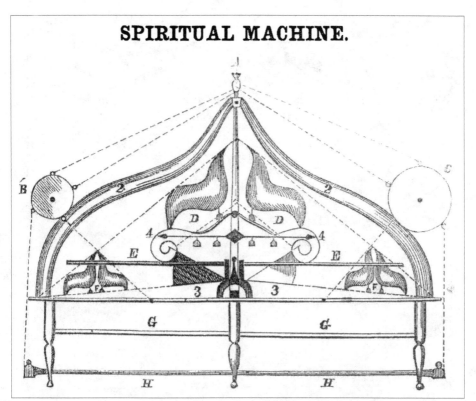

SPIRITUAL MACHINE.

2.2 Spiritualists believed that technological advances could help them scientifically prove the existence of spirits of the departed. Jonathan Koons built this "spirit machine" of wood and metal in 1852 to help the spirits concentrate their energy during séances. This device was called a battery, but some observers questioned its ability to conduct electricity. The drawing was published in 1854.

DIAGRAM
of spirit room

KEY:
- 1 Shelving
- 2 Drums
- 3 Spirit machine on table
- 4 Mediums' table
- 5 Chairs: J-J. Koons A-Abigail
- N-Nahum
- 6 Stove
- 7 Tiered benches

2.3 Artist's conception of the layout of the Koons Spirit Room as it was in 1852. Visitor accounts of the size of the building and number of windows varied but consistently reported that the spirit machine and the mediums' table were located within a semicircle formed by Koons family members and guests. Drawing by Sandy Plunkett.

2.4 Fiddle used by Jonathan Koons to initiate the séances in his spirit room. The fiddle is now owned by his direct descendant Alan Taylor of Oregon, along with the coffee mill that belonged to Jonathan's daughter Quintilla Koons Taylor. Photograph by Alan Taylor.

2.5 These dots and squiggles resembling shorthand appeared in *A Book for Skeptics*, an 1853 collection of Jonathan Koons's writings, and of poems and sermons supposedly transmitted by the spirit guide King and other entities. The image pictured here was said to be a message from the ancient angel Oress.

A CHART OF THE CELESTIAL SPHERES.

[See page 64.

2.6 The archetypal notion of seven heavens, shared by multiple world religions, was expressed through Nahum Koons in this 1853 drawing. The depiction of seven concentric rings surrounding Earth was created by the entranced Nahum and his spirit guide King. Published in *A Book for Skeptics*.

10

Mountain Tea

IN 1854 a petition drive, spearheaded by the New York publisher Samuel Byron Brittan, sought an official investigation of spiritualist phenomena by the US government. By that April the petition had garnered nearly 12,500 signatures nationally for presentation to Congress. Those signing the document (called memorialists) were not necessarily believers in spiritualism, but their willingness to sign showed a conviction that the subject was at least worth investigating by serious minds. Their spectrum of attitudes toward spiritualism was reflected in the notes some wrote beside their names; although some memorialists claimed to be mediums or believers, others were careful to note that they were an "unbeliever," and one even offered the disclaimer "signed at the request of Uncle Graham." Still others announced their professional qualifications such as apothecary or chemist, perhaps indicating that they took a scientific approach to the topic. The petition read in part:

> Two general hypotheses obtain with respect to the origin of these
> remarkable phenomena. The one ascribes them to the power
> and intelligence of departed spirits, operating on and through the
> subtile and imponderable elements which pervade and permeate all
> material forms. . . . Others . . . reject this conclusion, and entertain
> the opinion that the acknowledged principles of physics and

metaphysics will enable scientific inquirers to account for all the facts in a rational and satisfactory manner. While your memorialists cannot agree on this question . . . they nevertheless most cordially concur in the opinion that the alleged phenomena do really occur, and that their mysterious origin, peculiar nature, and important bearing on the interests of mankind demand for them a patient, thorough, and scientific investigation.

The petitioners listed many types of phenomena worthy of exploration, including lights of strange shapes and colors and "an occult force" that pushes heavy objects around in defiance of the laws of physics. Of particular interest were the various sounds supposedly produced by the spirits, from rapping noises to thunderous concussions that caused walls, floors, and entire houses to shake. "On other occasions harmonic sounds are heard as of human voices, but more frequently resembling the tones of various musical instruments, among which those of the fife, drum, trumpet, guitar, harp and piano have been mysteriously and successfully represented, both with and without the instruments; and in either case, without any apparent human or other visible agency," the document stated.

The organizers of the petition drive persuaded James Shields of Illinois to present the memorial to his colleagues on the floor of the US Senate. But their months of work were undone in just a few minutes on April 17 as Shields first correctly summarized the document—and then began to lampoon it, calling spiritualism a delusion among the poorly educated or those with "a partial derangement of the mental faculties." Shields's remarks were peppered with laughter from his fellow senators. One suggested tongue in cheek that the matter be referred to the Committee on Foreign Relations, in case Americans lost their citizenship after death. After a round of jokes they tabled the matter. Another attempt the next month also failed to gain any traction, and the matter was soon forgotten in the halls of Congress.

Although the petition failed to launch psychic anomalies into the realm of serious national debate, it did result in a historical document of considerable interest, a snapshot of various communities whose residents signed it. Not only did the memorialists include their names, they also listed their state, county, and township. Ohio was second only to New York State in the number of signers, with a total of 1,598 names coming from 48 of Ohio's 88 counties. All along Ohio's Lake Erie shore, from Ashtabula County in the east to Lucas County in the west, hundreds of people signed. Northeastern Ohio, which includes Cleveland, was a particular hotbed of interest; in fact, all but two counties in that section, known as the Western Reserve, had residents who signed. According to the author Emma Hardinge Britten, "Some of the earliest spiritual conventions were held in Cleveland, which formed a point of attraction from the number and enthusiasm of the friends located there. From thence, too, Spiritualism radiated throughout the entire of Ohio, rendering that State famous in the history of the movement." A visit by the iconic Fox sisters, who had conducted public séances in Cleveland in 1851, also had sparked interest in—and opposition to—the new religion.

In the sparsely settled hill country of southeastern and southern Ohio, interest in spiritualism did not seem to be widespread, but pockets of influence were evident from the clusters of signatures. Brown County, down on the Ohio River near Cincinnati, was an important conduit on the Underground Railroad and home to a committed band of abolitionists; there, too, interest in spiritualism ran high. Midway between Brown and Athens Counties lay Ross County, whose city of Chillicothe had been the original capital of the state. In both Ross County and its neighbor to the south, Pike County, several residents had signed the document.

In Athens County 106 residents inked the petition, mostly from the Athens and Amesville areas. Athens, the county seat and surrounding township, had 42 petitioners, while Ames Township and Amesville combined had 48, including some prominent people in both communities. Several of Jonathan Koons's neighbors in Ames had signed, including John Tippie (presumably Jr.); his wife, Anna Margaret; his brother Joseph and nephew Wesley; along with the Borders, Jonathan's former in-laws. Dover Township, where the Koons family lived, came in a distant third.

What is most compelling about the Dover listing is what is *not* there— not one signature from anyone living in Jonathan and Abigail's household. Of course Jonathan would have known about the petition because Anna Margaret and John Tippie Jr., who were frequent visitors to the séances, had signed it. The mystery is why Jonathan's family did not participate, as they were entertaining hundreds of people by 1854 and would have been in an ideal circumstance to collect large numbers of signatures. Jonathan certainly was not shy about entering into any kind of public fray that conceivably could promote the cause of spiritualism, but perhaps he did not welcome government scrutiny of his affairs.

Even with this strange omission, the document shines a light on the kind of people in Athens County and elsewhere who were willing to go on record as believing the phenomena were real and questioning their origin. Though risking ridicule from their neighbors, they shared a common belief that the progress of science would someday bring forth answers to the age-old questions surrounding death and the afterlife—answers heretofore arrived at only by faith.

JONATHAN Koons continued to draw more local people into his orbit that spring of 1854, including W. S. Beatty, editor of the *Athens (Ohio) Democrat*. In a brief letter to another newspaper, Beatty said, "Dear Sir—Like yourself I am a 'reasonable believer in Spiritualism,' and have been much favored by the kindness of Mr. Koons, in witnessing the manifestations at various times . . . and have only to say that I believe implicit confidence can be placed in his statements."

Likewise, George H. Carpenter of Athens wrote to a friend to vouch for the spectacular phenomena he was witnessing at the Koons Spirit Room. In addition to manifesting themselves through music and spirit writing, the invisibles would converse with the audience just as plainly as a human would chat with a friend. Beyond that, visiting clairvoyants claimed to see materialized forms "about twenty-seven inches high." "If the Spirits really do assume those diminutive forms," mused the *Spiritual Telegraph*, "the question may be asked whether the doctrine of *fairies* may not have had a real foundation in a similar phenomenon."

Gnome. Sprite. Elf. Puck. Fairy. The angels with their oversized hands and breeze-fanning wings now seemed to be shape-shifting into dwarfs. Maybe it depended on whether the seer was Christian. But all of the forms were of ancient origin, prone to finding their place in the archetypal mind.

AMONG the visitors tramping the leafy path up to Mount Nebo that May was a man known only as J. B., who had decided to visit the Koons Spirit Room on a lark. "I was a skeptic, and full of fun and frolic, I sought the place, expecting to witness a gross deception, and fully confident of my powers to expose it as such," he wrote. J. B. joined a crowd of 25 for an evening séance and was allowed to examine the séance table beforehand. Once he had taken his seat, satisfied with the setup, the light was extinguished. Although the cabin was dark as usual, viewing conditions seemed unusually good on this spring evening. Jonathan Koons had a habit of rubbing luminous phosphorus on moist sheets of sandpaper just before blowing out the candle, and he could control the amount of light by covering or uncovering the sandpaper. "A quantity of phosphoric light was placed upon the table which was sufficient to make us see distinctly what was going on," J. B. reported.

Five minutes later a piece of phosphorus rose from the table to the ceiling; within 30 seconds an object appeared. "We saw a hand, (exactly the shape of a human hand, except that it had only four fingers) holding the phosphorus and rubbing it on the fingers and the palm, of itself, so as to make it perfectly visible. The hand then commenced to dart about the room over our heads, with the speed of electricity," J. B. noted. As Jonathan Koons played the violin, the hand took up the drumstick and accompanied him "as well as any human drummer." After the drum, the flying appendage performed on the tambourine, triangle, and French harp before taking up the trumpet, from which a voice spoke. J. B. marveled at how the tambourine was keeping perfect time while sailing through the air. (In a typical Koons séance it was unusual for a hand to be clearly visible until the writing began.)

Upon returning to the table, the hand took up a pencil and began to write at an astonishing speed. To J. B.'s amazement the communiqué "covered half a sheet of foolscap on both sides," although it had taken only 90 seconds to scribble. By the time a voice bade the audience good night, J. B.'s skepticism had been washed away. Referring to the apostle Paul's text, J. B. later wrote, "The Spirits themselves (if they are Spirits) are most reasonable—for they wish none to believe without thorough tests and they say to all who go there: 'Prove all things, and hold fast that which is good'" (1 Thess. 5:21).

J. B.'s travelogue was published in the *Christian Spiritualist,* a New York weekly newspaper edited by the Irish-born minister John Henry Watson Toohey and a businessman, Horace H. Day. Evidently the story proved popular with readers, for the editors announced, "We hope soon to have completed such arrangement as will enable us to furnish to our readers a weekly account of the wonderful events that are of constant occurrence at Millfield." Perhaps Toohey and Day had recruited Jonathan Koons himself as the correspondent, for his letters began to appear often in the columns of the *Christian Spiritualist,* and he was even listed as an agent authorized to sell subscriptions.

The paper's Bible quoting may have held little sway with some segments of the Christian community; indeed the term *Christian spiritualist* might have seemed a misnomer to mainstream Christian pastors, who denounced spiritualism from their pulpits. Even though spiritualists sought to prove something that had long been an article of faith in the Christian church—the immortality of the soul—the new movement was a challenge to church authority. If practically anyone could become a medium and access "the other side" directly, the traditional role of the clergy was inevitably diminished. But some people of faith saw a much darker side to the table tippings and messages from the dead; if such things were real, they must have come from the devil.

The devil's tentacles could attach to a medium through body, mind, and soul. Critics argued that mediumship was physically dangerous, that it took a heavy toll on the person performing it. No wonder many such individuals had a history of chronic illness. Second, trance states were also harmful to the mind because the medium loses control of it for a while—squandering the God-given ability to reason. "How is it any better to stupefy and befool ourselves with mesmerism, than with alcohol or opium?" asked one opponent.

Frequent entrancements could blur the line between fantasy and reality, critics charged, driving the spiritualist insane. One convert, a sickly Circleville, Ohio, man whose condition defied medical treatment, turned to automatic writing and soon found his health improved. When the man refused to renounce his mediumship, his neighbors persuaded the local medical establishment to issue a certificate of lunacy. He was carted off to an asylum in Columbus, where he remained for seven weeks until friends on the outside were able to persuade officials to free him.

Beyond concerns for the practitioner's physical and mental health, ministers flatly declared that it was a sin for Christians to try to communicate with spirits of the dead. In an oft-cited example, nineteenth-century mediums were compared to the biblical Witch of Endor. When the ill-fated King Saul sought a prediction about his impending battle with the Philistines, he asked the witch to conjure up the spirit of the prophet Samuel, who delivered the news that Saul and his three sons would be killed in battle the next day. Aware that the king had outlawed sorcery in his realm, the witch risked her life to perform this service. According to the Old Testament book of Chronicles, Saul lost his life and his kingdom by disobeying the Lord on a previous occasion and by consulting a spirit rather than the Lord before battle. Looking beyond divination, Christians later argued that no one should regard mediums as spiritual teachers. God should be sufficient for everyone, and Christians can gain wisdom and gifts of the Holy Spirit through him. To seek other spirits for enlightenment was a repudiation of God.

Some spiritualists, on the other hand, found their beliefs entirely consistent with the New Testament—perhaps because they believed that the ability to enter altered states of consciousness was also a boon from the divine, a pathway to higher knowledge. In fact, proponents pointed specifically to 1 Corinthians 12:7 and its gift of prophecy bestowed by the Holy Spirit:

7 But the manifestation of the Spirit is given to every man to profit withal.

8 For to one is given by the Spirit the word of wisdom; to another the word of knowledge by the same Spirit;

9 To another faith by the same Spirit; to another the gifts of healing by the same Spirit;

10 To another the working of miracles; to another prophecy; to another discerning of spirits; to another divers kinds of tongues; to another the interpretation of tongues:

11 But all these worketh that one and the selfsame Spirit, dividing to every man severally as he will.

One of Koons's supporters, writing to the *Christian Spiritualist,* found no contradiction between the two religions. "While I see many things professing to emanate from Spirits, and much in our Spiritual literature that I disapprove, yet I have seen and read much of the higher Spiritual teachings of these latter days, that, to my mind, clears up many obscurities in the Bible, and gives us a more extended view of our future state than any thing contained in that sacred Book," the supporter maintained. "No man can be a good and pure Spiritualist without being a good and pure Christian."

✳ ✳ ✳

AS religious pundits debated the merits and pitfalls of spiritualism in far-off cities, Koons's life on Mount Nebo seemed to take on a magical quality such that strange things could happen if one were attuned. One evening he, Nahum, and another Koons son were on their way to a séance at a neighbor's house when an apparition darted before them out of the gloom. The image of a young man "in dark habiliments" suddenly appeared and then disappeared without speaking. The "haint" materialized a second time and again silently melted away. Upon their arriving at the neighbors' and forming the circle, the spirit—surely the one they had encountered on the path—began to speak through a medium.

Thus began a ghastly tale of a soul seeking justice. Thomas, a resident of eastern South Carolina while in the body, had worked as a farmhand to help support his widowed mother and three siblings. In July 1853 he demanded that his employer pay $25 owed to him in back wages. The farmer complied, and Thomas started toward home to share the cash with his family. As he passed through a lonely stretch of woods, two rifle shots felled Thomas and the money went missing. When Thomas failed to show up at home, the employer told the bewildered family that he had headed north after receiving his pay. Now, less than a year after his death, the vengeful ghost was here to tell Koons and his neighbors the truth: the employer had committed the heinous crime and concealed Thomas's lifeless body.

Eager to confirm the account, Koons wrote a letter to the *Spiritual Telegraph* relating the strange events but leaving out the name of the perpetrator. He also gave only the first name of the victim, even though the full name had been revealed at the séance. The newspaper ran a story based on Koons's report, concluding that "should this public statement provoke further inquiries, and lead to an expose of any such dark deeds as those alleged to have been committed, the utility, as well as the truth, of spiritual manifestations will stand conspicuously demonstrated."

It would not be the first or last time that psychic means had been used in an attempt to solve crimes, but the news item might well have reminded readers of the origins of spiritualism itself: the strange rappings heard in the John D. Fox household in Hydesville, New York, where in 1848 the ghost of a peddler—murdered for his money and wares—was supposedly making the noises. At the time of the disturbance, the spirit claimed to be one Charles B. Rosna, a hapless traveling salesman who was killed in the farmhouse by a previous tenant and buried in the basement. Soon after this message was received, neighbors attempted to dig up the basement but had to abandon the effort after it flooded. In 1904, long after the Fox family had moved out of the house and into the pages of history, a cellar wall began to crumble, exposing a human skeleton. A positive identification was never made, but an old-timey tin peddler's pack was found near the bones.

*   *   *

ALTHOUGH Ezra Tippie, the son of John Tippie Jr., was receiving much less press than his counterpart Nahum Koons, Ezra was coming into his own as a medium that summer of 1854. One night after a séance, when everyone had left, Ezra and James E. Cowee of Greensburg, Indiana, stayed behind in the Tippie Spirit Room for a private sitting. Cowee took his spot at the end of the rectangular battery table, and Ezra took the seat opposite. The candle was blown out, and a familiar voice inquired through the horn, "Would you wish to have the interview *strictly private?*" Cowee agreed. They lit the candle so that Ezra could position himself on the floor. He sat in front of his chair and leaned back against it. Cowee blew out the light and listened. "I could distinctly hear the passes made over the medium as the spirit-hands touched his person," Cowee wrote. "Soon his breathing notified me that he was asleep or in the mesmeric state."

Now the spirit King seized the horn and made a somewhat childish show of his powers. "See how long I can make Ezra hold his breath," he told

Cowee. The sound of Ezra's breathing went away, and nothing remained but a void of silence. Finally, King relented, and Ezra resumed breathing. "He caught his breath as a drowning man," Cowee recalled. King did the trick two more times, until the spirit, perhaps tired of the gambit, placed the horn over the table and began to speak in earnest with Cowee. All the while Cowee could hear Ezra's labored breathing from down on the floor. "I conversed half an hour, until I had gained all I sought; the knowledge obtained, far exceeding anything I could have gained from the combined wisdom of all the Tippies," Cowee exulted.

Besides the presumably personal advice Cowee received, he quizzed King on a technical point. Why was the little end of the trumpet often warm, and why was the big end moist? Not only did the spirit provide an answer, he promised to leave some moisture on the table. King commenced blowing through the horn, and soon Cowee heard some liquid dropping. "Good night," said the invisible, laying down the trumpet.

Cowee instantly lit the candle. Ezra had not moved. "He was still in the insensible state but shortly came to, utterly unconscious of the time spent and the business performed," Cowee reported. King, true to his word, had kept the conversation strictly private. On the table they found two or three tablespoons of a clear liquid that smelled and tasted like water. The Indiana man was convinced that Ezra could not have been behind the phenomenon. Cowee wrote:

> [The liquid] was as clear and limpid as spring water, and had no
> more taste. Now where did the water come from, if not produced
> by a spirit? If Ezra had produced it when speaking or blowing
> through the trumpet (supposing *he* did the talking) it would
> have tasted and smelt of tobacco, as he ever uses it, while I do
> not. There was no cup in the room, neither any water short of
> five rods to the spring. Now, considering all things, Ezra lying
> upon the floor, the horn talking above the table a foot or more,
> and afterwards blowing water through it; who can, unbiased
> by prejudice or skepticism, say that human beings and lips
> performed the whole?

✵ ✵ ✵

AS the Tippies and Koonses made their nocturnal visits to each other's spirit rooms, their steps may have been guided by some orange mushrooms glowing in the woods of a fall evening—the so-called jack-o'-lanterns. Other oddities of nature such as foxfire, or "fairy fire," had been known for centuries, the output of bioluminescent fungi feasting on rotting wood. But the commercial preparation of glow-in-the dark chemicals in the West goes back to 1669, when phosphorus was discovered by the German alchemist Hennig Brand as he was attempting to find the Philosopher's Stone. A fellow seeker named Krafft paid him $300 for the secret of how to obtain it— and its source turned out to be human urine. The phosphate-laden urine was evaporated down to a black residue, which was heated with sand to drive off impurities and ultimately to produce a white solid that Brand called "cold fire." Krafft's investment paid off handsomely, as he toured the courts of Europe, showing off the wondrous substance to nobles and royals.

According to the 1855 book *The Chemistry of Common Life,* "In appearance, phosphorus resembles bees'-wax; but it is more transparent, approaching the color of amber. Its name, which is derived from the Greek for 'light-bearer,' is indicative of its most distinguishing quality, being self luminous. Phosphorus, when exposed to the air, shines like a star, giving out a beautiful lambent, greenish light." Although some of the toxic effects of phosphorus on humans were already known by the 1850s, the Koonses routinely used the substance in their darkened spirit room to make visible the things that the spirits wished to show—sheets of paper or even a hand as it wrote messages or carried instruments around the room. It was no wonder that such a mysteriously powered substance would find its way into the séance. *The Chemistry of Common Life* mused, "Every other substance with which we are acquainted, can be traced to either earth or air; but phosphorus seems to be of animal origin. . . . Of all animals, man contains the most; and of the various parts of the body, the brain yields, by analysis, more phosphorus than any other. This fact is of no little moment. Every thought has, perhaps, a phosphoric source."

Many decades later, in the early twentieth century, phosphorus would play a role in the spiritualist Arthur Conan Doyle's mystery novel *The Hound of the Baskervilles.* The legendary supernatural hound that menaced a family in that Sherlock Holmes story turned out to be a mortal dog that had been painted with phosphorus to give it a more ghastly appearance, such that "its muzzle and hackles and dewlap were outlined in flickering flame."

＊　＊　＊

IN the fall of 1854 a man named Clark Williams ventured to the Koons farm. On Sunday evening, October 22, this "cautious observer" and "prudent, honest and successful man of business" entered the spirit room with about 20 others, including seven or eight members of the Koons family. Well versed in the who's who of spiritualist circles, Williams noticed Boston resident W. R. Hayden in the audience; Hayden's wife, the rapping medium Maria, had earned a name for herself in the movement by traveling to England and making several notable converts there. Jonathan Koons was joined by another fiddler, who sat next to him at the mediums' table. After the light was put out, the fiddlers played a tune together, the drums kicked in, and soon a voice began to sing through the trumpet. The tambourine flew around the room, playing as it went and sometimes touching the laps, heads, and hands of the visitors. "This music was kept up for some length of time, making the whole house roar so as almost to deafen us, during which time several different tunes were played," Williams later wrote. "Conversation was also kept up occasionally with Mr. Koons, wife and son, and others who might be suspected of trick, so that we could identify their positions and know that they were not beating the drums or playing the trumpet or tambourine."

The spectral hand then appeared right on schedule and wrote rapidly on paper about 2 feet from where Williams was sitting. He was so close he "could distinctly hear the crossing of t, and dotting of I as it wrote." The paper, however, went to Hayden, who was sitting farther back. When the light was restored, the spectators found a message "so beautifully written in such a short space of time" with the words neatly contained on the printed lines.

Despite his satisfaction with the evening's events, by Monday Williams was suffering from a stomach ailment and was thinking of cutting his visit short. That afternoon, he wrote, "I told Mr. Koons I felt so unwell that I thought I must leave in the morning for home, to which he replied[,] 'If anything is the matter with you just tell Mr. King (their presiding spirit) this evening, and he will direct some little thing that will make you well by morning.'"

When the time came for Monday evening's circle, Jonathan and Nahum made their customary visit to the spirit room near sundown "to inquire of the spirit what he would give us, if anything, that evening." Williams and a Mr. Boggs of Cincinnati stood eavesdropping outside the door. According to Williams, a voice replied through the trumpet that the evening's demonstration would consist of a "social chat" only. Later that night Nahum and his mother, "with a suckling child in her arms" (most likely son Joseph Britten, born in December 1853), hosted the session while Jonathan visited his sick nephew about 5 miles away.

With no one to play the fiddle, the group sat in silence for several minutes, waiting for the spirits to come. Suddenly a blow was struck to the table as if a chunk of ceiling had fallen on it. King had arrived for some light conversation with the visitors. Williams later reflected that "the spirit was sometimes joking and sometimes lecturing us so much like a human being that my skepticism would sometimes arise and cause me for a moment to doubt if it were not some kind of a trick, when immediately some feat would be performed with the trumpet which would satisfy us that it could not be any one in the body."

Williams found the movements of the horn quite convincing: at one moment it would rap the stovepipe near the ceiling and in the next would be on the other side of the room touching someone. The large end of the trumpet landed in Williams's lap, making contact with the back of his hand, and at his request the instrument touched his hand a second time, this time with the small end.

Perhaps Williams was so enthralled that he temporarily forgot about his stomachache. As the program neared its end, Boggs said to King, "Mr. Williams is not very well, will you look at him and tell him what to do to improve his health?"

"Certainly, sir—with a great deal of pleasure," the horn replied. The voice paused for about 60 seconds and then said: "His stomach is very much out of order, and he has pains."

"Will you tell him what will relieve him?" Boggs asked, pressing the matter.

"Oh yes, take a teaspoon full of sal soda, dissolve it in a pint of water, and let him drink it on going to bed and it will relieve him."

"I have not got the article about the house," interrupted Abigail Koons, who was still holding the baby in her lap. "Can you not give him something I have?"

"I will see," said King.

There was a longer silence this time, which prompted Abigail to guess that King was scouring the contents of the kitchen next door.

A couple of minutes later the voice came again: "Give him a bowl of mountain tea, or tea of pipsissewa."

"I have the pipsissewa," she replied.

"I know that," King said.

His prescription given, King bade the audience good-bye, wrapping up a session that had lasted 30 to 45 minutes.

The next morning Clark Williams awoke refreshed from a good night's sleep. The herbal tea that Abigail Koons had made him the night before, sometimes called wintergreen, had righted his stomach, and he spent part of Tuesday squirrel hunting with Nahum. Tuesday night's performance, however, was also expected to be another social chat, nothing like the spectacular effects of Sunday night.

On Tuesday evening a drowsy and probably distraught Jonathan Koons reported to the spirit room to host Williams and the other visitors. He had gone without sleep Monday night, tending to his nephew, who died before daybreak, and had worked all day Tuesday sowing wheat. Jonathan apparently did not take up the fiddle at all that night. After a few minutes of silence, he complained that King was slow in coming.

Finally King did arrive, chatting up the audience much as he had the night before but talking a bit longer, 45 minutes to an hour. Jonathan could not hold his eyes open and lay down on a bench, drifting off several times. Periodically King would yell, "Koons! Wake up, I will tell you an anecdote." As the program concluded, the entity enticed the audience with the promise of "a public exhibition tomorrow, Wednesday evening, if circumstances would permit." King also agreed to write a communication for Williams.

On Wednesday night the setup was much the same as for the past Sunday's demonstration, but no one was playing the other fiddle this time.

Jonathan played his as usual, but the second instrument remained on the table with invisible hands plucking the strings in the manner of picking a guitar. "There was a much greater variety of musical performance this evening than on Sunday evening," Williams recounted. "The drums were beat; tambourine played; and violin and harp. The sweetest music I ever heard to my ear was played this evening on the harp by the spirits alone, (viz.) no one in the body accompanying them."

After the music the ghostly hand appeared and seemed to take a special interest in Williams, teasing him by carrying the phosphorus-coated paper around the room, dropping it on the floor in front of him, and snatching it away as he bent down to pick it up. The hand came by on a second pass, again dropping the paper on the floor, but this time Williams was able to take the hand in his and feel it up to the wrist. The hand darted away without the paper, so Williams picked the sheet up and held it between his thumb and finger.

As the curious dance continued, the hand returned and took the paper, using its thumb and three fingers to secure it. "After this it came and shook hands with me the second time, letting me feel of the hand and arm, which I did to about half way to the elbow," Williams wrote. "I wished to get above the hand and arm, so as to say, as I have heard others say, that there was nothing above or beyond, but I did not; there was an arm as far as I felt, which was not to me as described by others—*cold,* but warm, rather warmer than that of a person in good health; it felt to me like a human hand somewhat feverish—dry and husky."

Williams's reverie was broken by the voice of the trumpet saying: "I cannot write to-night, leave paper and pencil on the table and I will try to write when you are gone." When the light was relit, the inquisitive visitor took a sheet of paper and scribbled on it, "Please write a communication for Clark Williams." The paper was left in the locked spirit room overnight, with Williams in possession of the key. The next morning he received a written message, purportedly from "the spirits of this room," which instructed him to publicize his experiences.

His quest completed, Williams left the Koons farm convinced of the authenticity of the demonstrations. That he felt a distinctly warm-blooded human-like hand in the dark did not seem to concern him, nor, apparently, did he entertain the possibility that there were extra keys to the spirit room door. Williams returned to Cincinnati and wrote an account for *Buchanan's Journal of Man*, having banished the specter of any "jugglery, sleight-of-hand, or trick."

Hayden returned to Boston and had his message from the spirits published in a spiritualist newspaper. He was evidently so impressed by what he had seen that he started a lecture tour to report the wonders of the Koons room, enlivening his presentation with diagrams and illustrations of what he had witnessed. "He has also a picture of that wonderful HAND in the process of writing . . . and besides these, he exhibits a picture of a *Spirit* in full form, which presented itself to beholders at that place. . . . All these are painted on large canvas so as to be distinctly seen by the whole audience," the *New Era* reported. Soon, eager listeners in Chelsea, Natick, Charlestown, Weymouth, and beyond would plunk down 10 cents each to hear of Koons's exploits.

THE ghostly hands that touched visitors—squeezing their hands and knees, whisking hats off their heads, carrying musical instruments, and even writing messages—were one of the strangest phenomena seen at the Koons cabin. But they were not peculiar to rural Dover Township, Ohio. Indeed, physical mediums in other locales were producing the same phenomenon, according to eyewitness accounts. One of the most famous of these mediums was Daniel Dunglas Home, who dazzled the nobility of Europe in the 1850s and beyond.

Home was born in Edinburgh, Scotland, in 1833 and emigrated to the United States with his aunt when he was about 9 years old. By the time he was 18, his apparent ability to create loud rappings and other poltergeist effects so distressed his aunt that she asked him to leave their residence in Troy, New York. Thus Home began his wanderings throughout the Northeast, where he attracted the attention of prominent spiritualists.

One of Home's first recorded séances took place in Springfield, Massachusetts, in early 1852, the same year that Jonathan Koons began his public demonstrations. Young Home astonished the circle by seemingly causing a table to move forcefully in different directions, pushing those seated around it back several feet. Next, the table levitated and remained suspended for several seconds. Finally, three participants sat on the table but could not restrain its movements. All the while the floor vibrated as if an earthquake or explosion were taking place.

After observing the phenomena on multiple occasions, the group, which included a Harvard professor and the poet (and editor of the New York *Evening Post*) William Cullen Bryant, issued a statement attesting to the wonders they had seen and their belief that no trickery was involved: "Mr. D. D. Home frequently urged us to hold his hands and feet. During these occurrences the room was well lighted, the lamp was frequently placed on or under the table, and every possible opportunity was afforded us for the closest inspection, and we admit this one emphatic declaration: *We know that we were not imposed upon nor deceived.*"

Upon moving to England in 1855, Home continued to win distinguished supporters, this time among the European aristocracy. Home's repertoire included several well-documented physical effects in addition to the table tipping; he was even said to handle hot coals without burning himself and to levitate not only pianos but his own body. It was not uncommon for an accordion to play when Home was holding it by the end—and sometimes when he wasn't holding it at all. At his séances hands—sometimes writing messages or carrying objects—would materialize in front of the sitters. Witnesses such as the British biologist Alfred Russel Wallace reported seeing a detached hand holding the accordion while the medium's hands were above the table.

Another sitter, the poet Elizabeth Barrett Browning, was present at Home's séance one evening when he directed such a hand to crown her with a wreath of flowers. As Home often conducted his demonstrations by lamplight, Browning was able to describe the image in a letter to her sister: "At the request of the medium, the spiritual hand took from the table a garland which lay there and placed it upon my head. The particular hand which did this was of the largest human size, as white as snow and very beautiful. It was as near to me as this hand I write with, and I saw it distinctly."

Home was extensively studied by the British physicist William Crookes, discoverer of the element thallium, who reported on his own encounters with the hands. On one occasion a hand ascended through a crack in a table and gave the eminent scientist a flower while Crookes restrained Home's hands and feet. The appendage "sometimes appears perfectly life-like and graceful, the fingers moving and the flesh apparently as human as that of any in the room," Crookes wrote. "At the wrist, or arm, it becomes hazy and fades off into a luminous cloud. To the touch the hand sometimes appears icy-cold and dead, at other times warm and life-like, grasping my own with the firm pressure of an old friend." When the physicist tried to hold on to the hand, it merely dissolved into vapor and faded away. Crookes's reports of these instances, however, were met with disdain by his colleagues, and his reputation as a scientist suffered as a result of his forays into the paranormal and his rumored dalliances with female mediums.

Home's reputation proved more resilient. Throughout a career spanning nearly 25 years, allegations of fraud were brought against him, but none was ever detected. A twenty-first-century biographer, Peter Lamont, concluded that "Home was a charlatan whose feats have never been adequately explained," while others argue that the phenomena were too elaborate to have been staged. In the nineteenth century Home's record was the gold standard against which other physical mediums' mettle would be tested. Back in the United States, the Koons family was able to produce the hands as well, but unlike Home's guides, the spirits at Mount Nebo demanded darkness, allowing only a glint of phosphorus to reveal their real-yet-phantom appendages. "'Light' must be the demand of every Spiritualist," Home wrote. "It is the single test necessary, and it is a test that can and must be given. By no other [means] are scientific inquirers to be convinced."

11

Sustaining "Brother Koons"

JUST AFTER Thanksgiving in 1854 the prominent head of a Buffalo, New York, firm paid a visit to the Koons and Tippie farms with three companions from New York City. The businessman, Stephen Dudley, had endured a two-day trip—first from Buffalo by train and then "seventy two miles of very unpleasant stage road" from Columbus—to reach the spirit room. Dudley was well known in Buffalo as a manufacturer and supplier of metallic items for steamboats and hotels. Cook stoves, steam and water gauges, railroad lanterns, and signal lamps all could be had from S. Dudley and Sons at 57 Main Street. The company's ad also offered a line of "planished table ware" "consisting of Coffee and Tea Urns, Steak and Fish heaters, Soup Tureens, Dish Covers, &c., &c., which we are constantly manufacturing in the most elegant style; and in beauty of finish unsurpassed by any other establishment in the United States." Besides Dudley's business acumen, a spiritualist newspaper observed that "high-toned moral sentiments and the most scrupulous regard to veracity are his prominent characteristics; and that his is not of the order of intellect which can be easily deceived, deluded, or stultified." Still, it was a matter of the heart that was most pressing to Dudley that fall: he was grieving the loss of his wife about a year before. He had come not only to witness the phenomena that were by then legendary in spiritualist circles but to find some evidence of her survival.

Traveling with Dudley were the acclaimed "test medium" J. B. Conklin of New York City and two women "who refuse to have their names published." The party arrived at the Koons farm on November 29 and tarried most of the day, inspecting the setup of the spirit room and getting to know the Koons family. "I spent several hours in listening to the conversation of Mr. K., whom I found a very intelligent man," Conklin wrote. About five in the afternoon he entered the spirit room with Nahum alone, hoping for a private audience with the spirits.

Conklin, who did not describe the lighting conditions, sat down at a table in the middle of the room with young Koons opposite. The trumpet was lying near the edge.

"Will the spirits speak to me in an audible voice?" Conklin asked.

The horn made a halting liftoff from the table, but instead of rising aloft it fell on the floor. When Conklin reached down to retrieve it, it was snatched from his hands and elevated just above his head.

"How do you do, Mr. C.? We are glad to see you," said a voice from the instrument.

Conklin felt a flutter of air across his face. He talked with the voice for several minutes, satisfied that he was in touch with a spirit. The trumpet floated in the air near his head the whole time. Though Conklin, as a medium himself, was a veteran of the séance, he could not figure out what was holding up the horn. More wonders awaited at the evening circle.

When the time for the seven o'clock séance came, Jonathan Koons graciously provided his out-of-town guests with good seats in the spirit room, reserving for Conklin and Dudley an honored place at the mediums' table. Dudley surmised that many of the guests lived nearby and that a majority were skeptical of what they were about to see. "It was a very inharmonious party," Dudley later wrote, "but the spirits did all they promised to do." After a short lecture by Koons in the darkened room, Dudley was amazed by the cannon-like boom of the bass drum, which signaled the arrival of the spirit band. "Then commenced what seemed to be the charging, by the spirits, of the electrical apparatus. . . . In this charging, the large table, on which the apparatus stood, shook like a tree in a gale of wind."

Next came the musical performance. As Koons played his violin, a second violin that had been placed on the mediums' table played an accompaniment, as did other instruments. Soon spectral voices joined in. "I think if anything can give an idea of heaven on earth, it must be such music as was made by that angelic band," Dudley recalled. "At the same time there was a most extraordinary exhibition of Spiritual pyrotechnics, seeming to consist of flying insects made of fire, which, in their motions, kept time with the music."

After the public circle had ended, Dudley and Nahum Koons returned to the spirit room for a private consultation. Unlike Conklin's appointment, this time the horn navigated without a glitch. When Nahum laid the trumpet on the table, it immediately levitated to head height and bade them good evening. Dudley asked the spirits whether his wife, father, and other deceased relatives were present. He was assured that they were. The trumpet told Dudley that it was his wife who had placed a tambourine in his lap during the circle that night. And although he had already touched a lifelike spirit hand and witnessed what appeared to be glowing insects whizzing around the room, Dudley told them that he desired to see even more evidence of their power. The spirits promised they would supply it "if all things were favorable." When asked to explain the cryptic comment, the trumpet replied that it wanted "a harmonious circle, and not such an one as we had previously that evening."

The next night a select group assembled in the spirit room: Jonathan and Abigail Koons and Nahum along with Dudley, his friend Conklin, the two female companions, and two unnamed gentlemen. Dudley was seated between Jonathan and Conklin on one side of the mediums' table. During a lull in the musical part of the program, Dudley asked the spirits to write for him. He had come prepared, with his own paper and pencil, which were directly in front of him on the table. Such a precaution would prevent the mediums from substituting paper that already had a message written on it. "The paper which we took with us was printing paper, unsized and unruled, and unlike any other paper that was there, or in that part of the country," Dudley reported. The spirits were to write with a "Fleesheim's Buffalo pencil" that he provided.

At once a luminous hand holding a pencil appeared over the paper and began to write. With the visitors hovering nearby, it scribbled faster than Dudley thought any human being could. Conklin leaned in so close that his face was nearly over top of the moving pencil, which suddenly reared up and struck him in the nose. The jab "gave him such a start that his head flew up as if the pencil had been sharpened at the upper end," Dudley wrote with some amusement. Soon both sides of the sheet were full, and the hand returned the paper—now folded—to Dudley, who later determined it was the same one he had brought from Buffalo. The hand proceeded around the room and shook the hands of all séance participants except one man who was too scared to touch it.

After the session was over and everyone except Nahum had gone, Dudley again tried to complete his mission. He believed his wife's spirit wished to communicate with him. The shade "tried to converse with me through the trumpet, but did not succeed," Dudley later reported. "Thereupon the presiding spirit apologized for her failure, and proffered to speak for her, which he did, giving her language, and we conversed for some ten or fifteen minutes. I can not express the gratification which this interview gave me, nor is it necessary that I should attempt it."

Stephen Dudley returned to Buffalo not only with this boon from the spirits but with their instructions to publish the writing the hand had given him. He submitted the message to the hometown *Age of Progress* but kept the original. It was part sermon, part cheerleading to workers in the field, and a veiled warning of things to come. With a swipe at two pillars of society, the spirits explained their purpose in inhabiting the spirit room: "We have labored, now, some considerable time in this place, to produce something more tangible and philosophical than the manifestations of the M.D.'s and D.D.'s of the world, for the elevation of mankind." The spirits' aim was to free individuals of doubt and fear about their future existence, to help people realize their potential for eternal self-improvement. "For when the proper knowledge of Man's own constitutional nature is once established, so as to enable him to know himself," their message continued, "the tyranny of superstitious fears can no longer enslave the mind."

But the spirits hinted that their largesse was not quite unconditional. "Yes, friends, was it not for the debt of love we owe our friends of earth, we would not labor in this great cause of reform and redemption of man; and how much longer we may be enabled to conduct our manifestations to this purpose and end, in this place, is a matter unsettled with us, as it depends upon the patience and perseverance of our mediums in this circle," they concluded. The extent of the mediums' endurance would depend in turn on the support of those who benefited from their revelations. How long such matters would remain unsettled was anybody's guess.

✳   ✳   ✳

A businessman from Sandusky, Ohio, having finished up his affairs at Chauncey, perchanced to call at the door of Jonathan Koons late on a November afternoon. Upon gaining admittance the businessman and his companion instantly realized that their timing could not have been worse. It had been hog-slaughtering day at the Koons farm, and parts of the butchered animal filled every corner of the cabin. The visitors could see that the family was exhausted. Although it was only about 6:00 p.m., some were heading off to bed while others dozed on chairs in the crowded interior. There would be no hoedowns played in the spirit room this evening. The spirits would not be invoked. Perhaps it was only politeness that kept Jonathan Koons from dismissing the callers out of hand.

The conversation was awkward at first, but Koons warmed to the task as the businessman—who later told of his experiences in a letter to the *Christian Spiritualist* that he signed "an Inquirer"—steered the talk toward spiritual matters, first contemporary and then ancient. From obscure biblical topics the two moved on to discuss geology, astronomy, chemistry, and physics, in all of which the host seemed remarkably conversant. "I was surprised . . . to find him so well posted in the conclusions of science," the Inquirer wrote. "In each department I inquired what books he had read, and he invariably answered, 'All I know on this subject is taught me by the spirits.'" Koons and the Inquirer went on to speak of the origins of the solar system, the progression of Earth through various geologic ages, and the evolution of the animal kingdom. Often Koons would preface his own remarks by saying, "They tell me," an apparent reference to his spirit guides.

> [Koons said] that in this and this period such and such animals
> existed, the monsters of the sea, of the air and the land, and
> frequently remarking, in considering a particular era in the earth's
> progress, that animals of a subsequent period did not then exist,
> because the conditions necessary to their existence did not then
> prevail. Thus he brought us down to the present or human period
> on the earth. He affirms the vegetable origin of coal, and spoke
> of the magnificent flora of that period, and the great mammals of
> the tertiary period. He then spoke of the effects of light on organic
> matter, of the universal diffusion of electricity and its importance
> in the economy of the universe. Then he discussed the nebular

hypothesis, affirming, as I understood, that one whole galaxial system was from a single nebula, which had condensed into suns, planets and satellites. His want of a scientific nomenclature made him somewhat obscure in this part of the discussion. He said that Spirits of different nebulae did not associate together until they had become archangels or seraphs in the spheres. Many of his positions in physics were in conflict with those of the present conclusions of science, but in almost every case he gave a reason for the difference, accompanied with such facts as made his difference probable.

By the close of the evening astonishment had turned to inspiration as the Inquirer reflected on Koons's vision of the universe: "As I heard him discussing these great subjects, blending the Spiritual with the Natural, and teaching the unity and harmony of God's works, I could not but reflect that such a scene might have been presented near two thousand years ago on the shores of the Sea of Galilee." The Inquirer imagined himself a time traveler at the feet of Jesus, listening to him amid the rank odors of a fisherman's hut: "Desirous to hear the great truths which He uttered, he [the traveler] would be oblivious to the odor and filth of the place, and his whole soul would be absorbed in the sublime contemplation of his own nature, and his relation to the future and to his Creator."

The Inquirer and his companion spent the night in the smelly log cabin, leaving the Koons family asleep the next morning. As the pair negotiated the path down from Mount Nebo, they may have taken a second look at the ground beneath their feet, which Koons had said was webbed with minerals that produced an active electrical field—a force believed favorable to spirit communication. The Koonses were in their element, rooted in this locale, but so were their persecutors. The Inquirer would both tell the world about his visit and try to undo some of the monetary damage caused by the burning of the Koonses' barn. The businessman came away from Athens County with a vision for the Koons ministry, if only enough people would join him.

BY 1854 the Koons farm was becoming a way station for mediums looking for fellowship or inspiration. One such seeker was Abraham P. Pierce of

Philadelphia, who traveled throughout much of the eastern and southern United States at the spirits' command, becoming entranced for hours or days on end as they wished. After a satisfying visit at the Koons Spirit Room, he and Jonathan Koons accepted an invitation from Jonathan's friend David Fulton to travel about 9 miles to his home in Amesville to conduct a circle there. They were accompanied by John Tippie Jr. and his son, along with a small cadre of followers. But a storm socked them in soon after their arrival at Fulton's. Unable to travel, the mediums instead held a series of séances over three days, in which they had "fine manifestations" and "many visitors attending." When the weather cleared, Pierce and two friends headed back toward the Ohio River, conducting circles in small villages along the way.

The wandering missionary must have made an impression on Koons, for some time later, when Pierce was at a low ebb of conflict and self-doubt regarding his ministry, an envelope from Koons arrived at his home. Inside was a message from the spirit guide King:

> *To A. P. Pierce:* We know your labor and your anxiety. By the favor of Heaven you will be protected. Salvation belongs to the *lost;* to those who are lost and astray in the wilderness of doubts and fears of meeting with an *angry God.* . . . Truth is eternal and must prevail, yet the seed of truth must first be incorporated in . . . the human family. So press onward in your Heavenly mission. . . . Sooner or later we will again hail you to the spirit room, where we can speak to you face to face, and give you a heavenly repast.

✻ ✻ ✻

UPON his return to Sandusky, the businessman calling himself the Inquirer was still dazzled by the backwoods philosopher he had found in Athens County. In his letter to the *Christian Spiritualist* in New York City he outlined his plan:

> I would suggest that [we] build him a house, in which his large family and the numerous visitors who are constantly going thither, may be accommodated; $2,000 would, with his labors, build a large house that would accommodate ten to fifteen visitors and furnish it. Erect a frame house, 44 x 30, with the dining room and kitchen

in the basement. The first floor to be divided into a suite of family rooms and a parlor. The upper floor may be divided into eight bed-rooms for guests. A housekeeper could be provided to take charge of the guests' apartments, so as not to impose any additional duties or labors upon the family, all of whom are mediums. Attic chambers might be added to give additional room. Stone and building materials are abundant here, and if 1,000 persons will contribute two dollars apiece, the work can be accomplished and no one burdened.—AN INQUIRER

The Inquirer's words found fertile ground. Jonathan Koons's tireless labors had not gone unnoticed in the spiritualist movement. After three years in the spotlight, he had come to be regarded as one of the most pre-cious assets of the new religion in the United States. Hundreds of people had witnessed the manifestations and left with the conviction that they were genuine. Not only did this Ohio farmer open his home day and night to strangers seeking enlightenment, he steadfastly refused to charge ad-mission to the séances, even while the Fox sisters were said to be bringing in $100 per day. "I reasoned with Mr. K. on the impropriety of his course," wrote David Fulton, who had urged Koons to reconsider the wisdom of providing free meals and lodging. "His reply was, 'there were so many skeptics in the country, that if he should charge, they would immediately say he had designed it as a money speculation.'"

Adding to Koons's bona fides was the oppression he had endured—the torching of his barn and crops in December 1852. The *Christian Spiritualist* noted in January 1855 that "it is intimated that the Methodists of Athens County, Ohio, where Mr. Koons lives, are responsible for this persecution." Although the Methodists may not have burned down the barn themselves, the article acknowledged, "some of the 'baser sort' have been worked upon and made the instruments of doing the 'dirty work' of sectarianism." If the Methodists were proved to have been the instigators, "what a deep and damning shame it will be for a denomination calling itself PROTES-TANT and *Christian* to be forced to the humiliating confession . . . that it has outraged every law, human and divine, in its *insane* desire to oppose *what it does not like.*"

Koons's friends at the *Christian Spiritualist* had already been discussing the idea of financial support for the medium—aid deemed long overdue.

Just as other religions paid missionaries in the field, so could they. The paper's publisher, a group called the Society for the Diffusion of Spiritual Knowledge (SDSK), boasted as officers such notables as the former Wisconsin governor Nathaniel Tallmadge, but Horace H. Day, the paper's editor and vice president of SDSK, provided the real motive power behind the society. Day was a wealthy industrialist—widely known as the Rubber King of New York—who was then wrangling with Charles Goodyear over patents for vulcanized rubber. In addition to funding the *Christian Spiritualist's* print operations, Day had hired mediums at the New York City office to interact with the public free of charge. Given that he was already spending about $25,000 a year on the SDSK, an investment in home construction in rural Ohio would have strained the bounds of Day's beneficence.

Rather than funding Koons from the coffers of the SDSK, the leadership of the *Christian Spiritualist* quickly latched onto the Inquirer's plan and began seeking donations from readers: "It is proposed that 1,000 names be obtained, each signer to pay the sum of *two* dollars, so as to raise two thousand, and present it to Mr. Koons, so that he may build him not only a barn, but a *home,* large and ample enough to accommodate the many visitors that go from the East and elsewhere to see the wonders of the 'Spirit Rooms.'" The editors suggested circulating a pledge drive throughout the spiritualist communities of Boston, New York, and Philadelphia to raise money for the Koonses by early spring. They went on to say that Jonathan had no advance knowledge of the public campaign they were launching on his behalf.

Fulton also called on readers of the *Christian Spiritualist* to support the project, noting that he and other local supporters had not been able to raise enough money to sustain the family:

> After the disgraceful event of burning his barn was enacted, an
> effort was made by some friends of the cause, to raise something
> for the support of the family for the time being, but it was soon
> found to be an uphill business, as the friends who dared to come
> out openly and acknowledge the cause were few in number,
> and the good old theological christians were not very friendly
> toward supporting a man who was "humbugging" the people and
> building collusion with the devil. Had he been disposed (like many
> in the East) to have taken advantage of the times and used his

opportunity for the sake of gain, he might have accumulated his thousands long before this time.

Koons must have been genuinely amazed to open his January 6 copy of the *Christian Spiritualist* and see the announcement of the fund drive. "I need not tell you my astonishment, mingled with the gratitude I felt as I read the communication of *An Inquirer*, in relation to myself and situation," he wrote to the newspaper. "It is impossible to put my feelings upon this subject on paper. . . . I leave it with you and the friends of progress."

But in a letter written soon after to a supporter in Cincinnati, Koons revealed misgivings about the plan to build him a spacious home and even supply a housekeeper to take care of his guests. He hinted that there could be strings attached to such a generous gift.

> You seem to rejoice in seeing a move in my behalf. Truly, the
> friends who set it on foot deserve our highest regards although it
> was done without my counsel or advice. The proposition is not
> enviable on our part, so far as the place [peace?] and quiet comfort
> of this life are concerned. When, however, we come to behold
> the sad and lamentable condition of our fellow mortals who are
> hungering and thirsting for the spiritual food and drink, which is
> received here, we cannot do otherwise than yield to the wishes of
> friends and spirits. We are aware that great burthens will fall on us
> under such license as the afforded aid presupposes.

The supporter, identified only as "a friend of fair play," sent Koons's letter to a Cleveland newspaper with an appeal for donations.

About a month into the fund-raising campaign, the *Christian Spiritualist* reported that some money had been collected—and five-dollar pledges promised—but the newspaper did not give any specifics. It steered readers' attention to the ongoing drive with the plaintive comment, "Shall Br. Koons be sustained in his mission of good, that he may be the instrument of converting thousands in the South and West?"

Three of Koons's supporters in Athens County wrote to the paper urging all "friends of reform" to donate. E. C. Porter, Seth Fuller, and Azariah Pratt outlined Koons's plight in the most forceful terms: though wildly popular with his visitors, he had been denounced by the public and subjected to "all manner of unkind things and abuse" since he began the public demonstrations more than two years earlier. "The man has been unfortunate. He is poor. His lodgings are unfit for any kind of comfortable accommodations," they wrote. "His barn was a good one, but this has been entirely destroyed, together with a year's crop, and the small amount of funds laid up for improvements about his house, were expended in providing the necessaries of life for his family and visitors. . . . The man must be sustained, and the cause sustained; and if we do not come up and do something, the phenomena here must cease."

A few weeks after his return from the Koons farm, Stephen Dudley, the Buffalo businessman, sought to put the piece of writing he had obtained from the spirit room to the test. Along with his friends Joshua R. Giddings, a member of Congress and vocal abolitionist from Ohio, and the trance speaker Emma Jay, Dudley paid a call on Jennie E. Kellog in New York City. Kellog was a psychometric medium, one who was said to be able to handle objects and tell of their origin. Dudley had seen the spirit hand scribble out the message to him with amazing speed. Now he deliberately avoided any mention of the source of the document or who had signed it.

Dudley tucked the paper into a fresh envelope and handed it to Kellog. Becoming entranced, she pointed upward and began to speak in a dramatic fashion: "A person of great might and—a power unknown. I can not compare him to anyone on earth. . . . I behold a sea of light extending everywhere . . . I'll call it a divine light. . . . It really seems to me this writing fell from Heaven untouched by mortal hands."

Now it was Jay's turn. The form of the message writer, she believed, was human but "developed to gigantic proportions. . . . He does not seem to be of earth, but to belong to another race of beings whose spiritual growth has continued for ages. . . . Could you once gaze on that being in all his transcendent beauty, you would value life as never before, and be quickened and strengthened to go forward to your immortality."

The ancient and wise King, grand master of the Koons circle, could not have said it better himself.

12

The Mesmeric Potion

ON A Sunday night in January 1855, Abigail Koons sat entranced, eyes unfocused, her mind combing the landscape of a faraway place. Her hand clasped that of a guest who was silently entreating her to visit his friend who was lying sick back home. How the preacher's daughter became acquainted with mesmerism is not known, although she and Jonathan may have taught themselves through their own private researches. And on this occasion it was Jonathan who had guided his wife into the hypnotic state.

When Abigail began to speak, she supposedly revealed the length of the friend's illness, laid out the prognosis, and offered a prescription. "I was perfectly surprised at the accuracy with which this old lady described the place, rooms, furniture, etc., with which I knew it was impossible for her to be acquainted," the pilgrim reported. "The general details, indeed, of my friend's malady were as truthfully described as if I had spoken them myself." Abigail's purpose accomplished, Koons brought his wife out of the trance by "reversing the motions by which he produced it."

Some healing mediums offered their cures in exchange for one dollar and a lock of the patient's hair, but Abigail Koons shared hers without charge. Although the visitor described her as an old lady, the 43-year-old Abigail, mother of an infant son, may well have been at the height of her powers.

* * *

AS early as the 1780s researchers in France had discovered that hypnotized subjects were able to display surprising abilities unknown to them in their ordinary lives. One of those abilities they eventually termed *clear seeing,* or clairvoyance—the power to view events at another place or time. For hundreds of years the common folk had had their own version of clairvoyance in the form of wise men and women, purveyors of the second sight. Even those without the gift could, on special occasions and through special rituals, call forth visions; for instance, on a late January night, the eve of the feast of St. Agnes, young maidens who performed certain rites before bedtime were assured to dream of their future husbands. But the so-called mesmerists, followers of the German-born physician Anton Mesmer, sought to put such mental phenomena on a more scientific footing and to harness them for healing, not just divination. They used hypnosis, or magnetizing, not only to treat their patients but sometimes to turn the patients into healers themselves. Some investigators believed that these gifted patients could use clairvoyance to look inside the bodies of others and make uncannily accurate diagnoses. Locks of hair, clothing worn near the stomach, or even something written by the sufferer could aid in the process.

The Frenchman Charles Poyen brought hypnosis to the United States in the 1830s, popularizing the practice through lectures and teaching it to physicians and medical students in Boston. Poyen soon teamed up with a textile mill worker from Rhode Island who displayed a talent for medical clairvoyance and successfully toured New England with her. After his return to France his American disciples carried on the work; within a few years Boston alone had 200 mesmerists. Mesmerism rapidly spread to Ohio and by the 1840s had become a form of popular entertainment, with eager audiences paying admittance to traveling shows.

The idea of consulting a clairvoyant for medical advice must have seemed much more plausible to the nineteenth-century mind than to the contemporary reader's. The line separating regular doctors and unconventional ones was much blurrier, and in the years leading up to the Civil War, medical practice of all types was largely unregulated. Moreover, nineteenth-century physicians sometimes inflicted harsh treatments upon their patients—prescribing toxic mercury compounds or opium- and alcohol-laced tonics, even draining their blood. Some doctors used homeopathy, but that did not always cure. For the desperately ill "religious or mental healing offered a rational alternative," the author Ann Braude writes. She further explains:

> "Medical mediums" and "clairvoyant physicians," most of them women, appeared throughout the country, offering an attractive choice of treatment for consumers of medical care. Some examined patients in trance, dispensing remedies prescribed by spirit doctors. Others healed through the laying on of hands charged with spirit forces, while still others used the clairvoyant state to see inside the diseased body. Spiritualism adopted from mesmerism the notion that entranced individuals could heal disease. But while mesmerism attributed the healing agency enabled by trance to a universal mesmeric fluid, Spiritualists transformed the healing trance into a form of mediumship.

When Jonathan began hypnotizing Abigail is not clear, although he seems to have engaged in self-hypnosis or deep meditation for years, allowing his mind to paint pictures on "visionary canvases." Through his writings he clearly stated his belief in mesmeric influence on both animals and people. "There are persons in my knowledge, who can exercise a magnetic influence over a dog, so that he will forsake his own master, and follow the operator in defiance of all the owner can do or say. They can also in a very few minutes exercise an influence on a horse, or colt, no matter how wild or fractious they may be, so that a child can lead or handle them." In his youth these charmers were often denounced as witches and wizards, but Koons now preferred to think of them as mediums through whom the spirits—some base and some exalted—chose to operate.

In his autobiography Koons related a story about two friends—one a believer and one a skeptic—who were discussing the subject of animal charming. The skeptic had two bulldogs guarding his home—animals so fierce that they would fight to the death to protect his life and property. The idea that any mental force could subdue them was simply incredible.

To prove his point, the dog owner cast forth a challenge to the believer, who was visiting his home: "Here I have a splendid melon patch joining my back yard, and I will agree to give you all the melons without charge that you can obtain after nine o'clock this evening."

"I am not in the habit of hooking melons," the other replied, "but if I can convince you in any reasonable manner, I will do it."

Between nine and ten o'clock that night, a knock was heard at the skeptic's door. The family was astonished to see the believer standing there, with no warning given by the dogs. "Where are your 'life guards' lodged tonight?" he asked.

The owner rushed to the backyard in search of his pets. He found them tied together by the tails with a small cord—one dog on each side of the melon patch fence. The skeptic would have to forfeit his prized crop.

In dissecting the case later, Koons guessed that the believer, obviously a charmer himself, had somehow "gain[ed] a magnetic control" over the animals during his daytime visit to the house, clearing the way for his return that night. Although this tale revealed a harmless and amusing show of force by the mesmerist, Koons pointed out that such powers can take a darker turn if not used wisely: "The principle of magnetism, psychology, and spirit correspondence, i.e., influx, may be considered the chief impellents in the productions of the mysterious wonders of all ages; yet, to say either or any of them are free from misapplication or abuse, would be preposterous in the extreme. . . . If the most refined and elevated seraph that flies the heavens was to offer an attempt at the elevation of the human family through a treacherous and debauched medium, he must inevitably fail."

* * *

PUSEY Graves had come all the way from his home in Fulton County, Illinois, to find out what lay behind the mysterious phenomena at the Koons farm. Now 41, he had arrived on the Koonses' doorstep by a circuitous route that led through many of the countercultural movements of the mid-nineteenth century. Reared in a Quaker home in Indiana, Graves as a young man concluded that the way the world worked was "fundamentally wrong." Thus began his quest to achieve a more equal and just society.

In 1836 he married Jane Witchell, a Hicksite Quaker whose parents held unorthodox views. A decade later he, Jane, and his in-laws joined a new communal farm in Randolph County, Indiana. The group had taken out a mortgage for the property, expecting to pay for the farm and have a surplus in the first year. But as Graves's son Charles later slyly reported in a biographical sketch of his father,

> One year was sufficient to make the demonstration. Human nature proved to be the same among these enthusiastic philanthropists that it had been for centuries before. The hard work and drugery was done by a few of the more enthusiastic members of this modern family while the more intellectual members sat in the shade or by the fire and expounded the true philosophy of human life to each other. Those who labored least and talked most were ready to select the best from what was produced for their own use and they always sat at the first table.

The farm went under, but the experience did not sour Graves on new ideas. At one point he fell under the sway of Grahamism, a dietary reform movement that emphasized the consumption of whole grains and chemical-free foods. More a lifestyle than a diet, Grahamism urged followers of the Reverend Sylvester Graham to avoid not only meat and white bread but alcohol and spices. Graves placed his family on a strict vegan diet, but this experiment—like the previous one—did not last. First eggs and milk were permitted, then fish and poultry, and finally they abandoned the diet altogether.

Beyond these personal concerns Graves's conscience was touched by the larger issues of the day. Deeply offended by slavery, he refused to use any product created by slave labor. Graves had once run for Congress on the antislavery ticket, but the citizenry remained unpersuaded, greeting him with "sneers, curses and stale eggs." Nonetheless he remained a staunch abolitionist whose home in Indiana had become a station for slaves escaping on the Underground Railroad.

A free thinker on religious matters as well, he came to believe that the Quaker faith was too outmoded to address concerns of social justice. Laying down the old religion, Graves dabbled in mesmerism. He got hold of a sensational new book by the medium Andrew Jackson Davis that was said to have been dictated while Davis was "under mesmeric influence and in a clairvoyant condition." First published in 1847, the tome was titled *The Principles of Nature, Her Divine Revelations and a Voice to Mankind.* The book's message was so shocking that Graves feared persecution from his neighbors just for having a copy. He invited "a few kindred spirits" to his house, where they read from the book aloud—but in hushed tones—in an upstairs room behind shuttered windows.

In the 800-page volume the unlettered Davis laid out his grand vision of the universe with remarkable eloquence, providing a basis for what later became known as the harmonial philosophy. According to the author Slater Brown, Davis "expounded a belief in universal and eternal progress; a faith in reason and nature, in the predominance of spirit as the cause of all things; and an assured hope in the future regeneration of mankind." Although Davis described God as the great creative force in the universe, many Christians considered *Divine Revelations* heretical because it did not acknowledge the divinity of Jesus and blamed many of the world's ills on the clergy. Davis's work deeply affected Graves, who became unsettled on religious questions. It was Graves's search for truth that had led the former California gold miner in January 1855 to a remote homestead in the Ohio woods, where Jonathan Koons was said to espouse the harmonial philosophy.

On the first evening Graves carefully inspected the Koons Spirit Room and, finding no evidence of chicanery, went on to enjoy a delightful musical program. Besides checking out the validity of the man he called Brother Koons, Graves had another reason for his odyssey. Long mistrustful of allopathic medicine, he was searching for unconventional medical advice for his ailing wife, Jane, who did not make the journey but sent a letter that may have described her condition.

On Saturday morning Abigail Koons fell into a trance to examine the case. She told Graves that one of the spirits had dictated a prescription for his wife. The recipe appears to be for a type of poultice to be used on the skin: They were to boil yellow root, sage leaves, and spring bark in water to make a concentrate. "Then strain and add a lump of alum and borax each the size of a large bean and a lump of virdigris as big as 2 beans," the recipe continued. "Apply twice a day[;] wash once a day with fine soap and rainwater." The entity, speaking through Abigail Koons, told Graves that the entire band of spirits would examine the recipe at their next meeting, to see if any alterations would be needed. Graves wrote down the recipe and left it in the spirit room for their inspection.

On Saturday evening the spirits again visited, this time adding writing to their demonstrations. As Graves recalled, "The Spirits began to rustle some sheets of paper that Mr. Braffit and I had put on the back table and had put a secret mark on it so that we know the paper was not changed. We left our pencils with the paper and directly two hands brought out each a sheet of paper onto the outer table and the two hands commenced writing about two feet apart." Graves was amazed to see that they wrote four separate messages in less than three minutes, including one to him by the spirit of his late mother, which he found to be "an exact simile of her hand writing."

During the Sunday night séance Graves took up some unfinished business: Had the spirits reviewed the prescription revealed to Abigail Koons the day before? The voice said they had, and that no changes were needed. Still, Graves pressed on with his agenda. In his pocket was a letter from a friend back home who wanted to present the Koons spirits with a test. The missive probably contained questions that only the writer of the letter—or someone with occult knowledge—could answer. But as Graves later recounted, the spirits demurred: "Then the spirit said (all the time talking through the trumpet) the spirit band of this room have consulted together and came to the conclusion not to answer such tests[,] for our mission to earth is to bring man into harmony with himself and into harmony with his brother and with his God or into harmony with the laws of nature." After a 10- to 15-minute exhortation, the voice said, "We will now lay away the horn, and answer your questions by rapping."

Soon the hands appeared, luminous as a result of rubbing against some phosphorus-laden sandpaper that Koons had provided. For yes they would rap their knuckles on the table, and for no they would rub their fingers back and forth across it.

"Is my father present?'
Rap. Rap. Rap.
"Was it he who wrote to me last evening?"
Rub.
"Was it Mother?'
Rap. Rap. Rap.
"Will my father shake hands with me?'
Rap. Rap. Rap.
A shining hand came forward and grasped his. Graves thought it was as real as any hand he had ever shaken.

"Now will the spirit of my father, to remove the last glimmer of a doubt, show me his hand plain and distinct?"

It came to within 18 inches of his face and remained about a minute. Graves's father had a peculiar hand, the son well remembered. "And I can affirm that was my father's hand and [indecipherable: no?] mistake he conversed with me by the rapping for some time," he later wrote.

Graves left the Koons home with his expectations met—the angelic musical performances, intercourse with shades who bore unmistakable marks of his parents, and a prescription for his wife, Jane. The visit evidently made an impression on him because he took the time to record it in a private journal that would survive for more than 150 years. It is not clear whether Jane ever used the prized remedy he had traveled to Ohio to get, but she would live until 1877—more than two decades after the spirits had divulged the healing potion through the mesmerized Abigail Koons.

Yet Pusey Graves did not remain a spiritualist, if he ever truly was one. Spiritualism was one port of call on his voyage through eternity. His son Charles recorded that late in life, having survived Jane and taken a second wife, Graves returned to the faith of his fathers. Before he died in 1899 in Kansas, well-regarded for a distinguished career of public service, he found his "chief pleasure" as a Bible teacher in the Society of Friends.

13

Not One Single Copper

AROUND THE time of Pusey Graves's visit, two Canadian pilgrims, Mr. and Mrs. E. V. Wilson, arrived at the Koons farm after eight days of travel. The unusually mild winter weather had made the interval a pleasant one. The last leg of the trip—250 miles by steamer on the Ohio—had taken them from Cincinnati to the little river town of Pomeroy. Thence they had journeyed overland to Athens, about 20 miles distant, and found their way to the Koons property. Jonathan greeted them before they could even step out of their buggy. To their surprise, he already knew their names and where they had come from.

E. V. Wilson, who was a mesmerist himself and an inspirational speaker, harbored a great curiosity about Jonathan Koons, scrutinizing the man who had become such a legend in spiritualist circles. Wilson would later write: "Mr. K. himself is about forty-eight years of age [actually about 43] and wears a long beard, which gives him a most patriarchal appearance, his exterior is rough, and though intelligent, is possessed of but a very limited education. His religious views are at present of the Harmonial or Davis school, formerly he was an infidel." Despite his lack of formal education, Koons was no doubt a literate person. During Wilson's stay he observed "the old man" engaged in extensive correspondence: "His answers [to letters] are all given through spiritual impression and those only are answered that he is directed to reply to by the spirits. His knowledge of Spiritualism is extensive, yet I cannot say that I agree with all his views respecting this subject."

Wilson also recorded his impressions of the rest of the Koons family. In 17-year-old Nahum—universally described as the principal medium—Wilson found "a tall, spare, and pale youth, with an unhealthy complexion, light hair, eyes hazel, or nearly so. In character and disposition he is a simple child of nature, honest, confiding, and trusting, yet in possession of a power through spirit assistance that few have been favoured with since the days of the prophets." When Nahum fell ill with a cold, chills, and severe headache, Wilson placed him in a hypnotic state for half an hour, suggesting that the pain go away. When the young man awakened feeling much better, the visitor declared Nahum to be "one of the best psychological subjects that I ever met with." Nahum's mother, Abigail, was noted to be both clairvoyant and clairaudial. The other nine children, though reputed to be mediums, appeared ordinary to Wilson and gave no outward evidence of special powers.

Like many other visitors before him, Wilson was struck by the unwavering courtesy of a family living in a space ill equipped to host large numbers of guests. "The house and every thing about it denote the unthrifty farmer, and is both untidy and uncomfortable," he reported, "yet the hospitality of the family is unbounded, all being anxious on our arrival to render us as comfortable as circumstances would permit, and all without the slightest idea or expectation of reward, in fact *they will not receive money* for any of their attentions to the visitors with which their house is constantly thronged" (emphasis added).

ALTHOUGH many visitors were flabbergasted and mystified by the audible wonders in Koons's dark room, others believed to possess psychic powers of their own reported actually seeing the spirits at work. One of those was Wilson, who witnessed a spirit performance in which he saw King wearing a bright star on his forehead and leading a band of seven other entities. King's spirit followers ranged from 18 inches to 3 feet tall and had black faces and long, straight hair. Their features were human-like and their eyes were "bright, mild and expressive of much intelligence."

At a signal from King, one wraith began charging the spirit machine with electricity, although Wilson did not explain how this was done. In his account one spirit took up a post by the bass drum and another by the tenor, while the others fanned out in a row between the machine and the wall. King sat or stood alone on the table. As Jonathan Koons began to play the fiddle, the ghostly visitors accompanied him on the drums, triangle, tambourine, harmonica, accordion, and horn. Not satisfied with instrumentals, sometimes the band would sing spirituals with minimal accompaniment. "And then was played one of the most difficult of Beethoven's pieces, and played on a common accordion, harmonica and tin horn, accompanied by four spirit voices," Wilson recalled. "This chant or song seemed to be one of praise, dedicated to God."

Another account by an unnamed séance participant found the little sprites quite boisterous, more like feisty leprechauns than 10,000-year-old spiritual guides. As the visitor bent over a piece of phosphorized paper, a ghastly hand suddenly appeared in front of his face. What followed seemed more like a comedy act than a séance.

"Some waggish spirit then commenced humming on the 'harmonicon' in the farther corner of the hut, under the beams," the visitor related. "The hand immediately grabbed the phosphorus paper and flashed with it through the air to the spot occupied by the performer. The noise was instantly stopped and the hand darted back again" under the man's nose. The riff was repeated twice more, as the music would start up again in a different corner and then under the table. "Nothing more was heard of the 'harmonicon' individual," the report continued. "The owner of the hand had probably strangled him to death. That little family quarrel having been settled, the hand came back, took up a pencil and wrote a communication on some general topic."

Such whimsy offered up an easy target for the mainstream press. Scribes at the *Wooster Republican* delighted in skewering spiritualism, pointing to these especially outlandish elements of the movement: "A little army of spirits giggling and laughing, looking on and poking one another in the ribs to give vent to their mirth! Who could imagine any exhibition, better calculated to occupy the attention and time, of serious candid and sober men and women? And who [could] fancy or even imagine any belief better qualified to take the place of the Christians? Verily here is a splendid substitute!"

Even the sprites' ruler, King, seemed to thrive on the slapstick humor that January of 1855. At one séance he turned his attention to J. G. Brice, a spiritualist lecturer based in New Orleans.

"Brice, I like you," King said, "and we would like to have you up in heaven. Koons, I wish that I had a rope, I would put it around Brice, and take him up to heaven with me tonight."

"I am ready and will go," Brice gamely replied.

King then repeated his call for Koons to bring a rope. Another medium in the audience hastily intervened. "King, had you not better let him remain a little longer to blow the spiritual trumpet?" he suggested.

"Well," King said, "I do not know but I had better do so. Yes, I had, I will not take him tonight."

GEORGE L. Barnard, a Boston merchant returning from a week at the Koons Spirit Room, not only had been converted but had left inspired, now possessing a "joyful confidence in a glorious immortality." He marveled at the lack of venality involved in the whole setup. "Visitors are admitted to the room free of charge, that being one essential condition on which the spirits consent to operate," explained the *Age of Progress*. Now he would build his own tabernacle, having been "assured by the intelligences who communicated at Mr. Koons' room, that if he [the merchant] will afford them suitable conditions in Boston, by fitting up a similar room, . . . and admit[ting] visitors free of charge, they will perform equally astounding and convincing things here." Soon, the spirits at Barnard's room at 13 Auburn Court would be conjuring up blue floating lights and turning water into red wine. Eventually, the proprietor of this room would charge 50 cents public admission or $1 for private parties.

An exchange in the newspaper between the Buffalo businessman Stephen Dudley and the Canadian medium E. V. Wilson revealed that the matter of money was also complicated when it came to Koons. Both men recently had visited the Koons farm and praised the manifestations in the spiritualist press. But Dudley wanted to make a correction to Wilson's account, which was published in a Canadian magazine. Wilson had written that the Koons family "will not receive money for any of their attentions to the visitors with which their house is constantly thronged."

Dudley found the remark misleading for, as he explained, "however peremptorily he [Koons] may have refused to receive any remuneration for his kindness and attention, from Mr. Wilson, in January, I had no difficulty, nor had those who went with me, in prevailing with him to accept what he considered a liberal compensation, in December. It is true that the extreme modesty of Mr. Koons would not suffer him to make a specific charge; but this did not prevent us from doing him justice; nor should it prevent any one who goes there and receives his hospitalities and friendly offices." Dudley called on Wilson to clarify his original statement, lest readers believe that giving an offering to Koons would be regarded as an insult. "I know that his circumstances will not admit of his entertaining company as he does without compensation; and I should be sorry if the idea should get abroad that he will not receive any," Dudley added. "Even without the entertainment of this mistaken idea, he is not offered half of what his services and kindness deserve."

Wilson swiftly responded in print, agreeing that donations to Koons were warranted.

> I mentioned in my communication to the "Anglo American" that Mr. Koons made no charge &c., simply from the fact that it is frequently thrown in my face that it was a speculation, and that the spirits would stop their performances at Koons rooms when the dollars stopped coming in.
>
> Now I know that there is not a faithful and true spiritualist in the world that would visit brother Koons, and come away without leaving an equivalent for the time, labor and attention bestowed upon them by Mr. Koons and his family, in giving them audience with the spirits. And my friend Dudley may rest assured that I did not leave brother K. without giving him a liberal compensation for the trouble we put him to.—Yours fraternally, E. V. Wilson

So Koons had to walk a fine line between not demanding money and not being loathe to accept it. His well-heeled admirers may have dazzled him with their cash, but others less well off sponged off him with little regard for their host. A joke made the rounds of spiritualist circles about two of Koons's freeloading guests—hangers-on who traded their supposed psychic insights for a place in the séance circle and a seat at the dining table. These so-called spiritual mountebanks had begun to decimate the family's supply of bacon and eggs. After several days or weeks of martyrdom Koons decided to act. He suggested that the two visitors could help earn their keep by removing a pile of logs lying outside in the yard. The pair set to work but soon abandoned the task. "Our guardian spirits have impressed us that muscular exercise is inimical to mediumistic development," they declared. Whereupon Koons, on advice of *his* guide, King, signaled the end of the free eggs and bacon. But more breakfast eaters soon would follow. Jonathan and Abigail perforce had become proprietors of an unprofitable hotel, and if an earthly ledger had been kept, those reading it would have concluded that whatever treasures the Koonses possessed must be stored only in heaven.

✳   ✳   ✳

BY spring 1855 the *Christian Spiritualist's* fund-raising drive was foundering. At an April forum attended by a number of New York City's leading spiritualists, the newspaper editor J. H. W. Toohey circulated a drawing of Jonathan Koons's "concentrating electric machine," all the while lamenting that donations for the Koons building project had largely failed to materialize. The success of the movement depended on reliable mediums who could reveal spiritual truths, but how were these talented individuals supposed to make a living? "We should permit it [charity] to knock on our pockets as well as on our heads," Toohey said.

The Reverend Uriah Clark, a former Universalist minister, disagreed, saying that such "eleemosynary appeals" were counterproductive. "He did not think this selecting mediums to be paid by contributions was the way to proceed," related a published report of the meeting, "for if the manifestations and evidences were worth seeing they were worth being paid for. The making of a charity business of Spiritualism was one way to disgust the world with it, and people who went to the medium's table should pay for the time they occupied." Clark worried that selecting and funding certain individuals could cause "invidious distinctions and heart-burnings."

When it came his turn to speak, a Mr. Benning took the floor to argue for the Koons fund-raiser. Benning, who had visited the spirit room himself, thought the manifestations were genuine and the family worthy of support. He alluded to Nahum, the principal medium, as "a young man seemingly without capacity or intelligence, and a very ordinary person indeed." Benning lamented the great financial hardship put on the Koonses by their visitors and insisted that pilgrims should at least pay for their room and board.

Evidently the pleas of Toohey and Benning failed to elicit any additional contributions for the Koons family. Toohey reported in the April 21 issue of the *Christian Spiritualist* that he had collected only a handful of dollars—10, to be exact. "It may be the hardness of the monied season through which we have just passed is more at fault than the feelings or sympathies of the Spiritualists on this subject, so that we shall not give up hope yet . . . and therefore conclude better times will give us more money and a better report," Toohey wrote. Moreover, he could not add even a dollar to the total, for his own office recently had been burglarized. His watch was swiped and more than $100 in cash and property stolen.

Toohey had dutifully sent Koons the $10 collected, along with a cover letter and something else, which prompted a thank-you letter. "Your kind letter of March 20th, came safe to hand with the * * * and the two five dollar bills from Seth Henshaw, and your venerable old friend, whose name is not given," read the letter from Koons that the *Christian Spiritualist* published. Apparently Toohey had chosen to redact Koons's reference to another, larger gift. In May, Toohey disclosed to his readers that "we did not state the full sum sent to friend Koons, because one of the donors wished it to remain private. The sum sent, however, came from *three* persons, and is very far from what was expected when the proposition was started, for some that promised aid, never gave it." Even with the undisclosed gift, apparently the amount raised was nowhere near the $2,000 needed to break ground on a house.

In his letter Koons seemed philosophical about what may have been an embarrassing letdown, agreeing with Toohey's observation that *"liberality does not generally exist where money is concerned."* Nonetheless Koons struck a theme of "I did not ask for this" and took the opportunity to lash out at his critics. First, he emphasized that the spiritual investigations he and his family had undertaken were private ones, which they had decided to "test experimentally" against Christian doctrine. Their eventual hope, he said, was to "lay these discoveries before the world."

"In this course of procedure, however, we failed, for it was impossible to keep the matter concealed," he explained. "The people rushed upon us, the doctrine of the Spirits as taught at my residence, became a theme of conversation. The neighboring pulpits were soon mounted by their respective occupants. Loud peals of anathemas were proclaimed from beneath the lofty domes of consecrated establishments, from the *sanctimonious shepherds* of their respective flocks against mediums. Their loud peals of *'devil, humbug, delusion, down with it,'* echoed from church to college." The religious leaders' fiery words had led to arson; it was they who "blew the bellows" on the flames that consumed his barn.

Next Koons underscored the point that he had expended no effort to recruit visitors to his spirit room; they had come unbidden. But his open-door policy caused frustration for his family because some guests *"are wise in their own conceit* and *think they know it all."* These skeptics tried to control the arrangements of the séances and demanded feats that the spirits "have not the power to perform." Some made "unreasonable demands" on the mediums and, when rebuffed, they cried fraud. Even so, Koons continued, if the Koonses did manage, with great effort, to convince the skeptics that they had no direct hand in the manifestations, "they then retire, and give it as their judgment that it is the *very old devil himself,* and such [people] of course would not think us worthy of *one single copper* for our time and pains with them."

After writing these bitter words, Koons toned down his rhetoric, insisting that he was not complaining. "We are well aware that every person acts out his own constituted nature and elevation, and cannot act otherwise for the time being. Yours as ever in love and labor, Jonathan Koons."

＊　＊　＊

A visitor to the Koons farm, himself a spiritualist, had left the place disappointed and perplexed after a stay of eight days in early March. According to the April 7 issue of the *New England Spiritualist,* the visitor "was obliged to leave unsatisfied as to the source of the phenomena. He, however, states his determination to visit the place again in a few weeks, when he designs to state fully the results of his investigations." Koons somehow got word of this and decided to get ahead of the opposition.

Koons claimed to have received a communication, purportedly written by a spirit hand, explaining once again why certain tests or restrictions were not permitted at a Koons dark séance. Rather than mount an unseemly defense of his own policies, Koons chose to send the message through a surrogate. He mailed the spirit writing to a believer in Chillicothe, James M. Killgore, with the following note: "Sir:—I submit the following communication into your charge and care. Use it as you deem proper. The communication was executed in the same way of that you received while at my Spirit Room [a phosphorescent hand writing with a pencil on blank paper]. This I will *swear.* You are therefore left to comment, and to use, and to judge its merits as you think proper." Koons went on to say that he had received the message "at a time when some of our visiters wished to know why the spirits would not consent to have our mediums haltered and muffled and confined during the manifestations."

Killgore forwarded the spirit writing to the *Spiritual Universe* in Cleveland with a brief explanation; the purpose of publication, he said, was twofold. First, "honest enquirers" could get answers, and, second, the message would counter the "pernicious effects of a few disaffected Spiritualists who are now preparing to denounce the wonderful manifestations and philosophical revelations made and given at Brother Jonathan Koons' 'Spirit Room,' because, forsooth, they are not twisted, and warped, and turned, to accommodate their every self-inflated whim and caprice."

The message itself, not signed by King or any particular entity, once again made the point that a harmonious atmosphere is necessary for spirits to produce their effects; when mediums are awash in negative emotions, "that places them out of their natural spheres of mind" and renders conversation with the spirits impossible. The communication seemed to target a specific person whose name was never mentioned but who clearly was from the spiritualist camp. "It is strange, 'passing strange,' that any distinguished teacher of the Harmonial Philosophy, should so far forget his teaching as to denounce a favorite resort of the Heavenly messengers, simply because the fixed and unalterable laws[,] which govern both them and us, are not there transcended." The writer referred to the Koons Spirit

Room as a "favorite resort" of the angels and as a "little humble Room," nearly the equivalent of the "Sanctum Sanctorum of God's green earth." (The author of the message made curious use of the pronouns *them* and *us*. He identified *them* as "the Heavenly messengers," but if the writing was produced by a spirit, who is *us*? Perhaps in his zeal the author inadvertently revealed his identity as a human being.)

The writing concluded with a reference to restraints placed on mediums, apparently for controlling their movements: "The picture that handcuffs, halters and chains would present of humanity to minds either *in* or *out* [of] the body, would be far from being elevating, attracting, or harmonizing." The Koons phenomenon had begun in the spirit of scientific inquiry, yet increasingly Koons's followers were being asked to believe in, rather than investigate, the wonders they beheld. "I speak from experience," the entity wrote. "The dove and child, confiding and harmless condition, as well as the serpent, one of wisdom, are indispensable requisites for the attainment of truth; for marvel not 'ye must become as little children, ere you can enter the Kingdom of Heaven,' or Truth."

14

Koons, King, and Company

LARKSPUR, VIOLETS, and wild geraniums laid a carpet of royal purple at the feet of pilgrims as they ascended to Mount Nebo in the spring of 1855, taking advantage of the good traveling weather. In early June, Koons wrote to the *Christian Spiritualist* to update readers on the family's activities, explaining that he had had little time for correspondence except on Sundays and foul-weather days: "We have labored under difficult and pecuniary circumstances the past spring. We found that there was no other alternative for us, save that of our own physical labor, in order to sustain ourselves and the cause in which we are engaged. We accordingly partook ourselves to unusually hard labor the present summer, so as to gain sustainance for ourselves and visiters. Our days were, therefore, devoted to the duties of our temporal lives, and the evenings, in general, to the support of our Spiritual requirements."

By saying the family had "no other alternative" than the hard work of farm life, Koons seemed to have given up on any financial rescue from his friends in the East. Apparently the money he received in March had not made an appreciable difference in his family's standard of living. Perhaps he had given up on further donations, but elsewhere in the letter he was careful to remind readers that his house was "constantly crowded with foreign visitors" whom he tried to accommodate despite his "limited means and circumstances."

Curiously, or perhaps ominously, Koons mentioned that he had recently had a visit from Charles Partridge, proprietor of the *Spiritual Telegraph,* and his traveling companion. "In consequence of the derangement
of our circle, we failed in giving them such attention as would have been
given under more favorable circumstances, for which failure we crave their
pardon and sympathy." Koons probably was referring to the near-cancellation
of a séance planned for the evening of Sunday, May 27, 1855, the day of
Partridge's arrival. On that night, like many others, Jonathan and Nahum
entered the spirit room before the demonstration to ask the spirits' guidance. Jonathan usually would call in out-of-town visitors to see who should
be given priority for admittance. In a preliminary meeting with Partridge,
King—speaking through the trumpet—praised the New York publisher's
work "in the most flattering terms" but announced that he [King] would
not be participating in the séance that night, as he was officiating elsewhere.
What ensued sounded almost like a family squabble between Koons and
the ghost. In Partridge's account:

> Mr. Koons expressed much regret at this announcement, and
> said he felt embarrassed and mortified, because several persons
> were there who had come a long way: some from New York,
> Pennsylvania, Virginia, Canada and other distant places. The Spirit
> said he was sorry, but he had engaged to attend a circle elsewhere
> (naming the place—a long distance away), and he must be there in
> fifteen minutes. Mr. Koons would not be satisfied with any excuses,
> but insisted that he (King) had agreed to preside over the circle,
> and meet the company who came there; and rather than be made
> the instrument of apology to others for the disappointment in the
> performances, he would abandon it altogether.

Koons's panic—and not so subtle threat to cancel the séance—seemed
to move King, who relented and agreed to send a portion of the spirit band
to the distant location. He would remain behind to preside over Koons's
circle, but King warned that "perhaps they would not be able to make so
good music, or have the full complement of the manifestations." For those
who believed that a spirit could transcend time and space, the hot words
that flew between Koons and King must have sounded rather banal, but if
viewed as a clash between a father and his teenage son, they make sense.

The exchange laid bare just how strongly Jonathan Koons had become invested in pleasing his audience, but if there were problems within the circle, few visitors would have been aware. Even Partridge, who heard the dispute, seems to have discounted its importance. Although Koons did not realize it at the time, Partridge would go on to write about his experiences in Koons's dark chamber as if they were one of the highlights of his life.

ONE guest in the audience that night was Selah Van Sickle. A self-taught painter with a mystical bent, Van Sickle had found a kindred spirit in Jonathan Koons. Van Sickle hailed from Delaware County, Ohio, where his parents had moved from New York State when he was a small boy. By the time the 43-year-old artist encountered Koons, who was about one year older, Van Sickle already was a well-traveled man. He eventually would earn a place in art history for his life-size portrait of Brigham Young, done in 1845 at Nauvoo, the Mormon enclave in Hancock County, Illinois. But Van Sickle had chosen not to follow the Mormon community on its trek to the West. By 1851 he had returned to central Ohio, where he spent about a year painting one of his major works, *The Panorama of the Life of Christ,* which he finished in 1854.

Described in a family history as a pantheist, Van Sickle found creative inspiration in the ruggedness of Koons's remote spiritualist homestead. Mount Nebo, whose ruling spirit was King, the Master of Paints, seemed like just the place for Van Sickle's art to flourish. He would rely on the spirits to direct his work—and thus he would depend on the Koons family to tell him what the spirits wanted. Soon he would build an art studio on their farm to channel the divine impulse, so that, day or night, his muses would be only footsteps away.

EVEN though the French mesmerist Joseph Barthet had found King's playing and singing distasteful, other visitors to the Koons séances found the performances both entertaining and spiritually uplifting. It is not clear whether the quality of the speech and music varied from night to night or whether it was a matter of differing perceptions and tastes. Joseph P. Hazard of Narragansett, Rhode Island, a businessman visiting in the spring of 1855, noted that "the spirits talk audibly through a trumpet, not with good articulation, but as if the process were mechanical." He found the invisibles much easier to understand if they spoke or sang through some of the other instruments. "Some of the music is seraphic, especially when they speak with the harmonicon, when it is more unearthly in its character than I should have been able to imagine." An Illinois pilgrim, also visiting at about that time, described "a kind of strange unearthly noise" that would sing along with the French harp and accordion. Sometimes, he said, Jonathan Koons engaged in conversation "with the voice in the horn and harp" between songs, which reinforces Barthet's impression that some of the musical instruments acted as a megaphone. On occasions when the audience members would become restive and start whispering among themselves, the horn would rebuke them with a shriek and admonish them to keep silent.

Out of the silence arose a groundswell that profoundly moved the publisher Charles Partridge:

> After the introductory piece on the instruments, the spirits often sing. I heard them sing. The spirits spoke to us, requesting us to remain perfectly silent. Presently, we heard human voices singing, apparently in the distance so as to be scarcely distinguishable; the sounds gradually increased, each part relatively, until it appeared as if a full choir of human voices were in our small room, singing most exquisitely. I think I never heard such perfect harmony. . . . So captivating it was, that the heartstrings seemed to relax or to increase their tension, to accord with the heavenly harmony. It seems to me that no person could sit in that sanctuary without feeling the song of "Glory to God in the highest, peace on earth, and goodwill to man," spontaneously rising in the bosom, and finding expression on the lip. I don't know that the spirits attempted to utter words with their song; if they did, they succeeded in this particular no better than modern singers. But it was hardly necessary for the spirits to articulate, for every strain and modulation seemed pregnant with holy sentiments, and language could scarcely signify more.

Like Partridge, no one in the other accounts of visiting the spirit room actually recalled any song lyrics whatsoever. Some suggested that the songs of the invisibles were akin to Gregorian chants, while others thought them similar to selections from a nineteenth-century hymnal. Visitors from Cleveland were impressed with communications coming through the harmonica: "While we heard tunes from it, we also heard words spoken and sung through it, and always in unison with the notes of the tunes," they told the *Plain Dealer* upon their return. "The words were sometimes Hymns of Praise, at other times remarks of a general character addressed to the circle."

Even so, the Cleveland visitors, like many before them, found the sounds hard to describe: "It is impossible to convey an adequate idea of the musical performances. While each of the musical instruments were used, the time was regularly and accurately marked, now on the drums, now on the triangle, now on the tambourine, and with the bell, and now with the use of all combined; and when all the musical instruments were simultaneously used, the effect was not merely novel but highly pleasing." While the band played, an invisible ringmaster spoke through the trumpet, conducting a sideshow all his own. "Through this horn many amusing and interesting comments on the instruments, the musicians, and their music were made, sometimes commending and sometimes severely criticizing," the Clevelanders reported.

Some spirits, however, did not seem to be competent musicians at all. One of the most bizarre of these instances was reported by Hazard, the Rhode Island spiritualist, who gained permission to spend the night in one of the Athens County spirit rooms (he does not say which one), describing them as "dark as Erebus, and rather lonesome places, in this wilderness." Far from counting down the seconds until sunup, Hazard seemed unfazed by any spookiness; in fact he found the spirits amiable. During the night he heard faint drumming and notes played on the violin. One new spirit, described as German, "played some things delightfully," but Hazard told how another one failed his audition: "One spirit attempted to sing through the trumpet, but could not make music; after each failure he would stop a minute, and then, very good-naturedly, say[,] 'I will try again.' This he did several times, when he added, 'What shall I do for you if I can't sing?' He at length took up an accordeon, and succeeded better on that; but I presume did not suit himself, as he would exclaim every once in a while, 'Oh, dear!' very despondingly."

From the sublime to the ridiculous, the music provided a veneer of entertainment to what seemed, to many, a serious spiritual endeavor.

✻ ✻ ✻

BY the summer of 1855 two new stars blazed in the spiritualist firmament. The brothers Ira Erastus Davenport and William Henry Harrison Davenport, mediums aged about 16 and 14, burst upon the scene as prodigies. Based in Buffalo, New York, these two sons of a retired police officer were able to produce manifestations "as marvelous as anything we have heard of, whether at Koon's or elsewhere," gushed the *Christian Spiritualist*. The boys' father maintained "an upper room" furnished with only a round hardwood table, a pine table, and some chairs. Like the Koonses', this was a family operation: the senior Davenport and his daughter also were mediums, whereas Ira and William were—like Nahum Koons—considered the principal actors in creating the physical effects. The two boys would sit at one table while the audience sat holding hands. On the table had been placed two violins, a tambourine, and a bell. Someone would tie William's and Ira's hands to the backs of their chairs; then the room would go dark.

Soon the violins would float through the room creating music while the tambourine shook wildly and the bell rang above the heads of the audience. Invisible hands would snatch caps and hats off the heads of the unsuspecting visitors. Strange lights and unintelligible voices filtered through the air. Drops of water fell upon the faces and bodies of the participants, although no one had observed a water source in the room. And astonishingly one of the boys would levitate to the ceiling, speaking aloud to let everyone know he was up there. And once the lights were back on, observers could see the red mark on the ceiling where he had made it.

All these feats had been performed without the aid of a retaining battery, like the strange contraption in Jonathan Koons's log sanctuary, or any type of machine. Such signs and wonders, the *Christian Spiritualist* said, would no doubt lead to "numerous conversions to the facts and faith of Spiritualism." That same summer a committee of nine men—including the *Age of Progress* editor Stephen Albro—declared that the Davenports themselves could not be responsible for the phenomena. For example, the investigators were "convinced beyond doubt" that the spirits had taken both Ira and William aloft, repeatedly banging their heads against the 12-foot ceiling of the Davenport spirit room. Later on, as the boys graduated from being tied to chairs to being restrained in a cabinet with a door and window, their fame would only increase.

One evening a skeptic recruited from the audience tied Ira and William up in the cabinet. Though their hands and feet supposedly were secure, a tin horn soon protruded from a window in the cabinet door, and a voice speaking through it began to take musical requests from the audience. The spirit pleased the crowd by playing a dozen or so airs on a violin. But the night turned ghoulish when a spirit hand was thrust through the window several times for the curious to touch. One of the gawkers pulled out a knife and slashed the hand, surprisingly drawing no blood. The hand's owner, supposedly a Swede who had died 230 years before, coolly replied, "You[r] knife is not sharp enough."

IN Ross County, Ohio, some 50 miles to the west of Mount Nebo, one John Q. Adams, "fresh from J. Koons room" in 1855, heard a voice instructing him to build his own tabernacle. After partitioning off 11 feet of his cabinetmaking shop, Adams tried to assemble a retaining battery. Like Koons himself, Adams at first had trouble. His own drawing, probably sketched from memory, was laughably inadequate. After much frustration and finally some help from a spirit calling itself Third King, Adams produced a design that was "almost a perfect *fac similie* of Messrs. Koons' and Tippie's machines."

Adams and his father-in-law both gained further instructions through automatic writing. They bought two drums, bass and tenor, "ten ear and three tea bells," and 20 yards of copper wire. The men strung up the bells and drums, presumably on a frame, and "connected [them] to the battery by the wire, after the same manner of those at Koons' and Tippie's." Adams did add his own imprimatur to the design, thus revealing his belief that the calling-up of spirits did not violate his reading of the Bible. A visitor to Adams's room described the machine in detail:

A cross—which Mediums are impressed is intended to represent
that one which the disciple toiled under as he ascended Calvary's
hill, and upon which the sorrowing and godlike Jesus was
crucified—is placed erect in the centre of the battery, having its
different parts penetrated by the ramifying wire, in as many as
four different places. Just above, and immediately over, the arms
of this cross, connected with the circuitous wire, are four plates,
each fashioned in the perfect form of a dove. The two over the
left are brass while the two over the right are copper. At the foot
of the cross there are two more of those dove plates. These mild
and innocent looking figures sit upon the wire facing each other,
in brass and copper pairs. I am inclined to believe that there is
some *meaning* in the construction of this battery, of which its
form and shape is a representation, which if properly understood,
would clear away some of the dark mysteries from the horizon
of Theology. The happy use to which the Spirits apply it for the
manifestations, i[s] its material, while its yet unexplained meaning
is its spiritual part.

At the same time efforts were under way in New York City to design
an electrified table similar to Koons's in the hope of manifesting the phenomena there. A cryptic item in the *Christian Spiritualist* gave few details
of the venture, except to say, "What the result will be, time, experiment
and observation alone can determine, but every effort should be made
to ascertain if the manifestations out West are indiginous to those lo-
calities by virtue of some peculiarity in the atmosphere, or the more
thorough passivity of the mediums and faithfulness of those composing
the Circle."

These passages make clear that the builders of these so-called batter-
ies had no concept of how the devices worked, if they did work at all. On
the one hand they thought that the use of such a machine *could* harness
forces like electricity that were little understood except by scientists, but
at the same time they felt that somehow belief (or receptivity to the divine) might be a necessary condition for the machines' performance. Just
a few months earlier a detailed drawing of Jonathan Koons's spirit table
had been reprinted in *Scientific American,* which framed it with a scathing
dismissal:

When a machine is invented by a human being, it can do something—has a relation and an arrangement of parts, and although it may have some defects, it evinces design, mind and genius. But here is a machine constructed under the direction of Spirits, who are claimed to be higher intelligences, and yet it exhibits the grossest ignorance of all science. But then it is like everything else connected with pretended spiritual revelations that we have read. It has no point, no aim, and has produced . . . no result but what can be witnessed in any juggling legerdemain establishment in Gotham.

Such pronouncements had scant impact, though, on witnesses such as Abraham P. Pierce who had sat through a Koons séance—and felt the room vibrate, "as if some fifty persons were coming into a large empty hall, causing the whole building to tremble."

EARLIER that year Koons had sensed trouble brewing, and in late July or early August 1855 it came calling at his door. An inquisitive visitor had returned to Mount Nebo to conclude the investigation he had begun in March. The Reverend J. H. Fowler had studied at the Cambridge Divinity School at Harvard University and was a spiritualist minister who, like Koons, followed Andrew Jackson Davis's teachings. Fowler had begun his missionary work in August 1854 with a notice to the *New Era* newspaper of his decision to enter the lecturing field. "They who desire his services will find him an able young man—one who understands his subject, is well imbued with its spirit, and has power to treat it intelligently and with effect," the *New Era* wrote. Although Fowler was based in the Boston area, he was busy on the Midwest lecture circuit in 1855, traveling to Columbus, Cincinnati, Indianapolis, Chicago, and St. Louis. Nothing delighted him more than to lead a skeptic into a verbal trap at a public lecture, as he had done with "a medical gentleman" in Cincinnati, making Fowler's audience "exceedingly merry."

Fowler needed no convincing that the spirits of the dead did indeed survive the transition from the earthly plane. He had seen evidence of amazing physical force used in a séance in New York State, where sitters clung to the top of a table as if it were a sinking ship and still were not strong enough to keep it from rising in the air. While in Cincinnati he had accompanied a healing medium to the Home of the Friendless, where they encountered a 17-year-old orphan girl, "a poor, sick, friendless creature," blind in one eye and given up for dead after a diagnosis of consumption. Fowler had watched as Mr. H., the healer and former mesmerist, began his treatment by passing his hand over the patient's head and neck, concluding that her cough was not caused by tuberculosis. Over the space of eight days, using only manipulations, he brought the bedridden girl back to health and restored sight to her eye, "which for eleven years had been cold and rayless as a stone." And Fowler had been most impressed with the drawings of a Columbus artist named Wolcott or Wolcutt, who sketched detailed portraits of deceased strangers, some of them spirit children, while sitting blindfolded. Most of all Fowler was convinced that he had heard from the spirits of his beloved father and sister, who had "spoken that precious word for which I would have travelled to the farthest verge of earth."

But he was equally convinced that half the spirit manifestations foisted upon believers were mere illusions performed by people still very much in the body. "Truth and Justice" demanded that he expose these frauds. "As for spiritualism, if it has not facts enough to sustain itself, let it go down," he wrote. "The truth will . . . shine all the more clearly."

Indeed, Fowler was a scholar who prided himself on his empiricism, even though, as one friendly critic put it, "the author deals, at times, more roughly with popular convictions than is needful or wise." His controversial paper *New Testament "Miracles," and Modern "Miracles": The Comparative Amount of Evidence for Each; The Nature of Both; Testimony of a Hundred Witnesses: An Essay Read before the Middle and Senior Classes in Cambridge Divinity School* had been published in book form and contained many eyewitness accounts affirming spirit manifestations. Now he was working on another collection, bidding the public to send him stories of remarkable healings and visitations from the departed. "Let the affidavits be concise, direct, unexaggerated," he specified. "Let the witnesses be none but reliable persons, and the names given in full."

His rational powers notwithstanding, Fowler initially had not expected to tread a debunker's path when it came to the celebrated Koons family.

In fact he had included in his book a signed statement from five pilgrims who attended a Koons séance in 1854—one of several cases that Fowler considered strong evidence of spiritual agency. On that particular occasion the spirits not only channeled through the visiting medium Abraham P. Pierce of Philadelphia but "played most sweetly on the trumpet; then took the harp, and brought both into tune, and played on both instruments, and at the same time sung with some four voices, sounding like female voices, and which, indeed, made the room swell with melody." When Fowler had arrived for his first visit to the Koons Spirit Room in March 1855, he had envisioned adding his own testimony to the glowing reports he had read, yet another part of him had remained unconvinced: "I resolved, as I have ever done on similar occasions, to assume the character of a skeptic, and not be deluded or influenced by my pre-convictions." Now, with his successful midwestern tour behind him, lack of clarity about the remarkable Koons performances had led him to return in late summer for a closer look.

Like countless investigators before him, Fowler was ushered into the spirit room and allowed to inspect the layout and seating arrangements. Not much had changed, appearance-wise, in the three years since the log building had opened in 1852. The oblong retaining battery table sat about 2 feet out from a short wall of the rectangle, with the smaller mediums' table in front of it. Just as the others had done, he quickly ruled out any possibility that "the electric retainer" actually functioned as a battery. He concluded that it had "no power to retain electricity or to excite it, because [it was] not in any way insulated or capable of being worked mechanically." But Fowler noticed something else. Why had the heating stove that squatted in front of the mediums' table, near the center of the room, not been moved out for the summer? "The spirits wish it [to stay] in order to pass things behind the funnel [stovepipe] to be more convincing to the people," Koons had explained.

The order of the seating—which "Mr. Koons is ever strict to observe"—also caught Fowler's attention. Nahum, *"without whom nothing can be done,"* invariably sat on the right side of the mediums' table, with his mother, sister, "and other known confidential media, if present" on his left. Only the most credulous believers sat on the right front row, while "the indifferent" took the back bench. Jonathan sat opposite Nahum on the left side of the mediums' table, having corralled all the skeptics on that side of the room. The stove acted as a divider between the two unwitting groups who had been so classified. In Fowler's estimation the setup gave Nahum free rein over the right side of the room and access to "the only passage-way leading—from his right—behind the long table, where are the toys, and where both drums may be played with pleasure." Even in the pitch black Nahum must have learned how to maneuver around the front of the little table, too, as doing so would allow him to touch the skeptical side of the audience with a drumstick or tambourine.

So far, though, all of Fowler's musings had amounted to a mere thought experiment, an amalgam of circumstances that proved nothing and could easily be shrugged off by true believers. Now it was time for the lights to go out. Jonathan rubbed phosphorus on some damp pieces of sandpaper and covered the glowing surfaces with regular paper, took his seat, and blew out the candle. Fowler marveled at the ebony blackness, the total absence of light. Something had to fill the void. "Give us music, yes, anything, one would almost say, but this dark foreboding," Fowler would later recall.

"Now the spirits are entering the room," Jonathan said. Fowler wondered about the little ones and the big ones—ranging from 6 inches to 6 feet tall, to hear Jonathan tell it. Next came what Fowler had come to expect, the "pretty good common music" from Jonathan's old fiddle and the crash on the table "as if t'would split the toughest oak."

But Fowler's ears were already attuned to the next part of the act. "Good evening," intoned a voice from the horn, although it was less distinct than Fowler would have liked. The voice repeated the phrase several times in call-and-response with the audience. As he would later write:

> Now mark. This voice, speaking through the horn, is pronounced by many of the most sanguine believers, to be Nahum Koons' voice, though I could not distinguish it. But they say Nahum finds the lungs for the spirits, and that will account for it! I think he does; and why not the *mouth*, also? That will account for it better still, since the SMALL end of the horn is frequently found to be warm when the talking ceases. . . . Nahum can never speak, nor can any one be permitted to put his hand over his (Nahum's) mouth, at the moment any sound is being made through the horn.

Fowler also was convinced that the Koons women were not mere passive vessels but active participants in the séance. One day at the Koons home Quintilla, the Koons daughter who was then about 13, came in the door singing something that seemed quite familiar to Fowler. Thinking back, he remembered "the *same female voice, tone, tune, and words*" that he had heard through the horn. He also suspected that Jonathan was not the only musician in the Koons tribe, despite their insistence otherwise. Nahum, Quintilla, and the others had had ample opportunity to learn the tunes, and no music except Jonathan's pieces was allowed in the spirit room. And Fowler believed that Nahum had the arm span required to play two drums at once with a single pair of drumsticks, using his right hand on the tenor and his left on the bass.

The minister also found it curious that the little vocal phrasings common to the Koons family wound up as utterances from the horn. When someone asked Nahum, "How do you do?" he had a laid-back way of answering: "Well I don't know as I could do any better." Or, if things were not going well, a Koons family member might repeat "O dear! O dear! O dear" in rapid succession. "Every *idea, phrase,* and *word,* smack too strong[ly] of the Koons to be mistaken." All in all Fowler found the voice bellowing through the horn full of "foolish talk," able to display only a "disgustingly vulgar wit."

"Let it be borne in mind that, according to Mr. Koons' own confession, he with his family spent the long evenings of half a year practicing in his room, previous to admitting any stranger," Fowler wrote. "What could they not learn to do, in the dark even, in this time?"

Buoyed by his suspicions, Fowler decided to act. During a séance he crept up to the unused stove and sat down on it. The tambourine was fluttering over the mediums' table. At some risk to himself, Fowler made a swipe at the instrument and grabbed hold of a hand. A warm hand. A man's hand. But the action was too fast for him to get a firm grasp. Now he could see why Jonathan insisted that the instruments were held aloft by electrical currents that should not be short-circuited by audience interference. It was, Fowler thought, "a pretty good way to keep hands off."

Toward the end of his visit Fowler landed a séance for himself alone, surely a mark of the importance with which he was regarded. Jonathan and Nahum took their customary seats across from each other at the mediums' table, while Fowler sat between them. As the mental chess game began, he heard thumps on the table and something touched Fowler several times.

Grabbing at the object in the dark, he encountered a wrist, "which dodged me instantly." Next a voice spoke through the trumpet. He tried in vain to get Nahum to speak at the same time. Fowler held his left hand as far away from Nahum as he could. "Put the horn in my hand, away out there," he commanded the spirits. The moment the metal touched his left hand, Fowler thrust his right hand toward Nahum to see if he was holding the horn. Each time he connected with what he thought was Nahum's arm. "It instantly withdrew," he later reported, "and with it the horn from my other hand. I caught his hand and arm in this way several times, but not so as to hold on upon it because of its peculiar sensitiveness." As a final test the minister asked Jonathan to hold Fowler's left hand with both of his and asked Nahum to do the same with Fowler's right hand. Then he waited. The silence was as profound as the blackness pervading the cabin. After 20 minutes everybody gave up. With the mediums' hands occupied, "not even a mouse was heard to move."

ON his return ride to Columbus, Fowler had time to reflect on how easy it was to fall under the Koonses' enchantment. "It is almost impossible for any person to sit in the darkness of that room during the performance, and not give way to the marvelous, and so become over-credulous. He will imagine, and be ready to believe, more is performed than really is; and if not careful, will boldly affirm it afterwards." Fowler had almost fallen down the rabbit hole himself during his last two evenings on Mount Nebo. Earlier he thought he had it figured out, was disgusted with the whole affair, and was ready to leave. But duty called when the child of Jonathan's sister died. Fowler was asked to preach the funeral, and he assented. Administering that holy sacrament made him feel more bonded with the Koons family, readier to look at the situation through fresh eyes. "By the occasion [I] allowed myself to be worked up into just that state of mind most susceptible to duplicity," he later recounted.

At the séance held the evening of the funeral, Fowler willed himself to be in a relaxed and receptive state. The parents of the dead child and other mourners filed into the spirit room for a sitting, hoping to receive information concerning their lost loved one. "The idea that such an imposition [imposture] should be practiced under these circumstances, seemed so horrible that I could not entertain it," Fowler wrote. "I had resolved not to disturb the performance by my skepticism, but be perfectly passive and receive what might come." Seated once again at a place of honor by Jonathan, Fowler let the wonders fill his soul. The tambourine flitted between the two drums like a singing bird, darting to the ceiling and then hovering at table level. The horn floated under the table and even passed once through Fowler's hands. By the next morning Fowler was agreeing with the others that these events really had taken place. Jonathan was confident that the credentialed cleric would leave his place as satisfied as the others had been.

But as Fowler's horse drew him farther and farther from Mount Nebo, doubt began to get the upper hand. Replaying the night in his head, sound but no picture, Fowler once again realized how Nahum could have been the author of these effects. Fowler also grasped how much his peers had influenced his belief. In regard to the horn passing under the table, "several persons, though they could not possibly know the fact, were so positive in affirming it, that I admitted it, for the time believed it, and the next day affirmed it as a fact." Even the room itself was "calculated to excite marvellousness to the highest degree." Now his confidence in the two magical evenings had vanished like the vaporous hands sometimes seen in the spirit room.

In fact Fowler had seen precious little of the spirit hands during his time at the Koonses'. (Perhaps they would have blamed it on the inharmony that Fowler brought with him.) Sifting through his observations, he remembered seeing a woman's hand, probably Quintilla's, lit by phosphorus on one occasion. And he had felt a man's warm hand carrying the tambourine, as well as a cold one that grazed his for just an instant. None would get close enough for examination. "Nor do I believe *any* doubting person has thoroughly examined them," he wrote. "They will not approach such persons."

He had heard worse things about the Tippies, in whose spirit room two spiritualists from Indiana had conducted their own investigation. "The gentlemen . . . at Mr. Tippie's, both affirmed, that one of them caught hold of the hand there exhibited, passed his other hand up the wrist, and felt the coat-sleeve as far as the elbow, when the hand was suddenly snatched away and could not be coaxed back on that or any subsequent evening,"

Fowler wrote. "I would ask how it is, that a *hand* and *arm* and *coat-sleeve* should be necessary to move a tambourine and other objects, which are 'moved by currents of electricity'?" These same men from Indiana, according to Fowler, had also heard Tippie's son and daughter playing the same tunes that played at the Tippie séances, despite the claim that no one in the household save the spirits was a musician. "I could mention other facts relative to Mr. Tippie's manifestations, which destroy all my confidence in them," Fowler snorted, "but I return to the Koons' room."

From one of Jonathan's neighbors Fowler had heard a curious story about the firing of pistols at a target in the darkened spirit room, a practice that had long since been discontinued: "Now a gentleman, living not far from Mr. Koons, publicly declared he would take oath that in the flash of a pistol he distinctly saw Nahum standing with the pistol in his hand, pointing under the table. Others began to state the same facts, when said performance was laid aside for philosophical reasons."

Yet another séance story—told by "a zealous friend" of Jonathan's— also pictured Nahum illuminated by flame. This time the phosphorus caught fire and blazed up, revealing Nahum standing with the tambourine in his hand. Believers explained away the apparent exposure by saying that Jonathan had told Nahum to smother the flame with the tambourine, and the boy had jumped up out of his seat to do it. In the process Nahum got phosphorus on his hands, which clearly marked his position for the rest of the performance. The show only got better as the séance resumed. To some this proved that Nahum had nothing to do with the spirits' demonstrations, but to Fowler it meant only that the Koons family was a band of confederates, and if one player was temporarily sidelined, another stood ready to take his place.

Upon his return to the East, Fowler would write, and then the world would know the truth about the great humbug of the West—the imposture he termed "Koons, King and Ko."

15

"An Artful and Designing Rogue"

FOWLER'S REPORT soon became front-page news in Boston's *New England Spiritualist,* which devoted four and a half columns to the minister's debunking of the Koons demonstrations. In Fowler's view, Jonathan Koons had thrust himself and his family into the public eye, so the remedy had to be public exposure. "I cannot longer refrain from giving to the public my experience at the celebrated Koons establishment," Fowler told readers. "Whenever any person gives to the world his testimony to facts involving great public interests, and particularly when those facts relate to his own personal experience, such person becomes a just subject for public criticism. Even his private life, his habits, his mental and physical constitution, everything about him, which may have the least bearing upon the facts alleged, become public property, and may be called in question by every lover of humanity."

Fowler immediately drew heavy fire from the spiritualist press for his explosive allegations. If he was correct, simple country folk, sometimes noted for their "absence of wit," had made fools of many of the leading lights of the movement. Even the Reverend A. E. Newton, the editor who had published Fowler's charges in the *New England Spiritualist,* was disinclined to believe them. *"The opinion of one who denies, since he has come away[,] what the evidence of his own senses compelled him to admit when on the spot,* will not be esteemed of much value on any point. There is such a thing as a mania of skepticism, as well as a mania of credulity; and we think Bro. F. manifests decided symptoms of the former disease," Newton wrote. J. W. H. Toohey, who reprinted excerpts of Fowler's article in the New York–based *Christian Spiritualist,* agreed with Newton and pointed to the many glowing reports of the Koons phenomena from eyewitnesses. Even as Toohey gave the challenger space in his paper, he termed the allegations mere *"suspicions, conjectures* and *statements"* of one J. H. Fowler.

Toohey later blasted Fowler for his "idiosyncrasy" when it came to investigating spiritual phenomena. Toohey had once attended a circle with Fowler when the latter insisted on marking a piece of paper before it was put on the floor for the spirits to write upon. Paper was marked to ensure that the medium did not pull a sleight of hand and substitute paper she had already written on. Others in the circle were offended, feeling that Fowler, a newcomer, did not know his place. "Brother Fowler, without any knowledge of the members, the previous investigations, or tests instituted by them, commenced, soon after his introduction to the Circle, an explanation of *his method,* which the Circle, through courtesy, adopted for the evening," Toohey complained.

The editors' chorus of dismissals was soon joined by a Michigan man who had visited the Koons Spirit Room at the end of June and found the demonstrations totally believable. In a letter to the *New England Spiritualist,* he wrote, "I have no doubt that Mr. Koons, Mrs. Koons, Nahum, and, indeed, the entire family, are strictly honest, honorable and truthful in regard to the so-called spiritual manifestations at their place; and that my opinion is, that they are but instruments used by Spirits to demonstrate to the world, in the best way they can, that information so eagerly sought; to wit, the continued life." He labeled Fowler's charges baseless, the product of "the wildness, and chimerical condition of his mind."

During the next couple of months Koons's supporters flooded the spiritualist press with testimonials, seeking to dismantle each of Fowler's arguments: (1) that Nahum or other family members got out of their seats and moved objects around; (2) that Nahum and perhaps others spoke through the horn; (3) that many of the Koons family members could sing and play instruments; and (4) that the hands were those of the Koons children, appearing only to "the credulous."

A Koons supporter, Hamilton Wade of New York, penned a lengthy account of his visit to the Athens County spirit rooms in mid-August 1855, shortly after Fowler had been there. Wade collected affidavits from several out-of-state visitors, who were boarding nearby at Southerton's Farm, and had them published in the *Spiritual Telegraph* along with his report. In advance of the Koons séances, Wade had devised mental tests to prove the authenticity of the performances. He felt that requests he sent telepathically would be heeded only by the spirits, not by mere mortals.

"In the five or six columns written by Mr. Fowler, I do not find a word to indicate that he used a single 'mental test,' and this appears all the more unaccountable when it is remembered that he said he devoted nine days to rigid investigation of the matter," Wade wrote. "I claim that a single reliable response to a mental request or question, constitutes stronger testimony than all the physical manifestations made in Mr. Fowler's presence, even were they unquestioned by him; for while Koons, Son & Co. might be tolerable jugglers, Mr. F. would hardly admit that in that densely darkened chamber any member of the above could see and respond to his *silent wish.*"

Eager to try his experiment, Wade crowded into the spirit room with about 20 others on the evening of August 13. As the tambourine floated overhead, he silently willed it to descend and hang on his closed hand. It instantly complied and stayed there several seconds. Wade repeated this gambit on a subsequent evening, and again the tambourine came to him, as if it were a trained bird alighting on its master. Wade deemed his mental exercises "a very satisfactory test."

More wonders had awaited on his final evening with the Koonses. Before the séance even got under way, Jonathan ushered Wade and a select group into the spirit room for a private consultation. The coterie included the artist Selah Van Sickle; his wife, Mary; Dr. Robert McKay of Louisiana; and a "Mr. Bruce." (There is no mention of Nahum's being present.) Van Sickle, who had been staying with the Koons family for the past three or four months, was seeking guidance on a painting he was working on. "It was Mr. Van Sickle's intention to consult the Spirits in relation to a certain 'Panorama of the Creation' that he is painting in a house erected (by direction of Spirits) about two hundred yards from Koons'," Wade explained. After the room was darkened and greetings were made, "Mr. Van Sickle then questioned the spirit as to the manner in which he should paint a certain scene in the panorama, and he received clear and satisfactory directions." The visitors then engaged the spirit in "a general conversation . . . relative to the nature of God."

Once the main performance began that evening, Wade and many of the others, including Abigail and Nahum, had the sensation of a cold hand being pressed against their faces, hands, and heads. Wade became so convinced that the hands were not human, he declared, "I think that unless some one through stronger tests explodes the whole manifestation as a cheat, I shall die in the belief that this night I felt a Spirit-hand."

When McKay asked the spirit to write, the table was moved to within 3 feet of him and Wade so they could better observe the process. Wade leaned over to put his face within 2 inches of the hand, its palm gleaming like foxfire. Unlike the hand that jabbed the medium J. B. Conklin in the nose with a pencil, this one seemed to welcome scrutiny. As a test Wade made a mental request for it to stop writing and lift itself up off the table so he could get a better look: "The hand was twice slowly elevated, its fingers spread apart, and . . . I deliberately examined the same."

All the while Nahum and his mother were chatting, as were others in the company. "I observed that Mrs. K. encouraged Nahum to talk, that Dr. McKay might know it was not his hand that wrote, nor his mind that composed the communication, and Mr. J. Koons was heard talking at least eight feet distant," Ward reported. At length the spirit hand gave McKay a "chaste and impressive" written message, purportedly from the doctor's late wife. Adding a final grace note to the evening's performance, three more hands blinked on, dashing and darting about the room.

❈ ❈ ❈

AS no trip to Athens County would be complete without a visit to the Tippies, Wade and McKay also called upon that family the same week in August. Wade found in 44-year-old John Tippie "a kind old farmer" who gave over his entire evening to the investigators without charging a penny. Unlike the Koons demonstration, no maestro was present to call forth music from the fiddle in the spirit room. Nonetheless a violin played and settled on Wade's lap several times during the concert. "I took it into my hands each time that it came to me, when 'thrumming' away it would rise towards the ceiling like a thing of life," he reported. Wade also got special attention from a cold hand whose fingers were "sporting" with his own. As with Koons, Wade felt the show was too complex and well orchestrated to have been the work of tricksters. "All the musical instruments (except the drum) were floating about and sounding in different parts of the room, over our heads and behind and before us at the same time, and I conclude that they were either supported by Spirits, or, as friend Fowler might believe, by six mundane performers trained by Jonathan Koons, to humbug the public, for the gratification of 'killing time' and neglecting and losing his crops."

Concluding his report to the *Spiritual Telegraph,* Wade said he had found "nothing unchaste" at either establishment, noting that Tippie's trumpet messenger had ended the program with a "truly Christian exhortation." Wade blamed Fowler for sullying the reputation of the Koonses in particular. Other than the dark séances—which the spirits required for materialization of the hands—"there is nothing about the establishment to encourage the idea of deception; and remembering the uniform kindness of the Koons family, added to the fact that during the several years these exhibitions have continued they have granted free admission to all, the absurdity and unfairness of the charge leveled against them by Mr. Fowler . . . seems so glaring; that were the writer a less worthy gentleman, I should certainly conclude that it was designed as a revenge for some personal pique."

James E. Cowee of Greenburg, Indiana, who in 1854 had had a private talk with King while Ezra Tippie lay unconscious on the floor, also wrote in to defend the Koonses and Nahum in particular. Trying to stay ahead of the opposition, Fowler had already written the *New England Spiritualist* to discredit the Indiana schoolteacher's testimony. Fowler thought that Cowee, though a medium himself, was too gullible—too caught up in "the sphere of credulity" to be a reliable informant. But the newspaper chose to publish Cowee's lengthy rebuttal anyway, giving it the same amount of space allotted to Fowler's salvo. It would be up to readers to decide for themselves.

"As to Nahum's finding lungs and mouth for the spirits to talk with, I believe it not, *for I know it is not so,*" Cowee wrote, stressing the verbal contrast between King and the teenage boy. "Nahum, in his most passive or excitable movements, has little language, and finds it difficult to express his thoughts upon any subject other than those of common conversation, while the spirits are very voluble—using terms and words of which Nahum can possibly have no understanding."

The Indiana pilgrim also recalled one evening during his three-and-a-half-month visit when some phosphorus fell off the sandpaper onto the floor of the Koons Spirit Room. A hand took the drumstick and tried to tamp down the phosphorus but succeeded only in getting the chemical stuck on the head of the drumstick, rendering it luminescent. Thus clearly marked, the drumstick began to whirl about the legs of the mediums' table, flew to the ceiling, and descended to beat one of the drums. Next the sitters saw it whizzing around the legs of a "stranger and skeptic" seated near Jonathan. "The drum-stick is going round my legs with nobody hold of it," the man shouted. Cowee, who was seated at the front of the mediums' table between Nahum and Jonathan, was convinced that Nahum could not have reached across the four-foot-wide table and twirled the stick around the stranger's legs. Cowee was equally certain that no man could have gotten up and slipped past him without detection—and definitely not a woman in her voluminous skirts.

Cowee also related the curious story of an after-hours encounter in the Koons Spirit Room that solidified his faith in the existence of the spirit hands, which Fowler had curtly dismissed. One evening after a séance Cowee and a Mr. Baggs of Cincinnati lingered in the cabin after everyone else had left. As they sat quietly in the dark, the trumpet was faintly blown and seemed to be moving around. Cowee quickly went next door to the Koons house and found Nahum talking with the rest of the family. He returned to the spirit room with the medium, and the three of them seated themselves as usual around the smaller table. To their amazement the wires of the electrical table started shaking, and a stand positioned in front of it began to move toward them. It sounded as if several hands were pounding on the stand as it came to a halt in front of the two visitors. Both Baggs and Cowee felt their hands grasped by "invisible hands," almost as if someone were greeting them. The hands lingered, allowing the two visitors to palpate them. One was large and the other much smaller, leading the men to conclude they were from two different spirits. Cowee even believed that one of the hands had combed his hair at a previous séance.

"There were but three of us in the room," Cowee wrote, "and yet there were the hands of five; the two hands suddenly appearing varying much in size. Nahum was ten feet distant, and his mother and sisters positively not in the room. The hands then passed over to Nahum, taking the table [stand] along, shook the long table as if it were a leaf, and departed." Cowee did not mention phosphorus and did not explain how he could trace the location of the hands, but he was sure he had experienced the miraculous.

Cowee was also present the evening that the phosphorus caught fire. "At the moment of the blaze, the tambourine was heard to fall upon the table, and in the sudden glare, none could tell how Nahum got it over the fire," he wrote. He was sure that Jonathan did not tell Nahum to use the tambourine to smother the flames. "But he blamed Nahum for getting up and so doing until he had first shown that he was in his seat and had not the instrument playing," Cowee reported. The eyewitness doubted that Mrs. Koons or daughter Quintilla, who were seated close to Nahum, could have carried on the show afterward in such a spectacular manner.

Above all, Cowee questioned what motivation the family would have for trickery, when their actions have caused them "to suffer loss of friends, of property and time, and to meet ills innumerable, and to bring want and poverty like grim giants, staring them in the face." He recalled the joyous visages of the Koons family members as they filed out of the spirit room after "some great, beautiful and loving demonstration of the spirit life. . . . They feed the starving in body and soul, and ask naught but to see them made happy. The poor and rich, the ignorant and wise . . . go away full in the knowledge of an IMMORTAL LIFE when this mortal habitation is dissolved."

Now it was the artist Selah Van Sickle's turn to push back against Fowler. A longtime sojourner like Cowee, Van Sickle had spent the summer living with the Koonses and working in his new studio on their property. Not only did he have intimate knowledge of the family in various moods and seasons, he had spent time with Fowler as well. Van Sickle was present at some of the same demonstrations that Fowler attended, and Van Sickle accompanied Fowler on a return trip, perhaps to the Columbus area.

"We left Mr. Koons' together, and I was in his company for six days after his departure, when his mind became tormented by those doubts which have since been given to the public as facts," Van Sickle wrote. His statement appeared in the *Spiritual Telegraph* along with Wade's.

Van Sickle believed that class prejudice may have helped form the conclusions of the Harvard-educated Fowler: "It was plain that his judgment was in great measure biased by Mr. Koons['s] personal appearance, as well as the apparent poverty of the establishment. It seemed really repulsive to his feelings that a man of so humble an appearance as Mr. Koons, should be chosen as the medium for such wonderful manifestations." Van Sickle went on to say, "I flatter myself that I have as great a regard for truth as Mr. Fowler, while I have rather the advantage of him in not being influenced by so great a regard to personal appearance, or biased by any orthodox views of philosophy."

The artist did not regard evidence of a hand protruding from a coat sleeve to be indicative of fraud, for if the spirits could produce a hand and arm, why not a coat sleeve? In particular he defended the teenage boy who had borne the brunt of the charges:

> I have frequently heard Nahum and the presiding spirit speak at the same time; I have been alone with Nahum in the Spirit-room, where I have held long conversations with the Spirits, upon subjects of which Nahum was entirely ignorant. I have also held these conversations while Nahum was snoring in his seat. I have sat beside Mrs. Koons, and heard the spirits sing, when there was no other member of the family present but the father, mother, and son. I have also heard Mr. Koons' daughter, who is accused of performing the singing part, sing in unison with the Spirit. In short, in all the manifestations that I have witnessed I have not the slightest suspicion of the family's practicing fraud.
>
> I beg to offer this slight sketch of my experience, as a set-off to Mr. Fowler's elaborate statement. No personal feelings of friendship shall hinder me from declaring the truth, and throwing back the charge of fraud and deception upon those who will not trust the evidence of their own senses; nor shall the humble appearance of Mr. Koons, though contrasted with

the showy exterior of his accuser, prevent my distinguishing an honest man from an artful and designing rogue. I have no other means of judging of facts, or of detecting fraud, than the evidence of my senses. If I disbelieve them with regard to these manifestations, I may as well call in question the reality of my own existence.

I am, gentlemen, your obedient servant, Selah Van Sickle.

NOW that the controversy had escalated to personal attack, Fowler fought back as best he could. In a second letter to the *New England Spiritualist,* which had printed his original allegations, he complained that part of his original article had been edited out. (In an editor's note Newton explained that the part taken out was too objectionable to be printed.) Fowler vigorously took exception to Newton's claim that Fowler had denied "the evidence of his own senses." He explained that he was very clear about the sounds he had heard in the dark séance, but his emotional state on those two magical evenings affected his *interpretation* of how those sounds were produced. Later, looking at the evidence in a less emotionally charged state, he realized he had been wrong to ascribe the sounds to a nonhuman source. If this caused him to lose credibility, "then, I fear, the opinion of most Spiritualists will be stale enough, for who of them has not had *good reason* to change his opinions in a similar manner, many times?"

Fowler also defended his actions at the circle of the newspaper editor Toohey by taking a swipe at the members' gullibility: "Different members of the circle . . . were so ready to receive and believe, that had I been disposed, they could have been egregiously imposed upon and delighted." Fowler went on to lament the willingness of so many in the movement to believe: "How wonderful is it to find a believer in spirit-intercourse, ready to *question* any of the wonders connected therewith! I have found no greater obstacle to thorough investigation of these phenomena than the credulity of Spiritualists. They are ever ready to decide every questionable point in favor of the marvelous. And if *their* judgment is not readily indorsed, they cry out *'skeptic,'* and have no patience to make further experiments. I am satisfied that the true philosophy of these phenomena cannot be discovered by such persons. Still, I repeat, my belief in the one great fact of spirit-intercourse is unshaken."

Even with this stout counterattack, Fowler promised more to come, for the part of his original article that the newspaper refused to publish "contains the most important evidence against Mr. Koons, and will be given to the public." Editor Newton, striking an evenhanded tone, responded that once that information became public, he would quote only from the parts containing *evidence*—"not doubting that the effect will be, as it has been thus far, to bring out the strength of the affirmative side more fully, as well as to give a healthful check to the 'credulity' of Spiritualists, if any such check is needed."

AS fur flew in the columns of the *New England Spiritualist,* a reader who called himself "Almost Believer" suggested the perfect solution to the dilemma of the dark séance, a "very reasonable one" in the eyes of the paper's editor. Almost Believer had a surefire way to determine who was playing the musical instruments—turn on the light:

> As many will not believe that the various instruments in music circles are played upon without the aid of human hands, why may not an arrangement be made to have the room suddenly lighted when the drums, tambourines, &tc., are being played? The playing would cease, no doubt, but the audience could see if the medium, and others near her and the instruments, were engaged in the performance. When I speak of *suddenly* lighting the room, I mean that it shall be done only by the consent of the medium and others conducting the performance. This might be done towards the last of the evening, in order not to deharmonize the circle before witnessing the usual phenomena.

Almost Believer laid out for readers a stunning tableau: the lantern flashes, the music stops, and the bow, drumstick, and tambourine fall to the floor. This would prove the spiritualist case handsomely, demonstrating not only that spirits were playing the instruments but that darkness was required for the manifestations. Such a confirmation would surely be worth the disruption. "Who would not lose an evening for the purpose of having his doubts removed?" the skeptic asked.

The final objection anticipated by Almost Believer was that the spirits would not allow such an experiment to take place—exactly the argument put forth by Jonathan Koons. Almost Believer insisted that blocking the proposal would be counterproductive. "How *can* they object, if their object in all these manifestations, is to convince us that they are from the spirits, and that we are to live again after shuffling off this mortal coil! Can they do this in any way more effectually than by removing all doubt as to the reality of these phenomena? Certainly not. And until some test, like the one I have proposed, shall be resorted to, the great majority of men will, I fear, retain their skepticism and their antagonism to the last."

16

Galileo in Eclipse

ON AUGUST 15, 1855, four days after Fowler's explosive charges first appeared in print, Jonathan Koons wrote a curious disclaimer to the *Spiritual Telegraph*. A vast rumor was spreading that "a great convention of mediums" would be held at or near his home in September, but Koons insisted, "I know nothing of the matter." In fact "urgent business" would require him to be gone most of the month. "I avail myself of the present opportunity to announce this fact to the public in general, in order to avoid disappointment to those who might feel inclined to visit me at that time, for the purpose of witnessing spiritual manifestations. I beg also to say, that the above mentioned report found its way into the world without my knowledge or sanction; consequently, I do not hold myself responsible in case those who have believed it should find themselves disappointed." According to a separate notice in the *Telegraph*, Koons planned to be away from home from September 1 to about September 20. "After this time he will be pleased to receive calls at his Spirit-room as before."

As it turned out, Koons was home after all at the beginning of September, threshing wheat by day and hosting yet another séance by night. Although his burnished image in the spiritualist community had been somewhat dimmed by recent allegations of deception, people kept coming; perhaps the controversy with Fowler made them more curious than ever. Pilgrims from Virginia, Tennessee, Michigan, Louisiana, and distant parts of Ohio descended on the Koons and Tippie households, boarding with the two families. It is not known whether Jonathan took his urgent business trip at any time during September. Perhaps he never intended to go in the first place, or his plans changed because of a crisis on the home front: his brother Michael, about 62 years old, lay gravely ill.

Jonathan soon got word that Michael was near death, not expected to live another hour. Jonathan quickly called Nahum, and the two closeted themselves in the spirit room. Some female visitors scurried after them and eavesdropped at the cabin door. For about 15 minutes they heard nothing. Finally, the interlopers could make out a conversation inside the spirit room.

"I don't think he's coming," Jonathan said.

"Well, Koons, what do you want?" inquired a voice they associated with the horn.

"My brother is very sick and I want to know what to do."

"He is very sick," agreed the trumpet, "and I apprehend will not recover. He is an old man, and is run down."

"But can you not prescribe something that will relieve him?" Jonathan persisted.

"Yes, give him what he can drink of a decoction of yellow-dock root. Then steam him over pennyroyal, and in half an hour afterwards, give him a tepid bath."

Jonathan emerged from the spirit room and told the curious pilgrims what the horn had prescribed. Then he hurried off to his brother's place 5 miles away to minister to him in his extremity.

Just as the spirit had foretold, Michael slipped away. His funeral was held on Sunday, September 2, probably at the Concord Church a few miles from Mount Nebo. But Jonathan had little time for private grieving, as a circle of strangers was awaiting him that evening in the spirit room.

Within the group of pilgrims was H. B. Champion, a well-known medium from Nashville, Tennessee. (Perhaps this was the basis for the rumor that Koons would be hosting "a great convention of mediums" at that time.) An admirer had hailed Champion as "one of the most remarkable mediums of the age." Like Jonathan Koons himself, Champion once regarded the claims of spiritualists as fraudulent—until the day in 1852 when a spirit informed him that he was a medium. Though he was a man seldom given to Bible reading or book reading in general, he soon was able to give informed discourse about the Holy Writ and the classics while in a trance state.

Champion and Koons would have had many things to talk about in addition to their dramatic, Saul-on-the-road-to-Damascus conversions. Both men had served as a conduit for Indian spirits, which here in this Western land were thought to still linger in the forests the native people had inhabited. In honor of his status as a medium, Champion was seated along with Abigail, Jonathan, and Nahum at the séance table.

Joining the Tennessee contingent that Sunday evening was Benjamin Lewitt of Fallassburgh, Michigan, who had been captivated at the Koonses' séance the night before by "disembodied spirits," first singing sweetly to Jonathan's lone violin accompaniment and then "shriek[ing] out in an unearthly voice." The Sunday night performance, though, turned out to be brief, as King appeared for only a chat, as he was engaged elsewhere. "He suddenly threw down the trumpet with which he was speaking, and left, disappointing Mr. and Mrs. Koons, as they evidently wished for further communication," Lewitt later reported.

On Monday evening the first King was entirely absent, and an entity calling itself Second King took his place, orchestrating "a splendid musical performance." And on this third night a spirit hand did appear but first had to hunt for paper because no one had thought to leave any on the electrical table. Somehow the hand found a pencil and some leaves from an old ledger book and brought them forward, scribbling one message for Lewitt and another for "the friends from the South." Although the advice seemed to have a cookie-cutter quality, exhorting them to "be of good cheer" and "let your light shine," these visitors left the Koons homestead satisfied that, as Lewitt put it, their hosts had allowed them to witness "some of the most convincing and astounding evidences of the blessed immortality of man, ever given to a bigoted and skeptical world." Any doubts stirred up by Fowler's report had been retired. After spending 10 days with the Koonses and Tippies, Lewitt concluded that the minister's attack on these "two innocent families" was brought on "by the fact that

Mr. Koons refused to give him [Fowler] complete control of his circle while he was there, as he wished."

❋   ❋   ❋

THAT fall a previous visitor to the Koons Spirit Room landed yet another salvo in the ongoing public relations war. A businessman from Marietta, Ohio, the historic river town east of Athens, wrote to a Cleveland newspaper to set the record straight, seeing as how, in his estimation, those reporting favorably on the Koons phenomena were "egregiously humbugged." The writer, identified only as "G.," claimed to have visited the scene of the wonders with an open mind. "I did not go there prejudiced against spiritualism," he wrote. "I was open to conviction. But I came away not one-half so favorable to it as when I went."

G. was traveling with a friend, and their first stop was the Tippie farm, where they arrived unannounced. With pressing business in Marietta the next day, G. and his companion were expecting to attend a séance that very night. But John Tippie demurred. "The spirits have left," he said. "I cannot now summon a band powerful enough to produce manifestations tonight." The Marietta men elected to stay over and were shown to a bed where they spent a miserable night slapping at bedbugs and fleas. After breakfast, which G. ungraciously complained was "fully in keeping with our lodging," they decided to go on to the Koons farm.

G. attended an evening séance there and was suspicious of the requirement for total darkness. He said Jonathan Koons had cautioned the audience members not to move around during the performance to avoid being hit by objects hurtling through the air. But if spirits could see in the dark, why wouldn't they know that someone in the room had changed position? G. also noticed how close the mediums were seated to the drums and other musical instruments, a juxtaposition he called "no very wonderful circumstance." He complained that even though the tambourine was flying about, it never paused in any visitor's hand long enough to be examined.

The Marietta resident was equally skeptical about the illuminated hand that had manifested itself in the space above the mediums' table, "flitting about in an area of three or four feet." He wondered whether someone with a phosphorus-dipped hand could be standing on top of the table. "The hand was very careful not to come within the reach of the spectators, and no hand was grasped except a little one that nestled lovingly in the hand of my friend," G. charged. "I am told that the phosphorus hand was grasped once, but pulled and struggled till it received its liberty." G.'s account of the hand's standoffishness was contradicted by other accounts in which the appendage did shake hands with people in the audience. However, G. believed those people were lying or deluded, "for Mr. Koons himself told us that spectators were not allowed to take hold of the hand."

When a skeptic proposed some tests for the mediums, G. believed that Jonathan Koons's bluff had been called:

> Hon. Mr. Welch, of Athens, proposed to cut an aperture in the head of a barrel, large enough to admit the drumsticks into it, but not large enough to admit a human hand, and to require the spirits to withdraw them from the barrel. This test was refused. He then asked to attach to some fine silk thread a hook, and to fasten this hook into the coat collar of the medium, and to be allowed the privilege of holding the extreme end of the thread in his own hand. *This* was denied him. He then asked that he might be allowed to attach the fore fingers of each hand of the medium together with a short thread, and see if they would be in the same position when the candle was relighted. This was also refused him, and every test that could have satisfactorily settled the matter has been denied.

But G. reserved his deepest scorn for the voice speaking through the trumpet. Though supposedly that of the ancient spirit King, the shrill voice sounded rather human. What's more, G. found the entity's mutterings banal, even inelegant. "Oh beneficent age!" he wrote sarcastically. "When we have the privilege of conversing with such elevated and elevating spirits, manifesting their luminous presence in a little box of a log hut, with the aid of phosphorus, tambourines and tin horns!"

✻ ✻ ✻

J. B. Conklin, who took a pilgrimage to the Koons Spirit Room with three friends in late 1854, had made his reputation as a test medium in New York

City. He routinely submitted himself to psychic challenges posed by strangers, a territory into which the Koons family seldom ventured. One test involved a newspaper editor who sent Conklin a combination lock with a dare attached: "If there was any truth in spiritualism, let the spirits open that, and he would be satisfied." The medium received the lock at 10:00 a.m., and by noon the spirits had spelled out the word *core,* which proved to be the right combination. A few years later Conklin would conduct séances for an anonymous client who turned out to be Abraham Lincoln, visiting New York City in 1860 during his first campaign for the presidency.

Conklin's experiences at the Koons farm had left him so impressed that he fired off a letter to a newspaper to describe the wonders. "While the spirits are communicating, there seems to be around all in the room, an unseen influence, which opens to a remarkable degree each person's interior man, to the reception of all ideas advanced by the spirits," he wrote. He found the ideas of King, especially, to be "of a very elevated nature."

About a year later, however, Conklin's ardor had cooled somewhat. Now he was suggesting that the Koons phenomena, though remarkable, were somewhat inconsistent. That would explain why sometimes the demonstration mainly would consist of King's chatting with the audience through the horn but at other times would include a light show of glowing phosphorus and flying instruments touching and teasing the audience. During one dark circle Conklin clasped and shook hands with a spirit hand, which "was withdrawn from me like a vapor, and held up before me." Conklin in turn held up a blank sheet of paper in front of the hand, prompting it to scribble "two hundred lines" on the sheet while it was suspended in air. He was gratified to see the most spectacular arrow in Koons's quiver, but the medium concluded that "there seems to be more difficulty in securing the requisite conditions for forming the spirit hand, than for a great number of other phenomena."

The hit-or-miss nature of the manifestations he blamed not on the mediums but on the discordant emotional state of the audience. "Ignorant and unbelieving persons have no idea that certain conditions are necessary to spiritual communications of a convincing or valuable character," Conklin wrote. When husbands, wives, and their various kin all insist on being admitted together, "one person coming in because another does"—or, worse, when people who are openly hostile to the process intrude—the mélange brings suffering to the mediums. If enough honest truth seekers are present, the manifestations may appear, "but in circles for the production of the creative phenomena, or the transmission of interior wisdom, no person should be allowed to come who is discordant to the circle, and more especially to the medium." If Conklin had been the doorkeeper at the Koons Spirit Room, critics like G. would never have gained a foothold inside.

✳ ✳ ✳

WHILE Koons's critics and surrogates battled in print, insight into his state of mind that melancholy fall of 1855 can be gleaned from an article he wrote for the *Lockport (PA) Messenger.* Its headline was "Spiritualism and Reform."

Koons began with a reference to one of his favorite historical figures—Galileo. Although he did not say so directly, Koons believed that both he and Galileo were victims of religious orthodoxy and unfavorable public opinion. "It is a lamentable fact, that men are too apt to suffer their reasoning powers to become clouded and swayed by the breeze of public sentiment," Koons wrote. "When Galileo discovered the movement of the heavenly bodies and the rotary motion of this earth, and proclaimed his discovery to the leading faculty of the world, he was hissed and scouted, and was ultimately compelled to recant his philosophy under the penalty of death." Koons went on to tell the familiar story (now considered apocryphal) of how Galileo recanted before church leaders but defiantly muttered to his followers that the Earth still moves. "Now look at the fruit of his discovery," Koons quipped. "It is not necessary at this age to teach the revolution of the world itself; but we do deem it necessary to teach the revolutions of its inhabitants."

Koons made no reference in the article to his life as a medium, but his lines appear tinged with regret: "Reformers are in the habit of talking about free love, liberty, peace, tranquility, wealth, fame and honors," he wrote. "They universally point out the captivating and flowery prospects of future enjoyments, but fail to set forth the amount of labor, suffering and long endurance, that naturally counteract the enjoyment of the objects of their pursuit." It would be far better for would-be reformers to look to the less glamorous side before choosing that lofty path, Koons said. "The better method for men to pursue would be: first, to compute the probable amount of sacrifices and privations that would naturally attend the pursuit and achievement of any desired object, purpose, or end; . . . and if any difference is considered necessary in estimating the loss and gain, let it be placed on the side of the unpleasant and counteracting influences, rather than that of the brighter prospects . . . and then the achieved treasure will be sure to merit a higher degree of real enjoyment and pleasure."

After operating the spirit room for more than three years, Koons seemed to be taking stock of his life. And although many spiritual teachers might say happiness comes with the journey, not the destination, Koons appeared to disagree. At age 44, he had received spectacular acclaim as a medium—and not just any medium but one of the elite who could deliver physical effects; through the trumpet and on the page he had delivered a message of love, harmony, and immortality to thousands, yet something seemed to be lacking. What was "the desired object, purpose, or end" that he craved? Could it have been financial security, respect from the local community, or perhaps even an end to a juggernaut he had created? Whether by accident or self-definition, Koons was all too often finding himself cast in the role of martyr.

EVEN as the first frosts came to Mount Nebo in October, Koons was unable to forget the fiery summer controversy and the anger left smoldering in his heart. Although many of his admirers had rallied to his aid in the spiritualist press, J. H. Fowler's charges had ignited in Koons an urge to defend his reputation. What vitriol must have dripped from his pen as he wrote a rebuttal to the *New England Spiritualist,* mockingly signing it with Fowler's words, "Koons, King & Ko." A. E. Newton—once again exercising his editorial judgment—decided not to run most of it. It contained, he said, mainly personal criticisms of Fowler and his methodology, whereas the real issue of importance to readers was "whether spirits cause the demonstrations that take place there." Newton preferred to save the space for reports from independent witnesses.

However, Newton did find a public interest in printing a small portion of Koons's letter. Koons called on *uninvited guests* to stay away from his séances unless they were willing to follow his rules for conducting the circle. He added sarcastically: "Whenever we give public invitations for all or any to visit and scrutinize the performances at this place, then of course, we will grant them the privilege to conduct matters to their liking, and then we will suffer ourselves to be bound hand and foot like martyrs, and be slobbered upon by tobacco-chewers and brandy-drinkers, as we did when animals in human form, of all ranks and characters, first began to intrude upon us."

In another part of the message Koons showed that he was still smarting from the attack by Fowler, whom he regarded as a snob with upper-class pretensions. "We place all upon a level, so far as personal respect is concerned, from the Emperor to the down-trodden slave," the self-educated Koons wrote, "and we set no extra value upon the polish of college or academical educations: and if any one will repudiate genuine ideas for the want of this sort of polish, we cannot view them in any other light than as slaves to form and fashion, and strangers to the merits of true honor."

To Newton, the editor, it now seemed that Koons was trying to put the genie back in the bottle, to distance himself from his celebrity role by claiming nothing and refusing further scrutiny. Newton found Koons's new policy to be rigid but nonetheless advised anyone who wanted to test the Koons séances to "govern themselves accordingly."

IN early October 1855 the St. Louis spiritualist and mesmerist A. Miltenberger was traveling through Ohio on his way back from Pittsburgh and intended to pay a call on the Koons circle in Athens County. However, when he stopped in Columbus, he somehow learned that Nahum was not at home and therefore decided the long trip across rough country would not be worth the effort. "As the *hand* was what I wanted to see and feel, I did not like to venture on seventy miles of *staging* to hear the physical manifestations alone," he wrote, evidently referring to the spirit music. After touring Columbus and visiting two local artists who drew under spirit impression, Miltenberger had the good fortune to land in Cardington, a Morrow County railroad station 38 miles north of the capital city. "Within a mile and a half I found an old quaker couple, Joseph Smith and wife, with whom Nahum Koons and Mr. Van Syckle were sojourning." Whether from a tip from other spiritualists or sheer good luck, Miltenberger had found the medium he sought—just a short jaunt away on the railroad.

A year earlier the Smiths had visited the Koons circle on Mount Nebo and had a life-changing experience. "They were sceptics, but remained eighteen days in close attendance, and at length were converted," Miltenberger wrote. The presiding spirit, King, promised the new converts that he would organize a spirit band to come to Cardington if they would prepare the way. Now at the Smith home Miltenberger found himself in a replica of the Koons Spirit Room, complete with the electricity retainer and musical instruments. However, the elderly couple had thus far been unable to conjure the entities consistently on their own, hence the need for Nahum's visit. According to Miltenberger, "Mr. Smith says at times he has all the effects that King produces (except the hand) but that it is very *uncertain,* and that he had invited Nahum there to *astonish the county,* in which I think he succeeded; for this was only his second night, and as many as two hundred people assembled there."

Despite the large crowd, Miltenberger managed to get a seat at the mediums' table, positioning himself across from Nahum. When the séance was over, Miltenberger was convinced that the musical instruments really did float about the darkened room: "The tambourine and horn performance satisfied me of this, *that the sense of hearing could follow round the horn and tambourine faster than the eye could have done had it been lighted,*" he later wrote. The other eerie effects, he thought, "*might* have been done by a spirit in the body. My *belief* does not amount to anything." But if the St. Louis spiritualist had hoped to investigate further, his mission was cut short. "I intended remaining there a few days, but King hurried them [presumably Nahum and Selah Van Sickle] off, without rhyme or reason, and they were in the habit of obeying him. I did not blame them for it, but it would not suit me to be a medium of that kind."

✳ ✳ ✳

BACK in Athens County on October 20, the Koons family was conducting yet another public séance. After they delivered their customary fare of fiddle tunes and conversation through the horn and harmonica, their visitors asked for the best token of all—the materialization of the famed spirit hand. A cloud soon appeared about a foot above the heads of the seated audience, at first so dark that it could scarcely be discerned from the inky blackness that surrounded it. Eventually the globe turned grayish and then white, producing a glow that illuminated the floor of the cabin. At the base of the cloud little lights—ranging in size from a candle flame to a five-cent piece—would blink on and off. Some lasted as long as 30 seconds whereas others vanished after just a few seconds. The color of the little lights resembled that of gaslight. After a while the room faded back to black, leaving the audience wondering what was next. The voice from the horn announced that the spirits "could not control the elements necessary to produce the hand."

Scarcely missing a beat, the horn then asked Jonathan Koons if he would like to hear a new tune. Without waiting for an answer, the harmonica struck up a lively melody and the tambourine joined in.

"I can beat that," Koons taunted after the song was over.

"Try it," said the horn.

Koons commenced to fiddle faster than usual, but try as he would, the tambourine stayed a little ahead.

"A little faster, Mr. Koons, a little faster," the trumpet goaded.

Koons switched to another tune at an even faster tempo, but the tambourine surged ahead once again.

"Go it Koons, go it Koons," screamed the horn above the din of the music.

Bested at his own game, Koons quit playing.

As a spectator later recorded, the parting shot came through the horn as a "shrill clownish laugh, directed at Koons as if to say, 'You can't come it.'" Koons had lost his musical dare but once again had proved his showmanship. The spirits' failed attempt to produce the hand was of little consequence to the spectators now. When the light was struck, the audience found all as it had been—the Koons mediums seated in their places, the instruments mute upon the table—as if all that had come between had been just a beautiful dream.

But the crowd-pleasing musical finale masked a hidden truth. The spirits—precisely as they had warned for the past year—were withdrawing from Mount Nebo. Just as the hand had failed to materialize, support

for Koons and his family had not coalesced. Now the Koonses were looking beyond Mount Nebo's sheltering slopes. Even the great Galileo had
quit Pisa for Padua largely for financial reasons. The days of the vaunted
spirit room were winding down.

17

An Arc of Golden Roses

AS THE waning year slid to its conclusion, Jonathan and Nahum were spending much more time on the road. November 1855 found them in the Columbus area, visiting friends in Cardington and Delaware Station, where the Smiths and Van Sickles lived. But the sharp-eyed Jonathan followed the newspapers wherever he went—and now a letter published in the *Spiritual Universe* of Cleveland had set him off. One F. F. Jones of Federalton, Athens County, Ohio, had somehow criticized, or at least questioned, the manifestations seen in the Koons and Tippie rooms, and Jonathan's fighting instinct was aroused. The feisty medium was as quick as ever to defend his reputation, penning his response on November 17. Koons suggested that Jones's letter was bogus, and that its author, who evidently claimed to be a spiritualist himself, was a fictitious person:

> Now without comment let me inform the readers of your invaluable columns that there is no such place as ["]Federalton," in Athens Co., and, in the second place there is no "spirit rooms" owned in said County by men bearing the names of "J. Coon" and "J. Tippy." It, however, appears evident from the tenor of the gentleman's letter, that his aims were to implicate the manifestations at the rooms of the respondent, and "J. Tippy's" in said County. Now as regards the investigations made at my room, I am in truth, bound to say, that I know of no such man as "F. F. Jones" in the county of

Athens; and, it is hoped, that the writer of said letter will locate his residence by some adjoining points so that I may be enabled to find him and witness some of his favorite spirit manifestations in the way of variety.

Koons had chosen to attack his opponent not on substance but on a technicality: Jones had misspelled the names Koons and Tippie. In a bit of sophistry reminiscent of Odysseus and the Cyclops, Koons said that *nobody* by those names owned spirit rooms in the county. To goad Jones further, Koons challenged him to give directions to where he lived, so that Koons could call on Jones to see what kind of manifestations *he* could produce.

Jones wrote back on December 10 from Federalton, an Athens County community in Rome Township where Federal Creek flows into the Hocking River—halfway across the county from Koons's home. (This time his initials were corrected to read "T. F." Jones.) As to whether he was real or imaginary, Jones responded that "if the gentleman will not believe what I have already written, he will not be likely to believe anything that I might write in reference to the matter." But Koons's rhetorical gambit had failed: Timothy F. Jones was not only a sentient being but a local leader, at various times a justice of the peace and township trustee. What's more, he was a minister of the Universalist faith.

In his rebuttal Jones went on to say that he did not claim to produce spiritual manifestations himself. He explained that his purpose in writing the first letter was not to "implicate" the phenomena at the Koons and Tippie rooms but to express his concern about the nature of dark séances. "I have thought that spiritualists, generally, set too high a value on that class of physical manifestations that can only be tested in the dark," Jones wrote. "Skeptics are led to the belief, from the very nature of such exhibitions, that the whole affair is but a grand cheat, which designing persons are endeavoring to palm upon the world."

The war of words in the *Spiritual Universe* did little to advance the understanding of spiritualism, but it did deliver some disturbing news. In the final sentence of his November 17 letter to the paper, Koons must have shocked many of his followers with an offhand, sarcastic announcement: "The spirit room at my residence, where those *gross* manifestations have been made, are closed for an indefinite period, which might be important for these to know, who are contemplating visits to that place."

✳ ✳ ✳

HIRAM Shenich was confounded upon reading Jonathan Koons's strange words in the *Spiritual Universe*. A clairvoyant healing medium who had relocated from Canada West to Athens County, Shenich wondered why Koons would deny that John Tippie Jr. kept a spirit room when they all knew he did. The Amestown resident had taken Koons's words quite literally and did not get the joke. Shenich had witnessed the dark circles of Koons and Tippie firsthand—and was something of a performer himself. Back in June 1855, at a Koons séance, he had jammed with the spirit band, playing a second fiddle while Koons played his. A guest at the impromptu concert found it "much more of a performance than usual," adding that Shenich played the violin very well.

A session at Tippie's that September had shown Shenich the extremes of brutishness and bliss. Although it was routinely reported that the Tippies didn't play musical instruments—the spirits did all of it—the invisibles would often call on a fiddler player from the audience if one was present. This night the lot fell to Shenich. After a few introductory tunes by the spirit band, a voice began to speak through the trumpet. Ten or 15 minutes into the address, a young ruffian rose from the audience and kicked the underside of the medium's table several times, upsetting it and bringing the show to a halt. The horn soon recovered and gave the young man a tongue-lashing, telling him to "go and remain in darkness and ignorance till nature develops you to a higher plane of intelligence." Once the unruly guest was banished, the presiding spirit commented that he was "very sorry that there were so many who had a predominance of animal propensities."

Shenich and the spirit band picked up the instruments again, perhaps to settle the crowd with a tune. While Shenich was playing in the dark, a spirit came up to him and asked for the fiddle. He handed over the instrument, which then flew over the heads of the audience, playing all the while. Another invisible felt inspired to snatch a string of sleigh bells off the wall and ring them in Shenich's face. "I said, if they did not take the bells away from my face, I would take them away from them," Shenich recounted. The spirit said, "That is just what we want."

Shenich lunged for the offending bells with his left hand and caught the spirit hand holding them. But the entity squeezed *his* hand so hard he begged to be let go. Instead Shenich was jerked up off the floor and levitated nearly to the ceiling in an almost horizontal position. In that position the invisibles flew him around the room for some time until they tired of the game and dropped him back on the table. Shenich's feet caught the edge of the table and shoved it about 2 feet. Somehow the spirits broke the bridge of the violin during their antics. Shenich meekly got off the table and took his seat, nursing a hand that would be sore for days thereafter.

Why the spirits would subject their musical collaborator to such rough measures is a mystery, but Shenich soon forgot his pain. "Then one of the spirits came and stood before me, and said 'Look!'" he later wrote. "I looked and saw him distinctly, with what he afterwards told me was one of the forms of glory on his head. It was something like the shape of a horse shoe, with the ends hanging down over his ears. It appeared of beautiful rainbow colors of diamond brightness; no earthly beauty can compare with the splendor of that sight." Next the spirit picked the tin horn up off the table and blew brightly colored sparks that shimmered and crackled in the dark. The séance ended with the spirit addressing the circle through the trumpet, explaining "how to live to be happy" and then bidding all a good night.

After witnessing such wonders at Tippie's, Shenich would not allow his host to be misrepresented in the *Spiritual Universe*. In December 1855, to counter Jonathan Koons's wordplay, the clairvoyant musician was about to make front-page news with his stout assertions that the Tippie demonstrations were alive and well:

> Dear Sir:—In looking over the columns of your valuable paper of Nov. 1855, I noticed a piece signed JONATHAN KOONS, which said that there was no spirit room in Athens County, Ohio, owned by J. TIPPIE. Now, many of the readers of your paper, know that that is an error; and it is very strange that Mr. KOONS should make such an assertion, when he has known J. TIPPIE for many years before there was any such thing known as Spiritualism, and knows that he has kept a circle for three years, and lives now where he has always lived, within 2 ½ miles of JONATHAN KOONS.' We think that it must be either a misprint or a gross mistake of Mr. Koons. But, be that as it may, for the sake of truthseekers, we think it should be rectified.

Though Shenich didn't mention it in his letter, he was in fact a business partner of John Tippie's. Just a few weeks earlier the two men had run an ad in the *Spiritual Telegraph* informing the public that spirits had led them to a "magnetic spring" near Tippie's spirit room, one that possessed "extraordinary healing qualities." In addition to the spiritual tourism that visitors to the Koons and Tippie farms found so appealing, now came the promise of physical blessings as well:

> After September, 1855, John Tippie will be prepared to receive patients, promising immediate relief to all inflammatory and painful diseases, and a speedy cure to all curable diseases. He will have Hiram Shenich, a clairvoyant healing medium, in attendance, who will examine and prescribe for all diseases, while under Spirit influence in the clairvoyant condition. With these advantages, he can say to the public with perfect confidence, that all reasonable expectations will be realized; and as no pains will be spared to benefit all, and no charges made for curing, and only a reasonable charge made for board and extra attendance, it is hoped that the public will avail themselves not only of these advantages, but also of the privilege of conversing with Spirits, who will talk audibly through the trumpet. All visitors can have private conversations with their Spirit-friends, who will be consulted in all matters ending to benefit mankind.

Shenich must have been dismayed by Koons's statement that the room of "J. Tippy" was not operating; on the contrary, Shenich believed that Tippie's phenomena—which occurred almost every evening—had steadily improved and were "better than they ever were." In fact "many who visit both rooms think that the manifestations at J. TIPPIE'S room are far superior to those at J. KOONS," Shenich declared. He explained that the spirits talked throughout the day using the trumpet, both in the house and in the spirit room; and in the evening they sometimes skipped the horn altogether and addressed the audience directly and audibly. Up to *four* phosphorescent hands could now be seen at one time, as they worked the crowd shaking hands with no signs of flittering away.

On a recent late fall evening, Anna Tippie was in the séance room during a demonstration, trying vainly to quiet the crying seven-month-old girl in her lap.

"Your child is troublesome," King announced, finally stating the obvious.
"Yes," Anna said, "and I wish you would take it, for I can't keep it still."
"Well, give it here," King acceded.

Two hands with arms materialized, took the child from Anna Tippie, and carried it around the room. Next, King "set it down on the table in the centre of the room, played music for it, sung and whistled, and talked to it for some time, then gave it back to its mother," Shenich recounted.

On another night King chose to materialize before the audience as a complete body, wearing "hat, coat, pants and boots." He stood on top of the mediums' table and struck a match off the side of a nearby stovepipe, illuminating his form for all in the room to see. Then he jumped down off the table and strolled about with the glowing match still in his hand. But just as the audience was growing accustomed to the friendly ghost, he "dissolved to the elements again."

Not only had the effects become more dazzling, but Tippie had been hard at work to improve his facilities. Shenich reported that Tippie initially had "a poor house and poor accommodations for visitors, but he has been building, and is now living in his new house, which is entirely completed, with ample room for many visitors." Tippie had also built a new spirit room to replace the original log building, and the family planned to start using it in a few days. Shenich explained that the new spirit room, with frame construction more airtight than that of the log cabin, would allow for more spectacular demonstrations, such as King's full-body materialization. "The spirits say that when they perform in the tight room, where the elements are confined, they will assume physicality in distinct forms, and perform with a burning lamp in the room, so all can see them, and all they do," Shenich continued. "And Mr. J. TIPPIE has been to a great expense to build and get things the spirits require, to manifest to the satisfaction of all who visit, for truth; and he intends to keep up the manifestations as long as he lives in the flesh. And in future the performances will be principally in the daytime."

If Shenich's report is to be believed, the Tippies were expecting a halcyon New Year, when they would bring the spirits into the light and dispel all suspicions about the dark séance. And surely with the coming of spring, pilgrims would flock to the magnetic healing waters on the Tippie farm.

✻ ✻ ✻

ALTHOUGH performances at the Koons Spirit Room were now suspended, Nahum and Jonathan were still very much practicing mediums as they contemplated a special invitation from Cincinnati. A private circle in that city had decided to finally solve the riddle of the battery that was said to power the spirit manifestations. The Cincinnati group had fitted up a spirit room and constructed its own machine, patterned after the one in the Koons Spirit Room, under conditions in which chicanery would have been impossible. "The principal apparatus, to which the name of Electrical Retainer was given by the spirits at Mr. K.'s, is a singular instrument. It contains most of the elements of a Galvanic Battery, and an ordinary Electrical Machine, but differently arranged, so that a person acquainted with such apparatus would not expect to witness the results of either," the *Spiritual Messenger* explained. Members of the circle had tried to activate the device and were rewarded with some raps on the supporting table and on the wooden part of the drum. They could also hear faint scratchings on the strings of a guitar. These weak effects were encouraging, considering that they were generated with no mediums present. Circle members could hardly wait until the real psychic talent arrived.

Hence the invitation came to Jonathan and Nahum to visit Cincinnati, which they did in mid- to late December, traveling with the painter Selah Van Sickle. The circle was a private one, but word leaked out of the mediums' engagement, and a large crowd gathered at the home of a Mr. Wilson. A newspaper correspondent, who was a member of the circle himself, insisted that the hosts had made no special arrangements for the Koonses' visit and had stuck to the usual room conditions and order of events. "Mr. Van Sickle was seated on one side of the room, and next to him Mr. Quinn, a member of the circle," the reporter recounted. "On the other side, Mr. Koons and his son; next to them, Mr. Wilson . . . next the writer . . . and the remainder of the circle and visitors promiscuously seated. If the mediums had been a company of well-trained jugglers, coming with the known purpose of deceiving us, the circumstances could not have been more favorable for preventing collusion."

As soon as Jonathan began fiddling in the darkened room, the audience heard loud reports near a table. Later examination revealed two gashes, evidently left by a drumstick, in its soft poplar surface. As the booms continued, the sitters observed a kind of phenomenon previously not seen at a Koons demonstration. An arc of lights resembling golden roses appeared near the ceiling and floated off to one side of the room. "This phenomenon was very beautiful, and was several times repeated," the writer reported. "Lights were then formed near the table, and passed in zig-zag lines with great rapidity, resembling forked lighting in minia- ture. We have witnessed some of the most brilliant pyrotechnic displays at different times in our life, but have never seen any approach to this in refined vividness and artistic beauty."

As the light show continued, observers noticed the energy of the room was ramping up. The drums began to beat faster, and the tambourine flew around the room with such rapidity that the sitters could feel the breeze as it passed. It struck the newspaper correspondent a smart blow to the right side of his head, causing the assembled party to cry out. "We protested that we were willing to believe upon reasonable evidence, without such forcible demonstration as that, and did not need a repetition," he wrote.

Jonathan Koons explained that even the spirits—once their forces were unleashed—sometimes found them difficult to control. But if they had erred in the slightest, it was on the side of the marvelous.

18

"Their Humbug Art"

THE ADVENT of 1856 brought glad tidings to the eastern spiritualist community. An anonymous benefactor was making it possible for Jonathan Koons—at long last—to visit New York City. On January 5 the *Christian Spiritualist* announced his upcoming trip in the most glowing terms. The spate of bad publicity during the past summer and fall seemed to have been forgotten. His visit, said the newspaper, "will be good news to many, as the presence of this family among us will enable those who may wish to compare the manifestations developed in the Davenport and other circles with those of the 'Koons Rooms' to do so."

Jonathan and Nahum had just come off their tour of Columbus and Cincinnati, which had lasted almost four weeks. In addition to the spectacular arc of golden roses produced at the Wilson circle in Cincinnati, they "had satisfactory manifestations on every occasion," Jonathan reported to the *Christian Spiritualist*. The New York trip would advance their national standing, but it had a surprising twist. Nahum would not be coming; his sister would appear in his stead. Although the article did not mention her name, the new player must have been Quintilla, then 13 or 14 years old. Jonathan explained the change as follows: "I have located my son near Delaware Station [Ohio], north of Columbus, for the purpose of assisting a Mr. Van Sickle in the execution of a panorama which is in progress at the counsel and direction of the Spirits, relating to the laws of matter. My daughter is developed for the same or similar demonstrations to those had in the presence of my son, and the arrangements of the Spirits appear to be, for her to fill his place for a season."

Jonathan may have felt a shiver of anxiety as he thought of the comparisons that would inevitably be made between his demonstrations and those of other mediums such as the teenage Davenport brothers, whose power as spiritualist performers seemed to match his own. Jonathan's attitude toward the new sensation from Buffalo is not known, but a flattering biography of the Davenport boys published more than a decade later makes it clear that they considered the Koonses to be their rivals. A New York family by the name of Cook was traveling to Ohio to visit the Koons rooms when they stopped by the Buffalo, New York, rooms of the Davenports. "They merely dropped in on their route, to see and hear what they could in Buffalo, not even dreaming that the Davenport manifestations were equal to those of Ohio, whereas, in fact, they were, and are to this day (July 22, 1869), not only superior to those of Koons, but to those of the Scotchman, Dan Hume, or any other medium now living," the biography boasted.

At a séance conducted "after the regular showman style," the spirits formed "spectral, then solid hands" that not only picked the ladies' pockets but took off their shoes and threw them on the séance table. The gathering took a comic turn when a Mr. Campbell, who complained of a lack of attention from the spirits, dared the invisibles to touch *him*. He was rewarded with a robust thrashing of his shins and "tender spots" by the trumpet—wielded by a hand and arm with no body attached—until "he fairly writhed with agony and rage." On a more serious note, one woman believed she recognized the materialized arm of her late sister, "for it had peculiar and unique marks and moles upon it, that could not possibly leave room to doubt its identity with the one now so strangely reincarnated." The Cooks were so bedazzled by the Davenport brothers that they decided not to visit the Koons circle after all.

In mid-December 1855 the mediums from Buffalo had arrived in New York eager to make their mark upon the city. They set up séance rooms at 195 Bowery. "The arrival of the Davenports has produced great excitement among the multitudes of our citizens who are anxious to witness the peculiar phenomena which take place in their presence, and we have no doubt that their rooms will be thronged with inquirers during the period of their proposed sojourn among us," wrote one anonymous enthusiast.

On Sunday afternoon, December 30, a group of 18 to 20 journalists from both spiritualist and mainstream periodicals accepted an invitation to see the Davenports in action. The private, press-only demonstration was first conducted in the light, with everyone holding hands around a table. Some visitors were astounded to see various musical instruments moving and sounding about the table and to hear bells ringing while Ira and William's hands were held fast by the other sitters. The boys' father and manager also had been restrained to avoid any collusion. The mystery only deepened when the lights were shut off for the second part of the séance. The same phenomena occurred with "greater force" than before, even though the boys were now tied to their chairs with cords and their hands bound together with handkerchiefs. When the lights came back on, the reporters saw the cords lying off to the side of the room. Strings and keys had been torn from a guitar and scattered about.

Some of the more hard-boiled observers were not convinced that they were witnessing the aftermath of untidy spirits. Only seven of the attending journalists would sign a statement vouching that some or all of these events actually took place without any signs of deception; one of those who did, the *Christian Spiritualist* editor Toohey, was outraged by the others' refusal, calling his reluctant colleagues "moral coward[s]."

Nine days later Toohey may have been shocked to learn that the Davenports' own manager, John F. Coles, was accusing them of hornswoggling the public. The boys' father, Ira Davenport Sr., had hired Coles to act as the mediums' agent while they were in the city, but Coles had soon become suspicious of the true cause of the spectacular effects. Coles bided his time through nearly two dozen séances while crafting a trap of his own. The Davenports held a séance on the morning of January 8 with the announced purpose of materializing a spirit hand for the benefit of the assembled sitters. Coles was in charge of the gas lamp, which was initially turned down just low enough for the participants to see ghostly fingers rising and dipping at one end of the table. "It was then rapped upon the table to completely darken the room by turning off the gas," Coles reported. "Instead . . . I turned it on to a full blaze, and suddenly jumping on Ira Jr., the elder boy, I discovered a glove drawn upon the toe of his right foot. The fingers of this glove had evidently been presented to us as the emanation of Spirits." A brief struggle ensued, and the manager was able to wrest from Ira the old woolen glove—its fingers stuffed—as proof of the humbug.

The disillusioned Coles had believed in the Davenports when he first saw them perform in Buffalo before taking them on as clients, but now he doubted whether any of their manifestations were induced by spirits. In his statement to a newspaper he wryly noted that the Davenports nonetheless planned to stay in New York, sitting in private circles for paying clients— but that their public séances were now suspended.

Jonathan's rivals were temporarily down on their luck, but the episode brought renewed criticism of the dark circle, a venue that Jonathan himself had pioneered and honed to near perfection. He no longer had to worry about being outdone by the Davenports, but now he would have to take care not to be caught in the same net of suspicion.

IN February 1856 the spiritualist press reported that the Koons family had reached New York City and was holding private circles for friends (or at least friendly strangers) at the Jackson Hotel. But the plan to leave Nahum with Selah Van Sickle for artistic inspiration had changed; Nahum was now in the lineup of mediums along with sister Quintilla. All was not well with Jonathan. "His visit, however, to this and other cities at present, is more for mental relaxation and fraternization with the friends, than for mani- festational purposes, as his health is somewhat impaired," one newspaper explained.

Jonathan may have been wise to lower expectations, for the Koons family probably had arrived in Gotham demoralized and jittery. Trouble had dogged them on this trip. En route to New York, the Koonses had spent much of January on tour in northern Ohio. Linus Smith Everett, the editor of the *Spiritual Universe* and a public speaker espousing the harmo- nial philosophy, invited the Koonses to his Cleveland home. Everett, then about 60, was a former Universalist minister who had served in the Buffalo area. A few years earlier he had left the church and converted to spiritu- alism along with his wife, who was said to be a medium. His newspaper was one of many that had helped elevate the Koons family to the realm of spiritualist royalty.

The guests from Athens County volunteered to hold private sittings for the Everett family. Everett was gratified to see the phenomena he had heard so much about duplicated in his own parlor—the voice speaking through the horn, music from the harmonicon, ghostly lights, and even the hand formed by spirits out of the elements. All went well for the first two evenings, with Jonathan, Abigail, and Quintilla conducting the circle. The third séance was even more spectacular: the illuminated hand touched Everett, his wife, and son several times and remained visible for a full 30 minutes. As a further demonstration, Jonathan asked King to raise the spirit hand from the table to the low ceiling. To everyone's amazement a blazing light suddenly illuminated the tableau, catching Quintilla in its glare. "A match, held by the spirit hand, ignited—and behold, there stood the medium, the daughter of Mr. Koons, revealed as the active and only performer in this solemn farce," Everett wrote in a shocking exposé.

Although the newspaper publisher was outraged by the humbug apparently going on under his nose, others thought that the Koonses—given their huge following and past record of success—should be given a second chance, another turn at proving themselves. With Nahum absent, perhaps the others had resorted to cheating out of desperation. So Jonathan was obliged to go to Delaware, Ohio, where Nahum was assisting the artist Selah Van Sickle, and return with his son. Now the Koons mediums would be expected to perform under a higher level of scrutiny than ever, perhaps to submit to tests that they formerly had rejected out of hand.

The séances were moved out of the Everett home and into a "new room" that had been constructed by Cleveland spiritualists. On at least two evenings circles were held there with the celebrated Nahum at the helm. But the demonstrations left Everett and others unsatisfied, as Jonathan was unwilling to perform under conditions that would have removed any doubt from their minds. Everett also felt that Jonathan was politicking, playing the more skeptical faction of the community against the faithful who still believed in his powers. "If honest, and if he had the good of spiritualism at heart, he would have been glad to embrace all possible opportunities to satisfy . . . inquiring minds on every subject concerning which reasonable doubts were entertained," Everett wrote. But Jonathan had refused, "preferring to confine his labors to circles composed of those known to have full confidence in his sincerity." Jonathan would turn to these friendly audiences as the family—now four mediums strong—made the long-awaited trip to New York.

MAINSTREAM newspapers pounced on Everett's story, gleefully spreading word of the Koons "jugglery" through Ohio and beyond. "As the Koons are going East to try to make money out of their humbug art, it is well that this expose should go with them," huffed a Cincinnati sheet. The *Daily Cleveland Herald* on January 26 quoted at length from Everett's article but could not resist a dig of its own: "From all accounts the baldest of impositions were . . . practiced under the name of spiritual manifestations and as with the Davenport family, scores of persons of ten times the intelligence of the humbugs themselves were duped."

Two days later Koons supporters landed a counterpunch when the *Daily Cleveland Herald* carried an item praising the family: "We see by the *Spiritual Universe* that the believers at Euclid Center have built a Spirit House 18 feet square, and fitted it up with musical instruments and spirit apparatus, after the fashion of Koons in Athens county. Mr. Koons and his family made some astonishing demonstrations there during their visit to this section. The demonstrations were voted genuine by those spiritualists who witnessed them."

To its credit the *Christian Spiritualist,* which had heavily promoted the Koons mediumship, carried the allegations of fraud, but its editor cautioned against jumping to conclusions: "We withhold comment until we get a full detail of the facts in the case and know both sides of the story. This reservation is due to Mr. Koons, as he and his family have been before the public for some years, having been tested and tried as mediums in almost every variety of form, by the many committees, who, from time to time, have met at his Spirit Rooms."

Despite the cloud of notoriety trailing them, the Koonses had gotten a friendly reception in Painesville, Ohio, a town in Lake County east of Cleveland. They spent six evenings there holding circles for 30 to 40 people nightly and boarding with a local family. Apparently the spirit machine, with its ear-splitting drums and purported electrical properties, did not travel with the Koonses on this trip. At the Painesville circles a brass horn, two tin horns, a tambourine, a harmonica, and two brass bells sat on a table in the center of the room. Jonathan followed his usual custom of playing the violin. The manifestations, though not quite as spectacular as those that unfolded back on Mount Nebo, seemed to satisfy the audience.

More than 20 people were so moved by the rushing wind, floating lights, and voices singing through the horns that they sent a statement to a spiritualist newspaper vouching for the troupe's authenticity. Most important, the Painesville participants said, care was taken to make sure that the Koonses remained seated throughout the séance. They were not physically restrained, but spotters stood near the chairs of Jonathan, Nahum, Abigail, and Quintilla to detect any movements. "Our special object is to say that we held such relative situations to Mr. Koons and all his company, during these sittings, that we know they did not leave their seats, which were some distance from the table. And indeed, the manifestations were frequently of such a nature, that they could not have been made by Mr. Koons and his family, *if they had been all on the table*" (emphasis added).

Certainly such watchfulness was something to which the Koons mediums were unaccustomed on their home turf. Perhaps the strain of it all was getting to Jonathan—making him physically ill and draining all his energy as he set up shop at the Jackson Hotel in New York City in early February 1856. But he was determined to go on with the show: over the next three weeks the Koons mediums would hold circles nightly at the hotel for handpicked audiences, sometimes as many as 30 "intelligent ladies and gentlemen." The publishers Charles Partridge and Samuel Brittan, along with their employees at the *Spiritual Telegraph,* frequently attended. The Koonses' "advent in this city has not been trumpeted to any great extent," the *Telegraph* observed, "and their circles have been rather of a private and select rather than a public and promiscuous character." The Koonses' critics claimed that the family had gone east to make money, but details of Jonathan's arrangements with his anonymous benefactor may never be known. Although invited guests probably did not pay for admission, clearly the New York tour was being underwritten by the sponsor, and Jonathan was known to have accepted donations in the past.

In the parlor of Mr. and Mrs. Jackson at 341 Spring Street, the Koonses managed to re-create the environment that had led to such phenomenal success at their spirit room back home. On the evening of February 24 George Washington Rains, a chemist and retired army officer, gathered there with friends to see the celebrated mediums at work. But before the demonstration could begin, Rains and his cohorts were bent on turning the premises upside down to detect any sign of deception. They carefully examined the setup: between the two front windows sat a rectangular table with a wood frame rising above it and drums attached on each side; various wires spanned the frame to connect with zinc and copper plates, and four small bells were suspended from a central post. One observer thought it looked like "a somewhat fantastically constructed apparatus"; perhaps it had been built especially for the Koons demonstrations in the city. A square mediums' table, covered in oil cloth, was positioned immediately in front of and touching the first table. But Rains could tell at a glance that the rectangular table was no battery, as so many had claimed. "An accurate description of this piece of furniture is not considered necessary, since from its construction it could not have been used either as a generator of statical or dynamical electricity, nor indeed of any species of force known in physics," he would later report.

On the smaller table were strewn the customary props for a Koons demonstration—"two tambourines, two tin trumpets or horns, about two feet long each, a small brass trumpet, a small bell, and an accordeon." But the rear table sported something novel. Instead of the sandpaper sheets tinged with phosphorus that were used at the Ohio séances, inspectors saw "a six-ounce large-mouth bottle, nearly filled with water and well corked, in which a stick of the ordinary phosphorus was immersed; near this was a box of lucifer matches." Rains's company insisted on removing the stick and examining it. Once they were satisfied that it was authentic, it was time for the circle to commence. But what unfolded did not follow the usual pattern.

Jonathan, Nahum, and Quintilla took their places at the square table, with the girl sitting alone in the center. Instead of sitting opposite each other as they did at home, both father and son sat on the right. Jonathan invited the onlookers to seat themselves wherever they wished. The rest of the group, three women and seven men, sat in chairs ringing the table in a tight semicircle, in an effort to cut off the mediums' access to the back of the room. Rains scrutinized the seating arrangements of the mediums themselves and saw a weak link: Nahum. Sitting on the extreme right and shielded by Jonathan, he alone might have the opportunity to rise from his seat for nefarious purposes. Rains resolved to keep Nahum talking so that his location could be known if he tried to move.

The lights were put out, and Jonathan began playing softly on the violin. Within seconds the stick of phosphorous in the jar began to glow, producing a vertical shaft of light through the cork top. What appeared to be a forefinger and thumb rose rapidly to the 12-foot ceiling and returned to the table, levitating and dropping several times in a row. Rains did not believe anyone could have stood on the mediums' table to make this happen without detection, given the tight quarters and the number of musical instruments cluttering the surface.

The luminous hand appeared to be more fully formed now, and as it gathered force the witnesses heard "a peculiar whistling sound resembling the blowing of the wind through a vessel's rigging in a gale." The hand swooped down to the table and snatched up a small tambourine, whirling and playing it over the heads in the circle. Someone suggested that Jonathan give his violin to the host, Mr. Jackson, who was sitting on the opposite side of the room. As Jonathan complied, the tambourine moved over the table and stopped in front of Jackson, maintaining a height of 6 to 8 feet off the floor.

At the same time the trumpet seemed to rise in front of the table, and an inarticulate voice spoke through it, trying to converse with the audience from 8 or 9 feet in the air. The voice responded to a few questions but apparently gave no sermons or revelations that night. Witnesses were impressed, though, that they heard the voice at various locations throughout the parlor. At one point "a strange sound resembling a continued shriek" resonated through the room, while the tambourine continued to dart about, even though the hand carrying it had gone dark.

Rains and his compatriots were listening intently as the phenomena were taking place, trying to make sense of what their ears were telling them. "Mr. Koons and son were frequently conversing in their seats," Rains's group later reported, "while the daughter was soundly asleep, seated next to one of the undersigned, who continually held a portion of her dress in his hands. At one period the speaking through the trumpet, the movements of the tambourine, and the whistling sounds occurred at the same instant in different parts of the room, while Mr. Koons and son were speaking to each other in their seats."

Now the performance came full circle, as the jar of phosphorus rocketed off the large table and climbed to the ceiling. It shook violently on its way back down, lighting the space around it, and came to a stop about 4 feet from an onlooker. Rains's company took immediate safeguards, asking that Nahum speak continuously to reveal his location. All members of the interlocking circle checked to make sure that no one else had gotten up. The phosphorus jar became even more luminous as it began to move about the room in various directions, satisfying the party that it was too far from any of the mediums for them to be manipulating it. In their report, published in the *Spiritual Telegraph,* Rains and company concluded by saying, "The undersigned feel entirely warranted in making a positive assertion, that no human being in the room had hold of, or by any machinery whatever, caused the motions of this bottle of phosphorus; and they are equally assured in their own minds that no deception, either voluntary or involuntary, took place during the evening of these remarkable occurrences."

The *Telegraph* also put its stamp of approval on the Koons family while contrasting them with the Davenports:

> We believe that all who have come in contact with Mr. Koons during his sojourn among us, have been impressed with his simplicity of character and honesty of purpose; and the manifest unsophistication and artlessness of his son and daughter are such that no one would be inclined to attribute to them the disposition, or to any extent even the capacity, to deceive; and notwithstanding the disadvantage of an existing prejudice arising from untoward developments in the presence of certain mediums who had just previously holden circles in our city, we believe that most persons who have visited the Koons have been satisfied both of their honesty and of the spiritual reality of the phenomena which occur in their presence.

When the glowing jar of phosphorus was carried hither and thither about the room, some sitters could even see "the forms of the Spirits' fingers grasping the bottle."

Jonathan must have left New York City feeling vindicated. His reputation had been sullied in recent months, dragged through newspaper headlines. But here he was, once again proving that things could happen if the spirits were right.

✳ ✳ ✳

JOHN Tippie Jr. and his children had also been traveling in early 1856, despite plans for their new spirit room back in Athens County. Late February found them visiting Cincinnati and giving public demonstrations—though performing in the dark as they typically had done. "Mr. Tippie, with his son and daughter, are here," read one local account, "as mediums for the musical manifestations of 'King.' A circle of twenty-five assembles each evening. Some of the most intelligent and influential of our citizens are among the attendants, and the manifestations have been very satisfactory."

Dr. Joseph R. Buchanan, proprietor of *Buchanan's Journal of Man*, had been out of town when Jonathan and Nahum put on their séances the previous December. He was determined not to miss the Tippies, whose demonstrations he knew were similar. On the Tippies' second evening in Cincinnati, Buchanan joined a crowd of mostly gentlemen as they gathered in a small darkened apartment to hear the spirits perform. After years of advocating for the Koonses and Tippies in the pages of his journal, Buchanan was expecting, as he later wrote, "something really marvellous."

John Tippie Jr., his son Ezra, and his daughter (likely Lucetta) took their seats around a small table with the familiar retaining battery rigged up with drums behind them on a second table. The three were joined by two female mediums who were friends of Miss Tippie's. In typical fashion John and Ezra sat opposite each other while the three women sat between the Tippie men and the audience. Buchanan couldn't help but notice how close John and Ezra were to the drums and how the positions of the three women around the table effectively shielded Ezra from any interference by onlookers. Once the lights were out, a member of the audience played the violin while the drums and tambourine kept time. A voice spoke through the horn, and the famed spirit hand grasped Dr. Buchanan's, but he left with the impression that all of it could have been done by 21-year-old Ezra.

Returning to another circle on February 29, Buchanan had devised a test of his own, which he covertly carried into the séance room. The evening started with a private audience with the horn at 6:00 p.m. He already suspected that the voice was "clumsily disguised" to sound like the spirit King but that Ezra was speaking. In the darkened room Buchanan pinpointed the sound as coming from young Tippie, who was 6 or 7 feet away. Buchanan could even hear Ezra catch his breath after uttering a long sentence through the horn. The doctor nonetheless kept his own counsel.

At the 7:00 p.m. performance he insisted on sitting at the mediums' table next to John Tippie and opposite Ezra. Buchanan believed that Ezra could produce most of the effects while sitting down—but to extend the tambourine over the heads of the audience or to offer the spirit hand, Ezra would have to stand on the table. From his coveted seat Buchanan was in a prime position to test his theory.

Once the lights were out and the music began, Buchanan closely followed the sounds of the tambourine in motion. Eventually it began circling the outer edge of the mediums' table. Buchanan thought that Ezra was doing this to drive back other people's hands or to sound out their positions. All at once the table, which had been slightly unbalanced, became firmly grounded, as if weight had been added. Now was the time to act. The doctor had secreted upon his person a fine cane that had been a gift from friends in Philadelphia. "I raised my cane which I brought into the room unobserved, and reaching over the table in the dark, felt the performer occupying the table on the opposite side, adjacent to the drum," the doctor related. "Before I had completely traced his dimensions, he seized the cane with violence, and endeavored to wrest it from my hands. During the struggle he slipped from the table, when I immediately called for a light and denounced the whole exhibition as imposture."

The stunned audience members began to debate the meaning of what they had just seen. One man agreed with Buchanan that it was all a fake, adding that on a previous evening he had felt a coat sleeve attached to the so-called spirit hand. Others argued that the sleeve was a spiritual garment; one claimed that "the man whom I detected on the table was not the medium, but a spiritual body, a whole man, created by the spirits, to play on the tambourine in the dark," Buchanan wrote.

To disprove this notion Buchanan made a simple proposal: let the dark séance continue and produce the spiritual body a second time, but with a twist. Let Ezra pin on his clothes a little piece of paper, dampened with luminous "phosphuretted oil," so that the audience could see his position at all times. The Tippies would have none of it, but neither could they explain what had just happened. Ezra gave his word that the demonstrations were "God-like." As Buchanan continued to press his point, the cornered medium shifted to the attack. Ezra began to speak of his past success, of the ill treatment he was receiving, of how they would all just leave town rather than face such insults. "We suppose now that God is whipped," added John Tippie, Jr., as the standoff wound down. Buchanan could see that this family would never agree to any true scientific tests of their claims.

In their critics' eyes the Tippies were not just ordinary mediums caught cheating but "pious frauds" hiding behind religion. To supporters they were simply out of their element among the doubting Thomases of the city. The family caught an early train out of Cincinnati the next morning. The Tippies would retire to their rugged fastness where they—and they alone—could set the rules.

THE *Christian Spiritualist* had recently warned that the integrity of the movement depended on self-policing. "The *true* Spiritualist [should not] shrink from saying the *plain* word, when he is conscious there is imposition associated with the manifestation, for if this *stern* duty is lost sight of, imposition and imposture will be sure to take advantage of the weakness, and degrade the manifestations into tricks of jugglery and necromancy." The irony could not have been lost on Buchanan. His own correspondents— men of judgment and discretion—had lavished praise on the Koons and Tippie demonstrations in the pages of his magazine. Now he found himself in a literal brawl with the presiding spirit of those rooms, or, as Buchanan now believed, one of King's earthly representatives. The doctor wasted no time publishing his exposé in his *Journal of Man* and also sent an article to the *Spiritual Telegraph*. The two families that had enjoyed such favorable coverage would now become the target of his barbed pen. Far from feeling like a fool, he chortled that his cane "had been well employed in overthrowing this most impudent scheme of imposture."

The publisher Charles Partridge, who had visited the Koons and Tippie spirit rooms, refused to take Buchanan's report seriously. He said the doctor was laboring under the false assumption that a spirit could not pull on a cane, that only a person could. Buchanan, Partridge said, "was rather hasty for a man of science." Partridge hoped that other members of the circle would file a report.

The Tippie camp fired back with a letter to the *Spiritual Telegraph* dated April 6, 1856, supplying the explanation they had been unable to muster when confronted by Buchanan. (Perhaps Partridge was reconsidering his position, as the letter did not appear in the paper until June 28—and then on a back page.) The Tippies' defense came from their loyal friend Thomas White, who hailed from the Quaker town of Mount Pleasant, Ohio, a station on the Underground Railroad and hotbed of abolitionist sentiment. White had spent nearly two weeks with the Tippie family in early 1855, writing a manifesto dictated by King and receiving encouragement from his own deceased daughter. In the process he found much to admire in John Tippie. "There is not a man in the State of Ohio whose character stands fairer," White had written in 1855. "So much so, that the enemies of the cause regret he engaged in Spiritualism, supposing that if he had not, they would have been able to have checked its progress, by virtue of other characters engaged in it."

Now White revealed to the *Spiritual Telegraph* that he was at the circle in Cincinnati when the battle over the cane took place. White contradicted Buchanan's assertion that he had called for a light; rather, he, White, had called for it, warning that someone was tampering with the tambourine. John Tippie instantly "struck a light" to reveal Buchanan picking himself up off the table. As King later explained it, Buchanan's prodding with the cane was "deranging the electrical circuits" and could have caused the whirling tambourine to fall on the heads of the audience. Other spirits helped King set the tambourine down so their leader could fight back.

In White's telling, "the Doctor gave his cane a jerk, and he (King) thought he would let the Doctor see he could jerk too, and gave him such a jerk as brought him sprawling at full length on the top of the table, and would have taken him clean over the table, and down under it, if a gentleman who sat next him had not caught hold of him and held on to him with all his strength." White wondered how Ezra, "a stripling of a youth," could have given the doctor "so merry an excursion" across the table. King, after all, hailed from a hardy race of giants.

Nevertheless the damage had been done. The influential Buchanan would do all in his power not only to spread news of the Tippies' alleged duplicity but to remind readers of the adepts from whom the Tippies had learned their rites in the first place: "Whether the performance of the Koons family is of any better character, appears extremely doubtful," he told his readers. "The relationship between the two families, the identity of their manifestations, and the fraud which has been detected in the Koons family by Mr. Everett of Cleveland, all conspire to indicate that the so-called spiritual phenomena of the Koons and Tippey families are among the grossest impostures of modern legerdemain."

❋ ❋ ❋

EVEN as the Koons Spirit Room remained shuttered in early 1856, something spectacular was happening at the home of two of Jonathan's converts, Mr. and Mrs. Joseph Smith. Since their pilgrimage to the Koons home about a year and a half before, the Cardington, Ohio, couple had waited for the spirits to occupy the special room that had been built for them. Even after Nahum's crowd-pleasing performance in their home in the fall of 1855, the entities too often had been both silent and invisible. "Opposed from without, assailed by jeers and laughter, and at the same time doubting the result, this old couple remained calm and serene, at times still strong in faith that the manifestations would come at last; and so they did come to reward their noble heroism," wrote the admiring St. Louis spiritualist A. Miltenberger.

Now the Smiths' spirit room was suffused with beautiful music from the harp and the accordion, and the tambourine kept time as ever with the drum. As many as 20 lights of different sizes would rise from the floor, float over the heads of the audience, and vanish like fireflies. Crowds of 100 to 200 people overflowed the spirit room, poured into adjoining rooms, crowded onto the porches, and milled about the yard in the hope of hearing the Spirit Kabel make its presence known through the trumpet.

A novel addition to these phenomena was Edward Rogers of Columbus, a tailor by trade but a medium with an unusual gift for drawing images of the dead. Rogers would sit in the Smiths' home blindfolded, with a set of colored crayons beside him and paper on his lap. "The influence seizes him and he is set to work, with a nervous rapid execution; first here—then there—then back again, dropping one color and seizing another, so rapidly that you can scarcely detect the changes," Miltenberger wrote in 1856. "In *thirty minutes* he handed me a beautiful *picture,* of a girl about ten years of age, and a *perfect likeness of a niece now several years gone to the Spirit-world.* To test the likeness, on my arrival home, *without any remarks,* I displayed it to my wife. She at once pronounced the name of the one it purported to be drawn for."

Another visitor, satisfied that no humans had wrought the marvels he had witnessed, recommended the Cardington spirit room to other pilgrims, noting that "Mr. Smith is an honest old Quaker, and invites investigation." Indeed, Joseph Smith had been a signer of the ill-fated 1854 petition to Congress that called for spiritualism to be perused by serious minds.

19

The Psychometrist

AS the wheel of the year turned to spring in 1856, Koons and his family returned from New York City to Mount Nebo to begin a new cycle of planting and reaping. A whiff of change was in the air. In his absence some ministers around Athens County had convinced a number of spiritualist converts to return to the fold and give up the new religion. Even with the spirit room closed and Koons taking a lower profile, he could not resist a fight, especially if theology was at issue. Soon he found an opponent on whom to focus his considerable energies.

That autumn the Reverend J. J. M. Dickey, described by Koons as "a Campbellite minister" in Chauncey, began distributing antispiritualist brochures locally. "Being thus equipped, he pitched his tent in the vicinity of the 'Spirit land,' and commenced cannonading," Koons recounted. Spoiling for a public confrontation, Koons and his spiritualist friends began casting about for a worthy opponent to debate Dickey.

Ironically, as Koons and his allies geared up to demolish arguments they considered sectarian and narrow-minded, the Campbellites no doubt regarded themselves as free thinkers within the realm of Christianity. The movement, begun by the Scots-Irish minister Alexander Campbell in the 1820s, opposed religious litmus tests that required a prospective church member to sign off on a list of beliefs before being permitted to join the fellowship. His teachings had found a firm foothold in the Sunday Creek Valley by the mid-nineteenth century. Campbell's evangelical swings through Athens County had netted many followers; nondenominational, locally governed churches sprang up in Chauncey, Glouster, and Trimble. According to a local history, settlers in the Sunday Creek Valley "read their Bibles and did their own thinking" when it came to religious matters—a habit of mind that Jonathan Koons surely would have applauded. Yet the followers of Dickey had come to an opposite conclusion: that spiritualism was wrong. Just as Alexander Campbell had debated the utopian socialist Robert Owen years earlier in Cincinnati, Dickey would debate another such opponent, someone recruited by the Koons team: William Denton.

Denton, born in 1823, was an English émigré who edited a spiritualist newspaper called the *Vanguard* in Dayton, Ohio. He was a nonconformist at an early age. After being dismissed from a teaching position in London for supporting mesmerism, he took a job with the Railway Service, only to be fired for "having promoted erroneous religious doctrines in the neighborhood." In 1848 Denton sailed for the United States to find space for his unconventional ideas but did not land in a New World utopia. He fled from a teaching job in Virginia (now West Virginia) when his antislavery views attracted the attention of an angry mob. Arriving in Ohio, he found a kindred spirit in Elizabeth Foote, whose progressive ideas also were known to draw a hostile crowd. Foote worked at a journal called the *Type of the Time* and dared to wear bloomers, which no doubt endeared her to the freewheeling Denton.

An avid collector of minerals, gems, fossils, and butterflies, Denton became a geologist in Dayton. After he and Elizabeth married in 1854, they traveled throughout Ohio and elsewhere lecturing on such reform topics as temperance, women's rights, free thought, spiritualism, and psychometry. He even debated the future president James A. Garfield about evolution.

In 1856 at Yellow Springs, Ohio, Denton's controversial ideas attracted an eager public, as he parsed theology with a Christian minister on 19 evenings. "If our friends in any other place can induce any minister to discuss the Bible question, they cannot do better than call out an opponent and let them go to work," Denton wrote. "'Agitation of thought is the beginning of wisdom.' I am prepared to answer calls of that description."

Denton followed the call to a nearly filled Christian church near Athens (likely in Chauncey), where he clashed with Dickey sometime in the fall of 1856. The resolution penned by Dickey stated: "Resolved—That Spiritualism is evil in its origin and tendency," whereas Denton's made a shocking proposition: "That modern Spiritualism reveals a better religion than the New Testament." Denton's resolution was so radical that some of his friends "trembled at the idea of 'going so far.'" After the combatants had swapped three rounds of speeches, Dickey abruptly cut off the debate, saying he could no longer allow his pulpit to be used for "spreading blasphemous opinions." The jarring finale left the crowd disappointed and Koons privately fuming.

In a letter to the *Spiritual Telegraph* in February 1857, Koons declared that Denton had come away with a clear victory, adding another win to the spiritualist scorecard. The local community had wanted to hear more from Denton, who stayed on in the county to deliver 10 or more lectures on such topics as spiritual manifestations, mental and physical slavery, and mental development. "His lectures were well attended," Koons reported. "The professors of the college and the presiding elders were present, at least upon some of the occasions. These incidents have awakened a deep interest in the minds of the people. . . . A number of church members within my own knowledge, have recently come out boldly, and declared they would perform their 'own thinking in future, and be mentally free;' which is all we ever demanded from any of them; and it is hoped that many more will follow their example."

Koons delighted in detailing his success to readers of the *Spiritual Telegraph,* but, significantly, he made no mention of plans to once again host public séances at his home. To the publishers Partridge and Brittan he wrote simply: "I have long since been impressed to write to you and other friends of New York; but I have been engrossed with other matters since my return from your city last spring, which have occupied all my time. I at length conclude to make it known through the *Telegraph* that I am still doing what I can in the dissemination of spiritual truth among the famishing souls scattered over the desolated plains of Christian theology."

Perhaps Koons was motivated to write the letter by a sense that fame was slipping away. No longer were glowing reports of the Koons magic—or even the growls of their detractors—making headlines. The *Telegraph* had taken more than two months to publish his letter. Other young, fresh faces were competing for space.

*   *   *

THAT October Koons proposed to the editors of the publication *Medium* in Lockport, Pennsylvania, that they publish his life story in their columns. Although his star was fading from the spiritualist firmament, Koons believed he was still under fire from his critics, and his letter of proposal has a dark, defensive tone. "Persons who appear to be at enmity with truth and spiritual intercourse" were circulating a report claiming that Koons was "a practical juggler." He wanted to put out a sketch of his life to counter these aspersions. Lashing out against the "monsters" and "Kings of Darkness" who doubted his veracity, he proposed to write "in defiance of ridicule and scholastic cannonading from the camps of the assailants." The publication accepted his proposal, prompting Koons to churn out twelve installments between October 1856 and January 1857.

In penning his autobiography Koons recalled many colorful folktales from his childhood in Bedford, several involving his friends, relatives, and neighbors. Now he reinterpreted these ghost stories in terms of spiritualist philosophy. The male and female healers who were branded wizards and witches were actually gifted mediums, and of the latter he now believed that "some of these women were highly susceptible of spirit influx, and would at this time be considered excellent psychomotrists." All the riddles of his youth suddenly made sense. Beyond his search for meaning, however, were Koons's thoughts about his legacy. He was not only addressing the readers of *Medium* but writing for history—trying to show that he was anything but a common fraud. His account of an active and engaged life would prove, he said, "that I had no time for 'jugglery' as has been imputed."

*   *   *

IN the waning months of 1856, even with the energy of the Koons Spirit Room now spent, the influence of that Athens County landmark was multiplying. South of Columbus, devotees of the movement had started their own spirit room. The new tabernacle, located 8 miles from Chillicothe at Samuel Wheelaland's place, had the ghostly guitar playing, bell ringing, and drum beating that people by now had come to expect. Beyond that, a heavy table "was lifted from the floor like a feather," and the audience had enough light to see the two mediums remaining in their chairs as the phenomena unfolded.

But the Chillicothe group's purpose was larger than mere spirit intercourse; the creation of the spirit room was only the first step. "It is located in a healthy region, where reside a large number of warm-hearted Spiritualists, who have laid all on the altar for truth's sake. They design to establish a Peace Union Society to cure diseases of body and mind," reported the *New England Spiritualist*. With the intention of "doing much good to mankind," the Chillicothe group planned to carry out its ministry while connecting with similar societies in Vinton County, Ohio (bordering Athens County) and Perry County, Pennsylvania.

Out in New Durham, Indiana, a wealthy farmer named Captain J. Davis also started a room of his own. While visiting at the Koonses' a year before, he had received a message from the spirits instructing him to outfit a hall with musical instruments and open it to the public. "Capt. Davis returned and followed their directions," the *Chicago Banker* reported, "the result of which is, that bands of disembodied men gather there and play the most charming music, and with a harmony truly divine. Let any one who wishes to know about all this, only spend the same amount of money in his railroad fare, as thousands now do for a week's cigars or lager beer, and they will see a pleasant country, besides the unfolding wonders of God's upper world."

Less than a mile from Davis's facility, a former member of Congress was not to be outdone. Charles W. Cathcart fixed up his own séance room, where amid ghostly music and strange lights he received "a series of beautiful pictures of the spirit land, painted by the late E. Rogers of Columbus, Ohio, and exhibited through the magic lantern." And in Dundee, Illinois, three wealthy men had constructed a circular house for the same purpose. "The most intelligent population of that region gather there weekly as learners in this great science, which promises to overshadow every one which has gone before it," the Chicago newspaper concluded.

And just as the *Chicago Banker* had sounded an optimistic note for the "science" of spiritualism, so did the publisher Charles Partridge for its religious side. As 1857 began, he believed that spiritualism had gained such a foothold that it was "likely to pervade and absorb all denominations of Christians, exert a moral and reformatory power among the nations, and inaugurate the millennial era."

BY the winter of 1857 Koons was a man restored in body and in mind. In an upbeat letter to the *Spiritual Telegraph,* he reported that the "general physical debility" from which he had suffered while visiting New York City the year before had been banished: "My physical health is apparently as good now as it ever was." Koons attributed his cure to the good offices of Mrs. French, a medium he had encountered during the trip. "She presented me with six bottles of her preparation, in New York, last winter . . . and I have used no other medicine since that time." Given his wife's talents as an herbalist and his general mistrust of authority, it is no surprise that Koons would seek out an alternative therapy. And while the potion was proving beneficial to his body, the massive writing project he had undertaken seemed an equally powerful tonic to his mind.

As he put the final touches on his autobiography, Koons still dreamed of changing the world. One night he sat up watching over three family members who had the measles. By three o'clock they had fallen asleep, and Koons himself retired. Soon his mind fell into "an abnormal condition" and he began to paint "busy scenes" upon his "visionary canvas." He saw a group of "airy castles" in which people were busily engaged in various professions. In the middle of it all was a dying oak tree—and a man was chopping it down. "The declining branches, and other external antiquated symbols of this monstrous oak, were unmistakable indexes in pointing out the conditions of its core," Koons recounted.

He recognized the man with the ax as none other than "the renowned A. J. Davis," the father of the spiritualist movement. In his dream Koons wished the seer success with his mission and watched while Davis made an incision around the entire base of the tree, exposing its decayed roots. But Davis, "the heroic operator," was surprised to find that the tree would not fall. While Davis was working, "I engaged myself in the examination of its connections with the surrounding castles, which seemed to have been overlooked by the ax-man. Seeing that he was nearly exhausted with labor, I begged leave to use his implement to separate the surrounding castles and tree while he took refreshment." Koons went around chopping down the braces that held up the tree. "While engaged in the separation of the last connecting branch, the tree commenced falling with a tremendous crash, and at this moment I aroused, ere the falling tree reached the ground."

The old order was falling, but in Koons's mind it couldn't fall fast enough. Certain connections to the castles in the air, society's delusions, had gone undetected by Davis. Koons, however, saw what it would take to bring down the mighty oak—and in his waking moments would tell anyone who would listen.

* * *

BACK home in Dayton a few months after the Athens County lectures, William Denton silently handed his sister, Annie Denton Cridge, an object wrapped in a piece of paper. William and Annie shared an interest in psychometry, the belief that a person's attributes can be discerned from an object they once possessed. Just as a medium might help locate a missing person by touching a piece of jewelry he or she once wore, so these spiritualists believed they might obtain extrasensory perceptions about people from other places and times.

According to the historian John B. Buescher, William

> discovered that his sister Annie could—to his satisfaction, anyway—
> read unopened letters through their still-sealed envelopes. Not only
> that, but she could also receive from the letters a rapid sequence
> of mental images that supposedly conveyed the scenes present
> when the writers penned them, as well as images of the writers
> themselves. Annie also had success with "psychometrizing" locks
> of hair, visualizing characteristics of the people from whom they
> had come. Having convinced himself that his sister had this power,
> in part because of her feminine sensitivity, William wondered
> whether she might help him in his geological research.

For several years William and Annie conducted hundreds of tests to determine whether these same principles could reveal Earth's ancient past through impressions received from rocks, fossils, other archeological artifacts, and meteorite fragments. Through practice Annie became quite adept at describing prehistoric animals in virgin forests, erupting volcanoes, and even oil deposits hidden underground.

The covered-up object that William gave Annie upon his return from the lecture circuit at first seemed no different than its predecessors. As she held it in her hand, Annie immediately thought it was a fossil. But try as she might, no mental pictures of a fossil popped into her mind.

"I feel like a flat-nosed Indian," she said. "I feel very strangely about my face." As the words rolled out of her mouth, a physiognomy began to emerge: a protruding mouth with the upper lip larger than the lower one, "very ugly" nose, eyes "very quick" and rounder than Caucasians', a forehead that "narrows up to benevolence."

"Seems to have been a hunter and watched for prey," Annie continued. "Feeling is different from any I ever had before. Intellect acts through perceptives, noting physical objects. With all this there is considerable dignity—felt as if he were the masterpiece of creation. . . . In his spirit I perceive something of the religious sentiment." As William listened intently, Annie went on to say that the subject was "an ingenious man" who commanded respect from others. "This man was, and felt himself, a superior. He had the feeling that a person would have who was looked up to."

"What kind of body did he have?" William asked.

"Tall, well made man, long arms, quite a muscular man, strong and tough," she responded. "Chest very healthy, no disease about stomach or lungs, so different from civilized persons. Neck short, broad across the shoulders. Ears large, he had a very fine perception of sound. Large feet, toes spread out—never wore shoes. He seems to move with perfect freedom and was full of animal life."

"What age?" William prodded.

"About 35 or 40."

"Can you tell the cause of his death?"

Annie paused, seeming to search for words. "Yes: he was killed by an arrow, or some kind of weapon, piercing the back of his head. Oh! I suffer intensely. I can say no more."

When Annie had recovered somewhat from the traumatic impression, her brother explained that the object in her hand was a skull bone given to him by Jonathan Koons when William visited him in 1856. William had begged for a piece for testing. It had come from the burial mound of Hommo, the ancient Indian chief whose spirit had made its presence known in the Koons Spirit Room in 1853.

* * *

BOUGHS of peaches and apples hung heavy in the drowsy heat of Koons's orchard. In the summer of 1857 Athens County farmers were enjoying a riotous blessing from Mother Nature. "Crops of all kinds were never more promising than they are the present season," reported a glowing bulletin from Amesville. "The number of acres and yield will almost double any previous crop. The midge did but little damage.—Oats and corn promise well. The weather continues hot, with an insufficiency of rain. We anticipate a fine crop of potatoes. Fruit of every kind will be abundant."

Koons nonetheless needed more to do than contemplate the harvest. With the spirit room gathering cobwebs and his family grown tired of public life, the 45-year-old was looking for ways to channel his restless mind. Writing to his friend William Denton, Koons was frank about this reversal of fortune: "You was misinformed, as to my traveling and giving tests. I might as well attempt to convert moonbeams into sunlight, as to attempt traveling, and giving tests at this time with my mediums. The gross abuses, and base misreprisentations that have been charged against them from time to time, has completely deterred, and discouraged them. So that they can no longer be prevailed upon to be public instruments for spirits to act [through]." Thus Koons's children and perhaps his wife had drawn the line at any more public performances. The steady drumbeat of claims of fraud had had an impact.

An important factor must have been Nahum's willingness to continue. No one else among his siblings had shown such standout ability. However, in the fall of 1857 Nahum's life took a more mundane turn when, at age 20, he married Ann Rebecca Bates, the daughter of George Bates, an Irish immigrant who had settled in Alexander Township in Athens County. The couple's first baby, George Bates Koons, arrived the following year. With his new wife and child, perhaps Nahum had little interest in sustaining his role as a public medium. It had been Jonathan's idea, after all. But Nahum, in a trance state, had seen the vision of heaven and helped the spirits render it on paper with his own hand. Later events would bear out that the young man had been forever shaped by his unearthly experiences in the Koons Spirit Room.

The ever-resilient Jonathan Koons was far from discouraged, though no longer regaling the public with his fiddle playing and mediumship. "My opinion is, that a great mental revolution is fast taking place but there must necessarily be some pioneers to hold the torch of reform, while minds are being freed from sectarian shackles," he had written in the summer of 1857. "As far as I am concerned, I intend to give the chains of mental slavery the best turn yet that I have in my shop, before I retire from my present stage of action."

Koons had chosen to reinvent himself as a writer—or perhaps it would be more accurate to say that he planned to greatly expand his list of publications, for he had been writing to the newspapers for years. Although his grammar and spelling were sketchy, his passion was hot and he felt he had something to say if he could "procure access to some of the abelest colums of reform publicating." Koons wrote to his friend Denton, the editor of the *Vanguard*, about a manuscript Koons was working on that ran "about 50 pages of foolscap paper." "As soon as I can see time, I will review it, and send it to you for criticism, and such use as you may deem most proper."

Koons closed his letter to Denton by inviting him to return to Mount Nebo, as he had enjoyed the time the lecturer spent with him in 1856. "I wish it so that you could pay us another visit. You wold meet with many more warm friends now, than when you was here. Why can you not come this fall? Please write me, and let me know your labor and whereabouts. Yours as ever, Jonathan Koons."

After the white-hot trajectory of the past five years, Koons had finally gone to ground. An important tool of reform—spirit manifestations—was no longer available to him, but he still craved the intellectual pursuits that he had barely dreamed of back in Bedford. How his life would play out off the stage was a script yet to be written.

3.1 Jonathan Koons, shown here in an undated photograph at what appears to be a formal event. Courtesy of Alan Taylor.

3.2 The geologist, spiritualist, and intellectual maverick William Denton, who became a
friend of Jonathan Koons's and corresponded with him in the late 1850s. This photograph was
taken sometime between 1855 and 1865. Courtesy of the Wellesley Historical Society, Wellesley,
Massachusetts.

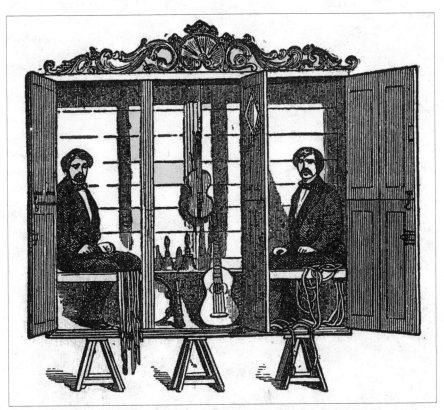

3.3 Ira and William Davenport of Buffalo, New York, became darlings of the spiritualist press in the 1850s before a number of exposures left their admirers disillusioned. The Davenport brothers became world-famous stage magicians touring the globe with their cabinet act. Some scholars believe they modeled their initial performances on those at the Koons Spirit Room. This illustration is from a 1902 book.

NANCY JANE WEBB PAGE

3.4 The widow Nancy Jane Page, née Webb, married the widower Jonathan Koons in May 1865, about a year after the death of Abigail Bishop Koons. Photograph courtesy of Sheila Cadwalader.

RANGE 14
TOWN 10
SECTION 9
FRACTION 3

MOUNT NEBO TABERNACLE.
EIGHT SIDES — 60 FEET WIDE
JANUARY 14, 1941.
W.E. PETERS
ATHENS, OHIO

3.5 William E. Peters, a surveyor, sketched his impression of what the 1871 spiritualist tabernacle on Mount Nebo might have looked like. Only three sides of the eight-sided structure are
seen here. Constructed by the Morning Star community, it burned or was torn down before
the turn of the twentieth century. William E. Peters Papers, Mahn Center for Archives and
Special Collections, Ohio University Libraries.

3.6 Photograph, published in 1947, shows a view of Mount Nebo, one of the highest elevations in Athens County, Ohio, at 1,024 feet. The Hibbard family's white farmhouse, built around 1868, would not have existed in Jonathan Koons's time there, but a 1950 article in the *Athens Messenger* said that an older building had existed on the site. The exact location of the Koons house and spirit room is uncertain. Photograph by William E. Peters. Courtesy of Southeast Ohio History Center, Athens, OH.

3.7 In the 1970s and 1980s an intentional community called Golgonooza flourished at the foot of Mount Nebo. Its founder, Aethelred Eldridge, an art professor at Ohio University, was inspired by the art and philosophy of the English poet William Blake. Shown here is the Primal Church of the Blake Recital, where Eldridge interpreted the poet in highly theatrical Sunday sermons. Photograph courtesy of Alexandra Eldridge.

3.8 Festivals and performances were part of the cultural fabric at Golgonooza. Here a dancer entertains the crowd at a Blake festival. Photograph courtesy of Alexandra Eldridge.

3.9 Millfield resident Shirley Tinkham (*left*) is shown here with the author in 2014 at the Koons family cemetery in Dover Township. The broken headstones of George and Filenia Koons are in the foreground. The site is believed to hold a third grave. Photograph by Jack Wright.

3.10 This historic home is located in Ames Township on the site where John Tippie Jr. opened a log spirit room in 1854. Tippie was said to have built a new home and spirit room in 1855. County auditor's records date the house to 1860, but it could be a few years older. The tree in the foreground is near the now-vanished Tippie family cemetery. The property owner, Ryan Harris, was restoring the residence in 2018. Photograph courtesy of Ron Luce.

20

Little Egypt

BY the late 1850s some seventy years had passed since the first settlers had planted their colony at Marietta. The frontier had long since moved on, and now "Western fever" was sweeping across Ohio, filling its sufferers with delirious visions of yet another golden new land. Real estate in Ohio and even in Indiana had gotten expensive. A poor man might have to work 10 years just to afford his 20 acres, and that with just a cottage instead of a spacious farmhouse. But even the not-so-poor were susceptible to infection: in Athens County the prosperous merchant Daniel Brown was enticed by tales from a cousin who had toured the West. Brown sold his general store in Amesville, set off with his family aboard a steamer on the Hocking River, and reached Iowa with $3,500 in gold coins—the payment for their new 200-acre farm—hidden in his wife's carpetbag.

Despite the lure of the West, such moves were a gamble not to be taken lightly, warned a farmer who had recently moved from northwest Ohio to Illinois. In a cautionary letter published in the *Ohio Cultivator,* the ex-Ohioan warned those who decided to sell their Ohio farms that a better deal might not be waiting out West. "Illinois is the best State west of Ohio," he wrote, "and I do not believe there is a farmer in Ohio that could buy a farm in Illinois, take into view the health, water, roads, schools and society, for double what he could sell his farm [in Ohio] for." Settlers who found dissatisfaction out West may be too ashamed to return home, while others couldn't afford the journey back East. If not for these constraints, "there would be as great an emigration to Ohio as ever there was from it," the farmer concluded.

But such caveats were easy to ignore. In Koons's neighborhood John Tippie Jr. had put his property up for sale. In early October 1857 Tippie had found two buyers for his extensive holdings in Ames and Dover Townships. Tippie sold 173 acres to Wesley Tippie, his nephew, for $3,000, but most of the Tippie farm went to a man named Peter Hixon, who ended up with 372 acres for $7,000. Tippie reportedly wrote to a spiritualist friend to say that "he sold out in Ohio in compliance with King's direction, and that he intends to follow his direction in all things, let the result be as it may." The Tippies were saying good-bye not only to their spirit room and magical spring but to the Tippie family graveyard where Grandfather Uriah, the old soldier of the Revolution, now slept.

On October 31, 1857, the *Vanguard* revealed that "Mr. John Tippie, of Athens county., O., has with his family removed to Southern Illinois, not too far from the junction of the Central with the St. Louis and Terre Haute railroads. A large quantity of good land has been secured by him and others at a low price, as a basis for a reform neighborhood, and as much of the co-operative element as can be practically carried out. The spirit calling himself 'King,' who has performed such remarkable feats at the spirit-room in Athens county, takes a peculiar interest in the undertaking." The junction of those two railroads was in Christian County in the town of Pana, located somewhat north of Little Egypt. This region, covering roughly the southern third of the state, had a culture distinct from that of the rest of Illinois and may have drawn its name from the delta where the Ohio joined the Mississippi.

If the newspaper report was correct, John Tippie Jr. was among many dreamers who envisioned a liberal community where spiritualism and other countercultural practices could flourish without barn burnings or other oppression. Such utopian projects were frequently announced in the pages of the spiritualist press in the hope of finding suitable recruits. A 440-acre settlement in Hardin County, Iowa, that was to be run "on entirely harmonial principles" was seeking members. A group out of Cincinnati, influenced by the ideas of the socialist philosopher Charles Fourier, was planning a community called a phalanx, to be located 40 miles southwest of the city in Dearborn County, Indiana. There the land was "elevated and free from all miasmatic influences," and the reformers touted it as "one of the most healthy sections of the State." The community, although relatively near Cincinnati by rail, would be mostly free of the sin found in cities and river towns: "The standards of morals is high; and intoxicating liquors are not to be found within its limits, or for miles around." In this settlement, the Cincinnati group promised, progressives could find the best of both worlds: "Come to the country and cultivate the land, you starving and suffocating city laborers; but to come with advantage, let us organize ourselves into a self-supporting society, so that we may retain all the advantages of social intercourse in the city, and at the same time enjoy the blessings of country life." Perhaps such an enclave was what John Tippie had in mind, yet he would soon find himself in one of the most dystopian communities in the United States.

❉ ❉ ❉

"THE subscribers, wishing to change conditions, offer their adjoining farms for sale, at reduced rates," read the ad in the *Athens Messenger* on March 12, 1858. "The same being under good improvement, well watered and timbered, near Mills and Market,—embracing the celebrated Fruit Farm of J. Koons. Each lot contains upwards of 200 Acres."

The "bug" that had bitten John Tippie Jr. the year before had alighted on the extended Koons family as well. Not only was Jonathan selling out and moving, but his nephew, 37-year-old Cyrus S. Hughes, had signed on to the plan. The Hughes family, which lived next door to Koons, originally included his sister Elizabeth, who perhaps had died by then; her husband, Joseph; their son Cyrus; and several other children, including their daughter Anna Margaret, who had married John Tippie Jr. The closeness of the two families went back a long way: in the 1840s they had worked together to start a district school, and in 1851 Koons had sent a Mr. Hughes (probably Cyrus) to Athens on the futile mission to find someone to preach Filenia's funeral. Now Cyrus shared his uncle Jonathan's vision of a new life farther west.

There is probably no single reason that Koons decided to leave Athens County. A generation before, he and most of his siblings had pulled up

stakes in Pennsylvania and headed to Ohio; perhaps the same sense of adventure that had prompted him to strike out from Bedford was stirring
in him once more. Maybe he sensed that he had played out his hand in
Athens County, and by finding a new home he could reinvent himself as
a less polarizing figure. Or, as he later suggested, he was buying up land
to give to his 10 children as an inheritance, figuring that the Mount Nebo
farm would not stretch far enough. Still, he and Abigail—now in their late
forties—were walking away from 20 years of toil to start over.

Jonathan and Abigail found a buyer for their 206 acres in Seth Fuller
of Chauncey, a friend who had attended their séances and publicly supported the *Christian Spiritualist*'s hapless campaign to build the Koons
family a new house. Apparently the Koonses by 1858 had less than half
the land they had started out with in 1836, but its value had appreciated
many times over. Fuller paid them $3,000 in June 1858 as part of a real
estate swap in which the Koonses purchased three tracts of Fuller's land
out west and paid him the same amount. These new properties included
80 acres in Council Bluffs, Iowa; 240 acres near Warsaw, Missouri; and 80
acres in southern Illinois. Abigail's land in Morgan County, Ohio—"123
Acres . . . situated on the East Fork of Sunday Creek, immediately above
J. M. Bishop's Saw-Mill"—also was sold that same month, along with the
Iowa property, for $2,000.

The couple set out in the latter part of September 1858 with their eight
unmarried children and an adopted daughter, Eliza, about whom little is
known other than that she was an orphan. Nahum, his wife Ann Rebecca,
and the infant George—born just a few weeks before—accompanied them.
Why the Koons family decided to move so late in the year is not known;
perhaps they had waited until Ann delivered her baby or the crops were
harvested. It was a timetable that was to have fateful consequences.

As they descended Mount Nebo for the final time, the family was facing a journey of more than 700 miles in horse-drawn wagons. The Koonses
were headed for Bates County, Missouri. Tucked up against the Kansas
border, it was prairie country, well watered by the Osage River and its tributaries. A visitor who was from Illinois and traveling through west-central
and southwestern Missouri in search of a new home extolled the virtues
of the region in a newspaper article. The mild climate was conducive to
growing fruit, which led him to predict that "in time, France will very soon

be excelled in quantity and quality of her wines." Perhaps Jonathan Koons envisioned re-creating the orchard he had been so proud of back on Mount Nebo. Cheap land could still be had, though that could change with the expected coming of the railroad. Most encouraging of all, the visitor from Illinois found the locale "more liberal than in most parts of Missouri," a place where people were "very intelligent" and "kind to strangers." He chose to settle in Jasper County, where "reformers in search of new homes would do well to locate themselves"; its seat is less than 80 miles due south of Bates County's. But the fact remained that the Koonses were planning to settle in a slave state, though they were almost certainly opposed to the practice. The desire for affordable land must have overshadowed all other concerns.

Midway through the journey, however, the Koons family's plans unraveled. In a letter to his friend William Denton, probably written in the spring of 1859, Jonathan explained that his new home was not in Missouri—but instead in Illinois, where he and Abigail had purchased a 160-acre farm in Franklin County. Koons had asked a friend, S. Webb, to personally deliver the letter to Denton, who was then in Kansas Territory.

Last summer, I sold my property in Ohio, or rather exchanged my real estate for lands in the middle and S.W. part of Missouri. I wrote you a letter of enquiry respecting sales of land in your vicinity; but received no answer; I therefore conclud you did not receive it. On the 22nd of September last fall [1858], I entered my trip with my family;—including my son Nahum and his wife. I was bound for Bates Co. Mo.—But when I came into Southern Illinois my youngest boy [Britten] was taken ill with fever and ague,—My wife was also very infirm, so as to render it unsafe to pursue our journey. Some of our horses were also badly jaded; but the worst of all, the incesant fall rains had set in, so as to render us circumstantially bound, and discomfeited. Under existing circumstances, I could do no better than haul in for winter quarters.

There then was another difficulty;—I had six head of horses on hand, and provender very scarce, and high in prices and to keep my horses would be robbing me of the means that were designed for other purposes. I therefore bartered two span of horses and wagons, for landed property near the place of my address in Franklin Co., Ill. So here we are in person, but,

> My heart is in Kansas,
> My heart is not here,
> My heart is in Kansas,
> Where sport the wild deer.

But [I] do not expect to be able for another move very soon, under existing auspices. I would be pleased to hear from you on the receipt of this.

In the letter Koons also mentioned that his friend John Tippie Jr. had reached Linn County, Kansas—just across the border from Bates County, Missouri—and was living with his family in either Moneka or Brooklyn (Brooklin). He made no mention of Tippie's ever having lived in Illinois, so it is not clear what happened with the proposed reform community there or whether the newspaper story was based on nothing more than a rumor. Perhaps Koons would rather have been in Kansas because his friends Denton and Tippie were already there, and, as his letter indicates, he had once considered looking for land in that territory as well.

Denton at the time was in Twin Mound, Kansas, where he was helping build another intentional community. "Socialism is, in my opinion, the goal of humanity," Denton had written in the *Vanguard*,

> but we cannot arrive there at a bound. . . . One good step towards
> it, would be to form neighborhoods of intelligent, reformatory
> persons; . . . I travelled through Texas on foot, looking for a suitable
> location, but found none; land was cheap, climate delightful; but
> far away from market, surrounded by semi-barbarians, it would be
> vain to attempt it in any part of Texas I saw. I have been through
> western Virginia; Pennsylvania, Ohio, Indiana, Illinois and a part
> of Iowa and Missouri, constantly looking out for a good place to
> establish such a neighborhood but never saw the place until I went
> to Kansas.

The land in that state was not only affordable but as fertile as in Illinois and "vastly superior" to Missouri's, in Denton's estimation.

Work at Twin Mound was proceeding apace under the direction of Henry Hiatt, an anarchist and visionary from Indiana. A quarter section had been laid out for a small town that might someday include a park with groves of trees "judiciously planted," a college, and "should we turn socialists, a unitary building to grace it." A hotel was under construction, a school and post office in the works, and the stagecoach called once a week. "Reformers, or those who incline to reform, most of them Spiritualists, own about three square miles of land in the vicinity, and there is every prospect of making a first-rate neighborhood," Denton wrote. Even more striking, another promoter of Twin Mound predicted that women would vote there just as soon as the town was officially organized—and that some of them would turn the established order on its head by becoming elected officials themselves.

While praising Kansas in the *Vanguard* article, Denton had expressed his disdain for Illinois and its citizenry. "In many parts of Illinois the land is cheap and very good, but the country is flat and unhealthy, and the people generally of the old fogey order," he declared. Whether Koons knew of his friend's opinion of Little Egypt is not clear, but his settling there had been driven by facts on the ground rather than ideology. In his letter to Denton from Illinois, Koons was feeling out of the loop with the intellectual and theological discourse he had savored over the years—and he had no sense yet of the cultural life in the new community where he had landed by happenstance:

> I can say but little on the subject of mental progression relating to this place [as] my time was so completely engrossed in domestic cares during the winter so as to deprive me of any extensive acquaintance and information on the subject.
>
> I have lost sight of all progressive publications, on any thing new on the subject. Pleas remember us to the vanguard in your correspondence to the same, and perchance its editors will favor us with a copy so as to learn its whereabouts, and renew our old acquaintance.
>
> If you should ever come within quarreling distance of this place, do not fail to call. This morning, we had a lively gale of a northwestern, that sprinkled us with a healthy shower of snow.— the air stil continues cold, much to the danger of loosing our fruit

crops. But nature must execute her laws, in defiance of the imputed attributes of mental discriminating supremises.

  Yours Fraternally,
  Jonathan Koons
  Mores Prairie
  Jefferson Co. Ill.

✻ ✻ ✻

EVEN though Koons had dropped out of sight in southern Illinois that fall and winter of 1858–59, his name still was mentioned occasionally in the spiritualist press. A letter from John Tippie's friend Thomas White, written in February and published in the *Telegraph*, flatly stated that Jonathan's (or Nahum's) magic had deserted him. "We are informed that Koons' trumpet medium has lost all his medium power, and is no longer subject to spiritual influence," White wrote. "This fact is good evidence of his honesty, for if he ever performed without the aid of Spirits, he could, and most likely would, do so yet; but he is not favored with either rap, tip, or any other evidence of Spirit presence. Yet he is too honest to renounce Spiritualism, as some others have done who once thought that they had been mediums also."

White had also been keeping up with his friends the Tippies: "I regret that I only know of one trumpet medium in the West at present, and I learn that he [Ezra] has gone with his father (John Tippie) to Pike's Peak," White told the *Telegraph*. "I received a letter from Mr. Tippie recently, informing me that Father King was with him; that they were all on their way to the Peak, and that they kept up their circles and obtained a great amount of useful information thereby." White's mention of Pike's Peak points to the possibility that John Tippie Jr. had been swept up in the gold-mining craze, which may have been part of the reason he moved west. Although the most famous gold rush occurred in California, starting in 1849, a second one in western Kansas Territory north of Pike's Peak (later Colorado) also captivated public attention 10 years later. Under the slogan Pike's Peak or Bust, the so-called Fifty-Niners raced in the spring of 1859 to see who could reach the gold first. Perhaps John Jr. and Ezra were among their ranks, but it is not clear whether the two ever made it to the vaunted mountain.

The Tippies' friend White was writing from LaPorte, Indiana, where he had attended three less-than-spectacular circles and was longing for the good old days. He addressed the *Telegraph* editor as "Brother Partridge" and lamented, "I have not forgotten the glorious times you and I enjoyed at the rooms in Athens county, Ohio, some four years ago; but O, the contrast between what we then witnessed and enjoyed, and the best that is being performed now! It reminds me of the Jewish fathers who mourned and wept at the dedication of the new Temple, when they remembered how far it fell short of the glory of the previous one."

Perhaps White was correct in writing during the winter of 1859 that the Koonses were at the nadir of their spiritualist practice, the dancing fiddle strings and the voice of the trumpet having gone silent. But as spring turned to summer Jonathan Koons was once again bouncing back. In a letter to the *Spiritual Telegraph* dated June 15, 1859, he was much more up-beat than when he wrote to his friend William Denton earlier that year. Koons had received five issues of the paper from Partridge, along with a letter, and set out to answer Partridge's questions. "My faith is firm as the granite pillar of Pike's Peak . . . and my knowledge . . . more precious than all the virgin gold it contains beneath its eternal snow-capped summit," he wrote. Koons sounded optimistic as he described his new surroundings: "The seeds of Spiritualism are already sown in this so-called Egyptian land (Southern Illinois)." A "venerable old clergyman" had converted to the cause, and regular circles were meeting at the home of Dr. Wilkey, where mediums were developing their talents for "trance speaking, writing, and physical demonstrations."

In his letter to the *Telegraph*, Koons explained the situation at his own home: "We have not been in a condition to hold public circles since our exit from Ohio to this place last fall. Recently, however, we became some-what hungry for spiritual nourishment, which led us to a renewed effort to receive manifestations. This we carried into effect in the presence of L. T. Dean of Ohio, and my own family, in which we reaped a consoling reward. We had a genuine Spirit-correspondence through the trumpet, and no mis-take. This effort has been since repeated with equal success."

The visit of Lovead T. Dean, a family friend, and the return of the Koons family's ancient spiritual guide must have cheered them as they tried to adjust to their new surroundings in Northern Township. At a private séance at Jonathan Koons's home, one involving a close circle of friends and relatives, Jonathan posed a question about the nature of God and got a detailed written answer from King, who styled himself as "First and Second Presidents of the Band of ancient and remote earthly dates." Along with Dr. Carter Wilkey, the circle included George D. Hascall, MD, and his wife; S. A. Bates; Joseph Border; Margaret Bates; Newcomb Graves; Alvis Taylor; J. R. Koons (Jonathan's son); T. M. Wilkey; Robert Taylor; Lydia Hughes; Jno. B. Tippie; and C. M. Brookins. The familiar Athens County surnames indicate that relatives outside Jonathan's immediate family had moved to Illinois as well—a Hughes niece and Nahum's in-laws, the Bateses. In addition, Dr. Hascall years earlier had made a pilgrimage from Rockford, Illinois, to the Koons Spirit Room. All signed their names below King's message, declaring their belief that "this was not written with mortal hands" but by the spirit himself. No mention is made of Nahum's being present, which could explain why the sermon was not delivered through the trumpet and written down by a listener on this particular occasion.

In his letter to the *Telegraph,* Jonathan Koons added that investigators had asked him to hold public circles for their benefit, but the Koonses "have as yet declined, for various reasons not necessary to enumerate." Koons does not explain why he "is not in a condition" to hold public circles. Perhaps he was referring to the bouts of illness suffered by Abigail and their son Brittan the previous winter. Jonathan hinted, though, that the spirits had been incommunicado for a time, leading to his "renewed effort" to hear from them. Reading between the lines, it seems clear that Koons did not want to reprise the life he had led in Ohio. He seemed content to conduct his private devotions and to promote spiritualism in more conventional ways, such as opening his "library of spiritual books" to interested parties at Salem, Illinois, and distributing copies of the *Spiritual Telegraph* that the editor, Partridge, had sent him. But even as the spirits returned, the Koons family was to be sorely tested before the year expired.

*　*　*

JONATHAN Koons got some welcome news that fall of 1859 when his nephew Cyrus Hughes finally found a buyer for his Athens County property. Seth Fuller, the man who had purchased Jonathan and Abigail's home place the previous year, scooped up the 202-acre Hughes farm for $2,500. Though they were no doubt eager to join relatives in Illinois, Cyrus and his wife, Eliza, revealed the bittersweet nature of selling out and moving in the words of the deed itself: "We reserve one fourth of an acre, including the Graveyard. Also the School house Lot and Meeting house Lots." In the graveyard in a high meadow slumbered not only Filenia and George Koons but a Hughes relative—perhaps Cyrus's mother, Elizabeth. They were leaving a part of themselves behind.

"THE fear of war has prevented many from going to Kansas that would otherwise have flocked there," wrote the territory's tireless advocate, William Denton, in 1857. "Others have been prevented by the dread of slavery. Both may lay aside their fears." Denton confidently predicted that Kansas would eventually be admitted to the Union as a free state, "though the pro-slavery party may not be willing to lie down and die for some time yet."

Denton was ultimately correct, but his rosy predictions had not come true by 1858, when the Tippies found themselves in Linn County in the eastern portion of the territory known as Bleeding Kansas. Linn County was just over the line from Bates County, Missouri, where Jonathan Koons had originally intended to settle. Violence had ruled the border region since the 1854 passage of the Kansas-Nebraska Act, which allowed the citizens of those territories to decide for themselves whether to allow slavery. As settlers from Missouri rushed in to claim Kansas land for slavery, migrants from the Northeast and Midwest stepped in to oppose it. Linn County was the scene of bloody clashes that pitted neighbor against neighbor, both individually and in militias. Many people who tried to stay out of the conflict found themselves the victims of robbery and intimidation—their homes, barns, and livestock looted.

In May 1858 the violence in Linn County escalated when a band of marauders from Missouri, led by Charles Hamelton, gunned down 11 unarmed

Free-Staters near Trading Post, executing five and gravely wounding five others. Only one escaped unharmed. James Montgomery's free-state militia, armed with Sharps rifles (popularly called Beecher's Bibles), pursued the gang across the state line but could not overtake them. When news of the massacre reached the abolitionist John Brown, he responded by building a fort near the scene. John Greenleaf Whittier immortalized the atrocity in a poem he called "Le Marais du Cygne," first published in the *Atlantic Monthly* in September 1858.

This was the place that the Tippie family chose to settle; whether ideological reasons played a part is not known. Migrating at about the same time as John Tippie Jr., his wife, Anna Margaret, and their large family were John's father, John Sr., and his wife, Elizabeth, who then were in their early seventies. Part of the attraction may have been that the Tippies already had a relative living just south of Linn County. Michael Tippie, a brother of John Sr., had been farming in adjoining Bourbon County since 1855 or earlier. Rhoda, a sister of John Jr., also moved to the area and may have shared a home with their elderly parents.

The bold adventure of John Jr. and Anna Margaret soon met with misfortune, not from the violence of Bleeding Kansas but from a more prosaic killer. Typhoid fever claimed John, then 47 years old, in September 1859. His elderly father and stepmother had died that summer within a month or so of each other. Even the new year brought no end to the suffering, for in February 1860 Anna Margaret's little daughter, Lydia, died of lung disease at age 8 or 9. The deaths of Anna Margaret Tippie's husband and in-laws left her with the responsibility of caring for her teenage stepchildren and the young children of her second family. Eventually a male guardian would be appointed to watch over four of the sons of John Jr. by his first wife—18-year-old Granville, 16-year-old Joe, 15-year-old Phillip, and 13-year-old Hathaway—freeing Anna Margaret to lead another life.

THE disease that had claimed the life of John Tippie Jr. in Kansas a month earlier struck the Koons household in October 1859. Just a year after their move from Ohio to Illinois, two of Jonathan and Abigail's children contracted typhoid, probably by ingesting tainted food or water. First would have come a low-grade fever that climbed each day, coupled with ab-dominal pain and a dry cough. No doubt Abigail would have administered her herbal remedies but to no avail. As the disease progressed, sufferers would eventually fall into a delirium in which they picked at the bedclothes or imaginary objects. Both children struggled for about 10 days. The first to die, on October 22, was 15-year-old Eliza, the adopted daughter. Two days later, 14-year-old Daniel succumbed.

The sudden loss of the youngsters might have made Northern Township feel like a hostile and blighted place, but Abigail and Jonathan still had to provide for their seven children ranging from 6 to 19 years old who were living at home. Their son Nahum lived nearby with his wife, Ann, and their toddler, George Bates Koons. By 1860 Jonathan's nephew Cyrus had moved to the community with his wife, elderly father, and several children. Later that year 18-year-old Quintilla would marry a local man and remain in the county. Just as family members had formed a tight cluster upon moving from Pennsylvania to Ohio, the next generation reconstituted their sup-port system in Illinois.

Jonathan's niece Anna Margaret Hughes Tippie, widowed in Kansas in 1859, also rejoined the family circle in Northern Township, perhaps as early as 1862. With two of her stepsons living with their oldest brother, Ezra Tip-pie, and other stepsons in the army, she probably felt free to make a fresh start with her four surviving children. Her son Charles, born soon after the death of his father, John Tippie Jr., had vivid memories of a harrowing trip in which the family crossed the Mississippi River that year, presumably heading to Illinois from Kansas. Charles became a musical prodigy by age 7, playing a violin concert for adoring adults at nearby Ewing College with his long golden locks cascading across his shoulders.

With the ongoing Civil War came a call for Illinois to fill its quota of sol-diers for the Union Army. Two of the Koons sons, Samuel G. B. and Roland (now going by the name James R.), signed on with the Forty-Ninth Infantry Illinois Volunteers at Centralia on February 25, 1864. That April they made their way to Camp Butler near Springfield to begin military service as pri-vates assigned to Company K. Camp Butler was not only a training camp for new recruits but also the site of a prison where more than 700 of 2,000 Confederate captives held there had died amid a smallpox epidemic in 1862. Twenty-two-year-old Samuel was just over 6 feet tall, with gray eyes, a dark complexion, and dark hair. James, 20, was fairer-skinned, with blue eyes, and a little shorter at 5 feet, 10½ inches. Presumably their years of rugged farm work made them able recruits. But something tragic must have happened when the brothers reached Camp Butler. Records state simply that Samuel died there on April 10 with no mention of his being mustered in; James was mustered in the following day and went on to serve for more than a year.

Back home in Franklin County—about 170 miles away—their mother, Abigail, died less than a week later, on April 16, at age 52. Whether she knew of Samuel's untimely death is not clear, although her son's body ultimately was brought back home for burial. The move to the West was proving to be a hard passage; death had claimed four Koons family members in the five and a half years they had been in Little Egypt.

On May 8, 1865, perhaps after observing the traditional year of mourning, Jonathan Koons, then 53, married a 42-year-old woman from the neighborhood, Nancy Jane Webb Page. A descendant of one of the pioneer families of the township, she had been widowed since 1859. First wed at age 15, Nancy Jane had borne 10 children, most of whom were adults by the time she married Jonathan. The 1870 census shows Nancy Jane and Jonathan living on his farm with his sons Cinderellus, 20; George, 18; and Britten, 16, along with her two sons from her previous marriage, 11-year-old Simeon and 13-year-old Alexander.

Koons had again chosen a minister's daughter as his mate. Nancy Jane's father, Charles Sweet Webb, was a Baptist preacher and later became a trustee of Ewing College, a Baptist-affiliated school founded in 1867. Her family had close ties to the college, and some of her relatives married faculty members there. Nancy Jane's brother, Solomon Munson Webb, probably was the friend who had delivered Jonathan's letter to William Denton in Kansas a few years earlier. According to Jonathan, he and Solomon found much to agree on. "Like ourselves, [he] is considered by some, to be somewhat fanatical; in consequence of the existing difference of opinion on theological views between himself and some others," Koons confided in Denton. "Such epithets are to myself however, marks of progression in the accused." Perhaps because of the persuasions of her new husband, Nancy Jane would practice spiritualism during their marriage.

✳　✳　✳

IN 1870 a book came along that plucked Jonathan Koons out of obscurity and recognized him as one of the early pioneers of spiritualism. Emma Hardinge Britten, a former British actress who became a medium and trance lecturer, published an influential account of the movement in her adopted country, a tome of more than 500 pages called *Modern American Spiritualism: A Twenty Years' Record of the Communion between Earth and the World of Spirits.* She devoted two chapters to the Koons and Tippie families, in effect guaranteeing their place in the history of spiritualism. Britten noted that the Davenport brothers were the most famous mediums who could produce spectacular physical effects in dark séances, but Jonathan Koons had paved the way with his innovations. "The initiatory experiments of 'the spirits' in this direction, and by far the most powerful which have ever been performed in modern times, owe their origin to the mediumship of Jonathan Koons and his family," she wrote. Britten had seen fit to give credit where credit was due. Later scholars would wonder whether the Davenports' father had visited the Koons Spirit Room, thus acquiring a blueprint that would guide his sons into becoming one of the world's most famous magic acts in the nineteenth century.

THE unprecedented campaign of the spiritualist and free love advocate Victoria Woodhull provides a clue to Koons's political beliefs as he settled into old age on the Illinois prairie. In 1872 Woodhull declared her candidacy for president of the United States and was organizing a convention for the Equal Rights Party—also called the People's Party—in New York City that spring. Woodhull's followers were disillusioned with the Democrats, the party of slavery, and had come to believe that the Republicans, the party of the interests, were economically corrupt. According to the *American Spiritualist,* a cornucopia of movements embodying "the revolutionary spirit of the country" was expected to converge on the city: "The National Labor Party, the International Workingmen's Association, the Woman Suffrage party, the Temperance party, the Peace party, the Spiritualists, the Liberal or non-Evangelical Christians, the Free Religionists, the Free Thinkers, the Free Lovers, the Land Reformers, the Socialists, Communists, Positivists, Harmonialists, etc." This radical melting pot was to coincide with the meeting of the National Woman Suffrage Association, whose leaders, Elizabeth Cady Stanton and Susan B. Anthony, had thrown their support to Woodhull.

It was only natural that Jonathan Koons was among those signing a People's Party petition that was published in several spiritualist newspapers shortly before the meeting. The petitioners hoped to solidify a new reform movement "which shall sweep over the country and purify it of dema-gogism, official corruption and party despotism; after which the reign of all the people may be possible through a truly republican government which shall not only recognize but guarantee equal political and social rights to all men and women, and which shall secure equal opportunity for education to all children."

Given the distance to New York City, it is unlikely that the 60-year-old Koons jostled in the throng of 600 iconoclasts who noisily nominated Woodhull for president. However, by sifting through the names of other petitioners in the newspaper columns, he would have encountered memorable ones from his past. Among the human rights advocates were Caroline "Carrie" Lewis, the wealthy free love crusader from Cleveland who had been awed by the Koons Spirit Room, as well as her spiritual godfather, John Murray Spear.

ALTHOUGH his days as a spiritualist performer were long behind him, Koons continued an active exploration of spiritual issues on the farm in Illinois. He was a contributor to the Chicago-based *Religio-Philosophical Journal,* finding in this paper an outlet for his strong views—which had become no less stri-dent over the years. "Dear Brothers," he wrote in the spring of 1875. "Please pardon me for writing you so often, but I must seek out some Spiritualist to whom I may venture to express my thoughts and experience, and I know none more worthy than your own dear selves. Since forming your limited acquaintance, your dear *Religio-Philosophical Journal* has been a star in the east in my family." He had even made the 300-mile trip from his home to the newspaper's office, apparently to pitch ideas for articles or books.

Koons shared an interest with others in the movement who explored alternative versions of the traditional Christian narrative, unorthodox histories that would raise the hackles of many believers. Thus he had decided to unveil some of his most controversial material yet—messages that he claimed a spirit had left in the locked Koons Spirit Room in Ohio decades earlier. He asserted that the texts, dealing with the origin of the Christian church, had been written and signed by "Jesus of Nazareth, the medium of the spirit Christ." Back in the 1850s Koons had deemed this material too offensive to Christians to disclose in its entirety. He had floated a trial balloon by giving one of the least abrasive of the articles to Abraham P. Pierce, the medium from Philadelphia who had visited Koons in 1854. Pierce had it published in the *New Era* newspaper of Boston that same year, but disclosure of the brief article led an anonymous source to accuse Koons or the spirit writer of plagiarism. Koons denied any wrongdoing and the *New Era* defended him, but the episode, Koons remembered, had caused "considerable excitement." Realizing that the documents were "unsafe to place before the Christian world," he had decided to keep the bulk of them—"some forty pages of legal cap, more or less"—under wraps for the time being.

By 1875 Koons had decided that society was ready for their release. "If said exposition could be placed in the hands of reasoning Christian believers, it would dislodge the last remaining brace to [the] modern sect[arian] party of Christendom, enabling the devotees of the Nazarene to appreciate their 'Lord and Savior Jesus Christ' in his true relations to heaven and spirit life," he wrote. Apparently Koons had received some encouragement from the editors of the *Religio-Philosophical Journal,* for he began compiling and copying the unpublished manuscripts. While engaged in his editorial task, Koons "felt the presence of a spirit throughout." After concluding the work at eight o'clock one evening, he held a private circle with his wife, Nancy Jane. Although he did not reveal his intent to her, Jonathan was hoping to find out who his control was. With Nahum the trumpet medium long gone from the household, the Koonses used a less spectacular means of spirit communication. "To her [Nancy Jane's] surprise, the signature appended to said article, was given alphabetically through her at the light stand by tips." The name spelled out—plus a horrifying dream or vision of a crucifixion later that night—convinced Jonathan that he was in direct communication with Christ. He revealed these latest developments in a dispatch to the *Religio-Philosophical Journal,* which by 1875 had become his staunch defender and advocate.

That spring the *Spiritual Scientist* of Boston published an unsigned article warning readers not to "act upon the advice of the spirits in opposition to your own convictions, or the dictates of common sense." The *Scientist* gave examples of those who had followed spirit direction a little too blindly: John Murray Spear, whose perpetual motion machine had been destroyed by a mob; the Elizabethan astrologer John Dee; and Jonathan Koons. "Mr. Koons, who had the most wonderful of the early physical manifestations in America, was brought to ruin and disgrace by allowing the spirits to control his business affairs," the article said. The writer did not explain the brief, enigmatic statement, and the *Religio-Philosophical Journal* was quick to brand the allegation a mistake. "He is now living on a farm in this State, one of the happiest and best of men," the *Journal* reported.

The one-time darling of the eastern spiritualist press now became a favorite of the Chicago paper. Referring to manifestations of "the most startling character" that had occurred at the Ohio spirit room, the editors of the *Religio-Philosophical Journal* announced they would reprint Koons's serialized autobiography, which had been published in a Pennsylvania paper in 1856–57. Over the summer of 1875 they ran his life story in 12 installments—thus introducing Koons's engaging history to a whole new generation of spiritualists. The newspaper series, along with author Emma Hardinge Britten's flattering portrayal, did much to restore Koons's reputation. Whatever doubts had been raised about his mediumship in the mid-1850s, the slate had been wiped clean.

IN 1877 the State of Illinois passed a law that ran contrary to Koons's passionate belief in nontraditional healing. Henceforth all physicians would be required to graduate from an approved medical school and obtain a state license before practicing medicine. Only those who had been active caregivers for the previous 10 years would be grandfathered in; the old practitioners would eventually die off. Given Abigail's experience as an herbalist and medical clairvoyant, Koons was contemptuous of the new law. His sympathy for medical outsiders extended to Dr. James A. Nolan and his wife, magnetic healers whom he believed were able to cure those given up for dead by the "diplomaed physicians." Charges of practicing without a license were brought against them in Benton, Illinois—the seat of Franklin County—but the couple's acquittal only added to their clientele. "Nolen and his wife were notified by a Ku Klux letter through the mail, to leave Benton within a stipulated time, or he would be visited by a mob, who would treat them to a feast of hickory withes," Koons wrote. "The inspired healers, however, continued steadfast in their angelic mission, in defiance of all threats and persecutions of the M. D.s. Nolen's persecutions remind me of my own," he added, citing the torching of his barn in Ohio.

Jonathan and Abigail's son Cinderellus had gotten his medical degree in 1876 from the American Medical College in St. Louis. The college was based on a philosophy of "eclectic medicine," with an emphasis on herbal remedies—perhaps just the sort of curriculum Abigail would have appreciated. The 27-year-old doctor began his practice in Franklin County and later moved to adjoining Jefferson County. A late nineteenth-century biography lauded him in the flowery language of the time: "Among the young and rising physicians of this county who owe their high standing and the confidence that the people place in them not to inherited wealth or fame, but to their own exertions and go-ahead spirit, we are glad to count him."

FIFTEEN years into their marriage, Jonathan and Nancy Jane evidently hit a rough patch that brought into focus the question of who would eventually inherit their real estate in Northern Township. Although Nancy Jane had routinely signed her X mark on Jonathan's land transactions for years, something changed in 1880. That year—and again in 1881—Jonathan bought more land in the neighborhood, but her mark was nowhere to be found on the paperwork. Instead the records specifically excluded Nancy Jane's interest in the new property with the notation "to Johnathan Koons and his lawful heirs by his first wife Abigal T. Koons, without reservation of dower in view of any after marriage alienation." The Koons heirs may have perceived the threat of at least some of the property going to Nancy Jane or her children; it is also plausible that something had indeed fractured in the marriage. But whatever the source of the disagreement, the couple continued to live together on the farm.

✻ ✻ ✻

AROUND 1881 Nahum, Ann, and their children moved back to Jonathan's homestead in Northern Township after living in Missouri for more than a decade. The youngsters—including the 4-year-old twins Samuel and Alice—would have found many cousins to play with, for most of Nahum's brothers, now married, had settled around Jonathan and Nancy Jane and were busy parenting the next generation. Nahum's only surviving sister, Quintilla—who would become the matriarch "Aunt Quint"—was caring for her large family with her postmaster husband, Alvis Taylor, at Taylor Hill, the community where Jonathan and Nancy Jane also lived.

Nahum and Ann's time in Missouri had been marked by both prosperity and tragedy. The family had settled in Wayne County, an area in the Ozarks whose vast timber resources were being exploited with the coming of the railroads. Nahum bought property in Piedmont, a village of about 1,000 people, and operated a sawmill and general store. Some members of Ann's family settled there, too, including her mother, Margaret, and younger brothers, George Jr. and Samuel A. Bates. The 1870 census shows Margaret and Samuel were living with the Nahum Koonses, whereas George Jr. resided separately with his wife and child. Samuel later became a physician who rose to prominence as a newspaper publisher and politician, and George would become one of the town's founding fathers—a successful businessman who also welcomed mediums into his home for séances.

The same railroads that were bringing commerce and excitement to the town brought misfortune to the Koons family in May 1873. Because Piedmont was the southernmost point on the St. Louis and Iron Mountain Railroad, the company had built a turntable next to the depot. The turntable was a rotating bridge used to turn the locomotives around. This unlocked and unguarded piece of machinery, somewhat like a merry-go-round, became an object of fascination for the children of the town. Tragically, Nahum's 9-year-old son, James, paid no heed to his father's warning not to play on the turntable. Caught between a stationary portion of the track and moving timbers on the machine, the little boy was accidentally crushed to death.

A protracted court battle followed in which the child's parents tried to collect damages, alleging negligence on the part of the railroad. The

Koonses won a jury verdict, but the railroad appealed the case to the Missouri Supreme Court and got the decision reversed. The appellate court ruled that the lower court had improperly admitted testimony about the dangers of the turntable from witnesses who were not qualified as experts to render their opinions. "Although we might concur in the opinion of these witnesses and that of the jury, the defendant was entitled to have the case tried according to law," the court said in explaining the reversal. The case was remanded to the Wayne Circuit Court, but it is not clear whether Nahum and Ann ever managed to hold the company legally responsible for the accident.

Both Jonathan and Nahum had clung to their spiritualist faith during their long separation. Though Nahum was no longer offering public demonstrations, he continued to hold private sittings with his family. Nahum and Ann's oldest child, 21-year-old George Bates Koons, had come to Illinois with his parents as a baby. Once his parents moved back to Northern Township, he made his home with 68-year-old Jonathan and 57-year-old Nancy Jane, helping run the farm. In the summer of 1882 he would bring home a bride tailor-made for the family: Polina May Jones was not only a medium but an accomplished fiddler.

21

"The Venerable Johnathan Koons"

THE CULMINATION of Jonathan Koons's religious thought was the publication, in 1881, of his book, *Truth Seekers' Feast; Composing a Savory Pic-Nic of Theological Knick Knacks, Relating to the Ground-work of Modern Christianity.* Printed by Exponent Power Press in Mount Vernon, Illinois, the book was written for an audience of "investigating truth seekers and free thinkers in general." What could have been a fascinating autobiography actually is a dense treatise that barely mentions his remarkable adventures in Athens County. In the introduction Koons, then about 70, alluded briefly to the arson that destroyed his barn in 1852, but in the 119 pages he largely stuck to his purpose of constructing an alternative history of Christianity. The "Ground-work of Modern Christianity" that he sought to upend was the Grand Council of Nicaea, a convocation of Christian bishops held in 325 CE during the reign of the Roman emperor Constantine. Koons delivered a message that, in ages past, would have gotten him burned at the stake as a heretic or, at best, banished to the far reaches of the realm.

Koons began his manifesto by expressing his distaste for organized religion. "It is an incontrovertible historical fact, and beyond dispute, that in place of cementing the social bonds, kindred relations and natural associations of the human family of all historic ages, theology has invariably been the entering wedge that effected their social dissolution and alienation." In Koons's view theology had also hampered the development of the arts and sciences: "Under the blood-stained banner of 'religion' all the most useful arts were, of necessity, developed in private study—outside of its sectarian folds—to avoid ecclesiastical persecution."

In his second chapter Koons took a long view of the history of religious persecution. He outlined the 250-year reign of terror forced upon the Christians by the Roman emperors from the time of Nero to Constantine but wryly noted that "no sooner than the fires of the Pagan persecution were extinguished by Constantine, the Christian bishops began persecuting each other." These conflicts over doctrine among early Christian leaders led to the Council of Nicaea, which, according to Koons, not only set the creed for the Catholic Church but backed its religious orthodoxy with the force of arms. For centuries the Catholics pursued heretics with a holy zeal, regarding them "no better than we esteem a sheep-killing dog; neither did they show them any more mercy, who considered themselves doing God's service to persecute them to the death." The tide began to turn with Luther's reformation, yet Koons gave his story an ironic twist: "Finally the persecuted Pilgrims found an asylum on the shores of North America, and unfortunately, brought a relic of the Eastern spirit of persecution with them, which was conspicuously exhibited after their landing in New England, under the Jewish Statute of Moses, to 'not suffer a witch or wizard to live'"—an apparent reference to the Salem witchcraft trials. "It is truly passing strange," Koons wrote, "that when a party faction of any denomination that has been sorely persecuted by other parties in power, in return, gain a victory over their persecutor, who become impaled with the military power of arms, in place of treating them with acts of kindness, the victors invariably try to excel, if possible, their vanquished persecutors in perpetrating the same and still greater atrocities against their powerless victims."

Koons saw the Nicaean transactions as another example of religious persecution, specifically, that of Arius, a Libyan priest who was excommunicated around 318 CE by his bishop, Alexander, because of Arius's views of the nature of Christ's divinity. But the ouster of Arius and his followers from Egypt did not end the controversy. In 325 CE Constantine, himself a new convert to Christianity, ordered bishops from throughout the empire to assemble in the Turkish city of Nicaea for the purpose of adopting a set of core principles of the faith, which later became known as the Nicene Creed. In Koons's narrative "a confederated conclave of Alexandrian bishops" in concert with Constantine decided which of the many gospels then in circulation were divinely inspired and culled out others, resulting in the 27 official books of the New Testament. "Their object, no doubt, was to condemn and destroy all the gospels extant, except those of their own selection and revision," Koons wrote. He charged that the bishops conspired to keep Jesus's other, more controversial, teachings a secret.

Koons's suspicions of the Nicaean proceedings would be echoed more than 100 years later in American popular culture of the twenty-first century. According to Dan Brown's historical thriller *The Da Vinci Code,* the Council of Nicaea suppressed texts that would have emphasized the humanity of Jesus in favor of those that celebrated his divinity. Unlike Koons's book, Brown's went on to sell millions of copies. And even though it was a novel, the work was severely criticized for historical inaccuracies, especially its claims about the history of the Christian church.

Historians of religion generally agree that the New Testament canon was not adopted at Nicaea. "The formation of the canon started centuries before Constantine, and the establishment of the four-fold Gospel canon of Matthew, Mark, Luke and John was virtually in place 150 years before his day," according to Bart Ehrman, an authority on the early Christian church. He maintains that the Nicaean council did not deal with matters of canon; the chief debate was about the manner in which Christ was divine—not whether he was divine. The issue was "whether Christ was a divine creation of the Father or was himself co-eternal and equal with God." Ehrman notes that the first mention of the 27 official books did not appear until 42 years later, in 367 CE, when Bishop Athanasius of Alexandria laid out his recommended scriptures in a letter to the Egyptian churches.

Another respected theologian, however, believes that the Council of Nicaea's decisions did set in motion a standardization of Christian doctrine that resulted in the suppression of diverse viewpoints about Jesus's life and philosophy. "From that meeting and its aftermath, during the tumultuous decades that followed, emerged the Nicene Creed that would effectively clarify and elaborate the 'canon of truth,' along with what we call the canon—the list of twenty-seven writings which would become the New Testament," notes historian of religion Elaine Pagels. "Together these would help establish . . . a worldwide communion of 'orthodox' Christians joined into one 'catholic and apostolic' church." Pagels points out that not only did Bishop Athanasius cite his version of the canon in his Easter Letter, he ordered the churches to cleanse themselves of apocryphal books. Monks living at a monastery near Nag Hammadi, Egypt, are said to have taken about 50 of these supposedly subversive texts from the library and hidden them in a jar on the mountainside to await their discovery nearly 1,600 years later, in 1945. These lost Christian writings are now known as the Gnostic Gospels.

Pagels contends that, had certain books other than the 27 chosen as the official New Testament been selected, the whole biblical perspective of human beings' relationship with the divine would have been transformed. For example, in contrasting the New Testament Gospel of John with the excluded Gospel of Thomas, she finds that "what John opposed . . . includes what the Gospel of Thomas teaches—that God's light shines not only in Jesus but, potentially at least, in everyone. Thomas's gospel encourages the hearer not so much to believe in Jesus, as John requires, as to seek to know God through one's own, divinely given capacity." So it is possible that, had the canon been formulated differently, the course of Christianity would have been altered.

Jonathan Koons, writing *Truth Seekers' Feast* without the benefit of later discoveries such as the Gnostic Gospels, seems to have come up with ideas similar to those expressed in them. Although it appears he may have gotten some facts about the Council of Nicaea wrong, his larger point was that the philosophy he said was hidden by the church fathers would have been more affirming to him personally. He believed that the bishops who prevailed at Nicaea "held the credulous mass of mankind spellbound under fears, superstitions and misapprehensions; all of which, I honestly confess, I partook freely in my young days, and which led me into a thorough investigation of the subject by day and by night; oft-times wishing myself annihilated; until, in A.D., 1852, the spiritual light of a higher life was shed down upon me and infused my yearning soul with a more supermundane effulgence of love, wisdom, order and divine beauty, than that which I had experienced beneath the cold shadow of an uncourtly oligarchy."

Koons spent much of *Truth Seekers' Feast* denouncing a philosophy that he rejected—weaving conspiracy theories about secret orders of knights and mysterious cabalists—but he devoted only a scant few pages to explaining what he did embrace. Toward the end of the book Koons professed his articles of faith, the truths that had been revealed to him through his longtime congress with the spirits. But here the writing broke down in strange words and long sentences that circle back on themselves, making his thinking largely inaccessible to the modern reader. Perhaps that was why he labeled this book volume 1, with the intention of publishing a second volume detailing what he called "the spiritual side of these subjects." "If I am favored with health, time, and the requisite means of support and assistance," he continued, "I will give the public the full benefit of the subjects embraced in this treatise in detail, as I received it from a band of prehistoric spirits; beginning at the date of June A.D. 1852, and thence, in broken doses, to the present date of A.D. 1881."

The question might well be asked whether Koons still believed in God, who was mentioned frequently along with Jesus Christ in Koons's early writings. At first glance the answer may appear to be no, for he wrote, "I believe there is no individualized spirit[,] god, angel, or devil, in existence, who is able to exercise the power of omnipresence, at the same moment, throughout the boundless depths of space. The only omnipresent power that I can recognize is the imponderable conduplicates, which manifest their presences simultaneously throughout the boundless universe." What he meant by "imponderable conduplicates" is difficult to conceive, but in another passage he made clear his new conception of the divine: "I find, in the course of my research, that the Bible Gods did not create man, but that man created the Bible Gods, in the image of human nature." He referred to "man's divine constitution," which suggests his belief in some form of inner consciousness or spirituality.

He chose to end his book with a poem by Lizzie Doten, a Massachusetts writer who composed her verses while in a trance state, imitating the styles of famous authors from Shakespeare to Poe. In "A Divine Idea" she expressed a somewhat Gnostic (or Eastern) worldview that resonated deeply with Koons. "The following lines of inspiration," he wrote, "come very near filling the bill of my own sentiments relating to the mythology of personal gods, in place 'of the life of God in man'":

> Gross by birth from his mother Earth,
> He needed some outward sign;
> So the artisan planned, with a cunning hand,
> A form of the Great Divine.

And Baal and Allah, and Juggernaut,
And Brahman and Zeus and Pan,
Show how deeply wrought was that one great thought,
In the worshipping soul of man.

Then his deity came in the morning's flame,
In the song of the sun-lit seas,
In the stars at night, in the noontide light,
In the woods and the murmuring breeze.
To the Great Divine, at the idol shrine,
By each and by every name,
Through the fiery death or the prayerful breath
The worship was still the same.

Like a grain in the sod grew the thought of God,
As Nature's slow work appears;
From the Zoophite small to the "Lord of all,"
Through the cycles and terms of years.
But the dark grew bright, and the night grew light,
When the era of truth began,
And the soul was taught, through its primal thought,
Of the life of God in man

* * *

Hour by hour, like an opening flower,
Shall truth after truth expand,
The sun may grow pale and the stars may fail,
But the purpose of God shall stand.
Dogmas and creed without kindred deed,
And altar and fane shall fall,
One bond of love, and one home above,
And one faith shall be to all.

Even in old age Koons continued to be fascinated by the religion he had learned at his mother's knee, yet he had reached a new understanding that filled him with a hopeful vision of the universe.

* * *

LITTLE is known about how Koons spent his time after the publication of his book. He may have forged ahead on the promised second volume, but age and ill health probably prevented it. Even in old age, though, he cut a striking figure as he drove across the prairie in his buggy, his long gray hair coiling around his shoulders. A short entry in *Tidbits,* a local publication, reported in March 1887 that "Uncle Jonathan Koons, an old resident of this Northern Township, was in town last Wednesday. He is 76 years old and has been in this county 29 years. His health has been bad last winter but is better now."

By the following year Koons had lived long enough to hear about the shocking revelations of 55-year-old Maggie Fox, the legendary medium who, along with her sister Kate, had started the spiritualism movement in 1848 with their mysterious raps. In an interview published September 25, 1888, in the *New York Herald,* Maggie Fox dismayed a nation of spiritualists by declaring that the whole business had been a fraud. The noises had not come from spirits but from her and her sister as they dislocated their toe joints. She claimed she had been pressured into a lifetime of deception by her older sister, Leah, who had been the family stage manager. "No, no, the dead shall not return," she told a reporter, "nor shall any that go down in hell. So says the Catholic Bible, and so say I. The spirits will not come back. God has not ordered it." Soon thereafter Maggie Fox gave a public confession and demonstration before hundreds at the New York Academy of Music, where she stood on a pine table in her stocking feet and produced loud raps throughout the auditorium. She proclaimed to the audience that "spiritualism is a fraud from beginning to end" and collected $1,500 for the exposé.

While skeptics gloated, Koons's favorite spiritualist newspaper, the *Religio-Philosophical Journal,* denounced Maggie Fox's confession in an article called "The Foxonian Cataclysm." "For thirty years this woman has been under Romish influence, and during all these years she has been gradually going from bad to worse until she has sounded the lowest depths of woman's degradation," it said. "The marvelous powers of mediumship she possessed always afforded her a groundwork on which to build deception and to impose upon the credulity of many and the friendship of many others."

The paper argued that the Fox sisters' own record spoke to the reality of spirit communication, as they and their sister, Leah, had produced hundreds of manifestations "from which every element of doubt, deception and error have been eliminated." The development of thousands of other mediums and the spread of spiritualism during the previous 40 years also spoke to its authenticity. "Showmen, religious bigots, Romish priests, a sensational press, and all the other powers of darkness combined cannot smother the spiritual fire burning in millions of homes," the newspaper concluded.

But that was not to be the end of the story. In November 1889 Maggie Fox confessed to the spiritualist newspaper *Banner of Light* that her earlier confession had been a lie, brought about by financial problems and pleas from officials of the Catholic Church, to which she had converted years earlier. With her reputation now destroyed and her mind at times clouded by drink, Maggie Fox died in poverty in 1893. As she lay on her deathbed in New York City, her doctor was said to have heard loud raps, even though she was incapable of moving her hands or feet.

✳ ✳ ✳

SPRING had returned once again to the Illinois prairie, and old man Jonathan Koons was surrounded by love—from the living and from the dead. On an April evening in 1892 he was at Nahum's home, bathed in the familiar and comforting ritual of the séance. He was perhaps too old to play the fiddle by then, but the spirits still made their heavenly music through the harmonica, tambourine, and dinner bell. Aerial lights prowled the velvet blackness as further proof that the spirits were with them.

Eighty-year-old Jonathan Koons could feel at peace with both the celestial and temporal realms. He had made out his will earlier that month. He would allow his wife, Nancy Jane, to have lifetime possession of the farm so long as she did not remarry, move off the land, or fail to pay the taxes. The property itself would go to the heirs of Abigail Koons: Nahum; the heirs of James R. Koons; Quintilla E. Taylor; John A. Koons; Cinderellus Koons; George E. Koons; and Joseph Britten Koons. Jonathan had appointed his sons John A. and Joseph Britten as executors. They would see to it that tombstones were erected for any deceased family member who didn't already have one, with the cost to be paid by Jonathan's estate.

With his earthly affairs in order, his thoughts could dwell on the continued life beyond. So many were on the other side by then. Filenia. Daniel.
Samuel. Abigail. James. His parents and brother Michael. So many. Familiar
voices were coming through the trumpet, perhaps welcoming him home.
But Koons was not yet done with this world. The next day he sent a dispatch to a newspaper about the séance, landing a headline that called him
"the Venerable Johnathan Koons."

Less than a year later, on January 26, 1893, Koons "passed to spirit." He
was 81 years old. His death was noted in *Tidbits:* "Jonathan Koons, a well
known citizen of Northern Township, died last week. He was noted as an
author and teacher of spiritualism for many years and had many followers
of this peculiar doctrine. He was a kind hearted man and had many friends.
He raised a large family of children and most of them live in this county."
Nancy Jane lived until 1898, dying at age 75.

Decades earlier Jonathan Koons had had an apocalyptic vision. It came
to him in a trance or reverie, which he later paused to record:

> First, the natural sun, moon and stars were represented in
> glowing and magnificent splendor, interspersed through a
> checkered canopy, under the display of every conceivable color.
> A small breach now takes place in the vertical firmament, a little
> south of the zenith. From this breach, innumerable lines diverged
> in every direction, very similar in appearance to those produced by
> a blow upon a piece of window glass. The breach now assumed
> a bright dazzling appearance, under an increasing magnitude. A
> voluminous flame of transparent light now burned forth from the
> breach, which seemed to absorb and extinguish the natural sun
> with all its systematized groups of surrounding bodies, while the
> element of the terrestrial heaven seemed to pass away in flying
> vapors. Meantime, far in the distance, another more bright and
> luminous firmament made its appearance, which occupied the
> place of the former, with a high degree of evolved animating and
> soothing influence, shed forth upon the habitable planet.

Like the biblical writer John of Patmos, Koons had foreseen a new
heaven and Earth, but unlike the former's, Koons saw no "lake which
burneth with fire and brimstone"—just a kinder, gentler world. As he

himself once wrote, "Not withstanding, I was an odd sheep in my father's flock, I can nevertheless boast of a successful enterprise in the achievement of what to me are inestimable treasures. And I deem it a privilege to communicate my experience to those who are travelers and pilgrims on my road."

Epilogue

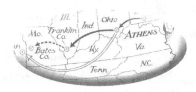

EZRA

IN 1870 Ed R. Smith, the popular clerk of the court at Mound City, Kansas, had just ridden 12 miles into the countryside to witness the marvels going on at the Round House owned by John Morrison. Smith could hardly believe the contours of the circular building sitting 200 feet from Morrison's home in Paris Township. The windowless house was 10 feet high, 14 feet in diameter, and crowned with a conical roof. A single tightly sealed door had opened to admit curious visitors, including some of the most prominent women of the community. In the dimly lit interior Smith saw some rough benches that could seat perhaps a dozen people. But his eyes were soon drawn to the table at the front: on a frame attached to the piece of furniture were strung cornets, fiddles, banjos, and two snare drums that must have been left over from the Civil War. Resting at the top of the assemblage was a long dinner horn.

As the crowd nervously took their seats, they were greeted by their hosts—Morrison and his fellow medium Ezra Tippie—who would conduct the séance. By acclamation the visitors chose Smith to be their spokesman in dealing with the spirits. The door was shut, and the ensuing dead silence caused them to shiver in the sweltering dark. Soon came the crash of the drums, the frail of the banjo, and rowdy notes from the fiddle. As the music died down something began to speak.

"Good evening," boomed a voice from the trumpet.

"Who do we have the honor of conversing with?" Smith asked.

"They call me Father King," the voice explained. "I lived on the earth thousands of years ago."

*　*　*

ELEVEN years before the séance at the Round House, the deaths of John Tippie Jr. and his parents had left the Tippie family adrift. Following that catastrophe in 1859, the 24-year-old medium Ezra had become administrator of his father's estate. While Ezra continued to have séances in his own home, it was rumored that he had grown fond of other spirits as well. According to papers filed on behalf of the estate of John Jr., "In 1860, Ezra Tippie was accused of becoming habituated to intoxication and that he was mismanaging and wasting the estate." It is unclear whether the accusation was founded in fact and exactly what was done about this matter. In late 1859 Ezra had married a woman named Catherine Daugherty, seven years his junior and, like her bridegroom, a native of Ohio. Perhaps Kate was a steadying influence, as she and Ezra would become life partners. She gave birth to seven children between 1861 and 1877 while they were farming in Linn County's Paris Township.

To many in eastern Kansas the advent of the Civil War seemed like a continuation of the violence to which they had long been accustomed. Ezra and four of his brothers spent time in the military during the war. Ezra and Granville served 17 days in Company K of the Sixth Regiment of the Kansas State Militia in 1864. Phillip and Hathaway were on active duty in the cavalry from 1863 to 1865. Joe entered the army as a teenager, served a six-month stint with a cavalry unit, and mustered out in 1862 at age 18. He rejoined the military at age 20 and was assigned to Company M of the Fifteenth Regiment; he went AWOL but returned in time to see action in Missouri in October 1864.

Joe's second stint in the army, however, was fraught with considerable violence not encountered on the battlefield. He spent time in military detention at Fort Scott for robbery, conduct prejudicial to good order and military discipline, and disobeying orders. Along with three other soldiers, Joe had terrorized residents of Greenwood County, Kansas, by breaking into their houses and robbing them at gunpoint late at night. Sometimes pretending to be bushwhackers or rebels, they plundered homes of guns, ammunition, tobacco, and cash. Among the charges leveled against Joe was that he "at the house of Mrs. Fairchild, forcefully broke down the door. Stole articles and burned her family Bible" and "at Mr. Pearmain's house, demanded money. Ordered him out of the house and threatened to hang him, but offered to release him if his wife would give them twenty dollars." Joe's troubles had continued off and on until he was mustered out in October 1865.

By the war's end all the adult Tippie brothers except Phillip still made their home in Paris Township. All but Ezra had developed a reputation among their neighbors as "hard characters." In April 1866 Ezra's four brothers allegedly became involved in a plot to steal from a rancher near Monmouth, Kansas, about 70 miles south of their home in Linn County. They had met the rancher, Ralph Warner, at Fort Scott and arranged to pay him several thousand dollars for his cattle. Their apparent plan was to go to Warner's ranch, drive off the herd, and then return to rob the rancher of the money they had just paid him. And they were said to have gotten the money by robbing one of their Tippie uncles a few weeks before. When two armed men burst into Warner's home at Monmouth, a struggle ensued and the rancher's son-in-law was shot and killed. Phillip and Hathaway Tippie, the two youngest of Anna Margaret Tippie's five stepsons, were believed to be the actual assailants; they failed to get the cash but escaped to Missouri. A posse overtook Joe and Granville, who were driving the cattle in a thunderstorm. They were subjected to a hasty jury trial, sentenced to death, and strung up on a tree. A citizens' league buried the executed men under the tree they were hanged on and turned over the cattle to the wronged Tippie uncle.

The episode left two brothers dead, two in exile, and two young widows with infants to care for. Perhaps Ezra had found private solace for these losses in his mediumship, but his friendship with John Morrison led to a reflowering of Ezra's public career. Sometime around 1870 he and Morrison began hosting séances in Morrison's home in Paris Township. Morrison had been the administrator of the estate of John Tippie Sr. a decade earlier and had been a guardian of the four ill-fated Tippie grandsons. As local historian William A. Mitchell described the duo, "Morrison was just an ordinary man without education whose manner of living had won for him a little bit more than the average of respect and confidence among those who knew him. Ezra Tippie was a near neighbor, a man of easy going habits and of such mild and inoffensive nature that visitors who went with much skepticism to the seances came away mystified and dumbfounded by what they experienced."

As the popularity of the circles grew, Morrison was unable to accommodate all the visitors to his modest home. Like Jonathan Koons before him, he constructed a spirit room next to his own residence, albeit with different geometry. The personality behind the "big booming voice" in the Round House was none other than King, the presiding spirit of the Koons and Tippie circles back in Ohio. This time he identified himself as Father King. Night after night the ancient one would answer visitors' queries on subjects large and small, from big philosophical questions to personal ones, even inquiries about the weather. He created such a sensation that "noted men came under assumed names and went away nonplussed," said the historian. "At each seance Morrison and Tippie were present as the media through which the spirit connections were established. Yet the language and the voice of Father King could not be that of either." The scientific knowledge displayed by the entity whispering through the trumpet also seemed unlikely to have come from the minds of two ordinary men. When asked to explain the phenomenon, neither man offered details. Tippie said "there was a mystery about it he could not solve," and Morrison said all was done at the direction of Father King, that he himself was "powerless to do otherwise."

Morrison and Tippie charged no fees and accepted no donations, building up a devoted following among the residents of Linn County. It is not clear how long the spirit room was in operation, but Mitchell reported that several hundred people visited in a year. King eventually became unreliable and often did not appear when summoned. Matters came to a head on January 1, 1872, in the wake of a train crash that left the engineer and fireman dead. When it was discovered that someone had placed an obstruction on the tracks, causing the accident, the locals appealed to Father King for clues to the identity of the perpetrator.

At King's direction a group of men (presumably including Tippie and Morrison) went to the scene of the train wreck and constructed a makeshift spirit room on that stormy winter night. They carried the musical instruments with them and placed them under blankets supported by poles to form a primitive tent. Soon came the boom of the drums followed by King's voice. Rather than divulge the name of the guilty party, King bade the devotees farewell, declaring that he was done with them forever.

Even so, a doctor in Marmaton, Kansas, wrote a letter to a spiritualist newspaper in 1874 suggesting that that part of the state would make an ideal location for a spiritualist colony. "We have the spirit, 'Father King,' of Athens County, Ohio, and Koons and Tippie notoriety, of twenty years ago, and others," he declared. "We have the once 'boy Tippie' here, and [he has] been here for years by spirit direction. John Morrison, the world-renowned positivist, is here, and [has] been here a long time, and others, though no stir about [it]. Ancient spirits that have been in the spirit world 21,000 years, have been concentrating power to this region for eleven years, though no stir about it."

PERHAPS Father King, his patience sorely tried by the inquiry into the train wreck, was having a peevish moment when he washed his hands of the whole business. Three years later he was writing to a newspaper in Fort Scott, where Ezra was performing in 1875. In the article "From 'Father King,'" an artful pretender defended the mission and character of "my medium, Mr. Tippy, and his friend, Mr. John Morrison," who had been censured by critics at a recent dark séance in that city. "The object of my visit was to prove the immortality of the soul, to demonstrate the fact of spirit communion, to teach the people, and make you all better and happier," he explained. Nonetheless the same questions that had surrounded the Koons and Tippie séances in the 1850s—about ventriloquism, darkness, deception—had found a whole new generation of skeptics to voice them, yet the tone of Father King's rebuttal was humorous and good-natured. "When I come again to town in about two weeks, call on me, mister," he wrote, addressing one foe. "We will give you a front seat, and perhaps I will be able by that time to show myself to you in person, so you can see as well as hear. Affectionately yours, Father King."

That same year at another dark séance in Kansas, where the admission was now 50 cents a head, a woman named Jennie Lapsey privately approached Ezra with a question before the program began.

"What would happen if the room should suddenly be illuminated?" Lapsey asked.

"My gracious, it might kill me by severing the electrical charge between myself and Father King," Ezra replied, evidently referring to the "nervo-vital fluid" that the angels had long relied on to connect with humans. "I do not fear anything of the kind," the medium hastened to assure her, "because Father King would know if there was any person present prepared to make a trial of the kind, and therefore would not appear."

The next night Lapsey returned to Ezra's seance with a concealed lantern. As Father King was speaking to the crowd, she turned it on. The horn tumbled to the ground and Ezra clutched his stomach, writhing in pain.

"Father King came once too often," crowed the *New York Tribune*. "He will never come again, at least to this particular part of Kansas."

Ezra left town the next day and a few years later moved to Oklahoma. The 1880 census still showed him living in Linn County with his wife, Kate, and six children at home, but perhaps the family relocated soon thereafter. A man who had frequently attended Ezra's séances in Kansas reported that "about the year 1880 Ezra Tippie moved west, and I am informed quit his mediumship altogether." Ezra died in 1903 at Seiling, Dewey County, Oklahoma.

Morrison's Round House in Paris Township was abandoned and gradually collapsed, leaving younger generations to quicken their steps as they walked past the ruins of the so-called ghost mansion. But some converts to spiritualism in that Kansas community went to their deaths convinced that they had indeed made contact with another world. One of those attending the séances became a trumpet medium himself, assuring that Father King's voice would not fall silent forevermore.

Back in Athens County the spiritualist influence lingered in the hills and hollows, particularly in Ames Township, where the Tippies had lived and where another spirit room was reported to have existed a few miles northeast of the Tippie farm. This third Athens County spirit room of the 1850s, of which little has been recorded, was at the home of George Keirns, one of two men who had witnessed Koons digging up Indian relics in the woods. Travelers waiting to gain access to the crowded spirit rooms of Koons and Tippie sometimes boarded at the even more remote Keirns home place, partaking of séances there.

"At one time spiritualism gained a number of followers in this township, especially in parts of the Hooper Ridge area. There were several who practiced certain acts of levitation, forms of healing and so on," a local historian wrote. What's more, the man who bought part of the Tippie farm established a spiritualist church. The two spirit rooms (log and frame) built at Tippie's home fell into disrepair, but the wealthy Peter Hixon, originally from Bedford, Pennsylvania, carried on John Tippie's tradition in a new building a mile or so away. "Not only did Mr. Hixon build his own church, but he also hired his own minister to expound the gospel," the historian added. Hixon's building is believed to have been torn down in the early 1900s; a private residence occupies the spot today.

NAHUM

AFTER Ann's death in 1899, Nahum spent most of his time in Illinois but lived a few years in both Oklahoma and Arkansas. In 1904, some 11 years after Jonathan died, a family friend, William A. Thompson of Murphysboro, Illinois, reported that Nahum was located at Temple, Oklahoma, where his son George Bates Koons had moved in 1902. "He [Nahum] is now about 68 years old," Thompson wrote, "and is by no means a wreck physically, mentally or morally. His character is above reproach, as is that of his two brothers. I am acquainted with them, both holding official positions. Their brother-in-law, Alvis Taylor, held the position of postmaster longer than any other man in Franklin county [Illinois]. Koons' youngest son, Britten Koons, is a human walking encyclopedia." During the last four years of his life, Nahum lived with his son Robert A. in Mount Vernon, Illinois, where Nahum died in 1921 at age 84.

Nahum's devotion to spiritualism was noted in his obituary:

He had been an avowed Spiritualist since early childhood, and had also been a medium for various Spiritul manifestations, having traveled quite extensively when a young man through eastern cities in the interest of the cause, and was the principal medium at his father's home in Athens county, Ohio, where seances for Spiritual manifestations were given under test conditions almost every day and night for ten [actually about four] years, where hundreds were convinced of the immortality of the soul and the possibility of communion between the mortal and the immortal life.

What the obituary did not reveal was the role that Nahum was said to have played after Jonathan died—a span of 28 years until Nahum's own death. According to the family friend Thompson, the faithful son had channeled communications from the departed Jonathan "many times."

KING

THE same spirit that first appeared to the Koons family as King and later to Ezra Tippie as Father King became almost a roving ambassador for spiritualism as the nineteenth century progressed, appearing through different mediums at various times and places. Two of the first people outside the Koons and Tippie orbit to latch onto King's persona had been the Davenport brothers, who reported "John King" as their control in the 1850s. John was even said to have a spirit daughter, Katie King, who became a celebrity in her own right and was involved in a scandal involving the British physicist William Crookes. In the post–Civil War era the machinery of the séance had grown ever more sophisticated, so that ethereal arms and hands were no longer the awesome spectacle they had been in the heyday of Jonathan Koons. Now séance goers expected to see full-body materializations of their favorite spirit characters, no easy task for the average medium. The spirit cabinet developed by the Davenport brothers—who went on to become internationally famous magicians—was essential to such a demonstration, as the medium would typically be restrained while the ghost appeared from behind the cabinet and interacted with the audience.

In the 1890s a man named J. H. Haughey—who had known Ezra Tippie's circles well—reported attending such a séance in Spring Hill, Kansas, where some 30 forms appeared. Among them was a "commanding presence" that "picked up a large tin trumpet that stood on the floor by the cabinet door and spoke the words, 'Good evening' to each one in the circle, then set the trumpet down and disappeared by settling down (seemingly) through the floor." About a week later Haughey was at another séance where the sitters were singing a rousing Methodist revival hymn. Suddenly the song was commandeered by a deep bass voice—the same "commanding presence" that Haughey had conversed with for 17 years. As an apparition began to take shape, the sitters could make out the features of a man's face. A "deep, coarse voice" proclaimed, "Good evening, friends" through the horn. "Father King," came the cry from Haughey. As the disciple would later recall, King "bowed in recognition, and seemed pleased to be identified, and disappeared from sight." To true believers some vestige of the pyrotechnic King who had danced on the tabletop at the Tippies' spirit room decades earlier was still roaming the earth.

Across the Atlantic another of King's devotees had tried to make contact. Joseph P. Hazard, the wealthy Rhode Island man who had "camped out" in one of the Mount Nebo spirit rooms and found himself thoroughly entertained by the spirits, attended two séances in London in 1879 hoping to connect with King once more. Hazard had fond remembrances of the amiable ghost from the week the businessman had spent at the Koonses' in the early 1850s. Hazard recalled how the spirit "was there every night, the leading genius of the manifestations" and remembered King as being most eager "to do whatever he was asked to do, for the satisfaction of *all* inquirers. . . . On the evening of my final departure he sat at a table by my side, and with his illuminated hand wrote a brief, but very gratifying note, which he presented to me."

King the pre-Adamite ruler—supposedly from a primordial order of wise ones—was now established in the popular imagination as John King and had even degenerated into an alter ego called the pirate captain Morgan, two terms of address that the Koonses had not used. In the 25 years between Hazard's visit to Ohio and his trip to London, he claimed to have seen John King in materialized form several times, once by *"nearly full or-dinary gas-light."* Now Hazard was curious to see if the John King mani-festing in England was the same one with whom he had conversed in the United States.

Hazard found himself attending a dark séance in Lamb's Conduit Street with people he did not know. He did, however, think he recognized the luminous head and inimitable style of John King. But when Hazard asked his old friend if he remembered him, the spirit replied that he did not. Hazard persisted, asking the same question of John King at the next séance, which was also dark, and got the same answer. Defeated, Hazard revealed his name to the medium, but still there was no hint of familiarity. As the séance wore on, Hazard finally got his due: "My identity gradually opened to his recognition, and without further aid or hint on my part. He then expressed great pleasure at meeting me again, and returned to me repeatedly during the evening with expressions of kindness and interest that were almost emotional in manner."

Despite John King's belated insight, Hazard soon was offering up an-other clue to keep the conversation going: "When I told him I had seen him in Ohio many years ago, he said, 'With the boys—the Davenports?' But when I responded, 'At Mr. Koons,' he made no reply, and I thought he might be unable, under existing conditions, to remember Mr. Koons at all."

MOUNT NEBO

SOME 13 years after Jonathan Koons packed up and left Athens County, another group of seekers was determined to breathe new life into the spir-itualist community in Dover Township. Led by an elderly Michigan man named Eli Curtis, these visionaries settled around 1871 on land that had been part of the Koons farm. Their 5-acre property encompassed the knoll that dominates the landscape on the east side of Sunday Creek, which they called Mount Nebo. Curtis had been contacted by a spirit he believed to be Jesus of Nazareth, who had instructed him to purchase the land "on which to commence the building of the City of the New Jerusalem, which in due time is to extend over the principal part of the Ohio State."

Curtis named his utopia the Morning Star Community and invited like-minded people to join him, especially mediums. Immediately upon buying the tract from the Hibbard family, Curtis renounced his rights to the land as a private citizen. "I claim no ownership nor right to said plat of land except an equal ownership as a member of the Morning Star Community with other members of the same," he stated. William D. Hall and Chauncey Barnes signed on to help Curtis realize his dream. Hall and Barnes agreed to serve as vice president and secretary, respectively, while Curtis took the lead as president.

It is not clear whether the Morning Star group bought the exact spot on which Koons's house and spirit room had sat, though Koons certainly lived in the vicinity of the knoll until 1858. The Koonses' 206-acre farm had been subdivided by Seth Fuller in 1863 and resold to three separate buyers, one of whom was a Hibbard. No one knows if the spirit room was still standing by the time Curtis moved to Mount Nebo. In any case his group had a time line for building a new tabernacle: they would lay the cornerstone by November 11, 1871, and have the structure completed by December 31. His colleague Barnes was optimistic that the edifice would be ready for dedication by Christmas. The Morning Star settlement would remain a separate community—and once resources could be secured, it would have its own newspaper called *Herald of the New Dispensation*. "We have promise, from our Celestial Spirit guides, that, ere long, we shall have accessional Mediums, and means in abundance, to carry out the plan of the Deific Blending, and Jesus of Nazareth, and his Celestial Messengers," Curtis wrote.

Curtis's selection of the name Mount Nebo carries some sad irony. In Deuteronomy, Mount Nebo was the hilltop from which Moses could view the Promised Land of Israel, which he was destined never to enter. Curtis's own vision of a new kingdom of God on Earth likewise was fated to be unfulfilled, as he met with misfortune soon after his arrival in Dover Township. That summer of 1871 he ran an ad in the paper offering a $500 reward for the return of $2,500 stolen from his home, and on December 15 his wife, Sally, died. Curtis himself passed away just 11 days later at age 78, with the construction project incomplete.

The octagonal building with doors or windows on each side, adorned with a cupola, was never finished. However, it was far enough along that séances or actual services of some kind were held there—much to the excitement of the participants. A story handed down through generations cannot be verified but gives a flavor of the times: A local man named Evertt had attended one of the rituals as an invited guest. As he and other participants stood in a circle, a disembodied hand appeared out of nowhere and made its way around the ring. Upon reaching Evertt, though, the appendage changed course and shot over his head. Other legends told of frenzied gatherings where the intoxication by spirits ran high and people were led to speak in tongues. But along with tales of wonder came a familiar theme known all too well to Jonathan Koons: some in the community believed the spiritualists were actually devil worshippers performing their rites in secret.

The dynamic Barnes was deemed Morning Star's most active member. According to the *Athens Messenger,* he "is said to have performed some wonderful feats under the alleged influence of spirits." He also embraced a new element of spiritualist practice: spirit photography. In his pocket Barnes carried dog-eared photos of himself and other spiritualists in which mysterious faces appeared as "shadowy spectres" in the background—and these he considered further proof of the spirits' presence. But the Morning Star community never attained the high profile that the Koonses' did, and it blinked out in 1875 when Barnes moved away.

Later on, some people would tell that the eight-sided building had been torn down around 1893. Others would insist that a bolt of lightning had touched off a fire that consumed it. But as late as 1927, an older resident known as Miss Hebbard, whose family had sold part of their land to the spiritualists, remembered the building on the knoll and recalled how the windows, shining like mirrors, could be seen from miles away. Today nothing remains of what was referred to as King Solomon's Temple.

✳ ✳ ✳

IN the wooded hills around Athens County, Mount Nebo is what passes for a holy mountain. The knoll continues to be privately owned and—perhaps because of the fascination it still commands—is off-limits to the public. A whole mythology has grown up around it, with Mount Nebo literally at the center of a pentagram linking five haunted cemeteries in the area. Some even believe that the locale does have peculiar electrical and magnetic properties.

In the spirit of Nahum Koons and Selah Van Sickle, Mount Nebo has also seen its share of artists over the years, including an intentional community founded by Aethelred Eldridge, an Ohio University art professor, in 1969. Inspired by the philosophy of the English romantic poet William Blake, Eldridge bought 80 acres near Mount Nebo and called his hippie paradise Golgonooza in honor of Blake's fictional city of imagination and art. Eldridge and his wife, Alexandra, and their friends dedicated a restored log cabin on the property as the Primal Church of the Blake Recital, with Aethelred as its minister. "It was a wonderfully creative time at the foot of Mt. Nebo," Alexandra Eldridge recalled. "We put on plays and pageants. Aethelred read and interpreted Blake every Sunday. Others read their own poetry, etc. We also had great dance parties there, and Aethelred would marry and baptize couples and babies."

One visitor recalled traveling from afar to attend a pageant at Golgonooza:

> Slightly off the road, nestled in a pasture among the verdant hills, a large log stage with a podium—more properly a pulpit—had been constructed, evidently just for the performance of "Hail the Depth of the Skin." It appeared as though the woods had been crawling with hippie artists, all of whom had emerged from the foliage to converge on the pasture. Figures carrying large cardboard cutouts of the sense organs—eye, nose, ear, tongue, lips, and genitals— moved all over the stage and throughout the audience as they took turns making prophetic pronouncements. All the while Æthelred Eldridge was declaiming from a pulpit in the style of an eighteenth-century Methodist minister, but rather than ascetic restraint from the Bible he preached imaginative excess and saturation of the senses from Blake's epic Milton. When the pageant was over the hippie artists vanished again, leaving us to our dark drive home with afterimages of the event dancing in our heads.

Though Blake was the ethereal muse at Golgonooza, inspiring both life and art, its residents were well aware of older associations with the land they inhabited. They had looked into antiquity, beyond the biblical reference to Nebo (originally Nabu), to find that it was the name of a Babylonian god. "Like the English Woden, the Greek Mercury, the Latin Mercurius, the Babylonian Nebo is the prophetic god of writing, the bringer of culture. Wednesday is his day, his planet Mercury, his animal a serpent-headed dragon, a chisel and engraving table are his tools, and the symbol of Nebo is the wedge upon an altar, upon the back of a beast," Alexandra wrote. They also looked to the recent past and found the story of the erstwhile resident Jonathan Koons. In their extravagantly illustrated newsletter, *Golgonooza Loose Leaf,* Alexandra and her compatriots retold the story of the Koons Spirit Room to a new generation of seekers. They collected and published oral histories of older residents of the area, recording shared tales about the Koonses and Tippies as well as the Morning Star community. All the while their writings expressed a cosmic sensibility: "Athens knows traditions more ancient than any folklore," one contributor wrote. "And Mount Nebo is a Hill of Vision. We come with fervor to keep the Hill, to stir the iron stream in its core, to draw forth the life within."

The Golgonooza colony flourished into the early 1980s. In 1987 the log building in which Aethelred staged his Sunday performances burned down. He suspected arson, vengeance based on the mistaken belief among some in the area that he worshiped the devil. Aethelred continued to live on the property and teach at Ohio University, eventually gaining notice in the 2000 edition of the *Dictionary of the Avant-Gardes,* but the third great wave of spiritual activity on Mount Nebo had subsided.

ABIGAIL

GREAT blue herons now peer into the depths of Burr Oak Lake in Morgan County, Ohio, where Abigail Bishop Koons's 123 acres once occupied dry land. Nearly a century after she sold her property along the East Branch of Sunday Creek and moved west, a dam was built for flood control and the valley inundated. The houses and covered bridges were burned before the dammed-up waters could overtake them. On the wooded lakeshore today, occasional breaks in the tree line reveal where the Bishop family's houses once stood. The home of Abigail's sister Almira is said to have been haunted.

Afterword

Koons in Legend: Gold and Dross

"In the lives of mortals, the best days are the first to flee," the poet Virgil once observed. So, too, with religious movements. In her 1870 book *Modern American Spiritualism,* published about 15 years after the Athens County spirit rooms closed, Emma Hardinge Britten seemed to be yearning for the old-time religion, the golden age:

> Premising that the manifestations . . . transpiring in the spirit rooms of Koons and Tippie, are special, and remarkable for clearness and force, it is asked, Why do they come no more in such a form? Are they passing away or diminishing in excellence? And if so highly instructive and useful as we have represented them, why are they not continued with even increasing force and beauty? To these queries we answer generally. These phenomena were evolved at that particular period when, in the incipiency of the movement, their use was most manifest and essential. They cease to some extent with the cessation of the conditions of their production, which were fervent zeal, devotion, earnest singleness of purpose, and lavish expenditure of time and means.

No more zealous servants could be found than Koons and Tippie; Britten acknowledged that "these faithful workers expended thousands of dollars and incurred a loss of time, property and position that at length culminated in financial burdens impossible to be borne any longer." Why, then, would the spirits not help them prosper so that the important work could be continued? Why had the spirits deserted them, as some people claimed?

In Britten's analysis the success of John Tippie Jr. and Jonathan Koons in Athens County rested upon their having large families of "highly-mediumistic" children situated in a locality with a peculiar electrical nature. As the children reached adolescence, their "mediumistic aura" waned. With a change in these conditions "the spirits could do no more." On a practical level she reported that the resources of the Koons and Tippie families had become "utterly exhausted":

> Some change, then, was imperatively demanded; and still unwilling to sacrifice their splendid gifts to sordid necessity, they were induced to organize traveling parties for the purpose of giving the manifestations a wider field of action. Whether the mediums missed the influence of their highly charged spirit rooms, and the strong electrical current of their pine forests and ancient hills, or whether the public interest had waned by familiarity with these marvels cannot be correctly determined. Certain it is that though very powerful evidences of spirit presence still followed them in their missionary wanderings, they were no longer regarded as the marvelous and exceptional mediums they were once deemed. Others entered rival claims for public favor, and the Koons and Tippie families seemed somehow to glide out of the page of supersensuous celebrity.

In the end Britten concluded that Jonathan Koons was a nineteenth-century Job, albeit not a perfect one. "[He] is not the first and will not be the last man, who, in a good cause, has pushed devotion beyond the bounds of worldly prudence," she wrote. "[But] if . . . the thorns of martyrdom must inevitably pierce the reformer's feet, the blossoms that spring up out of them are worth all the pain endured."

The publication of *Modern American Spiritualism* was only one step among many that Emma Hardinge Britten took to secure for Jonathan Koons a place in the constellation of spiritualist luminaries. In 1872 her newsletter, the *Western Star,* included a humorous piece—probably fictionalized—about a seeker named Amodeus who goes to the Koons farm and engages in a lively colloquy with King. But the seeker is driven out of the hayloft sleeping quarters later that evening by a messianic roommate who wants to make Amodeus a disciple. Much later, in 1888, Britten wrote a sober historical sketch for another of her newsletters, *Two Worlds,* to remind a new generation of readers of Jonathan's sacrifice: "After infuriated mobs had burned good Jonathan Koons's barns, pelted his children, broken up his own and his family's peace; after he had been preached against, prayed against, his substance had been wasted—necessity obliged him to break up the overwhelming burdens he had imposed on himself" and move west. His family "became scattered far and wide in search of employment." The last she heard about Jonathan Koons's whereabouts, he had written to Charles Partridge from "the mining camps of Pike's Peak, Missouri," where he supposedly described his plight in dramatic tones: "The end is near at hand; the battle nearly fought out; but say of me, my friend—if there is never a monumental stone to record my assertion—He was faithful unto death; and when the serpent of temptation would have swayed him to disown or turn aside from the glorious light of immortality, revealed and proved alone by the presence of the immortals, he aye answered, 'Mine eyes have seen the glory of the coming of the Lord,' and 'What shall a man give in exchange for his soul.'"

Britten's account is suspect for several reasons. There is no independent verification that Jonathan's children were pelted or beaten, and Koons evidently did not leave Athens County because of arson or other persecution. Koons himself wrote, "The conflagration of my barn, containing the avails of a year's labor, however, atoned for all, after which we enjoyed peace and safety, and I pursued my investigation unmolested."

The lofty quote attributed to the dying Jonathan Koons resembles Britten's own writing style more than his, and Britten had a habit of editing quoted material. Further, the reference to Pike's Peak, Missouri, is interesting because Koons alluded to Pike's Peak and "its eternal snow-capped summit" in an 1859 letter to Partridge. However, Koons probably was referring to a mountain in what would become Colorado, rather than a lower peak in Missouri. Though a visit to Missouri cannot be ruled out, in 1888 Jonathan was in fact very much alive in Illinois, secure in his old age and surrounded by his wife, children, and grandchildren. But in one respect Britten was right: he had kept the faith.

In 1892, the year before Koons died, Emma Hardinge Britten yet again brought his name before the public, although this time in England. In her last newsletter, *Unseen Universe,* she serialized chapters of a novel called *Ghost Land Volume 2* (a sequel to *Volume 1,* published in 1876). The book is presented as the autobiography of a wandering spiritual seeker who briefly visited the Koons Spirit Room during his travels through the United States.

Britten was the editor of *Ghost Land,* which was published under the pen name of Louis, supposedly a German-speaking diplomat of aristocratic lineage. Scholars have disagreed about the identity of the author, but some recent analysis suggests that Britten herself wrote at least part of it. An even larger question is the degree to which *Ghost Land,* even if based on an actual person's experiences, was fictionalized. The scholar Joscelyn Godwin maintains that *Ghost Land* may be regarded "as fact, as fiction or as a mixture of the two." He concludes, "Given so uncertain an identity, we can only take Louis's autobiography as fiction. But even if it is only a novel, it is a very good one." Whether derived from imagination or from actually witnessing or hearing about the Athens County phenomena, the story of Louis adds an interesting dimension to the saga of the Koons family.

In the second volume of *Ghost Land,* a mysterious stranger ascended the hill to the Koons farm in the company of his friends, "Mr. D" (alias John Cavendish Dudley) and "Monsieur Lotti" (from India), along with "two Hindoo servants." The three gentlemen are traveling from New York City under assumed names. The year is not known, but the text suggests it might have been in the early days of the Koons Spirit Room. The stranger, whose fictional name is Chevalier Louis de B——, later wrote of what he found:

> The place we at length arrived at was a wild, stony district in the midst of bare hills, clusters of tall pine trees, mountain ranges destitute of vegetation, and strewed with ancient boulders scratched over with stony histories of their far and wide travels in tens of thousands of years ago. The habitations in this lonely spot were few and far between. Two rude ill-kept houses of public entertainment had been set up to accommodate the crowds of people who flocked to the scene of wonders, but these at the time of our arrival were so full that we had to drive to a more promising scene some miles further on.

After a wait of several days the New York visitors gained entrance to the pine-logged spirit room of Jonathan Koons. Louis noticed that the walls were decorated with "spirit writings and drawings stuck up against the logs." Even though "most of the instruments were strung up to the roof, and quite out of reach," they were "played on with masterly skill" in the darkened room. Louis found pages of writing "thrown upon the table in pencil, and often in wet ink." And the spirits conversed with him and Mr.

D through the trumpet, impressing them with "answers quickly, sharply and wittily given." Louis found further evidence of "the intelligence of our strange visitors":

> That their knowledge of us far surpassed that which we had of them, was shown by the fact that they addressed Mons. Lotti, Mr. Dudley, and me by our real names, and asked after some of our friends by name in India and England. Of Emma Hardinge they spoke as if she were one of themselves, one voice jocularly shouting out, "She is going to put me in her book" (a book not written till some eighteen years afterwards). When I questioned, "How do you know her, and who is she?" such an answer was given as convinced me they knew of her through me—and that correctly, too.

One night, as Louis and his party were sitting in the circle, a thunderstorm assailed Mount Nebo, rocking the Koons Spirit Room to its very core. Even though the room was dark as usual, Louis reported that "the Spirit house was constantly illumined by successions of zigzag blue lightnings, and bells rung above our heads." A bolt of lightning must have struck nearby: "One mighty and distracting peal of heaven's artillery shook the Spirit house . . . whilst a succession of blinding wild fire seemed to pierce the roof, walls and atmosphere around, forming to my perception one vast, boundless amphitheatre of rushing flame, dazzling every eye but mine, and causing every human being present but myself to bury their faces simultaneously in their hands; then it was that I alone sat watching and gazing up calmly at the unveiled and gracious face of a mighty planetary angel."

In Louis's vision the roof became transparent, allowing him to see the angel's head filling the entire sky. It was a being that he had known for some time, although in previous encounters it was always veiled. Seeing the angel clearly was a transcendent moment for this seeker: "He of whom I alone had knowledge in that place, looked for an instant lovingly, protectingly into my eyes; an instant in which I lived a lifetime."

An enormous spirit hand thrust a roll of papers into Louis's hands. Sensing the private nature of the communication, he hid it in his bosom for later perusal. A voice spoke through the trumpet, calling him by his real name and assuring him that the message was from the ancient angel called Oress. And then the storm was over, the fiery sky vanishing, the thunder muted, and the face gone. Louis heard some "signal raps" that indicated the close of the circle. The lamps were relit. It was, Jonathan said, the worst thunderstorm he had experienced since moving there.

Characterized by one researcher as a "spiritualist propagandist," Britten spent more than two decades promoting Jonathan Koons's good name in her publications. The controversies that swirled around him during his colorful career—mostly set in motion by other spiritualists—fell victim to her editing pen. Nonetheless she did more than any other person in the nineteenth century, with the exception of book editor J. Everett, to ensure that Jonathan Koons's story would live on.

OTHER CONTEMPORARY VIEWPOINTS

Others were less kind in assessing Koons's impact on the spiritualist movement. One of the most scathing articles was published in 1865 in *Knickerbocker* magazine. The anonymous author lampooned the gullibility of spiritualists in general—all the while taking a swipe at Dr. Robert Hare, an elderly chemist who had converted to spiritualism after an eminent scientific career at the University of Pennsylvania. In his 1855 book Hare had furnished glowing eyewitness reports of the Koons demonstrations, noting that "my spirit friends confirm the truth of the account received." The *Knickerbocker* writer could scarcely conceal his disdain:

> Should any one be desirous of finding an example of the strongest character, of the extent to which men of reputed intelligence may suffer themselves to be duped, let him open the pages of the book of Dr. Hare, of Philadelphia, on "Spirit Manifestations," at page 295, and read what he inserts in reference to the "believing" visitors, at the establishment of Jonathan Koons, in Athens county, Ohio; and then let him look up the report of the self-constituted committee of "unbelievers," who attended the manifestations of Koons some time afterward, and exploded the whole imposture, by seizing the illuminated "spirit hands" which played the musical instruments, etc., and found good-sized Hocking [Athens] County girls attached to them. We should imagine that the gentlemen who so eloquently describe the proceedings, and attest their truthfulness so positively, must have felt themselves in no enviable position when the humbug was exploded.

(Although several investigators came and went over the years, the identity of the committee and where the report ended up are not clear.)

In 1859 the spiritualist newspaper *Banner of Light* had offered a more nuanced critique by the writer called Phoenix, "an old spiritualist" who claimed to have seen the Koons séances firsthand. Phoenix was the pen name of James J. Mapes, an agricultural chemist from New Jersey who had converted to spiritualism. "Professor Mapes having become satisfied that a great truth lay at the root of it, though mixed up, as he thought, with fanaticism and some charlatanism, determined to see everything for himself; and wherever he heard of new wonders, he packed up his portmanteau, and without regard to time or expense, started off to make a personal investigation," one commentator explained. Although written in an oblique style, Mapes's opinions made their way into the columns of the *Banner of Light*:

> In the last letter we gave Phoenix's views of the manifestations given by the Davenport boys. He also saw the manifestations by the Koons family, many of which he believes to be tricks; some, however, were doubtless genuine, and entirely beyond the control of the mediums themselves. It is his opinion that but few mediums, who are enabled to exhibit physical manifestations, are sufficiently well balanced in mind to withstand the temptation to deceive. They may commence as mediums with the most determined honesty of purpose, but they cannot long avoid being pleased with the surprise of those who attend their séances, and when the manifestations do not occur, this desire to please strongly tempts them to attempt an imitation of what has before occurred without their assistant.

Mapes may well have been one of the "first-class scientific professors" who Koons said had investigated the séances, but if so Mapes missed an opportunity to submit the Koons family to the rigors of science. He apparently did not do any experiments on the mediums he visited, and perhaps Koons would not have agreed to the test conditions anyway. Instead the chemist played the role of participant-observer and published his impressions in the spiritualist press under a pseudonym. Still, his conclusion that the Koonses were a mixture of gold and dross is an important one.

The Koons family operated in an era before the formal science of parapsychology was born. Until the establishment of the Society for Psychical Research in London in 1882 and the creation of an American branch three years later, few physical mediums were subjected to systematic scientific studies. Even if one concludes that many of the séance manifestations were akin to magic tricks, the role of telepathy and remote viewing in the various Koons phenomena cannot be ruled out.

THE PSYCHOLOGY OF THE MEDIUM

The question must be asked: Why did Jonathan Koons—16 years into his marriage—turn his family life upside down with his obsession? Was it his own peculiar version of "middle-aged crazy"? Profit was not the primary motive, so he must have gained other benefits from his notoriety. For one, he was drawn to the spotlight. He loved playing music and explained in his autobiography that his fiddling skills had garnered him entrée to a higher level of society than he could otherwise have accessed. Thus he recruited his wife and children to engage in a complex form of performance art that drew in an even larger circle than his fiddling had. Attracting a devoted following that included East Coast millionaires, intellectuals like William Denton, and artists like Selah Van Sickle must have been a heady elixir for a man of humble circumstances.

Koons also had long searched for a philosophy of life that was essentially full of hope. Christianity had disappointed him, but he still sought something to believe in. In the early 1850s he undoubtedly experienced an epiphany. With spiritualism he was able to banish fears of damnation and despair, nurturing his soul while offering a vision of a benevolent universe to his fellow men and women. He was willing to do practically anything to share that vision—even deception. Something of his worldview may have been captured in the statement of a former medium who recanted to Houdini in 1926: "I really believed in spiritualism all the time I was practicing it but I thought I was justified in helping the spirits out. They couldn't float a trumpet around the room. I did it for them. They couldn't speak, so I spoke for them. I thought I was justified in trickery because through trickery I could get more converts to what I thought was a good and beautiful religion."

Similarly, in probing the motivations of mediums, the scholar R. Laurence Moore explores a factor more subtle than outright fraud—self-delusion. "Unless we assume that mediumistic phenomena were genuine (i.e., produced with the aid of spirits) or, alternatively, that they were all the contrivances of conscious fraud, then we must suppose that honest mediums on some psychic level were kidding themselves," he writes. Moore notes that a medium's belief in his or her psychic powers sometimes had positive effects by literally enabling them to rise from their sickbeds, recover their health, and become public performers. On the other hand, "crippling damage" may be inflicted on the self-deluded medium's psyche if the medium is caught in trickery and forced to confront a flawed self-image. Whether this was the case with Jonathan Koons, following the 1856 incident involving Quintilla at the Cleveland home of Linus Smith Everett, the editor of the *Spiritual Universe* (see chapter 18), is mere speculation, but Jonathan was physically ill around that time.

THE PSYCHOLOGY OF THE SEEKER

The psychology of the séance may be a thicket of mixed motives on the part of the medium, but the emotional state of those on the receiving end of the services must also be considered. Is the audience at a bogus séance simply being rooked, or are they receiving something of value? A few years after Jonathan Koons moved to Illinois, a sensational court case arose in Buffalo, New York, that many hoped would actually prove whether spiritualism was real or fake. The 1865 case involved a medium named Charles J. Colchester, who had developed a following for his seeming ability to summon ghostly music, read sealed envelopes, and make writing appear in red, blood-like letters on his arm. When Colchester—who claimed to be the illegitimate son of a British nobleman—moved from Washington, DC, to Buffalo, he refused to purchase the juggler's (or magician's) license required to practice his profession. Colchester was hauled before a federal court, where his lawyers argued that he was practicing his religion and that the case should be dismissed on First Amendment grounds.

Colchester was an unlikely preacher. While in Washington he had briefly held séances for Mary Todd Lincoln until he was accused of trying to blackmail her. A Lincoln family insider learned of the threat and exposed Colchester at a musical dark séance, reaching toward the sound and getting whacked on the forehead by a drum the medium was shown to be holding. Colchester had boasted to a friend that he could easily cheat certain clients whom he regarded as fools.

Colchester's associates at his trial in Buffalo testified that he had taught them magic tricks such as blood writing, which seemed to prove that he was indeed a magician. The medium was found guilty and ordered to pay a fine plus court costs. But the trial raised the question of what exactly is meant by a religious experience versus a secular one.

Defense witnesses who had consulted Colchester for private readings—including a judge and a journalist—testified that their time spent with him had been worthwhile. The defense argued that even a performance of humbug could be of religious significance for the person seeking advice from a medium. The issue was not so much whether the information provided by the medium was true but whether the interchange between the psychic and the seeker was meaningful. The scholar David Walker cites the testimony of the defense witness Lester Day in particular. Day believed that spirits of the dead exist but that they do not communicate with humans. Although Day did not consider himself a spiritualist, he was "most grateful for the opportunity they [Colchester's manifestations] provided to imagine a life lived *as if* such communication were possible—even as he distinguished that imagination from his notion of a noncommunicative spiritual reality," Walker writes.

CURRENT ASSESSMENTS FROM SCHOLARS

Fred Nadis, in his book *Wonder Shows,* also argues that such performances transcend the real/fake dichotomy. "The sort of 'magic' that public performances of Spiritualism, telepathy, mind reading, and hypnosis offered often had a spiritual component," he writes. "Such performances provided new marvels to an age stripped of the older order of miracles, while bolstering arguments for the realities of a spiritual realm and an expanded vision of human powers. This restoration of humanity to its 'Adamic powers' has long been a millennial religious goal." And although it is easy to dismiss the medicine show performers as frauds, Nadis believes they helped to smooth the social fabric during tumultuous times: "They were not just simple charlatans, dangers to public health and morality, but in their own monstrous way guardians of older values. If the medicine they sold in bottles did not cure anything, their shows offered an antidote to the alienation and dehumanization that accompanied the mechanistic philosophy."

Similarly, the scholar Catherine Albanese notes that the more outlandish displays of spiritual performers should not be simply dismissed as a kind of vaudeville of an earlier time: "A deeper reading . . . points to its connections to social, economic, and religious dislocation as the nation moved inexorably into a future in which the old verities no longer held and traditional communities dissolved under the impact of serious social change."

Instead of mediums' being hucksters exploiting the bereaved and naive, as Houdini liked to say, perhaps they were performing valuable therapeutic functions. In this light Jonathan Koons—and certainly his son Nahum—may be regarded as a kind of shaman, not just performing but actually inventing rituals that many people found transformative. In so doing they may have been reenacting—albeit in a format new to the nineteenth century—the ancient rites performed centuries before on the plains of the Hocking River below Mount Nebo.

Marc Demarest, curator of the Emma Hardinge Britten online archive, contends that Koons's innovations have earned him a notable spot in the history of the spiritualism movement. "Jonathan Koons is, no matter how you look at it, the well-spring of physical manifestations in Modern Spiritualism," he writes. "At least: dark seances, and spirit trumpets. Possibly: spirit music and automatic writing. And if you allow for chemical assist (in his case, phosphorus, spread on sheets of paper, if memory serves): partial-form manifestations (of spirit hands)."

Demarest argues that Koons has gotten short shrift perhaps because of the reported exposure of his fraudulent séance. Although Emma Hardinge Britten lavished praise on Koons in *Modern American Spiritualism,* other nineteenth-century chroniclers of the movement, such as Sir Arthur Conan Doyle, scarcely mentioned him. Regardless of the humbug eventually brought to light at the Everett home in Cleveland, some of Koons's followers had been so moved by their experiences in the Koons Spirit Room that they went back home and started their own sanctuaries based on his model. The Athens County spirit room was copied throughout the Midwest and elsewhere: the Ohio locales included Chillicothe, Cleveland, Cincinnati, and Morrow County, while other spirit rooms popped up in Indiana, Illinois, and far-flung locations such as New York City and Boston. The rituals that took place within their walls morphed into traditions that became part of the spiritualist lexicon. (How some of these physical effects were actually created—and how the knowledge was passed on—is a puzzle yet to be deciphered.) Today physical manifestations do not figure as large as they did in the nineteenth century, but they are a part of the tradition that has given spiritualism its colorful legacy. Demarest has concluded that Jonathan Koons "is *at least* as important for the subsequent history of the Spiritualist movement as the Fox sisters."

THE HAUNTED GROVE

Five-year-old Jonathan Koons is digging up briars near a Pennsylvania farm field as his older brothers plow some distance away. The little boy is grubbing around a chestnut stump when he hears a rumbling coming out of the earth where he has just inserted the hoe. He strikes a second blow to see if there is any response from the monster under the ground. The sound is different this time—a cacophony of bells, glass, and iron tinkling and chiming against each other. Invisible hands snatch him up off the ground by his shoulders, casting him into the air, and he loses time. Jonathan awakens to find the field deserted; his brothers have unhitched their horses and gone home for lunch. He runs to the house but is too terrified to speak of what had happened to scare him so. His family's urgent questions go unanswered. They can only look at the child and see how unnerved he has become.

Jonathan's silence continues for several years until he has another vision. He is again at the haunted spot, and a snow-white steed and rider are approaching. Their brightness eclipses the landscape, and they pass through the forest that skirts the field as if the trees were not even there. Jonathan stands his ground as the figure comes within arm's length, and this time, he remains conscious.

"What in the name of God is your errand?" he inquires of his visitor.

"A rich treasure has been reserved for you, through many ages," the being replied, handing Jonathan a purse. But that is not the only boon; he then gives Jonathan a small rod. As soon as Jonathan touches it, the stranger built of light disappears. Jonathan wakes up not knowing exactly what was in the purse but intuits that it is a "precious gift."

The teenage Jonathan decides to tell his family about both of the incidents at the chestnut stump. His intrigued relatives want to go to the spot to look for buried treasure, but Jonathan will have none of it. He has developed a dread of the place—a horror that persists through age 19 when he leaves home.

Writing his life story decades later, Koons still had not forgotten his otherworldly experience in the field; he wondered if it really happened or was just a vivid impression from another realm of consciousness. "Whether or not these things are significant to any part of the history of my life, is a matter to be judged and decided by those who peruse it," he wrote in 1856. "I only give the facts."

As someone who has perused Jonathan Koons's history for several years, I hope you will allow me to supply an interpretation: Koons eventually overcomes his terror of numinous powers he can't control; by accepting the stranger's gifts he begins to make a space in his life for magic to operate. But in Jonathan's dream life he needs a third episode to complete the triad, a way to see what was inside the bag. Perhaps that is what his journey into spiritualism was all about—claiming the treasure as his own and returning it to the community. His path took him from rough-hewn farmer to showman, from adulation to disgrace and back again. That he was an imperfect guide there can be no doubt.

Acknowledgments

The writing of this book has been an eight-year journey in which I've received help from many individuals and institutions. I appreciate all the information and support I have been blessed with, while acknowledging that opinions about religion are diverse and passionate; I alone am responsible for any mistakes, misinterpretations, or omissions in the telling of this story.

I found many archival documents used in this study through the website iapsop.com, the home of the International Association for the Preservation of Spiritualist and Occult Periodicals. Its collection of nineteenth-century spiritualist newspapers is one of the most comprehensive available to researchers in this field. It has been a pleasure to meet Brandon Hodge, an IAPSOP board member who has researched and published about the Koons and Tippie families. I thank him for providing the rare photographs of Jonathan, Abigail, and Nahum Koons that appear in Gallery 1 of this book.

One of the key findings of my research came from the archives of the Wellesley Historical Society in Wellesley, Massachusetts, which contain three letters written by Jonathan Koons to his friend William Denton. The curator Kathleen Fahey and the staff were gracious in providing me with those documents and a picture of Denton.

Here in Ohio I was assisted by the staff of the Western Reserve Historical Society in Cleveland, especially Ann K. Sindelar and Vicki Catozza. I wish to thank Shannon Kupfer of the State Library of Ohio at Columbus, who digitized a copy of *A Book for Skeptics*. The friendly people at the Southeast Ohio History Center in Athens, Ohio, also have been a key resource; thanks go to Sara Green, Bosha Green, Eli Jablonski, Lynne Newell, Jessica Cyders, and Tom O'Grady. John Cunningham in particular spent countless hours sharing with me his extensive knowledge of local history and sources. I also deeply appreciate his reviewing and commenting on portions of the manuscript.

Alden Library at my alma mater, Ohio University, has been a welcoming facility. Its Robert E. and Jean R. Mahn Center for Archives and Special Collections provided photographs and other materials, and lorraine wochna helped me access an important collection of online archival documents. Many staff including Doug McCabe, Sara Harrington, Janet Carleton, Lucy Conn, Shari Gabriel, Chasity Gragg, Judy Markins, Barbara Fiocchi, and others have assisted me over the years. In 2016 the library also invited me to its Authors@Alden series, where I was interviewed by Kelee Riesbeck and read from a portion of this book as a work in progress.

For legal documents I turned to the Southeast Ohio History Center, Athens County Recorder's Office, Morgan County Probate Court, Morgan County Recorder's Office, and the Moritz College of Law at the Ohio State University. To explore the fate of the Tippies and Koonses after they left Ohio, I received help from the Linn County, Kansas, Historical Society and the Frankfort Area Genealogical Society in Illinois. I also acknowledge the Bedford County (PA) Historical Society, which provided me with documents relating to the Koons family in that state. The Library of Congress has preserved Jonathan Koons's 1881 book, *Truth Seekers' Feast,* and made a copy available to me.

Kim Toney of the American Antiquarian Society in Worcester, Massachusetts, went the extra mile in locating a rare spiritualist newspaper. Additional materials came from Earlham College, which has the diary of Pusey Graves in its collection. Historian Elizabeth Isenburg of St. Louis generously shared with me the diary of a visitor to the Athens County spirit rooms. Joscelyn Godwin, author of *Upstate Cauldron* and other helpful books, provided valuable insights through email correspondence.

A wonderful perspective on the more recent history of Mount Nebo came from the artist Alexandra Eldridge, who lived and made art there during the 1970s and 1980s. My late friend Sandra Sleight-Brennan also shared reminiscences about that locale with me, and her creation, the angel sprite, presides over my writing room and adorns this section.

I am indebted to Leslie Lilly and Marta Mills, two friends and fellow writers who read an early draft of this book and offered suggestions. Alan Taylor, a descendant of Jonathan Koons, graciously shared photos and family genealogy with me. Thanks also go to Shirley Tinkham, Paul Bircher, Michelle Ajamian, Bob Castro, Star Castro, Ivars Balkits, Lisa Trocchia-Balkits, David Wakefield, Connie Davidson, Donna Allison, Ryan Harris, Ron Luce, Carla Ankrom, Sandy Plunkett, Brian Collins, Adrian Hartman, David Koontz, Chuck Otterson, Steve Riesbeck, Patsy Sims, Silas House, Richard Dean, Todd Dean, Maureen Jennings, the late Connie Brosi, and all who have contributed to this work.

I wish to thank Gillian Berchowitz, director of the Ohio University Press, and her talented staff including Sebastian Biot, Nancy Basmajian, Sally Welch, Jeff Kallet, Samara Rafert, and Beth Pratt. On matters of scholarship and the writing craft, I appreciate the valuable input of Jeffrey Kripal and Nancy Rubin Stuart. Shortly before this book went to press, the Ohio Arts Council gave me an Individual Excellence Award to continue my development as a writer. I thank the council for providing this support.

Finally, I am grateful for the encouragement of my brothers, John Hines and Benjamin Hines, as well as the good energy sent my way by Karen Kornmiller, Tim Murphy, Nyoka Hawkins, Gurney Norman, Kate Black, Carrie Kline, Michael Kline, Jack Spadaro, Robert Gipe, Darnell Arnoult, Pat Isaacs, Steve Conley, Bonnie Proudfoot, and Roxanne Groff. My husband, Jack Wright, has also been with me every step of the journey—visiting archives and spiritualist enclaves, reading drafts, and providing a sounding board for my endless speculations about the Koons and Tippie families. Without supporters like these, it would have been much harder to pursue the writing life.

The voyage of discovery that began with my exploration of Jonathan Koons's life and times has continued well beyond publication of the hardcover edition of *Enchanted Ground*. In early 2021 Jonathan Taylor of California, a great-great-great-grandson of Jonathan and Abigail Koons, contacted me regarding his family's holdings in Ohio. Over the generations the family has preserved mystical drawings, song lyrics composed in 1890 about the Koonses' history, and the painting of Jonathan and Abigail that is the frontispiece of the paperback edition. I am grateful to Taylor and his cousin Erin Waggoner for sharing images of these heirlooms with me.

Notes

ABBREVIATION KEY FOR FREQUENTLY CITED PUBLICATIONS

AP: *Age of Progress*
CS: *Christian Spiritualist*
NES: *New England Spiritualist*
RPJ: *Religio-Philosophical Journal*
ST: *Spiritual Telegraph*
SU: *Spiritual Universe*

Issues of the above publications can be found at the online archive of the International Association for the Preservation of Spiritualist and Occult Periodicals in Forest Grove, Oregon (www.iapsop.com). Due to the rarity of these newspapers, complete runs may not be available for each one. Additional issues of the *Spiritual Universe* are archived at the Western Reserve Historical Society in Cleveland, Ohio. Microfilm of the *New England Spiritualist* can be obtained through library loan. In addition, microfilm of the *Athens Messenger*, published in Athens, Ohio, is kept at Alden Library, Ohio University.

EPIGRAPHS

vii   Koons, *Truth Seekers' Feast*, 66.

vii   Nichols, *Religions of the World*, 122.

vii   McCabe, *Spiritualism; A Popular History from 1847*, 58.

vii   Goss, *Northern Township Franklin County, Illinois*, 2:382.

1: THE FRENCHMAN'S VISIT

1   In the 1850s sightseers could tour: Barnum, *Barnum's American Museum Illustrated*, 3, 5.

1   Joseph Barthet had heard: du Potet de Sennevoy, *Traité complet du magnétisme animal*, 517–31.

2   had organized mesmerists in New Orleans: Bell, *Revolution, Romanticism and the Afro-Creole Protest Tradition*, 198–99.

2   he could hear a tune whistled: Frank Brown, "The Koons Spirit Room," The Voice Box, 2007, http://www.the-voicebox.com/koonsspiritroom.htm.

2   Tonight, with violin in hand: du Potet de Sennevoy, *Traité complet du magnétisme animal*, 517–31.

7   "persons of undoubted respectability": E. V. Wilson, "Spiritualism in Ohio," *Anglo American Magazine*, January–June 1855, 348.

7   an estimated 2,000 mediums: Haller, *Swedenborg, Mesmer, and the Mind/Body Connection*, 154.

7   one to two million Americans: Ibid.

7   The federal government had removed: PBS, "Indian Removal, 1814–1858," Resource Bank, accessed June 17, 2017, http://www.pbs.org/wgbh/aia/part4/4p2959.html.

8   Mediums, also called instruments: Albanese, *A Republic of Mind and Spirit*, 181–85.

9   "the work of an invisible intelligent power": Clark Williams, "Visit to the Koons Family," *Buchanan's Journal of Man* 5, no. 2 (February 1855): 44–49.

9   the French mesmerist Barthet: du Potet de Sennevoy, *Traité complet du magnétisme animal*, 517–31.

2: "THE PLACE OF MY NATIVITY"

10   corn was said to grow 14 feet high: *The Ohio Guide*, 6.

10   the juice of wild strawberries: Walker, *History of Athens County, Ohio*, 110.

10   For over 30 years his fellow Pennsylvania Germans: *The Ohio Guide*, 115.

10   signs were printed in both English and German: Ohio History Connection, "Lancaster, Ohio," Ohio History Central, accessed July 27, 2012, http://www.ohiohistorycentral.org/entry.php?rec=740&nm=Lancaster-Ohio.

10   just completed an apprenticeship: Jonathan Koons, "Biography of Jonathan Koons," *RPJ*, June 19, 1875, 106. The *RPJ* reprinted the autobiography in 12 installments; it originally was printed by a Pennsylvania paper, also in installments, in 1856–57.

11   Gump had built a house: Robert Howsare, "Brief History of Ancestors of Belle (Logue) Gump in Rainsburg, Pa." Vertical File 2012.11.16.54, Bedford County Historical Society, Bedford, PA.

11   "vast plain of social relations": Koons, "Biography of Jonathan Koons," *RPJ*, June 19, 1875, 106.

11   "some were praying, some laughing": Ibid.

12   "of German extraction throughout": Jonathan Koons to Francis Marion Koons, January 26, 1878, Koontz file, Bedford County Historical Society, Bedford, PA.

12   "I became afflicted with rheumatic affections": Koons, "Biography of Jonathan Koons," *RPJ*, June 19, 1875, 106.

12   "In that age I did not doubt": Account of his spiritual crisis given in Koons, "Biography of Jonathan Koons," *RPJ*, July 3, 1875, 126.

14   a neighbor woman named Mrs.——: The original text does not give the woman's name.

14   "that old rib" and all subsequent quotes in this story: Koons, "Biography of Jonathan Koons," *RPJ*, July 17, 1875, 142.

17   erstwhile wearers of coonskin caps: H. Brown, *Grandmother Brown's First Hundred Years*, 98; Inter-State Publishing, *History of Hocking Valley, Ohio*, 742.

17   "with an abundance of liberty but no property": Walker, *History of Athens County, Ohio*, 22.

18   brandy flowed from underground springs: Ibid., 97.

18   farmland "need only to be tickled with the hoe": *The Ohio Guide*, 15.

18   the estimated 15,000 Indians: Worldmark Encyclopedia of the States, "Ohio: History,"
      City-Data.com, 2016, http://www.city-data.com/states/Ohio-History.html; Rusler, *A
      Standard History of Allen County, Ohio*, 136.

18   The Indians were forced to cede: Walker, *History of Athens County, Ohio*, 106.

18   In 1797 several families from Marietta: Ibid., 115.

18   "40 miles by water from the Ohio": Ibid., 129.

19   "Enroute for home, I purchased the property": Koons, "Biography of Jonathan Koons,"
      RPJ, June 19, 1875, 106.

19   bought 262 acres in Dover Township: Athens County, Ohio, Deed Book, 7:100. Microfilm
      copies of the Athens County deed books cited are held by the Southeast Ohio History
      Center, Athens, OH.

3: PUTTING DOWN ROOTS

20   "was a member of the Episcopal Methodist church": Jonathan Koons, "Biography of
      Jonathan Koons," *RPJ*, June 19, 1875, 106.

21   "threatened the wandering and disconsolate pilgrim": Ibid.

21   "without a literary education": Ibid.

21   "ideas that ring like true metal": J. B. Conklin, "Twenty Years Ago: The Spirit Room
      of J. Koons, Athens County, Ohio," *RPJ*, September 11, 1875, 206.

22   Bishop acquired 1,600 acres: Athens County, Ohio, Deed Book, 2:310.

22   wedding at the Pittsfield Meeting House: Josiah Carpenter, "Importance of right views
      in matrimony," n.p.

22   "a good and virtuous example": Bishop, "An Eulogium on the Death of Gen. George
      Washington," 409.

22   Bishop divided his Athens County property: Athens County, Ohio, Deed Book, 7:127–29.

22   Abigail and Almira received: Ibid., 128. Notably absent from the land distribution was
      Samuel's eldest daughter, Caroline, who still lived in Coos County, New Hampshire.
      In 1825, when she was 24, she had married Samuel J. Brown, a widower nine years her
      senior and the father of three children. For some reason the Reverend Bishop must have
      balked at the match, for he brought a civil suit against the man who had performed the
      marriage ceremony, alleging that proper certificates had not been filed with the clerks
      of the towns where Caroline and her groom resided—paperwork that would have
      publicized their intention to marry. A high court ultimately ruled against the aggrieved
      father. Caroline and Samuel Brown would go on to have several children before his
      death in 1837. Caroline would eventually marry his younger brother and climb aboard
      an ox-drawn wagon bound for Oregon, half a continent away from her Ohio relatives.
      *S. G. Bishop v. J. Marshall. Reports of Cases Argued and Determined in the Superior Court
      of Judicature for the State of New-Hampshire*, vol. 5 (Newport: French and Brown, 1832),
      407–8; and "Caroline Bishop Brown," findagrave.com, https://www.findagrave
      .com/memorial/46499714/caroline-brown.

23   "a plat of house lots containing . . . a common": Athens County, Ohio, Deed Book, 7:128.

23   "the love and goodwill that I bear": Ibid., 150–51.

23   "at a reasonable price": Ibid.

23   "furnish materials for mechanics": *Bishop Fraternal Calvanistic Seminary v. Samuel G.
      Bishop*, Athens County, Ohio, Clerk of Courts, Chancery Records, 2:147. Southeast Ohio
      History Center, Athens, OH.

23 "one ear of corn to be paid": Athens County, Ohio, Deed Book, 7:207.

23 Abigail would sell this land back: Ibid., 9:847.

24 his mother, Margaret, fell gravely ill: Koons, "Biography of Jonathan Koons," *RPJ*, September 4, 1875, 198.

24 "honest, amiable, kind and affectionate": Koons, "Biography of Jonathan Koons," *RPJ*, July 3, 1875, 126.

24 Jonathan's brother Lewis wrote to him: Ibid., September 4, 1875, 198.

24 a second real estate purchase he had made: Athens County, Ohio, Deed Book, 7:774.

24 students reciting the words of Cassius and Brutus: H. Brown, *Grandmother Brown's First Hundred Years*, 88.

25 "contains two stores": Richard Dean, Nathan Dean Era/Mudsock (1820–1840s), March 11, 2013, https://people.ohio.edu/ deanr/msockcomm.htm.

25 crossing the main street on horseback: H. Brown, *Grandmother Brown's First Hundred Years*, 98.

25 created the Western Library Association: Beatty and Stone, *Getting to Know Athens County*, 45–55.

25 a "strong Abolitionist": C. H. Harris, "Visits to Little-Known Areas of District," *Athens Messenger*, March 6, 1952, 11.

25 One Ames resident recalled: Eli Brown to ——, March 18, 1892.

25 A philanthropist as well as Marietta's former mayor: "The Ward Room," The Hackett Hotel, accessed June 12, 2010, http://thehacketthotel.com/rooms/nahum-ward-room/.

26 In June 1838 they moved: Koons, "Biography of Jonathan Koons," *RPJ*, June 19, 1875, 106.

26 "Having a theoretic knowledge": Ibid., August 7, 1875, 166.

26 "I do not claim, however, that I was instrumental": Ibid.

27 "possessed of powerful magnetic forces": Ibid., July 10, 1875, 130. Although he writes about the "powwow system of healing" in an approving manner, Koons curiously did not like his father to be called a powwow doctor. Jonathan Koons's preferred term for Peter and the other healers was *exorcists*.

27 Jonathan's siblings soon joined an exodus: So many families from Bedford County chose Ohio for their new home that reunions of the Bedford County Pennsylvania Association of Ohio were held as late as the 1920s and attended by Koons descendants.

28 Their sister Mary, who went by her nickname, Polly: In June 1845 Jonathan Koons's sister, Polly Koons Border, died in Athens County; she was in her early forties. She had given birth to her ninth child, a girl named Emeline Theresa, less than two months earlier.

28 In 1838 Jonathan and Abigail had sold: Athens County, Ohio, Deed Book, 9:254.

28 George wed Chloe Weimer: Athens County, Ohio, Marriages, 1–2:1822–1856, 165.

28 dowry consisted of: Athens County, Ohio, Probate Court Estate Files, Box 204, "Estate of George S. Koons." Southeast Ohio History Center, Athens, OH.

28 Michael had come west with his wife: Athens County, Ohio, Deed Book, 9:583.

28 "agree to build . . . a comfortable school house": Ibid., 17:428.

28 no classes were ever held: Harris, "Visits to Little-Known Areas of District," 11.

29 the trustees sued: *Bishop Fraternal Calvanistic Seminary v. Samuel G. Bishop*, Athens County, Ohio, Clerk of Courts, Chancery Records, 2:143 and 2:190. Southeast Ohio History Center, Athens, OH.

29 "in the hands of the said Samuel G. Bishop": Ibid., 2:151.

29   Bishop's property was sold: Athens County, Ohio, Deed Book, 19:648.

29   Jonathan Koons's ancestors had been blessed: Jonathan Koons to F. M. Koons, January 26, 1878, Koontz file, Bedford County Historical Society, Bedford, PA.

29   his father's 385 acres in Monroe Township: Peter Koontz estate papers, Bedford County Courthouse.

29   the exact amount of Peter's legacy: Athens County, Ohio, Probate Court Estate Files, Box 204, "Estate of George S. Koons." Southeast Ohio History Center, Athens, OH.

29   his father had sent him an affectionate poem: J. Everett, *A Book for Skeptics*, 94.

30   "The time will come": "Athens County," *Ohio Cultivator* (Columbus), July 1, 1849, 202.

30   had a family of seven children: US Census, 1850, in Ancestry.com.

30   Sanders: Various handwritten census records for this child have been interpreted as Sanders, Sandes, and Rolandis. In later life he would use James R.

30   a more manageable 160 acres: Entry for Jonathan Koons, US Census Non-Population Schedule, 1850 to 1880, for Dover Township, Athens County, Ohio, November 28, 1850, 443, line 11, Ancestry.com.

30   From their ridgetop fields they produced: Ibid.

31   "homemade manufactures": Ibid.

31   April 20, 1850: This is the date engraved on George's tombstone. In his autobiography Jonathan Koons gives the date as April 21, 1851, but a receipt for a coffin in George Koons's estate papers indicates that 1850 is correct.

31   Jonathan Koons walked steadily up the path: For Jonathan Koons's account of George Koons's death see Koons, "Biography of Jonathan Koons," *RPJ*, September 4, 1875, 198.

4: "A STRIKING SPECIMEN OF BEAUTY"

40   "There were no churches or meeting-houses": Walker, *History of Athens County, Ohio*, 581.

41   "News! Fresh from heaven": Swedenborgian Church of North America, "Early Swedenborgian History in America," 2017, www.swedenborg.org/EarlySwedenborgiansInAmerica.aspx.

41   the "good news" Chapman was spreading: For a discussion of Swedenborg's theology, see Cathy Gutierrez, "Dead Reckonings," in *Handbook of Spiritualism and Channeling*, 52–53.

41   Chapman had begun his wanderings: Means, *Johnny Appleseed*, 135.

41   owned land in eight Ohio counties: Silverman, *Core of Johnny Appleseed*, 97–101.

41   planted apple orchards: Ibid., 91–95.

42   Ohio by 1843 had several hundred members: Ibid., 65.

42   In Meigs County: Philip and Nan de Maine, "A Brief Informal History of the New Church in Middleport, Ohio," *New Church Life* 112, no. 6 (June 1992): 259–63.

42   stopping to spend the night: Peters, *Athens County, Ohio*, 1:74–75.

42   a solitary meal of "pone and meat": Walker, *History of Athens County, Ohio*, 199–200.

42   Methodist societies eventually formed: Daniel, *Athens, Ohio*, 63.

42   Methodists built a brick church: Walker, *History of Athens County, Ohio*, 221.

42   The Presbyterians followed: Ibid., 222.

42   At least three presidents of Ohio University: Daniel, *Athens, Ohio*, 99.

43   In 1828 the elders set their sights: The conflict between the Presbyterians and the Prudens is detailed in the Robert L. Daniel papers at the Southeast Ohio History Center library in Athens.

43 "Our ancestors drowned old women": *New Harmony (IN) Gazette*, editorial, April 11, 1827, 222; *Popular Freethought: A Guide to the Periodic Writings of American Infidels, 1825–1865*, accessed November 22, 2016, https://popularfreethought.wordpress.com /browse-by-title/new-harmony-gazette-1825-1828/.

44 "We charge you with questioning": Daniel papers.

45 barred from testifying in a civil suit: Pruden Family Papers, 1819–1950, MSS17, Series II: Civil War Letters and Essays, file 16, Robert E. and Jean R. Mahn Center for Archives and Special Collections, Alden Library, Ohio University, Athens.

45 In 1840 he and Mary built: Inter-State Publishing, *History of Hocking Valley, Ohio*, 227, 328.

45 the number of churches in Athens County: Walker, *History of Athens County, Ohio*, 166. Walker's tally does not seem to account for the Churches of Christ (also called Campbellite) that sprang up in the Sunday Creek Valley in the 1840s.

45 "I had become an advocate": Everett, *A Book for Skeptics*, 21.

46 "Let us strictly avoid": Koons, *Truth Seekers' Feast*, 15–16.

47 a kinder, gentler religion: R. L. Moore, *In Search of White Crows*, 56.

47 Twelve-year-old Filenia: Jonathan Koons, "Biography of Jonathan Koons," *RPJ*, June 26, 1875, 114.

47 "Her disease . . . bid defiance": "Died—," *Athens Messenger*, September 12, 1851. The word *communicated* at the end of the poem is baffling, as Filenia died seven months before Jonathan began to investigate spiritualism, according to his published statements.

47 Abigail gave birth to a boy: Koons, "Biography of Jonathan Koons," *RPJ*, June 26, 1875, 114.

47 "What rendered the occurrence": Ibid.

48 a scathing letter signed "A Friend": *Athens Messenger*, September 12, 1851.

49 a Whig: Ibid., August 30, 1850.

49 Reverend Alfred Ryors . . . tossed back a biblical salvo: Ibid., October 3, 1851.

49 frequently attended the Methodist Church: "The Funeral of Miss Koons Again," *Athens Messenger*, October 17, 1851. Jonathan Koons reportedly attended the Episcopal church at one time; perhaps this refers to the Methodist Episcopal church. If Koons did attend a Methodist church, perhaps it was during his courtship of Abigail, who had been a Methodist, although evidently not a member of the Athens congregation.

50 Koons sent a somewhat conciliatory letter: *Athens Messenger*, October 24, 1851.

50 "the churches of the village": Daniel, *Athens, Ohio*, 98.

50 "Membership tended to confer": Ibid., 100–101.

51 Reflecting on the incident five years later: Koons, "Biography of Jonathan Koons," *RPJ*, June 26, 1875, 114.

5: AT THE SPIRITS' COMMAND

52 Word of mysterious rappings: Charles Partridge, "Letter from Mr. Partridge. Spirit-Manifestations in Athens Co., O., Number One," *ST*, June 23, 1855, 2.

52 "there arose quite an excitement": "Letter from Mr. Jonathan Koons" [an article containing Koons's letter, two letters from other people, and comments from the editors], *CS*, June 3, 1854, 3.

52 "causing so much fear and alarm": Everett, *A Book for Skeptics*, 22.

52 He assumed it was all: Ibid.

52 hoping at the same time: "Letter from Mr. Jonathan Koons."

53 "I gave myself little or no alarm": Jonathan Koons, "Biography of Jonathan Koons," *RPJ*, August 28, 1875, 190.

53 had lived at the old Fletcher place: For the entire account see the August 28, 1875, installment of Koons, "Biography of Jonathan Koons."

54 "One of these luminous forms": Ibid.

54 "My own personal experience": Ibid.

54 The spiritualist fervor had entered Athens County: "Letter from Mr. Partridge." I have used the spelling in Partridge's account. However, it is possible that the last name was Herrold, a local family with ties to Indiana.

54 one Mary Jane Paston: A search of Ancestry.com reveals two 1850 federal census records that could confirm the identity of Mary Jane Paston. A Mary Paston, then 18 years old, lived in Canaan Township with her family: parents, John and Isabel, and siblings, Elias and Samuel. A Mary Jane Poston, then 14 years old, lived in Athens Township with her family: parents, Elias and Amanda, and five siblings. Although the spelling is slightly different, I believe the latter family was the one Jonathan Koons visited. The Indiana medium gave the girl's place of residence as Dover Township, but either the family moved between 1850 and 1852 or the medium got it wrong.

55 taking up the Pastons' time: "Letter from Mr. Partridge."

55 Around February 1852, Paston invited: Ibid. Koons told the *ST* in 1855 that the pivotal séance took place at the home of Mary Jane Paston, although in an earlier account he had identified the medium as "a daughter of Mr. S." Everett, *A Book for Skeptics*, 22. Perhaps he initially was attempting to protect the family's identity.

55 "But as far as this matter concerned": Everett, *A Book for Skeptics*, 22.

55 "Is there a spirit present?": "Letter from Mr. Partridge."

55 "was not very satisfactory to me": Everett, *A Book for Skeptics*, 22.

56 "seized by some strange influence": "Letter from Mr. Partridge." Partridge's dramatic account of Jonathan's initiation is somewhat contradicted by Koons's letter to the *CS* of June 3, 1854, in which he says the phenomena first presented in his household as faint raps and later progressed to writing through the hands of the Koons mediums. This prosaic fashion of gradual development was much more typical.

56 he by then had nine children: Everett, *A Book for Skeptics*, 22.

56 son Cinderellus . . . as well as an adopted daughter: US Census, 1850, for Dover Township, Athens County, Ohio, Ancestry.com; and Jonathan Koons page, accessed October 19, 2015, http://person.ancestry.com/tree/13540148/person/12251354126/facts; see also Perrin, *History of Jefferson County, Illinois*.

56 writing out messages: "Letter from Mr. Jonathan Koons."

56 "these strange spiritual gifts": Everett, *A Book for Skeptics*, 22.

56 "one for rapping": "Letter from Mr. Partridge."

56 "During the latter part of the summer 1852": Jonathan Koons to William Denton, March 6, 1857, Denton Family Papers, William Denton Correspondence, Series 1, Box 2, Wellesley Historical Society, Wellesley, MA.

57 Koons grew increasingly perplexed: "Letter from Mr. Partridge."

57 "After communicating with Spirits of every grade": Ibid.

57 Koons began to feed his manuscripts: Ibid.

58 Nahum Koons took up a pencil: Charles Partridge, "Spirit-Manifestations in Athens Co., O., Number Two," *ST*, July 7, 1855, 2.

58   "Being in a state of gloom": Ibid.

59   "A few moments after the circle was formed": Ibid.

59   "collecting and focalizing the magnetic aura" and "novel battery": Britten, *Modern American Spiritualism,* 308.

59   "retainer of electricity": Clark Williams, "A Visit to the Koons Family," *Buchanan's Journal of Man,* February 1855, 44.

59   "spirit machine": *Cleveland Plain Dealer,* November 4, 1854, 1.

59   "a wire woven into a kind of net work": E. V. Wilson, "Spiritualism in Ohio," *Anglo American Magazine,* January–June 1855, 348.

59   metal plates were made of copper and zinc: Britten, *Modern American Spiritualism,* 308.

59   a horizontal wooden bar: *Cleveland Plain Dealer,* November 4, 1854, 1.

59   "The spirits wrote on the table": Partridge, "Spirit-Manifestations in Athens Co." This article contains a full account of securing the musical instruments.

60   The house consisted of two cabins: Wilson, "Spiritualism in Ohio," 347.

61   "One end of the dwelling": David Fulton, letter to the editor, *CS,* February 24, 1855, 3.

61   the spirit room was up and running: Partridge, "Spirit-Manifestations in Athens Co." In Koons's account in *A Book for Skeptics,* the spirit room and electrical table were constructed *before* the musical instruments were obtained. In this version of the story the Koonses placed paper and pencil in the spirit room, and the spirits wrote their demand for musical instruments on the paper without the assistance of any medium. Everett, *A Book for Skeptics,* 23. Partridge's report in the *ST* is ambiguous as to whether the instruments were gathered before or after the room was built. But Partridge makes clear that the electrical table was constructed in Jonathan's residence. Presumably the drums were added later. Neither Koons's nor Partridge's account gives a date for construction of the spirit room.

62   18 feet long by 15 feet wide by 9 feet high: Partridge, "Spirit-Manifestations in Athens Co."

62   16 feet by 12 feet by 7 feet: Robert Hare, *Experimental Investigation of the Spirit Manifestations,* 298.

62   shuttered windows: Accounts vary as to the number of windows; perhaps the building changed over time.

62   "common cherry breakfast table": Williams, "A Visit to the Koons Family."

62   "a common fall-leaf table" Hare, *Experimental Investigation of the Spirit Manifestations,* 298.

62   a coal-burning stove: Wilson, "Spiritualism in Ohio," 348.

62   "old shoes and other old trumpery": Hare, *Experimental Investigation of the Spirit Manifestations,* 298.

62   Koons's list of props: Everett, *A Book for Skeptics,* 23.

62   "of more ancient date than Adam": Ibid., 26.

62   lived 14,000 years earlier: "The Antiquity of the World," *CS,* March 17, 1855, 2.

63   "King, Servant and Scholar of God": Everett, *A Book for Skeptics,* 43.

63   exotic spirits such as Native Americans or Chinese: Ibid., 60–61.

63   "he had lived in Africa": Mary S. Gove Nichols, ed., "The Life of a Medium; Or, the Spiritual Experiences of J. B. Conklin," *Nichols Monthly,* October–November 1855, 289, http://www.iapsop.com/archive/materials/nichols_monthly/nichols_monthly_1855_oct-nov.pdf.

63   a bejeweled chariot: Nichols, *Religions of the World,* 121.

63   "spent the afternoon in examining papers": J. B., "Wonderful Spiritual Manifestations in Ohio," *CS*, May 13, 1854, 3.

63   "doctrines taught by our spiritual correspondents": Everett, *A Book for Skeptics*, 24.

63   with the dedication "To My Mother": Ibid., 63.

6: A BURIED MAN'S INSTRUCTIONS

65   sometimes called the Huckleberry Knobs: N. P. H., "Responses from the Rural World—Athens County," *Ohio Cultivator* (Columbus), May 1, 1858, 135.

65   the Hocking Canal: The name of the river running thorough Athens County was eventually shortened from the Indian name Hockhocking to Hocking.

65   for another four years: Beatty and Stone, *Getting to Know Athens County*, 242.

65   "about 50 years behind the age": Nichols, *Religions of the World*, 122.

65   "I staged over a country": Hamilton Wade, "Four Days at the Koons and Tippie Rooms," *ST*, September 15, 1855, 4.

66   "the miles bear no correspondence to the hours": Hare, *Experimental Investigation of the Spirit Manifestations*, 297.

66   "Fare, hog and hominy": *ST*, reprinted in "A Short Trip to Ohio," *SU*, November 22, 1855, 4.

66   "The way to Mr. Koons' house": J. B., "Wonderful Spiritual Manifestations in Ohio," *CS*, May 13, 1854, 3.

66   "When you finally get into Koons's vicinity": Hare, *Experimental Investigation of the Spirit Manifestations*, 297.

66   "there is something in the locality": Ibid., 295.

67   "owing to the peculiar geological formation": Nichols, *Religions of the World*, 120.

67   "the enchanted ground": Ibid., 122.

67   "a plain, unvarnished farmer": *CS*, February 24, 1855, 3. Perhaps Fulton is exaggerating here; Jonathan owned well over 100 acres, although not all the hilly land would have been suitable for farming.

67   "from thirty to fifty men sitting on stones": Hare, *Experimental Investigation of the Spirit Manifestations*, 302.

67   Benning . . . "was suddenly impressed": *Spiritual Age*, February 12, 1859.

68   "was aware of our coming": Pierce, *Revelator*, 16.

68   Koons digging for treasure: Everett, *A Book for Skeptics*, 55.

69   gave his name as Jewannah Gueannah Musco: Ibid., 56.

69   "persued [*sic*] them unto death": Koons to William Denton, March 6, 1857, Denton Family Papers, William Denton Correspondence, Series 1, Box 2, Wellesley Historical Society, Wellesley, MA.

69   take two neutral observers: Everett, *A Book for Skeptics*, 55.

69   others were afraid to live there: S. B. Brittan, ed., *The Telegraph Papers* (New York: Partridge and Brittan, 1855), 6:132, http://www.iapsop.com/archive/materials/spiritual_telegraph/spiritual_telegraph_papers_v6_1855.pdf.

69   a 3-square-mile complex of earthworks: Lepper, *Ohio Archaeology*, 97.

69   reminded them of an old fort: Walker, *History of Athens County, Ohio*, 7.

69   as ceremonial theaters: Lepper, *Ohio Archaeology*, 99–102.

70   They had walked southward: Koons to Denton.

70   With the two witnesses looking on: Everett, *A Book for Skeptics,* 56.

70   "Periods of duration have elapsed": Ibid., 29.

70   a river of Nile-like proportions: Beatty and Stone, *Getting to Know Athens County,* 5–7; Walter Sullivan, "A Great Lost River Gets Its Due," *New York Times,* November 29, 1983, http://www.nytimes.com/1983/11/29/science/a-great-lost-river-gets-its-due.html; Jean Backs, "Ohio's Ancient Nile, The Teays River," Ohio Department of Natural Resources, 2011, http://www.dnr.state.oh.us/parks/magazinehome/magazine/sprsum04/teaysriver/tabid/364/Default.aspx.

71   extinct valleys and dry riverbeds: GeoFacts No. 10, "The Teays River," explains that "remnants of the valley of the Teays River are preserved as flat-bottomed valleys in hilly, unglaciated southern Ohio and as deep valleys now filled with sediment in the glaciated [northern and western] portion of the state." Ohio Department of Natural Resources, Division of Geological Survey. www.OhioGeology.com.

71   "has been successively inhabited": Everett, *A Book for Skeptics,* 29.

71   Ruminations on the role of ancient Scythians: Barnhart, "Early Accounts of Ohio's Mounds," 237–50.

71   "I am in possession of a history": Koons to Denton.

71   "your sinful ignorance": Everett, *A Book for Skeptics,* 29.

72   Gone were his crops: "Fire—Incendiarism," *Athens Messenger,* December 24, 1852, 4.

72   "The fat was in the fire": Jonathan Koons, "Biography of Jonathan Koons," *RPJ,* June 26, 1875, 114.

72   "a gang of drunken rowdies": "Fire—Incendiarism."

72   "While my property was consuming": Crowell, *Identity of Primitive Christianity and Modern Spiritualism,* 1:517–19.

72   "We sympathize with our friend": "Fire—Incendiarism."

72   "The clergy denounced me": Koons, *Truth Seekers' Feast,* II.

73   "I was well informed": Jonathan Koons, "Modern Martyrs," *Woodhull & Claflin's Weekly,* July 26, 1873, 5–6.

7: THE TRUMPET MEDIUM

74   "The circle is hereby notified": Jonathan Koons to William Denton, March 6, 1857, Denton Family Papers, William Denton Correspondence, Series 1, Box 2, Wellesley Historical Society, Wellesley, MA.

74   the bow and arrow were replacing the spear: Lepper, *Ohio Archaeology,* 183.

74   But his purpose was the same as Musco's: For an account of the excavation, see Koons to Denton. Could "M. Handsberry" be James M. Hansberry of Ames Township, who later signed a petition requesting an investigation of spiritualism?

75   "The creation of objects that could *talk*": Patrick Feaster, "Framing the Mechanical Voice: Generic Conventions of Early Phonograph Recording," *Folklore Forum* 32, no. 1/2 (2001): 61, http://hdl.handle.net/2022/2334.

75   "by a certain inspection of the stars": Ibid.

76   an "enchanted head": Ibid., 62.

76   "direct voice" communication: J. Gordon Melton, ed., *Encyclopedia of Occultism and Parapsychology,* 5th ed. (Detroit: Gale Group, 2001), 2:1590.

76   "a tin trumpet about two feet in length": "Spiritual Manifestations in Athens Co., Ohio," *Cleveland Plain Dealer*, November 4, 1854, 1.

76   "As one who for 35 years has been freeing himself": Harry Houdini, "How I Unmask the Spirit Fakers," *Popular Science Monthly*, November 1925.

78   Houdini's contemporary E. J. Dingwall: Dingwall, *How to Go to a Medium*, n.p.

79   "I left the house fully convinced": J. B., "Wonderful Spiritual Manifestations in Ohio," *CS*, May 13, 1854, 3.

80   Colonel Nathan Dean Jr., had been an entrepreneurial force: Richard Dean, interview by author, May 29, 2015, Athens, Ohio.

80   "New fields disclose": Everett, *A Book for Skeptics*, 94.

81   participants . . . included John Tippie Jr.: Ibid., 19.

81   David Fulton also received a snippet of verse: Ibid., 64.

81   Lending credibility to the séances was George Walker: Ibid., 83; Walker, *History of Athens County, Ohio*, 417–20.

81   Walker signed an affidavit: Everett, *A Book for Skeptics*, 19.

81   Judge Robert A. Fulton visited the Koons circle: Ibid., 83; Walker, *History of Athens County, Ohio*, 162. I was unable to determine whether David Fulton and Robert A. Fulton were related.

81   "affirm to have seen and conversed with spirits": "Evidence of Immortality," *AP*, July 7, 1855, 4.

81   "an inveterate opposer": Jonathan Koons, "Biography of Jonathan Koons," *RPJ*, July 31, 1875, 158.

81   "found it necessary to support his hat": Ibid., August 21, 1875, 178.

8: COMMUNICATION FROM ANGELS

83   Dr. J. Everett, a Columbus physician: Everett, *A Book for Skeptics*, 2.

83   visited the Fox family: Ibid., 10.

83   "performed with a skill and excellence": Ibid., 17.

83   he felt breezes: Ibid., 18.

83   shook hands twice: Ibid., 17.

83   "The exhibition which I have been permitted to witness": Ibid., 18.

84   "Many of the communications thus written or spoken": Britten, *Modern American Spiritualism*, 312.

85   "I [could] only give the substance": Jonathan Koons to William Denton, March 6, 1857, Denton Family Papers, William Denton Correspondence, Series 1, Box 2, Wellesley Historical Society, Wellesley, MA.

85   "There was nothing at all angelic": Editor's note, "Visit to the Koons Family," *Buchanan's Journal of Man* 4, no. 11 (November 1853): 323.

85   "mental and spiritual conditions were more simple": "John King," *Medium & Daybreak*, January 24, 1879, 9.

85   drawing of the celestial spheres: Frontispiece in Everett, *A Book for Skeptics*.

85   King supposedly had drawn: Ibid., 71.

85   King revealed what the diagram stood for: Quotations regarding the diagram are found in ibid., 64–71.

87   something must have gone wrong: Ibid., 84.

88   "a man was knocked down with a drum-stick": "Spiritual Manifestations in Athens County," *Cleveland Morning Leader,* December 19, 1855.

88   one tambourine would be broken: "The 'Manifestations' at Mr. Koons'," *NES,* August 11, 1855, 1.

88   M. B. Ashley was advised by a medium: "The Spirits Pay a Board Bill. A Visit to Jonathan Koon's Spirit Room," *Progressive Thinker,* July 9, 1892, 5.

89   a "letter from Ohio": S. B. Brittan, ed., *The Telegraph Papers* (New York: Partridge and Brittan, 1854), 3:267.

89   "reports . . . have been industriously circulated": Ibid., 3:352.

89   "base and untruthful charges": Ibid., 3:353.

90   "the mediums of my family": Ibid., 3:354.

90   "responsible men for publication,": Ibid., 3:353.

90   his house had been searched repeatedly: Koons probably is referring to the spirit room and its attic, rather than his residence next door.

90   Koons found two baby birds: In her rewrite of Jonathan's letter, which she does not acknowledge as such, Emma Hardinge Britten soft-pedals the incident as follows: "The only thing that was ever found concealed in it [the house] was two young, unfledged birds, which one of my boys, boy-like, had got out of a nest, intending to rear. Not approving of the act of robbing a nest, I wrung off the heads of the birds." Britten, *Modern American Spiritualism,* 323–24.

9: ALLIES AND KIN

91   "arrangements are being made for another circle": S. B. Brittan, ed., *The Telegraph Papers* (New York: Partridge and Brittan, 1854), 3:268.

92   farming, a war pension, and work as a cobbler: Dodd, *Story of Uriah Tippie of Ohio,* 14.

92   his wife, Betsy: John Sr. and Betsy Lyons married in 1814, which means she may have been his second wife and therefore the stepmother of John Jr., who was born in 1811.

92   Phebe Denman . . . who had died around 1846: Moore, *Tentative Tippie Tabulations,* 5th ed., 19.

92   married a much younger woman: Ibid., 25.

92   had eight children living with them: US Census, Year: 1850; Census Place: Ames, Athens, Ohio; Roll: M432_660; Page: 127A; Image: 258. Ancestry.com.

92   "the Tippie family did not manage": du Potet de Sennevoy, *Traité complet du magnétisme animal,* 525.

92   "The children . . . were clairvoyant": "The Spirits at Mr. Koon's in Doon [*sic*], Ohio," *AP,* October 21, 1854, 4.

92   boosted the spirits' "signal": Nichols, *Religions of the World,* 120.

92   Tippie won the gratitude: Anonymous, "Journal of Trip East, Fall of 1855." Private collection of Elizabeth Isenburg, St. Louis, MO.

93   signed an affidavit: Everett, *A Book for Skeptics,* 19.

93   "while in a somnambulic or clairvoyant state": Ibid., 95.

93   "rooms and manifestations [are] very much alike": Hare, *Experimental Investigation of the Spirit Manifestations,* 302.

93   seating arrangements nearly identical: du Potet de Sennevoy, *Traité complet du magnétisme animal,* 525.

93   "more varied and interesting": "Astounding Manifestations at Koons'," *AP*, November 4, 1854, 3.

94   "a short interval of darkness": Nichols, *Religions of the World*, 123.

94   "truly significant and beautiful": "Astounding Manifestations at Koons'."

94   "The violin was not on the table": Ibid.

94   "we advise any and all": Ibid.

95   "Were it possible that such manifestations": "Spiritual Manifestations in Athens Co., Ohio," *Cleveland Plain Dealer*, November 4, 1854, 1.

95   followers of the spiritualist John Murray Spear: Buescher, *Remarkable Life of John Murray Spear*, 89–90.

95   destroyed by a mob in New York State: Spear's biographer, John Buescher, speculates that Spear sent Brown, Lewis, and the other Clevelanders to check out Jonathan Koons's electrical table so they could gain ideas for additional projects of their own (326n14). A detailed drawing of the table accompanied the Cleveland group's report in the *Plain Dealer*.

96   "opposition to marriage as an institution": A. Braude, *Radical Spirits*, 127.

96   Supporters of free love: Ibid., 128–29.

96   The trance speaker Lizzie Doten: Ibid., 134.

96   scandalized Cleveland society: Buescher, *Remarkable Life of John Murray Spear*, 90.

96   "I am married to all men": Ibid., 154.

96   Brown believed: For a sketch of her life see Buescher, *Other Side of Salvation*, 155–58.

96   "true soul unions": A. Braude, *Radical Spirits*, 132.

97   "The doctrines taught there": "Spiritual Manifestations in Athens County," *Cleveland Morning Leader*, November 19, 1855.

10: MOUNTAIN TEA

103   the petition had garnered nearly 12,500 signatures: Marc Demarest, "The Do-Nothing Congress: April 17, 1854," *Chasing Down Emma* (blog), February 20, 2013, http://ehbritten .blogspot.com/search?q=Petition+to+Congress+1854.

104   the matter was soon forgotten: Ibid.; John Buescher, "Petitioning Congress: 1854 Memorial of the Spirit Rappers," http://spirithistory.iapsop.com/spiritualists_petition _to_congress.html.

105   "Some of the earliest spiritual conventions": Britten, *Modern American Spiritualism*, 303.

106   "'reasonable believer in Spiritualism'": W. S. Beatty, "Letter from Jonathan Koons," *CS*, June 3, 1854, 3.

106   George H. Carpenter . . . wrote: Four years later Carpenter would renounce spiritualism in favor of Christianity. In 1858, ill and often bedridden, he revealed to a newspaper that he had been an infidel prior to witnessing the Koons séances. The performances had convinced him to shed his materialism. "These manifestations are interesting and instructive as touching the immortality of the soul, for they prove that mind can and does exist, separate and apart from what we call *physical matter*," he wrote. "As soon, however, as a man is satisfied of that fact, his safer and *only safe* way is the adoption of the Christian faith." Letter to Dr. Hoyt, *Spiritual Age*, September 8, 1858, 2.

106   "about twenty-seven inches high": "The Spirits at Mr. Koons'," *ST*, April 8, 1854, 2.

107   "I was a skeptic": J. B., "Wonderful Spiritual Manifestations in Ohio," *CS*, May 13, 1854, 3.

107   rubbing luminous phosphorus: See for example "The 'Manifestations' at Mr. Koons'," *NES*, August 11, 1855, 1.

107   "'Prove all things:'" J. B., "Wonderful Spiritual Manifestations in Ohio," 3.

108   "furnish to our readers a weekly account": "Letter from Jonathan Koons," *CS*, June 3, 1854, p. 3.

108   challenge to church authority: R. L. Moore, *In Search of White Crows*, 40–45.

108   "to stupefy and befool ourselves with mesmerism": Porter, *Spirit Rappings*, 50–51.

108   a sickly Circleville, Ohio, man: Britten, *Modern American Spiritualism*, 402.

109   the biblical Witch of Endor: See 1 Sam. 28:3–25 and 1 Chronicles 10:13–14, King James Version.

109   no one should regard mediums as spiritual teachers: Porter, *Spirit Rappings*, 51–52.

110   "While I see many things": An Inquirer, "Correspondence," *CS*, January 6, 1855, 3.

110   "in dark habiliments": "Digest of Correspondence," *ST*, May 6, 1854, 2.

111   an old-timey tin peddler's pack: Stuart, *Reluctant Spiritualist*, 17. The farmhouse later was moved from Hydesville to Lily Dale, New York, where it burned in 1955. Barbara Weisberg notes in her 2004 book *Talking to the Dead* (267) that "a peddler's trunk, still on view at the Lily Dale Museum, was rescued from the remains, although skeptics question whether it actually belonged to the infamous Charles Rosna."

111   Ezra and James E. Cowee of Greensburg, Indiana: All quotations in this account appeared in "'The Manifestations at Mr. Koons'," *NES*, September 8, 1855, 1.

113   when phosphorus was discovered: Phosphorus Element Facts, Chemicool.com, October, 17, 2012, http://www.chemicool.com/elements/phosphorus.html.

113   "In appearance, phosphorus resembles bees'-wax": James Johnston, *The Chemistry of Common Life*, quoted in "Facts Concerning Phosphorus," *NES*, April 4, 1857, 4.

114   "its muzzle and hackles": Arthur Conan Doyle, *The Hound of the Baskervilles*, chapter 14.

114   Clark Williams ventured to the Koons farm: Williams's account appears in *Buchanan's Journal of Man* 5, no. 2 (February 1855): 44–49. He said the first séance was on Saturday, but the 1854 calendar shows it was on Sunday.

118   He was evidently so impressed: "Dr. Hayden in the Field," *New Era*, December 23, 1854, 3. American Antiquarian Society Historical Periodicals Collection: Series 4. See also ibid., November 25, 1854, 3. Around that time the *New Era* even announced that Jonathan Koons would be coming to Boston, but I have not been able to confirm whether he ever did visit. "Jonathan Koons," ibid., January 6, 1855, 2.

118   attracted the attention of prominent spiritualists: S. Braude, *Limits of Influence*, 63.

118   One of Home's first recorded séances: Ibid., 67–68.

119   "Mr. D. D. Home frequently urged us to hold his hands and feet": Ibid., 68.

119   Alfred Russel Wallace reported seeing: Ibid., 80.

119   "At the request of the medium": S. Brown, *Heyday of Spiritualism*, 253–54.

119   a hand ascended: S. Braude, *Limits of Influence*, 93.

120   "sometimes appears perfectly life-like" S. Brown, *Heyday of Spiritualism*, 254–55.

120   "Home was a charlatan": Peter Lamont, *First Psychic*, 277.

120   "'Light' . . . is the single test necessary": D. D. Home, *Lights and Shadows of Spiritualism*, 394.

11: SUSTAINING "BROTHER KOONS"

121   "seventy two miles of very unpleasant stage road": "Wonders at Koons' Spirit Room," *AP*, December 16, 1854, 3.

121   "planished table ware": "S. Dudley & Sons," *AP*, June 9, 1855, 1.

121   "high-toned moral sentiments": "Wonders at Koons' Spirit Room."

122   "I spent several hours in listening": J. B. Conklin, "Twenty Years Ago: The Spirit Room of J. Koons, Athens County, Ohio," *RPJ*, September 11, 1875, 206.

122   he entered the spirit room with Nahum: Ibid.

122   an honored place at the mediums' table: Ibid.

122   "It was a very inharmonious party": Dudley's report of the séances comes from "Wonders at Koons' Spirit Room."

124   "manifestations of the M.D.'s": According to "Wonders at Koons' Spirit Room," this reference is to medical doctors at Buffalo who held the knees of the Fox sisters to prevent them from making rapping sounds during an investigation.

125   A businessman from Sandusky, Ohio: An Inquirer, "Correspondence," *CS*, January 6, 1855, 3.

126   Abraham P. Pierce of Philadelphia: His account given in Pierce, *Revelator*, 16–24.

127   Upon his return to Sandusky: An Inquirer, "Correspondence."

128   the Fox sisters were said to be bringing in $100 per day: Albanese, *A Republic of Mind and Spirit*, 223.

128   "I reasoned with Mr. K.": Letter to the editor, *CS*, February 24, 1855, 3.

128   "the Methodists of Athens County": "A Proposition in Behalf of Brother J. Koons," *CS*, January 6, 1855, 2.

129   Horace H. Day . . . provided the real motive power: See Marc Demarest, "Horace H. Day (1813–1878): The Sinews of War–Spiritualism as Political Manipulation," *Chasing Down Emma* (blog), September 20, 2011, http://ehbritten.blogspot.com/search?q =Charles+Goodyear; Marc Demarest, "Horace Day: The Marriages," *Chasing Down Emma* (blog), September 21, 2011, http://ehbritten.blogspot.com/2011/09/horace-day -marriages.html?q=horace+day; Britten, *Modern American Spiritualism*, 133–35; and Pat Deveney, database for the *Christian Spiritualist*, February 3, 2009, http://www.iapsop .com/archive/materials/christian_spiritualist/.

129   "It is proposed that 1,000 names be obtained": "A Proposition in Behalf of Brother J. Koons," *CS*, January 6, 1855, 2.

129   "After the disgraceful event": David Fulton, letter to the editor, *CS*, February 24, 1855, 3.

130   "I need not tell you my astonishment": "Letter from Jonathan Koons," *CS*, February 3, 1855, 2.

130   "You seem to rejoice": "Mr. Koons and his Visiters [*sic*]," *SU*, February 10, 1855, 2.

130   "Shall Br. Koons be sustained": "Br. Jonathan Koons' Rooms," *CS*, February 3, 1855, 2.

130   "all manner of unkind things and abuse": "Correspondence," *CS*, February 3, 1855, 3. It is not clear whether the signer of the letter was Azariah Pratt Jr. or Sr.

131   Dudley paid a call on Jennie E. Kellog: His account of the psychometric reading is given in *ST*, reprinted in "Interesting Experiment," *AP*, January 27, 1855, 3.

12: THE MESMERIC POTION

132   Abigail Koons sat entranced: E. V. Wilson, "Spiritualism in Ohio," *Anglo American Magazine*, January–June 1855, 441.

132   Some healing mediums offered their cures: A. Braude, *Radical Spirits*, 146.

133   gifted patients could use clairvoyance: S. Brown, *Heyday of Spiritualism*, 6.

133 Poyen brought hypnosis to the United States: Ibid., 14–15.

133 teamed up with a textile mill worker: Ibid., 16–17.

133 Boston alone had 200 mesmerists: John C. Spurlock, *Free Love*, 85. Cited in Albanese, *A Republic of Mind and Spirit*, 195.

133 form of popular entertainment: S. Brown, *Heyday of Spiritualism*, 18–19.

133 medical practice . . . was largely unregulated: A. Braude, *Radical Spirits*, 143.

133 "religious or mental healing offered a rational alternative": Ibid., 145.

134 "'Medical mediums' and 'clairvoyant physicians'": Ibid., 146.

134 "exercise a magnetic influence over a dog": Jonathan Koons, "Biography of Jonathan Koons," *RPJ*, July 31, 1875, 158.

134 In his autobiography Koons related: Ibid.

135 had arrived on the Koonses' doorstep: The story of Pusey Graves's visit comes from P. Graves, "Pusey Graves's Journal," Friends Pamphlet Group 6: Pusey Graves, and "Biographical Sketch of Pusey Graves by Charles B. Graves," Friends Manuscript Series 2: Pusey Graves Collection, both from Friends Collection and Earlham College Archives, Richmond, Indiana.

137 Davis "expounded a belief in universal and eternal progress": S. Brown, *Heyday of Spiritualism*, 97.

137 many Christians considered *Divine Revelations* heretical: Ibid., 104.

137 Graves carefully inspected the Koons Spirit Room: P. Graves, "Pusey Graves's Journal."

139 did not remain a spiritualist: C. B. Graves, "Biographical Sketch of Pusey Graves."

13: NOT ONE SINGLE COPPER

140 "Mr. K. himself": E. V. Wilson, "Spiritualism in Ohio," *Anglo American Magazine*, January–June 1855, 347.

141 "a tall, spare, and pale youth": Ibid., 443.

141 "The house and every thing about it": Ibid., 347.

141 "bright, mild and expressive of much intelligence": Ibid., 442.

142 "Some waggish spirit": Nichols, *Religions of the World*, 121.

142 "A little army of spirits giggling and laughing": *Wooster (Ohio) Republican*, February 23, 1854.

143 "Brice, I like you": Wilson, "Spiritualism in Ohio," 349.

143 "joyful confidence in a glorious immortality": "The Spirits at Mr. Koon's in Doon [*sic*], Ohio," *AP*, October 21, 1854, 4.

143 the Koons family "will not receive money": Letter to the editor, *AP*, April 14, 1855, 2. Koons himself wrote in November 1853 that he had "repeatedly refused compensation when offered," but hundreds of visitors later, his resistance evidently had waned. S. B. Brittan, ed., *The Telegraph Papers* (New York: Partridge and Brittan, 1854), 3:353.

144 "however peremptorily he [Koons] may have refused": Ibid., April 7, 1855, 2.

144 "I mentioned in my communication": Ibid., April 14, 1855, 2.

144 A joke made the rounds: R. T. Hallock, "Spiritual Lyceum and Conference: New York Conference," *ST*, May 1, 1858, 3.

145 proprietors of an unprofitable hotel: The same scourge that assailed the Koonses also hit the Tippie family, perhaps even the same two freeloaders. According to *Tiffany's Monthly*,

two men claiming to be "wonderful mediums, for the highest order of spirits only" had wormed their way into both the Koons and Tippie circles, where they "assumed much authority over the sittings." "Sometimes they would take a ramble in the woods, and come out with a new light or a coal direct and blazing from the altar of divine wisdom," the journal said with no little irony. The pair eventually overstayed their welcome. In a variation of the Koons story, John Tippie Jr. persuaded the men to lend a hand in hoeing corn, but they soon abandoned the field. The itinerant mediums bundled up their belongings, tied them to sticks they would carry on their shoulders, and headed for greener pastures (Reprinted from the *Telegraph*, January 1859, 350-351).

145 April forum attended by . . . leading spiritualists: "Abstract of the Proceedings at the Conference at No. 555 Broadway, Tuesday Evening, April 10," *CS*, April 21, 1855, 2.

146 a Mr. Benning: Could this be the Reverend Benning who visited the Koons room and purportedly received a message from his deceased wife? *Spiritual Age*, February 12, 1859.

146 "Your kind letter of March 20th": "A Letter from Jonathan Koons," *CS*, May 12, 1855, 3.

148 "Sir:—I submit the following communication": "Letter from Chilicothe," *SU*, May 12, 1855, 3.

14: KOONS, KING, AND COMPANY

150 "labored under difficult and pecuniary circumstances": Letter to the editor, *CS*, June 16, 1855, 2.

151 "Mr. Koons expressed much regret": Charles Partridge, "An Evening at Koons' Spirit Room," *ST*, July 21, 1855, 3.

152 hailed from Delaware County, Ohio: Van Sickle, *A History of the Van Sickle Family*, 209.

153 "the spirits talk audibly": Hare, *Experimental Investigation of the Spirit Manifestations*, 295.

153 "a kind of strange unearthly noise": Ibid., 299.

153 "After the introductory piece on the instruments": Ibid., 305.

154 "While we heard tunes from it,": "Spiritual Manifestations in Athens Co., Ohio," *Cleveland Plain Dealer*, November 1, 1854, 1.

154 "dark as Erebus": Hare, *Experimental Investigation of the Spirit Manifestations*, 296.

155 "as marvelous as anything we have heard of": "Manifestations in Buffalo," *CS*, August 11, 1855, 3.

155 The two boys would sit: Description of the Davenport phenomena comes from *Buffalo Republican*, qtd. in ibid.

156 "convinced beyond doubt": "Spiritual Manifestations at Davenports," *AP*, June 30, 1855, 2.

156 "You[r] knife is not sharp enough": *Vanguard*, March 7, 1857, 4.

156 "fresh from J. Koons room": *ST*, quoted in "Spirit Manifestations in Ross County, Ohio," *CS*, July 21, 1855, 4.

157 "A cross—which Mediums are impressed": Ibid.

157 "What the result will be": Ibid., 2.

158 "When a machine is invented": "Spiritual Machine," *Scientific American*, February 3, 1855, 2.

158 "as if some fifty persons": Pierce, *Revelator*, 17.

158 had studied at the Cambridge Divinity School: *A Catalogue of the Officers and Students of Harvard University*, 45.

158 "They who desire his services": "J. H. Fowler in the Field," *New Era*, August 16, 1854.

158   busy on the Midwest lecture circuit: "Letter from J. H. Fowler. Visit to Mr. Koons," *NES*, April 7, 1855.

158   making Fowler's audience "exceedingly merry": "Agitation of Thought," *Buchanan's Journal of Man*, May 15, 1855, 140.

158   a séance in New York State: "Letter from J. H. Fowler."

159   "a poor, sick, friendless creature": *Cincinnati Daily Times*, reprinted as "Spiritual Therapeutics," *Buchanan's Journal of Man*, May 15, 1855, 134–35.

159   Fowler had been most impressed: "Letter from J. H. Fowler."

159   "spoken that precious word": Fowler, *New Testament "Miracles," and Modern "Miracles,"* 100.

159   "As for spiritualism, if it has not facts": J. H. Fowler, "The 'Manifestations' at Mr. Koons'," *NES*, August 11, 1855, 1.

159   "the author deals, at times": "Editor's Table," *NES*, April 14, 1855, 2.

159   "Let the affidavits be concise": "Proposal from Bro. Fowler," *NES*, July 21, 1855.

160   "played most sweetly on the trumpet": Fowler, *New Testament "Miracles," and Modern "Miracles,"* 67–68. Fowler does not give the publication date of the report in *New Era*, but it was certainly 1854. The passage from the *New Era* does not appear in the second edition of Fowler's book, published in 1856. Fowler told his readers that the testimony about the Koons séance was now deemed unreliable (101). He also revealed that, years earlier, upon reading aloud a summary of the book at the Cambridge Divinity School, his professor had denounced Fowler as "unfit to preach in any Christian pulpit" (102).

160   "to assume the character of a skeptic": Fowler recounted his experiences in the Koons Spirit Room in "The 'Manifestations' at Mr. Koons'." All quotations are from this article.

15: "AN ARTFUL AND DESIGNING ROGUE"

166   I cannot longer refrain: J. H. Fowler, "The 'Manifestations' at Mr. Koons'," *NES*, August 11, 1855, 1.

166   "*the opinion of one who denies*": A. E. Newton, "The Wonders at Mr. Koons' Rooms," *CS*, August 18, 1855, 2.

167   mere "*suspicions, conjectures and statements*": Ibid.

167   "Brother Fowler, without any knowledge": J. W. H. Toohey, "J. H. Fowler," *CS*, October 6, 1855, 2.

167   "I have no doubt": John M. Kinney, letter to the editor, *NES*, September 1, 1855.

168   "In the five or six columns": Wade's detailed account can be found in "Four Days at Koons and Tippies' Rooms," *ST*, September 15, 1855, 4.

168   seeking guidance on a painting: According to a family history, "Under the supposed direction of the presiding spirit of the circle, he [Selah Van Sickle] executed a work of art denominated an 'Illustration of the Philosophy of Nature or the Subdivision of the Celestial and Terrestrial elements and mental conditions, divided into seven grand spheres with the God sphere or the heaven of heavens, which he regards as the true Cabalistic Philosophy'." Van Sickle, *A History of the Van Sickle Family*, 207–9. This painting sounds somewhat like King's/Nahum's 1853 drawing of the seven heavens (see chap. 8). It is not clear whether *Illustration of the Philosophy of Nature*, noted in the family history, and *Panorama of the Creation*, mentioned by Wade, are one and the same or two separate works. Only three of Van Sickle's paintings—all portraits—were known to exist as of 2016.

170   "As to Nahum's finding lungs": Cowee's account comes from "'The Manifestations at Mr. Koons,'" *NES*, September 8, 1855, 1.

173   "We left Mr. Koons' together": Selah Van Sickle, "Another Letter about Koons' Spirits," *ST*, September 15, 1855, 4.

174   Fowler fought back: "Note from Bro. Fowler," *NES*, September 29, 1855.

175   a reader who called himself "Almost Believer": "Musico-Spirit Circles.—An Experiment Suggested," *NES*, August 25, 1855, 2.

16: GALILEO IN ECLIPSE

177   "I know nothing of the matter": Letter to the editor, *ST*, September 1, 1855, 3.

177   Koons planned to be away: "Absence of Mr. Koons," *ST*, September 1, 1855, 3.

178   his brother Michael . . . lay gravely ill: Account of Jonathan Koons's herbal treatment given in David Quinn, "The Manifestations at Mr. Koons,'" *NES*, October 13, 1855, 1.

178   Within the group of pilgrims was H. B. Champion: "Correspondence of the *AP*," *AP*, October 20, 1855, 18–19.

178   "one of the most remarkable mediums of the age": Nichols, ed., *Supramundane Facts in the Life*, 82.

179   "shriek[ing] out in an unearthly voice": Lewitt's report appeared in "Correspondence of the *AP*," *AP*, October 20, 1855, 18–19.

180   "I did not go there prejudiced": The Marietta businessman's account appeared in "Spiritual Manifestations in Athens County," *Cleveland Morning Leader*, November 19, 1855. The editor noted that he had received the letter "some time ago."

182   a combination lock with a dare attached: *NES*, April 21, 1855.

182   turned out to be Abraham Lincoln: John B. Buescher, "Across the Dead Line: Lincoln and the Spirits during the War and Reconstruction Era [in] Washington," 3, accessed November 5, 2016, http://spirithistory.iapsop.com/jb_buescher_across_the_dead_line.pdf.

182   "While the spirits are communicating": J. B. Conklin, "Twenty Years Ago. The Spirit Room of J. Koons, Athens County, Ohio," *RPJ*, September 11, 1875, 206.

182   "was withdrawn from me like a vapor": J. B. Conklin, *Nichols Monthly*, October–November 1855, 286–90.

183   "It is a lamentable fact": Jonathan Koons, "Spiritualism and Reform," reprinted in *CS*, September 22, 1855, 4.

184   he wrote a rebuttal to the *New England Spiritualist*: Jonathan Koons, "Koons, King & Ko.," *NES*, October 6, 1855.

185   "As the *hand* was what I wanted to see": A. Miltenberger, *ST*, reprinted in "A Short Trip to Ohio," *SU*, November 24, 1855. This account makes no mention of Jonathan Koons's being present.

186   "They were sceptics": A. Miltenberger, "A New Manifestation," *ST*, reprinted in *Yorkshire (England) Spiritual Telegraph*, September–November 1856, 101.

186   "Mr. Smith says": Miltenberger, "A Short Trip to Ohio," 4.

186   "the tambourine and horn performance": Ibid.

186   Back in Athens County on October 20: "Letter from J. B. Trembley," *SU*, December 22, 1855, 2–3.

17: AN ARC OF GOLDEN ROSES

189   One F. F. Jones of Federalton: Jonathan Koons, "Who Is F. F. Jones?," *SU*, November 24, 1855, 3. I could not find a copy of Jones's original letter to the newspaper.

189   "Now without comment let me inform": Ibid.

190   community in Rome Township: Beatty and Stone, *Getting to Know Athens County*, 123. According to Inter-State Publishing, *History of Hocking Valley, Ohio*, Federalton was the original name of present-day Stewart, Ohio (528).

190   "if the gentleman will not believe": T. F. Jones, "Who F. F. Jones Is," *SU*, December 22, 1855, 3.

190   Timothy F. Jones was . . . a local leader: See Walker, *History of Athens County, Ohio*, 500–501, 509.

190   "I have thought that spiritualists, generally": T. F. Jones, "Who F. F. Jones Is."

190   "The spirit room at my residence": Koons, "Who Is F. F. Jones?"

191   he had jammed with the spirit band: Account of John Gage in Hare, *Experimental Investigation of the Spirit Manifestations*, 300.

191   A session at Tippie's that September: Hiram Shenich, "Extraordinary Spirit Manifestation," *ST*, reprinted in *Los Angeles Star*, October 6, 1855, 4.

192   "Dear Sir:—In looking over the columns": Hiram Shenich, "J. Tippie's Spirit-Room," *SU*, December 22, 1855, 1.

193   "John Tippie will be prepared to receive patients": "New Spiritual Magnetic Spring," *ST*, November 3, 1855, 5.

193   Tippie's phenomena . . . had steadily improved: Shenich, "J. Tippie's Spirit-Room," 1.

195   as they contemplated a special invitation: *Spiritual Messenger*, quoted in "Spirit Room at Cincinnati," *NES*, January 5, 1856, 3.

195   a large crowd gathered: For a report of the séance see ibid.

18: "THEIR HUMBUG ART"

197   "will be good news to many": "Jonathan Koons and Daughter Coming to New York," *CS*, January 5, 1856, 2.

197   "had satisfactory manifestations on every occasion": Ibid.

197   the new player must have been Quintilla: The only other female child in the Koons home was the orphan Eliza, then about 10 or 11 years old. Koons referred to her as his "adopted daughter." It seems more likely that Quintilla is the "daughter" mentioned here.

198   "They merely dropped in on their route": Randolph, *Davenport Brothers*, 131–32.

198   They set up séance rooms at 195 Bowery: "The Members of the Press Invited to Investigate the Manifestations at the Davenport Circle," *CS*, January 5, 1856, 2.

198   "The arrival of the Davenports": Marc Demarest, "A Series of Cheap Magical Soirees to Amuse the Million: Amherst's Hierarchy of Manifestations," *Chasing Down Emma* (blog), November 29, 2014, http://ehbritten.blogspot.com/2014_11_01_archive.html.

199   The private, press-only demonstration: "The Members of the Press Invited."

199   John F. Coles was accusing them: Demarest, "A Series of Cheap Magical Soirees."

200   at the Jackson Hotel: "The Koons in New York," *ST*, February 30 [*sic*], 1856, 2.

200   "his health is somewhat impaired": "The Koons Family in New York," *CS*, February 9, 1856, 2.

200 was a former Universalist minister: Buescher, *Other Side of Salvation*, 59–60.

201 "A match, held by the spirit hand, ignited": Linus Smith Everett, "John Koons, the Humbug," *Cincinnati Commercial*, reprinted in *New Albany Daily Ledger*, February 4, 1856, 2.

201 Jonathan was obliged to go to Delaware: "John Koons and His Family," *Daily Cleveland Herald*, January 26, 1856.

201 "If honest, and if he had the good of spiritualism at heart": Ibid.

202 "make money out of their humbug art": Everett, "John Koons, the Humbug."

202 carried an item praising the family: *Daily Cleveland Herald*, January 28, 1856.

202 "We withhold comment": "'The Phantasy Disappearing!'" CS, February 16, 1856, 2.

202 a friendly reception in Painesville, Ohio: "The Koons Family in New York."

203 The Koonses' "advent in this city": "The Koons in New York." The CS of February 9, 1856, hinted that better days were to come, for "he expects to return to the city ere long, for other and more public reasons."

204 George Washington Rains . . . gathered there with friends: The Rains group's report appeared in "Testimony from a Koons Circle," *ST*, March 8, 1856.

204 Jonathan, Nahum, and Quintilla took their places: The New York accounts make no mention of Abigail Koons's participating in the séances. On at least one occasion the hostess, Mrs. Jackson, who was also a medium, joined the Koons family at the mediums' table. *ST*, February 30 [*sic*], 1856, 2.

206 "his simplicity of character and honesty of purpose": Ibid.

207 "Mr. Tippie, with his son and daughter": "Spiritualism in Cincinnati," *NES*, March 8, 1856, 3.

207 determined not to miss the Tippies: For accounts of J. R. Buchanan's tussle with the Tippies, see Celsus, "Another Exposure of Spiritualism," *Boston Investigator*, April 23, 1856. See also "Buchanan's Journal of Man," *ST*, March 22, 1856, 2.

209 Buchanan made a simple proposal: Celsus, "Another Exposure of Spiritualism."

209 "The *true* Spiritualist [should not] shrink": "Dark Circles and Unexpected Developments," CS, January 12, 1856, p. 2.

210 refused to take Buchanan's report seriously: "Buchanan's Journal of Man."

210 the Quaker town of Mount Pleasant, Ohio: *The Ohio Guide*, 469.

210 "There is not a man in the State of Ohio": White, *An Essay on Spiritualism*, 2.

210 Now White revealed: Thomas White, "Another Side of the Story," *ST*, June 28, 1856, 7. White also said he had prepared a "full and impartial report of all that transpired" in Cincinnati. I was unable to find a copy of this document.

211 "Whether the performance of the Koons family": Celsus, "Another Exposure of Spiritualism."

211 "Opposed from without, assailed by jeers": A. Miltenberger, "A New Manifestation," *Yorkshire Spiritual Telegraph*, September–November 1856, 101.

212 "The influence seizes him": Ibid., 102.

212 "Mr. Smith is an honest old Quaker": William H. Smith, "Spirit Room at Cardington, Ohio," *NES*, January 5, 1856, 3.

19: THE PSYCHOMETRIST

213 "Being thus equipped": "Letter from Jonathan Koons," *ST*, April 11, 1857, 3.

213   opposed religious litmus tests: "Campbell, Alexander (1788–1866)," *Encyclopedia.com*, accessed October 25, 2016, http://www.encyclopedia.com/people/philosophy -and-religion/protestant-christianity-biographies/alexander-campbell.

214   churches sprang up in Chauncey, Glouster, and Trimble: Blower, *A Brief History of Trimble Township*, 101.

214   "read their Bibles": Inter-State Publishing, *History of Hocking Valley, Ohio*, 742.

214   Denton . . . was an English émigré: "Timeline," Finding Aid for Denton Family Papers, 1, Wellesley Historical Society, Wellesley, MA, accessed October 25, 2016, http://www .wellesleyhistoricalsociety.org/documents/Denton%20Family%20Papers%20 -%20Research%20Guide.pdf.

214   found a kindred spirit in Elizabeth Foote: Beth Hinchliffe, "Borne on the Wings of History," *WellesleyWeston Online*, May 19, 2011, http://www.wellesleywestonmagazine .com/summer11/wings.htm.

214   An avid collector: Ibid.

214   "If our friends in any other place": William Denton, "Notes from the Lecturing Eield [*sic*]," *Vanguard*, March 7, 1857, 4.

215   Christian church near Athens: Ibid.

215   left the crowd disappointed: Ibid.

215   "His lectures were well attended": "Letter from Jonathan Koons," *ST*, April 11, 1857, 3.

216   "who appear to be at enmity with truth": "Letter from Jonathan Koons," *RPJ*, June 12, 1875, 99.

216   "were highly susceptible of spirit influx": Jonathan Koons, "Biography of Jonathan Koons," *RPJ*, July 10, 1875, 130.

216   "I had no time for 'jugglery'": Ibid., June 19, 1875, 106.

217   located 8 miles from Chillicothe: The description of the group's activities appears in Joel Watson, "Another Point of Spirit Attraction," *NES*, September 27, 1856, 3.

217   Out in New Durham, Indiana: *Chicago Banker*, reprinted in "Spirit Hall at New Durham, Indiana," *NES*, December 13, 1856.

217   "a series of beautiful pictures of the spirit land": Britten, *Modern American Spiritualism*, 341.

217   And in Dundee, Illinois: "Spirit Hall at New Durham, Indiana."

218   "likely to pervade and absorb all denominations of Christians": Charles Partridge, "The Spiritual Telegraph," *NES*, January 17, 1857, 2.

218   "She presented me with six bottles": "Letter from Jonathan Koons," *ST*, April 11, 1857, 3.

218   mind fell into "an abnormal condition": Dream or vision recounted in Koons, "Biography of Jonathan Koons," *RPJ*, September 4, 1875, 198.

219   "discovered that his sister Annie": John B. Buescher, "Across the Dead Line: Lincoln and the Spirits during the War and Reconstruction Era [in] Washington," 58, accessed November 5, 2016, http://spirithistory.iapsop.com/jb_buescher_across_the_dead_line.pdf.

220   William and Annie conducted hundreds of tests: Ibid., 59–60.

220   Through practice Annie became quite adept: A few years later Annie would apply her talents to the solar system, claiming to visit Jupiter and the other planets through remote viewing. On Jupiter she found an advanced race "who bore no sign of care or want," each married to all the others. Buescher, "Across the Dead Line," 62–63. Her interest in utopian societies took a feminist turn several years later when William published her visions as *Man's Rights; Or, How Would You Like It?*, a satirical novel in which gender roles are reversed.

220 The covered-up object that William gave Annie: William Denton, "Remarkable Spiritual and Psychometric Test," *Vanguard*, March 7, 1857, 2–3. Denton calls the Indian chief Hommo in this account, but the details of the story more closely resemble that of the other Indian chief, Musco, who was supposedly killed in battle.

221 William had begged for a piece for testing: Denton, "Remarkable Spiritual and Psychometric Test."

221 "Crops of all kinds": A., "Athens County," *Ohio Cultivator* (Columbus), August 1, 1857, 228.

221 "You was misinformed": Jonathan Koons to William Denton, July 25, 1857, Denton Family Papers, William Denton Correspondence, Series 1, Box 2.

222 "a great mental revolution": Ibid.

222 "about 50 pages of foolscap paper": Ibid. Denton did eventually publish one of Jonathan's religious essays in the *Vanguard*.

20: LITTLE EGYPT

233 The frontier had long since moved on: The exhibit "Early Visions of Ohio 1765–1865," curated by Christopher Busta-Peck, stated that "by 1865, the rural areas of Ohio had reached what could be called a climax settlement landscape, supporting as many people as the land was capable of supporting." Further growth occurred in towns and cities. Decorative Arts Center of Ohio, Lancaster, September 12–December 31, 2015. In the late 1850s this trend was no doubt well under way.

233 Real estate in Ohio: William Denton, "Kansas the Place for Reformfrs [*sic*]," *Vanguard*, October 31, 1857, 4.

233 the prosperous merchant Daniel Brown: H. Brown, *Grandmother Brown's First Hundred Years*, 102.

233 hidden in his wife's carpetbag: Ibid., 106.

233 "Illinois is the best State west of Ohio": J. S. Robinson, "About Moving West," *Hardin Co. Republican*, quoted in *Ohio Cultivator* (Columbus), September 1, 1857, 258.

234 Tippie sold 173 acres to Wesley: Athens County, Ohio, Deed Book, 24:518.

234 Hixon, who ended up with 372 acres: Ibid., 285. A curious story suggests that Tippie's exit from Athens County may have been tied to some failed prospecting ventures. As the story goes, he became consumed by a quest to find lead ore in the county, just as others of his generation had been bitten by the "gold bug" that took them to California. Prompted by a spirit message that lead was to be found in Ames Township, Tippie borrowed thousands of dollars from Hixon and sought the ore in vain. Undeterred, Tippie set his sights on another lead prospect in Waterloo Township. To obtain a second loan from Hixon, Tippie put up his farm in Ames Township as collateral. When the Waterloo venture fizzled as well, he signed over his property to Hixon and moved west. However, the deed never mentions minerals or mortgages and describes only a straight real estate transaction between Tippie and Hixon. William E. Peters Papers, reprinted in *Athens County Family History 1987*, compiled by Beverly Schumacher and Mary L. Bowman (Athens, OH: Ancestree, 1987), 201.

234 "he sold out in Ohio": "Spirit-Rooms at the West," *ST*, March 26, 1859, 8.

234 Tippie family graveyard: The buyer, Peter Hixon, resided in a large two-story farmhouse with a view of the cemetery—perhaps the same house that John Tippie Jr. had built in 1855. While Hixon was alive, the cemetery was maintained, but after his death the new owners removed the marble tombstones to make way for the plow, obliterating

the graves of Tippie family members. See Peters Papers in Schumacher and Bowman, *Athens County Family History 1987*, 201.

234   "removed to Southern Illinois": Three weeks later the *Vanguard* noted that the address of John Tippie was "in demand at this office, for ourselves and others" (November 21, 1857, 7). On March 6, 1858, the *Vanguard* followed up on the story, telling readers that John Tippie reportedly "is establishing some sort of a reform neighborhoo[d] or community" in Illinois, on the northern edge of a region called Little Egypt. "Several [people] would like to know where, but we have not hitherto been favored with information" (1). Do these statements suggest that Tippie may not have been in Illinois after all, or was he merely keeping his address private?

234   settlement in Hardin County, Iowa: "Community Movements," *Vanguard*, October 31, 1857, 6.

235   "elevated and free": *Phalansterian Record*, quoted in "The 'Fourier Phalanx' Located," *Vanguard*, February 13, 1858, 1.

235   perhaps had died: I have been unable to establish a death date for Elizabeth Koons Hughes. According to W. E. Peters, a third person was buried in the Koons family cemetery beside George and Filenia Koons, "probably a Hughes." However, the sandstone grave marker had crumbled by the time Peters photographed the cemetery in 1939.

236   Fuller paid them $3,000: Athens County, Ohio, Deed Book, 24:628. It is not clear why the 1850 agricultural census listed the farm as covering 160 acres but the Koonses ended up selling 206 acres in 1858. Deed Book, 21:556, shows that Jonathan purchased 15 5/16 acres from Henry Brown in 1854, but this does not account for the entire amount of acreage listed as sold four years later. Jonathan also sold land in 1854 to Alex Danes (Deed Book, 28:94).

236   real estate swap: Franklin County, Illinois, Deed Book, H:313. Available on microfilm from familysearch.org.

236   "123 Acres . . . situated on the East Fork": *Athens Messenger*, March 12, 1858.

236   sold that same month . . . for $2,000: Morgan County, Ohio, Deed Book, 3:423. The buyer was David Clayton of Athens County. The Morgan County deed contained one exception: Jonathan and Abigail had already sold a quarter acre of the property to the Homer Township Board of Education for use as school grounds (Deed Book, 4:435). Perhaps to sweeten the deal, Jonathan and Abigail sold Clayton the 80 acres at or near Council Bluffs, Iowa, in addition to the Morgan County, Ohio, acreage, all for $2,000.

236   "France will very soon be excelled": J. Kershner, "South Western Missouri," *Vanguard*, January 2, 1858, 2.

237   "lands in the middle and S.W. part of Missouri": Jonathan Koons to William Denton, n.d., Denton Family Papers, William Denton Correspondence, Series 1, Box 2. Wellesley Historical Society, Wellesley, MA. The letter suggests that Koons had multiple properties in Missouri. He mentioned Bates County as his destination but also had purchased land at Warsaw, which is in Benton County to the east. Today the two locations are about an hour's drive apart.

238   "bartered two span of horses and wagons, for landed property": In his letter Koons never mentioned the 80 acres in Illinois that he and Abigail had bought before they left Athens County. Why they bought the Northern Township land is not clear; perhaps they had already sold the first tract in yet another real estate deal, or the land may have been unsuitable for farming.

238   Denton at the time was in Twin Mound, Kansas: William Denton, "Kansas the Place for Reformfrs [*sic*]," *Vanguard*, October 31, 1857, 4.

239 predicted that women would vote: Joseph Treat, "Agitator Communications. Papers on Woman. No. IV," *Agitator*, November 15, 1858, 27.

240 "Mores [*sic*] Prairie Jefferson Co. Ill.": Koons's original mailing address was in Jefferson County, but he apparently lived in adjoining Franklin County. Perhaps this was the closest post office.

240 "We are informed that Koons' trumpet medium": "Spirit-Rooms at the West," *ST*, March 26, 1859, 8.

240 "gone with his father (John Tippie) to Pike's Peak": Apparently the Tippies were already living in eastern Kansas and had gone on a prospecting trip.

240 the so-called Fifty-Niners raced: Calvin W. Gower, "The Pike's Peak Gold Rush and the Smoky Hill Route, 1 (1859–1860)," *Kansas Historical Quarterly* 25, no. 2 (summer 1959): 158–71, https://www.kshs.org/p/kansas-historical-quarterly-the-pike-s-peak-gold-rush-and-the-smoky-hill-route/13151.

241 "I have not forgotten the glorious times": "Spirit-Rooms at the West."

241 "My faith is firm": "Letter from Jonathan Koons," *ST and Fireside Preacher*, July 9, 1859, 2.

241 at the home of Dr. Wilkey: Ibid., 3. This is probably a reference to Carter Wilkey, MD, although Carter had a son, James Henry Wilkey, who was also a physician. Carter Wilkey was reported to have attended a séance at Jonathan Koons's home at an unspecified date.

242 a private séance at Jonathan Koons's home: "Jonathan Koons. One of the Old Workers Whose Materializing Circles in Ohio Created World-Wide Attention," *Progressive Thinker*, May 7, 1904, 2.

243 scooped up the 202-acre Hughes farm: Athens County Deed Book, 27:579.

243 "The fear of war": "Kansas the Place for Reformfrs."

243 found themselves in Linn County: Dodd dates the arrival in Kansas of John Tippie Sr. as September 10, 1858. She says that John Jr. arrived in the vicinity "at this time or soon after" (17).

244 Beecher's Bibles: The rifle's nickname refers to the abolitionist minister Henry Ward Beecher, who raised money for 50 of these weapons to be sent to Linn County. Mitchell, *Linn County, Kansas*, 387.

244 John Greenleaf Whittier: Kansas Historical Society, "Marais des Cygnes Massacre Site," *Kansapedia*, July 2016, https://www.kshs.org/kansapedia/marais-des-cygnes-massacre-site/11870.

244 Michael Tippie . . . had been farming: Linn County Historical Society files. Some sources list Michael's occupation as physician; another as a minister.

244 Rhoda . . . also moved to the area: Dodd, *Story of Uriah Tippie*, 18.

244 may have shared a home: Magley, *Descendants of John Tippie Sr.*, 2.

244 met with misfortune: *U.S. Federal Census Mortality Schedules Index, 1850–1880*, Lykins County, Kansas, record for John Tippie, Lydia Tippie, Elizabeth Tippie and J. Tippie [John Sr.], Ancestry.com. *U.S., Federal Census Mortality Schedules Index, 1850–1880* [database online]. Provo, UT, USA: Ancestry.com Operations Inc, 1999.

244 at age 8 or 9: The *U.S. Federal Census Mortality Schedules Index* cited above says 8 years; the Linn County Historical Society record says 9 years. Also listed in the death records for early 1860 was 80-year-old Charlotte Tippie, whose relationship to the family is not clear.

244 a male guardian: "Genealogy Report: The Descendants of Uriah Tippie, Generation No. 4," Genealogy.com, accessed October 24, 2016, http://www.genealogy.com/ftm/d/o/d/June-E-Dodd-KS/GENE3-0004.html.

244 contracted typhoid: *U.S. Federal Census Mortality Schedules Index, 1850–1880*, Franklin County, Illinois, record for Eliza Koons and Marcellus Koons, National Archives and Records Administration (NARA); Washington, DC; *Non-population Census Schedules for Illinois, 1850–1880*; Archive Collection: T1133; Archive Roll Number: 58; Census Year: 1859; Census Place: Avon, Fulton, Illinois. Available on Ancestry.com.

245 a low-grade fever: For information about typhoid, see Mayo Clinic Staff, "Typhoid Fever," mayoclinic.org, July 11, 2015, http://www.mayoclinic.org/diseases-conditions /typhoid-fever/basics/symptoms/CON-20028553; and A. Verghese, "The 'Typhoid State' Revisited," *American Journal of Medicine* 79, no. 3 (September 1985): 370–72, https:// www.ncbi.nlm.nih.gov/pubmed/3898837.

245 14-year-old Daniel: *U.S. Federal Census Mortality Schedules Index* lists the 14-year-old boy as Marcellus Koons. However, the tombstone says "Daniel M." The most straightforward explanation is that Marcellus was his middle name. There are also discrepancies in the ages of Eliza and Daniel; I have used those on the mortality schedule.

245 rejoined the family circle: US Census, 1860, Linn County, Kansas; US Census, 1870, Franklin County, Illinois; David E. Goss, *Northern Township Franklin County, Illinois*, 2:14. Anna Margaret apparently lived out her days in that locale, dying on November 27, 1897, at about age 71 (Ancestry.com).

245 privates assigned to Company K: Office of the Illinois Secretary of State, "Koons, Samuel G. B." and "Koons, James R.," Illinois Civil War Detail Reports. For Samuel Koons see http://www.ilsos.gov/isaveterans/civilMusterSearch.do?key=143382, and for James Koons see http://www.ilsos.gov/isaveterans/civilMusterSearch.do?key=143380, both accessed November 7, 2016.

245 Confederate captives held there had died: "Camp Butler National Cemetery, Springfield, Illinois," National Park Service, accessed November 7, 2016, https://www.nps.gov/nr /travel/national_cemeteries/illinois/Camp_Butler_National_Cemetery.html.

245 Twenty-two-year-old Samuel: Illinois Civil War Detail Reports.

246 brought back home for burial: Frankfort Area Genealogical Society files, West Frankfort, IL.

246 had close ties to the college: Sheila Cadwalader, email to author, September 2, 2016.

246 "considered by some, to be somewhat fanatical": Koons to Denton.

247 "The initiatory experiments": Britten, *Modern American Spiritualism*, 307.

247 "the revolutionary spirit of the country": E. F. B., letter to the editor, *New York Herald*, reprinted in "A Sign of the Times," *American Spiritualist*, May 4, 1872, 4.

248 had thrown their support to Woodhull: Woodhull split with Stanton and Anthony on the first day of the meeting, choosing to hold her human rights convention at another location. See Mary Gabriel, *Notorious Victoria: The Life of Victoria Woodhull, Uncensored* (Chapel Hill, NC: Algonquin, 1998): 166–69.

248 a People's Party petition: *American Spiritualist*, May 4, 1872, 5.

248 Among the human rights advocates: Ibid.

248 "Please pardon me": "Letter from Jonathan Koons," *RPJ*, April 24, 1875, 42.

248 Koons shared an interest: For a discussion of spiritualists' interest in alternative Christian narratives, see Buescher, *Other Side of Salvation*, 20.

249 his most controversial material: "Letter from Jonathan Koons."

249 Pierce had it published in the *New Era*: Koons misidentified the newspaper as "New England 'Spirit Messenger.'" Ibid.

249   Koons denied any wrongdoing: The anonymous *New Era* reader sent in a clipping from a different newspaper that contained the same paragraph—ascribing the authorship not to Christ, but to De Witt Clinton, a US senator and New York governor who had died in 1828. The skeptic concluded that either Koons had staged a fraud, or the spirits themselves were not above plagiarizing published works. The *New Era* conceded that the writing appeared to be Clinton's but urged its readers not to jump to hasty conclusions regarding Koons. "With regard to Mr. K., we can only say that we have, from different sources, what appears to be satisfactory evidence that he has acted truthfully in the matter," it said. "There surely have been real wonders enough enacted at his place, to render it unnecessary, as well as extremely unwise, for him to attempt to fabricate any false stories." A full exploration of this controversy is not possible in 2018, as the issues of the *New Era* that contained the article (or paragraph) Pierce sent in and the anonymous letter alleging plagiarism may no longer exist. For the *New Era*'s position, see "Alleged Plagiarism," *New Era*, December 2, 1854, 2. For Koons's response, see J. Koons, "That Communication Signed 'Jesus Christ,'" *New Era*, January 6, 1855, 2. Both are in the American Antiquarian Society Periodicals Collection: Series 4.

249   "was given alphabetically through her": Koons's account is puzzling, given that Nancy Jane signed her name with an X on legal documents. If unable to write, how could she spell out a word through tipping? Perhaps she knew the alphabet and called out the letters.

250   "brought to ruin and disgrace": *Spiritual Scientist*, April 15, 1875, 6.

250   "He is now living": "Timely Advice," *RPJ*, May 8, 1875, 60.

250   reprint Koons's serialized autobiography: "Letter from Jonathan Koons," *RPJ*, June 12, 1875, 99. Buescher notes that the *RPJ* "tried to dampen spiritualist enthusiasm for the more sensationalistic phenomena produced at séances" and was a "skeptical counterweight" to the *Banner of Light* (*Other Side of Salvation*, 124). The editors' decision to give space to Koons's life story shows the high regard they must have had for his mediumship.

250   obtain a state license: "Jefferson County, Illinois: Early Doctors," Genealogy Trails, accessed November 22, 2016, http://genealogytrails.com/ill/jefferson/earlydoctors.html.

250   Abigail's experience as an herbalist: In December of that year, he applied for a patent for "Dr. Koons' Sanguifying Usqnibaugh," which may have been a tonic for fortifying the blood. Jonathan Koons, Dr. Koons' Sanguifying Usqnibaugh, US Patent 1,316, filed December 18, 1877. "Usqnibaugh" may have been inspired by the Gaelic word *usquebaugh*, which means "water of life" and may be the basis for the English word *whisky*. "A Brief History of Scotch Whisky," 1995–2011, www.whisky.com/history.html.

251   "notified by a Ku Klux letter": Koons, *Truth Seekers' Feast*, 11.

251   Cinderellus had gotten his medical degree: See Perrin, *History of Jefferson County, Illinois*, 21; "Biographical/Historical Note," American, Barnes and National Colleges Collection, Bernard Becker Medical Library Archives, Washington University School of Medicine, http://beckerarchives.wustl.edu/?p=collections/findingaid&id=8693&q=&rootcontentid=38394#biographical-hist-note.

251   moved to adjoining Jefferson County: Perrin's history says Cinderellus moved in 1878, but the US Census of 1880 finds Cinderellus living in Franklin County and working in a sawmill.

251   "Among the young and rising physicians": Perrin, *History of Jefferson County, Illinois*, 21.

251   excluded Nancy Jane's interest: Franklin County, Illinois, Deed Book, 8:213 and 304.

252   Nahum, Ann, and their children moved: "Jefferson County IL Obituaries. Nahum Ward
      Koons." Copyright 1997–2004 by Misty Flannigan. Copyright 2005 by Cindy Ford. October 24,
      2016, http://www.rootsweb.ancestry.com/~iljeffer/obits/koons-nahumwardjcobit
      .htm; and Ellinghouse, *Missouri: A Sesquicentennial History,* 72. Although the obituary
      gives the date of Nahum's return as 1880, Ellinghouse says "around 1881," which is
      supported by census data showing Nahum still living in Missouri in 1880.

252   a village of about 1,000 people: *Koons v. St. Louis & Iron Mountain Railroad Company,* 65
      Mo. 597 (1877).

252   operated a sawmill: George W. Smith, *History of Illinois and Her People,* (Chicago:
      American Historical Society, 1927), 6:138. This book contains errors about Jonathan
      Koons and should be consulted with caution.

252   Some members of Ann's family: "Koons, Nahum," US Census, 1870, Benton Township,
      Wayne County, Missouri, 2, Ancestry.com; and Liz Budzowski, Bates Family Genealogy
      Forum, July 30, 2000, http://genforum.genealogy.com/bates/messages/3243.html.

252   Samuel later became a physician: Ellinghouse, *Missouri: A Sesquicentennial History,* 71–73.
      For more information about Nahum's brother-in-law Samuel A. Bates, see Ellinghouse,
      Swindled, 1874.

252   The same railroads: The story of the child's tragic death is found in *Koons v. St. Louis &
      Iron Mountain Railroad Company,* 65 Mo. 592–98 (1877).

252   Nahum's 9-year-old son, James: In the 1870 census the child is called Rolandus, which
      suggests he was named after Nahum's brother James Rolandis.

253   private sittings with his family: Frank Brown, "The Koons Spirit Room," The Voice Box,
      2007, http://www.the-voicebox.com/koonsspiritroom.htm.

253   Polina May Jones: Ibid.

21: "THE VENERABLE JOHNATHAN KOONS"

254   "investigating truth seekers": Title page of Koons, *Truth Seekers' Feast.*
254   "an incontrovertible historical fact": Ibid., iii.
255   "Under the blood-stained banner": Ibid., iii–iv.
255   "no sooner than the fires": Ibid., 13.
255   led to the Council of Nicaea: Ibid., 13–14.
255   "no better than we esteem": Ibid., 14.
255   "It is truly passing strange": Ibid., 12.
255   Arius, a Libyan priest: For a sketch of the Council of Nicaea controversy, see Pagels,
      Beyond Belief, 171–81.
256   "Their object, no doubt": Koons, *Truth Seekers' Feast,* 20.
256   suppressed texts: D. Brown, *Da Vinci Code,* 234.
256   "The formation of the canon": Ehrman, *Truth and Fiction in* The Da Vinci Code, 93. For
      another rebuttal of Brown's views, see Tim O'Neill, "History Versus the Da Vinci Code,"
      2006, http://www.historyversusthedavincicode.com/chapterfiftyfive.htm#christpower.
256   "whether Christ was a divine creation": Ehrman, *Truth and Fiction in* The Da Vinci Code, 23.
256   laid out his recommended scriptures: Ibid., 93.
256   "From that meeting and its aftermath," Pagels, *Beyond Belief,* 170.
257   "what John opposed": Ibid., 34.
257   "held the credulous mass of mankind spellbound": Koons, *Truth Seekers' Feast,* 70.

258 "the spiritual side of these subjects": Ibid., 117.

258 "If I am favored with health": Ibid., 98.

258 along with Jesus Christ: Koons reported back in 1854 that he and his circle had received "a sixty days visitation from the spirit of Christ—during which time, we were favored with a view of one of those angelic forms, which was very bright in appearance, holding an emblem of a cross in his hand." It is not clear whether he believed the messenger was divine or simply a wise teacher. J. Koons, "That Communication Signed 'Jesus Christ,'" *New Era*, January 6, 1855, 2. In his book *Upstate Cauldron*, Joscelyn Godwin notes that interpretations of religious visions are often culturally based: "When our nineteenth-century visionaries met a luminous being, they took it to be a dead relative, an angel, or Jesus, and it spoke to them as such." By contrast, Godwin says, a mystic from the Greco-Roman period might have perceived it as "a daimon: a member of a class of beings intermediate between humans and gods" (303).

258 "I believe there is no individualized spirit": Koons, *Truth Seekers' Feast*, 96.

258 "I find, in the course of my research": Ibid., 66.

258 "man's divine constitution": Ibid., 92.

258 "The following lines of inspiration": Ibid., 118. Koons reprinted only four of the nine stanzas of Doten's poem as it was later published in 1895. See Lizzie Doten, "The Divine Idea," 231–34, in *Poems of Progress* (Boston: Colby and Rich, 1895). Assuming he had access to the complete version in 1881, he had edited out the first three, in which God plants a longing for the divine in humanity while creating the world. In these lines Doten also compared the relationship of God and humans with that of parent and child. Koons also eliminated stanzas 7 and 8, which celebrate the awakening of the soul in lofty language. These changes probably were not made for space considerations but rather to focus more precisely on the parts of the poem that best fit his philosophy of life.

260 he drove across the prairie in his buggy: Alan Taylor, email to author, September 2017.

260 "Uncle Jonathan Koons": Frankfort Area Genealogical Society files.

260 Maggie Fox dismayed a nation of spiritualists: Stuart, *Reluctant Spiritualist*, 298–99.

260 "For thirty years this woman": *RPJ*, October 20, 1888, 4.

261 As she lay on her deathbed: Stuart, *Reluctant Spiritualist*, 312–13.

261 On an April evening in 1892: "The Venerable Johnathan Koons," *Progressive Thinker*, April 23, 1892.

261 He would allow his wife: "Last Will and Testament of Jonathan Koons," Illinois Probate Records, 1819–1988, Franklin County, Wills 1875–1911, vol. B:65–66, https://familysearch.org/ark:/61903/3:1:939J-K8TN-5?i=91&wc=SFKG-3TG%3A162587401%2C162620301%3Fcc%3D1834344&cc=1834344.

262 he sent a dispatch to a newspaper: "Venerable Johnathan Koons."

262 His death was noted: Frankfort Area Genealogical Society files.

262 had an apocalyptic vision: Jonathan Koons, "Biography of Jonathan Koons," *RPJ*, September 4, 1875, 198.

263 "I was an odd sheep in my father's flock": Ibid., August 14, 1875, 170.

EPILOGUE

265 the Round House owned by John Morrison: Account of séances given in Mitchell, *Linn County, Kansas*, 313–14.

266   Ezra had become administrator: "Genealogy Report: The Descendants of Uriah
      Tippie," accessed October 24, 2016, http://www.genealogy.com/ftm/d/o/d/June-E
      -Dodd-KS/GENE3-0004.html.

266   Ezra continued to have séances: "Father King. He Has Been in Spirit-Life 20,000 Years,"
      Progressive Thinker, September 13, 1890, 3.

266   "In 1860, Ezra Tippie was accused": "Genealogy Report."

266   Ezra and four of his brothers: Magley, *Descendants of John Tippie Sr.*, 8.

266   Joe entered the army: Ibid., 11.

266   fraught with considerable violence: Ibid.

267   made their home in Paris Township: Linn County Historical Society files.

267   a plot to steal from a rancher: J. F. Price, editor of *Cherokee Sentinel*, quoted by A. J.
      Georgia, "General History of Crawford County," in Home Authors, *A Twentieth Century
      History*, 25–27.

267   Morrison had been the administrator: "Genealogy Report."

267   "Morrison was just an ordinary man": Mitchell, *Linn County, Kansas*, 314.

268   "noted men came under assumed names": Ibid., 315.

268   scientific knowledge: "Father King . . . in Spirit-Life 20,000 Years."

268   "there was a mystery about it": Mitchell, *Linn County, Kansas*, 315.

268   Matters came to a head: Ibid.

269   "We have the spirit, 'Father King,'": *Kingdom of Heaven* 4, no. 4 (May 1874).

269   an artful pretender defended: "From 'Father King,'" *Fort Scott Monitor*, reprinted in *RPJ*,
      January 9, 1875, 5.

269   another dark seance in Kansas: "Spiritualism in America," *Clutha Leader*, June 3, 1875,
      accessed at https://paperspast.natlib.govt.nz/newspapers/CL18750603.2.34.

270   "Ezra Tippie moved west": "Father King . . . in Spirit-Life 20,000 Years."

270   Morrison's Round House . . . was abandoned: Mitchell, *Linn County, Kansas*, 315–16.

270   became a trumpet medium: "Father King . . . in Spirit-Life 20,000 Years."

270   This third Athens County spirit room: Anonymous, "Journal of Trip East, Fall of 1855."
      Private collection of Elizabeth Isenburg, St. Louis, MO.

271   "spiritualism gained a number of followers": O'Neal, *McDougal Story*, 21.

271   After Ann's death in 1899: "Jefferson County IL Obituaries. Nahum Ward Koons."

271   "He [Nahum] is now about 68 years old": William A. Thompson, "Jonathan Koons.
      One of the Old Workers Whose Materializing Circles in Ohio Created World-Wide
      Attention," *Progressive Thinker*, May 7, 1904, 2. Perhaps due to a typesetting error,
      Franklin was misidentified as a county in Pennsylvania.

271   Nahum lived with his son Robert: *Mount Vernon Register*, October 26, 1921.

271   "He had been an avowed Spiritualist": "Jefferson County IL Obituaries. Nahum Ward
      Koons."

272   son had channeled communications: "Jonathan Koons. One of the Old Workers."

273   "picked up a large tin trumpet": "Father King . . . in Spirit-Life 20,000 Years."

273   attended two séances in London: *Medium & Daybreak*, January 24, 1879, 9–10.

274   Michigan man named Eli Curtis: "Spiritualism," *Vinton Record* (McArthur, Ohio),
      November 25, 1871, 2.

275   "I claim no ownership nor right": *Athens Messenger*, January 31, 1896.

275 farm had been subdivided by Seth Fuller: Athens County Deed Book 28:364.

275 In any case his group had a time line: "Spiritualism."

275 he ran an ad in the paper: "$500 Reward," *Athens Messenger*, June 29, 1871.

275 Curtis himself passed away: Theodore Rancour, "Eli Curtis 1793–1871," Ancestry.com, http://person.ancestry.com/tree/50077857/person/20281554876/story.

276 A local man named Evertt: Daren Neglia and Alexandra Eldridge, "Round the Area in Memory," *Golgonooza Loose Leaf* (Millfield, Ohio: Church of William Blake, 1973), n.p.

276 Morning Star's most active member: Harris, *Harris History*, 148–49.

276 "performed some wonderful feats": *Athens Messenger*, January 31, 1896, 5.

276 In his pocket Barnes carried: "Mount Nebo," *Athens Messenger*, November 2, 1871, 3.

276 blinked out in 1875: Harris, *Harris History*, 148–49.

276 had been torn down: Don Baird, "Mountain Is Rich in Occult Tales," *Columbus Dispatch*, October 28, 1984, B-1.

276 an older resident known as Miss Hebbard: Neglia and Eldridge, "Round the Area in Memory." "Hebbard" is a variant spelling of "Hibbard."

277 an intentional community: For a detailed account of the Golgonooza years, see John Murphy, "Building Golgonooza in the Age of Aquarius," in *William Blake in the Age of Aquarius* (Princeton, NJ: Princeton University Press, 2017), 161–81.

277 "a wonderfully creative time": Alexandra Eldridge, email to author, October 31, 2017.

277 a pageant at Golgonooza: Thomas Csordas, "The Church of William Blake," frequencies: a collaborative genealogy of spirituality, September 26, 2011, http://frequencies.ssrc.org/2011/09/26/the-church-of-william-blake/.

278 "Like the English Woden": Alexandra Eldridge, "Nebo," *Golgonooza Loose Leaf* (Millfield, OH: Church of William Blake, 1973), n.p.

278 Athens knows traditions more ancient than any folklore: Daren Neglia, "The Spirit Room in Athens," ibid.

278 He suspected arson: Nancy Gilson, "Burning Bright," *Columbus Dispatch*, October 29, 2001, 8-E.

279 is said to have been haunted: Carla Ankrom, personal communication with author, July 2016.

AFTERWORD

281 "Premising that the manifestations": Britten, *Modern American Spiritualism*, 332.

282 "Some change, then, was imperatively demanded": Ibid., 324.

282 "[He] is not the first": Ibid., 332.

282 included a humorous piece: *Western Star*, September 1872, 231–35.

282 "After infuriated mobs had burned": Britten, "Historical Sketches," *Two Worlds*, March 16, 1888, 256. In this article Emma Hardinge Britten also claimed to have visited an Athens County séance: "In Hardinge's 'History of Modern American Spiritualism' . . . are a number of lucid and interesting letters, furnished to different papers by prominent American citizens, describing in detail the wonders they witnessed at Koons' and Tippie's spirit rooms, and the many marvellous tests of intelligence they received. . . . These descriptions, though given by persons totally unacquainted with each other, tally in general features, and all agree with the experience of the Editor, who herself enjoyed the unspeakable privilege of visiting the far off scene of these matchless wonders."

Koons's Spirit Room had closed by November 1855, and, although no exact date is known, the Tippie room is thought to have closed at about the same time. The English-born Britten did not arrive in the United States until 1855 and did not begin her career as a medium until 1856. The window of time in which she could have visited the Athens County spirit rooms is exceedingly narrow.

283   "The conflagration of my barn": Jonathan Koons, "Biography of Jonathan Koons," *RPJ*, June 26, 1875, 114.

284   Britten herself wrote at least part of it: Marc Demarest, "Introduction to the Annotated Edition," in *Art Magic*, ed. Emma Harding Britten (Forest Grove, OR: Typhon Press, 2011), xlvii.

284   "as fact, as fiction or as a mixture of the two": Godwin, *Theosophical Enlightenment*, 209.

284   can only take . . . as fiction: I concur with Godwin. For example, *Ghost Land* recounts that Koons traveled to Rochester, New York, to investigate spiritualism. According to his own published statement, he wanted to go but couldn't afford to.

284   "a very good one": Godwin, *Theosophical Enlightenment*, 207.

284   the story of Louis: Britten, *Extracts from Ghostland*, 2:32–34. Also see *Unseen Universe*, August 1892, 231–35.

284   "Two rude ill-kept houses of public entertainment": Could this refer to the Koons and Tippie Spirit Rooms' being full, requiring the visitors to drive further to the George Keirns farm to await a vacancy?

286   "spiritualist propagandist": Marc Demarest, "Back from Jerusalem: Emma Hardinge Britten, Spiritualist Propagandist," accessed August 2, 2017, http://www.ehbritten.org/video/ehb_life_bw_version.pdf.

286   "my spirit friends confirm": Hare, *Experimental Investigation of the Spirit Manifestations*, 295.

286   "Should any one be desirous": "Observations on Horseback," *Knickerbocker*, January 1865, 85.

287   a more nuanced critique: Phoenix, "An Old Spiritualist—No. 6," *Banner of Light*, April 9, 1859.

287   pen name of James J. Mapes: Britten, *Modern American Spiritualism*, 142.

287   "Professor Mapes having become satisfied": Benjamin Coleman, "Spiritualism in America," *Spiritual Magazine*, October 1861, 443.

287   "we gave Phoenix's views": Phoenix, "An Old Spiritualist—No. 6."

288   "I really believed in spiritualism": Jaher, *Witch of Lime Street*, 370.

288   "Unless we assume": R. L. Moore, 124–25.

289   court case arose in Buffalo, New York: David Walker, "The Humbug in American Religion: Ritual Theories of Nineteenth-Century Spiritualism," *Religion and American Culture: A Journal of Interpretation* 23, no. 1 (2013): 49; Fornell, *Unhappy Medium*; and Terry Alford, "The Spiritualist Who Warned Lincoln Was Also Booth's Drinking Buddy," *Smithsonian Magazine*, March 2015.

290   defense witness Lester Day: Day stepped forward at the conclusion of the 1865 trial and paid Colchester's fine and court costs, sparing the defendant a jail sentence. Day believed that the spiritualist community would repay him. Colchester died in 1867, and Day spent his later years as a destitute old man. By 1874 spiritualist newspapers had started a fund for Day, raising more than $300 toward the debt he had incurred for the cause. *New York Herald*, August 23, 1865, 4; *RPJ*, June 6, 1874, 5; *Woodhull and Claflin's Weekly*, February 14, 1874, 14.

290   "The sort of 'magic'": Nadis, *Wonder Shows*, xiii.

290   "They were not just simple charlatans": Ibid., 9.

290   "A deeper reading . . . points": Albanese, *A Republic of Mind and Spirit*, 224.

291   earned him a notable spot: Marc Demarest, "Sanguifying Usquibaugh: Koons-Hunting," *Chasing Down Emma* (blog), January 25, 2014, ehbritten.blogspot.com.

291   "is *at least* as important": Marc Demarest, "The Lesson We Desire to Teach: E. V. Wilson at Koons' Spirit Room, January 1855," *Chasing Down Emma* (blog), August 24, 2014, ehbritten.blogspot.com.

292   *he then gives Jonathan a small rod:* The image of the rod being handed to Jonathan by the mysterious treasure-bearing stranger echoes the history of another spiritualist leader, Andrew Jackson Davis, "the Poughkeepsie seer." Davis was about 15 years younger than Koons, but Davis was the founder of the Harmonial School of spiritualism that Koons would come to embrace. At age 17, about 1843, Davis had a spiritual revelation that also involved a rod. Galen, the legendary Greek physician, appeared to Davis in a graveyard and showed him a staff with "a slender rod of highly polished silver" at its core. The strips that encased the rod listed all diseases known to humans as well as their cures. The vision had enormous personal significance for Davis, who went on to become a clairvoyant healer who made medical diagnoses while in a mesmeric state. His autobiography, published in 1857, was fittingly called *The Magic Staff.* S. Brown, *Heyday of Spiritualism*, 85–90.

293   Writing his life story: Jonathan Koons, "Biography of Jonathan Koons," *RPJ*, July 10, 1875, 130.

Bibliography

Albanese, Catherine L. *A Republic of Mind and Spirit: A Cultural History of American Metaphysical Religion*. New Haven, CT: Yale University Press, 2007.

Barnhart, Terry A. "Early Accounts of Ohio's Mounds." In *Ohio Archaeology: An Illustrated Chronicle of Ohio's Ancient American Indian Cultures*, edited by Bradley T. Lepper, 237–50. Wilmington, OH: Orange Frazer Press, 2005.

Barnum, P. T. *Barnum's American Museum Illustrated*. New York: William Van Norden and Frank Leslie, 1850. http://lostmuseum.cuny.edu/archive/american-museum-illustrated -guide-book.

Beatty, Elizabeth Grover, and Marjorie S. Stone. *Getting to Know Athens County*. Athens, OH: Stone House, 1984.

Bell, Caryn Cossé. *Revolution, Romanticism and the Afro-Creole Protest Tradition in New Orleans, 1718–1868*. Baton Rouge: Louisiana State University Press, 1997.

Bishop, Samuel G. "An Eulogium on the Death of Gen. George Washington." March 1800, Gilmanton, NH. The New York Public Library Collection of Washington Eulogies. Reprinted 1866. *Bulletin of the New York Public Library, Astor, Lenox and Tilden Foundations* 20, no. 1 (1916).

Blower, James Girard. *A Brief History of Trimble Township, Athens County, Ohio, Its Towns, Villages and People*. Athens, OH: Author, 1965.

Braude, Ann. *Radical Spirits: Spiritualism and Women's Rights in Nineteenth-Century America*. Boston: Beacon, 1989.

Braude, Stephen E. *The Limits of Influence: Psychokinesis and the Philosophy of Science*. Lanham, MD: University Press of America, 1997.

Britten, Emma Hardinge. *Modern American Spiritualism: A Twenty Years' Record of the Communion Between Earth and the World of Spirits*. New York: Author, 1870.

———, trans. and coll. *Extracts from Ghostland Vol. II, Or Researches into the Realm of Spiritual Existence*. Published by the Emma Hardinge Britten Archive. Accessed August 1, 2017. http://www.ehbritten.org/texts/primary/ehb_ghostland_V2.pdf.

Brown, Dan. *The Da Vinci Code*. New York: Doubleday, 2003.

Brown, Harriet Conor. *Grandmother Brown's First Hundred Years*. Boston: Little, Brown, 1929.

Brown, Slater. *The Heyday of Spiritualism*. New York: Pocket Books, 1972.

Buescher, John B. *The Other Side of Salvation: Spiritualism and the Nineteenth-Century Religious Experience*. Boston: Skinner House Books, 2004.

———. *The Remarkable Life of John Murray Spear: Agitator for the Spirit Land*. Notre Dame, IN: University of Notre Dame Press, 2006.

Carpenter, Josiah. "The importance of right views in matrimony, set forth in a sermon, delivered March 19, 1800, at Pittsfield Meeting House, Rockingham County, state of Newhampshire, at the celebration of marriage between Samuel G. Bishop, preacher of the Gospel, son of Bille Bishop of Connecticut, deceased, and Abigail Tuck, the youngest daughter of the late Reverend John Tuck, of Epsom, deceased." Evans Early American Imprint Collection. Accessed October 4, 2016. http://quod.lib.umich.edu/e/evans/N37417.0001.001/1:1?rgn=div1;view=fulltext.

A Catalogue of the Officers and Students of Harvard University, for the Academical Year 1844–45. Cambridge, MA: Metcalf, 1844. http://guides.library.harvard.edu/hds/1st-100/1840-1869.

Crowell, Eugene. *The Identity of Primitive Christianity and Modern Spiritualism.* Vol. 1. New York: G. W. Carleton, 1874.

Daniel, Robert L. *Athens, Ohio: The Village Years.* Athens: Ohio University Press, 1997.

Davis, Andrew Jackson. *The Magic Staff.* New York: J. S. Brown, 1857.

Demarest, Marc. "Introduction to the Annotated Edition." In *Art Magic,* edited by Emma Harding Britten. Forest Grove, OR: Typhon Press, 2011.

Dingwall, E. J. *How to Go to a Medium: A Manual of Instructions.* Exeter, UK: F&W Media International, 2012. First published 1927 by Kegan Paul, Trench, Trubner (London).

Dodd, Gladys. *The Story of Uriah Tippie of Ohio (1759–1848) and of Some of His Kansas Descendants in the Nineteenth Century.* Arvada, CO: Gladys Dodd, 1991.

du Potet de Sennevoy, Jean. *Traité complet du magnétisme animal: Cours en douze leçons.* 4th ed. Paris: G. Baillière, 1879.

Ehrman, Bart D. *Truth and Fiction in* The Da Vinci Code: *A Historian Reveals What We Really Know About Jesus, Mary Magdalene, and Constantine.* New York: Oxford University Press, 2004.

Ellinghouse, Cletis. *Missouri: A Sesquicentennial History.* Marceline, MO: Walsworth, 2006.

———. *Swindled: Wayne County's Turbulence, 1868–1904.* Bloomington, IN: Xlibris, 2012.

Everett, J. *A Book for Skeptics: Being a Communication from Angels, Written with Their Own Hands; also Oral Communications, Spoken by Angels through a Trumpet, and Written Down As They Were Delivered, in the Presence of Many Witnesses. Also a Representation and Explanation of the Celestial Spheres, As Given by the Spirits, at J. Koons' Spirit Room, in Dover, Athens County, Ohio.* Columbus, OH: Osgood and Blake, 1853.

Fornell, Earl Wesley. *The Unhappy Medium: Spiritualism and the Life of Margaret Fox.* Austin: University of Texas Press, 1964.

Fowler, James Hackett. *New Testament "Miracles," and Modern "Miracles": The Comparative Amount of Evidence for Each; The Nature of Both; Testimony of a Hundred Witnesses: An Essay, Read before the Middle and Senior Classes in Cambridge Divinity School.* Boston: B. Marsh, 1854; 2nd ed., 1859.

Godwin, Joscelyn. *The Theosophical Enlightenment.* Albany: State University of New York Press, 1994.

———. *Upstate Cauldron: Eccentric Spiritual Movements in Early New York State.* Albany: State University of New York Press, 2015.

Goss, David E. *Northern Township Franklin County, Illinois: A History.* 2001.

Gutierrez, Cathy, ed. *Handbook of Spiritualism and Channeling.* Brill Handbooks on Contemporary Religion. Leiden: Brill, 2015.

Haller, John S., Jr. *Swedenborg, Mesmer, and the Mind/Body Connection: The Roots of Complementary Medicine.* West Chester, PA: Swedenborg Foundation, 2010.

Hare, Robert. *Experimental Investigation of the Spirit Manifestations, Demonstrating the Existence of Spirits and Their Communion with Mortals. Doctrine of the Spirit World Respecting Heaven,*

Hell, Morality and God. Also, the Influence of Scripture on the Morals of Christians. 5th ed. New York: Charles Partridge, 1858.

Harris, Charles H. *The Harris History.* Athens, OH: Athens Messenger, 1957.

Hoagland, Edward. "The Quietly Compelling Legend of America's Gentlest Pioneer." *American Heritage,* December 1979.

Home, Daniel Dunglas. *Lights and Shadows of Spiritualism.* New York: G. W. Carleton, 1877.

Home, [Mrs.] Daniel Dunglas. *D. D. Home: His Life and Mission.* London: Trubner, 1888.

Home Authors. *A Twentieth Century History and Biographical Record of Crawford County, Kansas.* Chicago: Lewis Publishing Company, 1905.

Inter-State Publishing. *History of Hocking Valley, Ohio.* Chicago: Author, 1883.

Jaher, David. *The Witch of Lime Street: Seance, Seduction and Houdini in the Spirit World.* New York: Crown, 2015.

Johnston, James. *The Chemistry of Common Life.* Edinburgh: Blackwood, 1855.

Koons, Jonathan. *Truth Seekers' Feast; Composing a Savory Pic-Nic of Theological Knick Knacks, Relating to the Ground-work of Modern Christianity.* Mount Vernon, IL: Exponent Power Press, 1881.

Lamont, Peter. *The First Psychic: The Peculiar Mystery of a Notorious Victorian Wizard.* London: Abacus, 2006.

Lepper, Bradley T. *Ohio Archaeology: An Illustrated Chronicle of Ohio's Ancient American Indian Cultures.* Wilmington, OH: Orange Frazer Press, 2005.

Magley, Marsha C. Squires, comp. *Descendants of John Tippie Sr.* Bird City, KS: Author, 1992. Available at the Southeast Ohio History Center, Athens.

McCabe, Joseph. *Spiritualism; A Popular History from 1847.* New York: Dodd, Mead, 1920.

Means, Howard. *Johnny Appleseed: The Man, the Myth, the American Story.* New York: Simon and Schuster, 2011.

Mitchell, William Ansel. *Linn County, Kansas: A History.* Claremore, OK: Country Lane Press, 1928. Reprinted 1987 by Linn County Historical Society, Pleasanton, KS.

Moore, Josephine Carroll, comp. and ed. *Tentative Tippie Tabulations.* 5th ed. Athens, OH: Athens County Historical Society and Museum and Athens County Genealogical Chapter, O. G. S., 1996.

Moore, R. Laurence. *In Search of White Crows: Spiritualism, Parapsychology and American Culture.* New York: Oxford University Press, 1977.

Nadis, Fred. *Wonder Shows: Performing Science, Magic and Religion in America.* New Brunswick, NJ: Rutgers University Press, 2005.

Nichols, T. L. *Religions of the World, An Impartial History of Religious Creeds, Forms of Worship, Sects, Controversies, and Manifestations, From the Earliest Period to the Present Time.* Cincinnati: Valentine Nicholson, 1855.

————, ed. *Supramundane Facts in the Life of Rev. Jesse Babcock Ferguson, A.M., LL.D., Including Twenty Years' Observation of Preternatural Phenomena.* London: F. Pitman, 1865.

The Ohio Guide. Compiled by Workers of the Writers' Program of the Work Projects Administration in the State of Ohio. New York: Oxford University Press, 1940.

O'Neal, Harold. *The McDougal Story.* Ohio, [1966?].

Pagels, Elaine. *Beyond Belief: The Secret Gospel of Thomas.* New York: Random House, 2003.

Perrin, William Henry. *History of Jefferson County, Illinois.* Chicago: Globe, 1883.

Peters, William E. *Athens County, Ohio.* Vol. 1. [Athens?] 1947.

Pierce, Abraham P. *The Revelator: Being an Account of the Twenty-One Days' Entrancement of Abraham P. Pierce, Spirit-Medium, at Belfast, Maine, together with a Sketch of His Life.* 2nd ed. Boston: Adams, 1870.

Porter, James. *The Spirit Rappings, Mesmerism, Clairvoyance, Visions, Revelations, Startling Phenomena, and Infidelity of the Rapping Fraternity Calmly Considered, and Exposed.* Boston: James P. Magee, 1853. Western Reserve Historical Society, Cleveland, Ohio.

Randolph, P. B. *The Davenport Brothers, the World-Renowned Spiritual Mediums: Their Biography, and Adventures in Europe and America.* Boston: William White, 1869.

Rusler, William. *A Standard History of Allen County, Ohio.* New York: American Historical Society, 1921.

Silverman, Ray. *The Core of Johnny Appleseed: The Unknown Story of a Spiritual Trailblazer.* West Chester, PA: Swedenborg Foundation Press, 2012.

Spurlock, John C. *Free Love: Marriage and Middle-Class Radicalism in America, 1825–1860.* New York: New York University Press, 1998.

Stuart, Nancy Rubin. *The Reluctant Spiritualist: The Life of Maggie Fox.* New York: Harcourt, 2005.

Van Sickle, John Waddell. *A History of the Van Sickle Family, in the United States of America.* Springfield, OH: Author, 1880.

Walker, Charles M. *History of Athens County, Ohio and Incidentally of the Ohio Land Company and the First Settlement of the State at Marietta with Personal and Biographical Sketches of the Early Settlers, Narratives of Pioneer Adventures, Etc.* Cincinnati: Robert Clarke, 1869.

Weisberg, Barbara. *Talking to the Dead: Kate and Maggie Fox and the Rise of Spiritualism.* San Francisco: HarperSanFrancisco, 2004.

White, Thomas. *An Essay on Spiritualism.* St. Clairsville, OH: A. H. Balsley, 1855.

Index

Page numbers in italics denote illustrations. The family relationships of Jonathan Koons are shown in parentheses.